REACHING YOUR POTENTIAL:

PERSONAL AND PROFESSIONAL DEVELOPMENT

FOURTH EDITION

Robert K. Throop
Marion B. Castellucci

WADSWORTH
CENGAGE Learning

Australia • Brazil • Japan • Korea • Mexico • Singapore • Spain • United Kingdom • United States

27-L-93

Reaching Your Potential: Personal and Professional Development, Fourth Edition

Robert K. Throop, Marion B. Castellucci

Senior Sponsoring Editor: Shani Fisher

Director of College Success and Developmental English: Annie Todd

Assistant Editor: Daisuke Yasutake

Editorial Assistant: Cat Salerno

Associate Media Editor: Emily Ryan

Marketing Manager: Kirsten Stoller

Marketing Coordinator: Ryan Ahern

Marketing Communications Manager: Martha Pfeiffer

Content Project Manager: Alison Eigel Zade

Senior Art Director: Linda Jurras

Print Buyer: Julio Esperas

Text Permissions Account Manager: Margaret Chamberlain-Gaston

Production Service: Priya Sundaram/ S4Carlisle Publishing Services

Text Designer: Cia Boynton

Senior Photo Editor: Jennifer Meyer Dare

Photo Research: Kelly Franz, Pre-PressPMG

Cover Designer: Carol Maglitta/One Visual Mind

Cover Image: Dave Lesh

Compositor: S4Carlisle Publishing Services

For product information and technology assistance, contact us at **Cengage Learning Customer & Sales Support, 1-800-354-9706**

For permission to use material from this text or product, submit all requests online at **www.cengage.com/permissions.** Further permissions questions can be e-mailed to **permissionrequest@cengage.com.**

Library of Congress Control Number: 2009925789

Student Edition:

ISBN-13: 978-1-4354-3973-3
ISBN-10: 1-4354-3973-2

Wadsworth
20 Channel Center Street
Boston, MA 02210
USA

Cengage Learning is a leading provider of customized learning solutions with office locations around the globe, including Singapore, the United Kingdom, Australia, Mexico, Brazil and Japan. Locate your local office at **international.cengage.com/region**

Cengage Learning products are represented in Canada by Nelson Education, Ltd.

For your course and learning solutions, visit **www.cengage.com.**

Purchase any of our products at your local college store or at our preferred online store **www.ichapters.com.**

Printed in the United States of America
1 2 3 4 5 6 7 13 12 11 10 09

This is for my father, Ken, who lives within me; for my mother, Joie, who always made me feel unique; for my wife, Joyce, who provides me with unconditional love; and for my daughters, Tracey, Wendee, and Bethany, who fill me with resounding joy.
—*Robert K. Throop*

•

For my mother, Agatha Eken Bonney.
—*Marion B. Castellucci*

Contents

Preface

Self-belief is the foundation of success in all personal, educational, and professional endeavors. In order to succeed, students must deal with personal, economic, and societal problems and make a commitment to work to achieve their goals. A solid sense of who they are and who they might become is the springboard for overcoming obstacles and succeeding in school and all other areas of life.

Reaching Your Potential is designed to help students take control of their lives and improve their self-belief. The text provides a blend of concepts and applications to help students discover their emotional, intellectual, physical, and social potential. Through a process of learning and self-examination, students discover their values, increase their commitment to personal goals, and challenge themselves to grow and learn. While gaining practical knowledge and skills, students will discover their emotional, intellectual, physical, and social resources. They will learn that they can improve their lives by changing the way they think about themselves—and then acting accordingly.

Coverage   *Reaching Your Potential,* Fourth Edition, is divided into five units and fourteen chapters. Unit 1, "Developing Your Emotional Potential," discusses the fundamentals—values, self-belief, commitment, and goal setting. Unit 2, "Developing Your Intellectual Potential," explores the thinking skills, creativity, and study skills needed for school and professional success. Unit 3, "Developing Your Physical Potential," discusses how a healthy diet, exercise, and rest contribute to well-being and provides information on overcoming substance abuse and preventing the spread of sexually transmitted diseases. Unit 4, "Developing Your Social Potential," stresses the importance in today's diverse society of good communications and human relations skills, including avoiding miscommunication, active listening, speaking, ethical conduct, conflict resolution, group interaction, and leadership. The fifth and final unit, "Developing Your Action Plan," provides suggestions for dealing with stress and change, managing money, and choosing and pursuing a career.

How to Use This Book

Because people learn best from their own experiences, *Reaching Your Potential* offers a unique format that involves students in active learning. Before they begin, students fill in self-assessment questionnaires—benchmarks against which they will measure their progress. Please note that an online version of the self-assessment is also available on the Premium Website.

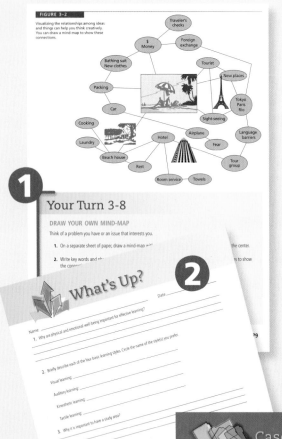

1 As students work through the text, they apply the concepts they learn to their own situations in the "**Your Turn**" activities that are interspersed throughout each chapter. Through these activities, students participate in a process of self-discovery, which engages and holds their interest.

2 At the end of each chapter, students test their comprehension by answering "**What's Up**" questions.

3 Students also apply the knowledge they have acquired with the **case studies** in each chapter. They can use their critical thinking skills to solve the problems.

4 Each chapter ends with a **journal activity** in which students reflect on the contents of the chapter as it pertains to their lives and their futures.

Finally, when students finish the text, they reassess themselves and the progress they have made toward reaching their potential.

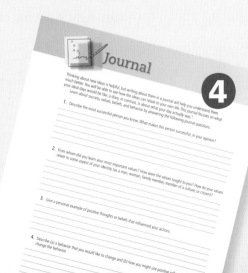

Your Turn 2-1

WHAT ARE YOUR DREAMS?

Take a few minutes to write down what you've always dreamed of doing.

"Service to others is the
you pay for your room
on earth."
MDMA

FIGURE 2-1

Short-term goals take a y...
from five years to accomp...

Short-term
goals

Now

TABLE 8-1 The Most Common Club Drugs

Drug	Form	Short-Term Effects	Potential Health Effects
MDMA *Ecstasy, XTC, E, X, go, hug drug, disco biscuit*	Tablet or capsule	■ Stimulant: increased heart rate, blood pressure; feelings of alertness and energy; mild hallucinogenic effects	Depression, sleep problems, anxiety, impaired memory and learning
GHB G *grievous bodily harm, goop, max, soap, juice, liquid ecstasy, fantasy*	■ Clear liquid, white powder, tablet, or capsule ■ Often made in home laboratories	■ In high doses, can lead to high body temperature, dehydration, and death ■ Depressant: reduced heart rate, blood pressure; reduced pain and anxiety; feeling of relaxation and well-being; reduced inhibitions ■ In high doses, can lead to drowsiness, loss of consciousness, coma, and death	Unknown
Ketamine *K, special K, kettle mine, cat Valium, jet, super acid*	■ Liquid for injection, powder for snorting or smoking ■ Used legally as an anesthetic, usually for animals	■ Used as a date rape drug ■ Depressant: hallucinations; poor judgment; poor coordination ■ In high doses, can cause delirium, amnesia, depression, respiratory problems, heart rate abnormalities, and death	Memory loss; numbness; nausea and vomiting
Rohypnol *Roofies, roaches, forget-me drug, Mexican valium*	■ Pill or powder	■ Depressant: reduced heart rate, blood pressure; reduced pain and anxiety; feeling of relaxation and well-being; reduced inhibitions ■ Visual and digestive disturbances; urine retention ■ Used as a date rape drug	Loss of memory for period while under the effects of the drug
	■ Used legally in Europe as a sleeping pill		

36 UNIT 1 Developing Your Emotional Potential

Additional features make the text attractive to students. Its format and concise coverage make the book easy to read and comprehend.

⑤ Full color **photos, diagrams, graphs,** and **tables** provide visual interest as well as reinforce concepts.

Taking the First Step

Old habits and ways of living are powerful forces. Taking the first step toward a major goal can be hard. But procrastinating, or postponing a task that ought to be done now, is the sure way to fail to reach a goal. People who procrastinate usually have a "good" reason. Danielle may say, for example, that she will start studying for a course as soon as pressure eases up at work. In fact, Danielle knows she should start studying now, but she gives herself an excuse not to start.

"The best way to get something
done is to begin."
ANONYMOUS

Postponing a task will not make it easier. Rather, when you are tempted to put off something important, you should carefully think about what is holding you back. You may be feeling shy, indecisive, fearful, negative, or bad about yourself. You feel you can't do something, so you don't do it. The result is inaction.

To overcome procrastination, you can change your beliefs and you can change your behavior. In Chapter 1, we discussed the power of positive self-talk in improving your self-belief. If you are a procrastinator, now is the time for some serious conversation with yourself. Danielle, for example, should be telling herself, "Studying is important. I want to study to pass the course. I can start now despite pressures at work. When I'm at home I'll study from 8 to 10 each evening."

Tips for Getting Started   One approach for people who procrastinate is to start by doing a little bit. There are several techniques you can use to get yourself started on a task:

■ **Set a deadline for getting started.** By focusing on a starting date, you will find the energy to begin because you have made a

⑥

⑥ **Quotations** from great leaders, artists, thinkers, and other role models serve to inspire students to succeed.

⑦ A diverse array of people who have overcome challenges and succeeded in life are profiled in **"Whatever It Takes,"** providing motivation for students to do the same.

WHATEVER IT TAKES
⑦ Becky Zaheri and the Katrina Krewe

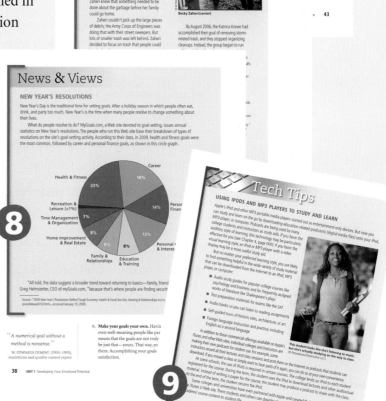

In September 2005, a week after Hurricane Katrina flooded New Orleans, Becky Zaheri visited the city to check on her house. She expected to see storm debris, water damage, and empty neighborhoods. What she didn't expect to see was trash all over the streets. Her family had planned to return to New Orleans in a few months. But Zaheri knew that something needed to be done about the garbage before her family could go home.

Zaheri couldn't pick up the large pieces of debris; the Army Corps of Engineers was doing that with their street sweepers. But lots of smaller trash was left behind. Zaheri decided to focus on trash that people could

Becky Zahevi (center)

By August 2006, the Katrina Krewe had accomplished their goal of removing storm-related trash, and they stopped organizing cleanups. Instead, the group began to run

hat can get
 write
king up the
ork on the
tes you will
t part and
 self-talk.
don't have
household
s, teachers,
time. How

43

News & Views

NEW YEAR'S RESOLUTIONS

New Year's Day is the traditional time for setting goals. After a holiday season in which people often eat, drink, and party too much, New Year's is the time when many people resolve to change something about their lives.

What do people resolve to do? MyGoals.com, a Web site devoted to goal-setting, issues annual statistics on New Year's resolutions. The people who run this Web site base their breakdown of types of resolutions on the site's goal-setting activity. According to their data, in 2009, health and fitness goals were the most common, followed by career and personal finance goals, as shown in this circle graph.

Career 18%
Health & Fitness 23%
Personal Finan... 14%
Recreation & Leisure (<1%)
Time Management & Organization 7%
Home Improvement & Real Estate 8%
Family & Relationships 8%
Education & Training 8%
Personal ... & Interest 13%

"All told, the data suggest a broader trend toward returning to basics—family, friend... Greg Helmstetter, CEO of myGoals.com, "because that's where people are finding securit...

Source: "2009 New Year's Resolutions Reflect Tough Economy; Health & Travel Are Out, Nesting & Relationships Are In, pressReleease016.html>, accessed January 19, 2009.

⑧ **"News & Views"** highlight trends, topics, or issues of particular interest to students.

⑨ **"Tech Tips"** provide suggestions for using technology in college, in personal life, and on the job.

Tech Tips

USING IPODS AND MP3 PLAYERS TO STUDY AND LEARN

Apple's iPod and other MP3 portable media players started out as entertainment-only devices. But now you can study and learn on the go by downloading education-related podcasts (digital media files) onto your iPod, MP3 player, or computer. Podcasts are being used by many college students and instructors as study aids. If you favor the auditory style of learning, this technology may be particularly effective for you (see Chapter 4, page 000). If you favor the visual learning style, an iPod or MP3 player with a video display may be a more useful study aid.

But no matter your preferred learning style, you are likely to find something helpful in the wide variety of study material that can be downloaded from the Internet to an iPod, MP3 player, or computer:

■ Audio study guides for popular college courses like psychology and business and for frequently assigned works of literature like Shakespeare's plays

■ Test preparation materials for exams like the SAT

■ Audio books so you can listen to reading assignments

■ Self-guided tours of historic sites, architecture, or art

■ Foreign language instruction and practice, including English as a second language

In addition to these commercial offerings available on Apple's iTunes and other Web sites, individual colleges and instructors are making their own podcasts for student use. For example, some instructors record all their lectures and class sessions and post them on the Internet as podcasts that students can download. If you missed a class or simply want to hear parts of it again, you can do so at your own convenience. During the term, the student uses the iPod to download lectures and other audiovisual material. Instead of writing a paper for the course, the student may produce a podcast to share with the class. At the end of the term, the student returns the iPod.

Some colleges and universities have even partnered with Apple and created their own sections on iTunes U Web site. There students and others can download podcasts that range from campus tours to academic course content to student life.

This student looks like she's listening to music, but she's actually studying on the way to class.

6. **Make your goals your own.** Havin... even well-meaning people like par... means that the goals are not truly be just that—yours. That way, yo... them. Accomplishing your goals satisfaction.

"A numerical goal without a
method is nonsense."
W. EDWARDS DEMING (1900–1993),
statistician and quality-control expert

38 UNIT 1 Developing Your Emotional Potential

196 UNIT 4 Developing Your Social Potential

© 2011 Wadsworth, Cengage Learning

New to the Fourth Edition

Although computers and the Internet played a small role in our lives when the first edition of *Reaching Your Potential* was published, technology's influence, especially in higher education, is far more pervasive today. To improve the effectiveness of the text, we have increased the fourth edition's coverage of technology with a new feature, "Tech Tips." These sections appear in each chapter, followed by a "Your Turn" activity so students can explore and apply the aspect of technology covered in the chapter. The "Tech Tips" sections focus on the following topics:

- gaining an **overview of computers and other technology** used in college and accessing computers and technology resources on campus (Chapter 1)

- effectively using **course management systems such as Blackboard** and learning to adapt to individual instructors' online styles (Chapter 2)

- understanding the special challenges of taking **online and blended courses** and assessing whether one has the computer skills and personal qualities needed to succeed in these courses (Chapter 3)

- using the **library's online catalog and databases** and exploring its resources (Chapter 4)

- using the Internet's many features and **searching for and evaluating information found on the Web** (Chapter 5)

- understanding what personal, topic, and corporate **blogs** are and exploring the blogosphere (Chapter 6)

- writing appropriate **e-mail messages** and using the send, cc, reply, and reply all functions properly (Chapter 7)

- using **iPods and MP3 players** and downloading and/or producing course-related podcasts (Chapter 8)

- exploring **cell phone** functions and using proper cell phone etiquette (Chapter 9)

- using **online social networks** like Facebook and MySpace and being aware of privacy issues (Chapter 10)

- understanding the norms of **course discussion boards** and using them effectively (Chapter 11)

- minimizing **technology-related stress** and using technology to keep in touch with others and cope with stress (Chapter 12)

- exploring **personal finance resources on the Internet** and using them for budgeting, finding financial aid, evaluating credit cards, and performing other money tasks (Chapter 13)

- using **career guidance and job search Internet resources** and exploring careers, internships, and entry-level job opportunities. (Chapter 14)

Our second goal for the fourth edition was to revise and update the instructional content and activities to make them more useful to students and relevant to their needs.

- In Chapter 1, a new "Your Turn" activity about positive psychology prompts students to explore this new subfield of psychology.

- In Chapter 4, on study skills, the treatment of learning styles has been revised to focus on a model based on visual, audio, kinesthetic, and tactile learning, and a new "Your Turn" activity helps students identify their preferred learning style(s). The section on previewing while reading has been expanded to cover previewing a Web site, with an accompanying "Your Turn" activity on previewing the FEMA site. Finally, a new section explains that students with special needs must take responsibility to navigate their college's academic services on their own.

- In Chapter 5, the approach to food groups and a balanced diet has been updated to reflect the *New Dietary Guidelines for Americans 2005*. A new fast-food quiz helps students learn to identify healthy menu choices when eating out.

- In Chapter 6, on health, a new bar graph shows the number of calories expended during common activities. The section on drug abuse has been updated with the latest statistics on smoking and drinking alcohol, a new student self-test on alcohol abuse, and new information about methamphetamines, which have become the illegal drug of choice in many regions of the country.

- In Chapter 9, on speaking, a new "Your Turn" asks students to do research on the Web about spoken English and its variants.

- In Chapter 12, on stress, new sections on the causes of stress and the cognitive and physiological responses to stress are based on up-to-date stress research findings. A new "Your Turn" provides a brief stress assessment test.

- In Chapter 13, the section on credit cards has been expanded to cover the marketing of cards to students and the special pitfalls for students of overusing credit cards. The section on banking has been updated to cover online banking.

- In Chapter 14, on careers, a new section emphasizes the importance of keeping up with economic trends such as globalization and outsourcing as well as technology developments, and making decisions with these factors in mind. New sections on internships and using social networking sites for job-related tasks reflect students' approaches to the job market. The career resource and job-hunting information has also been updated to reflect the availability of so much information on the Internet.

Throughout the text, there are many new News & Views features on various current topics: how the average amount of physical exercise varies considerably from state to state (Chapter 6), the relationship of noise and health and how to protect your hearing (Chapter 8), the study of proxemics, or our comfort zone (Chapter 10), identity theft and how to prevent it (Chapter 13), and job growth projections through 2016 (Chapter 14). Other News & Views features have been expanded and updated.

The Whatever It Takes profiles have been updated with new profiles of people from all backgrounds and walks of life. Among the new profiles are those of three young friends who became doctors, a post-Katrina volunteer, a man who develops high-tech study aids for limited-sight people, a recovered drug abuser who lobbies for drug treatment programs, a successful young politician, a soccer coach for a team of refugees, a jockey, a venture capitalist, and an illegal immigrant who became a surgeon.

Photos have been updated in all chapters. As in the previous editions, we have tried to show engaging and diverse people in a wide range of activities to increase the appeal of the text to students.

Complete Learning and Instructional Package

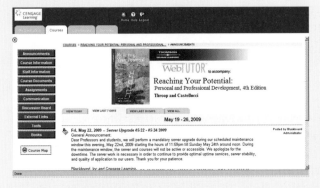

WebTUTOR™ on WebCT™ Printed Access Card
WebTUTOR™ on Blackboard™ Printed Access Card

Student Resources

Premium Web Site

The Premium Web Site, which contains various resources such as Tutorial Quizzes, Flashcards, PowerPoints, Web Links, Discussion Questions and Video Skillbuilders, can be accessed by visiting www.cengage.com/success/throop/potential4e. Students will need a passkey to access the site. Instructors request a package of the main text plus the passkey if they are interested in assigning material on the Web site.

Premium Web Site Printed   ISBN 0-4958-9936-4
Access Card

WebTUTOR™

Available in both the WebCT™ and Blackboard™ platforms, WebTUTOR™ allows for instructors to easily communicate with their students in an online learning management system. The WebTUTOR™ provides students with content such as Tutorial Quizzes, Flashcards, PowerPoints, Web Links, Discussion Questions and Video Skillbuilders that will enrich and complement the material in the main text.

ISBN 1-4354-3974-0
ISBN 1-4354-3976-7

Instructor Resources

A printed Instructor's Manual (ISBN 1-4354-3975-9) written by the authors offers teaching suggestions, additional resources, and answer keys to text activities. A PDF of the Intructor's Manual is also available on the PowerLecture CD (ISBN 1-4354-3977-5), a resource that contains an ExamView® Test Bank, PowerPoints, and Discussion Questions.

An additional service available with this textbook is support from **TeamUP Faculty Program Consultants**. For more than a decade, our consultants have helped faculty reach and engage first-year students by offering peer-to-peer consulting on curriculum and assessment, faculty training, and workshops. Our consultants are educators and higher education professionals who provide full-time support helping educators establish and maintain effective student success programs. They are available to help you to establish or improve your student success program and provide training on the implementation of our textbooks and technology. To connect with your TeamUP Faculty Program Consultant, call 1-800-528-8323 or visit www.cengage.com/teamup.

Acknowledgments

We would like to acknowledge all the students who have proven that education—both through teaching and writing—is the ultimate profession, and that there could not have been a better path for us to have traveled.

Cengage Learning and the authors thank the following instructors, who reviewed the manuscript of the fourth edition of this and provided valuable suggestions for improving it:

Aleyenne Johnson-Jonas
The Art Institute of California-San Diego

Robert C. Noyes
Tidewater Community College

Wendy Parker
Minnesota School of Business

Jan Pitera
Broome Community College

Dave Parmenter
Wright Career College

Mary Rhiner
Kirkwood Community College

Liese A. Hull
University of Michigan

Sharon Zygowicz
GateWay Community College

Lisa Ledeboer
Mt. San Antonio College

Cengage Learning and the authors are also indebted to the following instructors, who reviewed the previous edition's of this text and made many helpful suggestions.

Tricia Berry
Hamilton College

Jonathan Hayward
ITT Technical Institute

Thomas Bledsaw
ITT Technical Institute

Lisa Hoover
ITT Technical Institute

Sally Combs
Atlanta Technical Institute

Susan Klemm
Lincoln School of Commerce

Joann Driggers
Mt. San Antonio College

Herman Kuminkoski
ITT Technical Institute

Marianne Fitzpatrick
Bauder College

Thom Perrino
City College

Nancy Gleason
Hamilton College

Maris Roze
DeVry Institute

Carolyn Hagaman
Western Kentucky University

Louise Sundermeier
Lynn University

Martha Hannah
Valdosta Technical Institute

Diana Wyatt
Danville Area Community College

Because so many of the improvements in this text have come from your suggestions, we always welcome comments. Send us your thoughts care of Cengage Learning, 20 Channel Center, Boston, MA 02210 ATTN: College Success, or e-mail us at rthroop@ec.rr.com or marioncastellucci@verizon.net.

Robert K. Throop

Marion B. Castellucci

Introduction: To the Lifelong Learner

Your values, beliefs, and thoughts make you the person you are today. They influence your current and future behaviors. But if you are like most people, perhaps you feel that you could be more than you are today. Perhaps your values, beliefs, and thoughts are limiting your ability to make the most of the present and grow toward a better future. To improve your life, you must change the way you think about yourself and your potential.

Reaching Your Potential is based on the simple idea that you can be what you want to be. Through a process of self-examination and self-discovery, you can change your life. But to change, you must understand the various aspects of yourself and how they interrelate to form the whole you.

Four Areas of Potential Growth

Each of us has four areas of potential growth. We have:

1. **Emotional potential:** how we feel and what we want
2. **Intellectual potential:** how we think and learn
3. **Physical potential:** how we maintain our body's well-being
4. **Social potential:** how we relate to other people

Each of these four potentials will be discussed in this book separately so you can develop insight into that aspect of your own character and life. But it is important to remember—and we will keep reminding you—that these areas are interrelated and are simply parts of the whole you. It is vital that you develop all these potentials as an ensemble.

How can you develop to your fullest potential? You must change the way you think about yourself and create a mind shift—a new way of looking at things. And the way to do this is through learning. Learning is the critical key to achieving success.

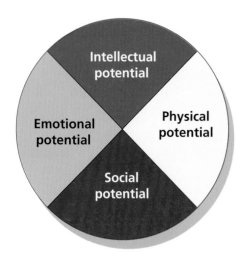

Each person has emotional, intellectual, physical, and social areas of potential growth.

Through learning we re-create ourselves. Through learning we become able to do something we were never able to do. Through learning we re-perceive the world and our relationship to it. Through learning we extend our capacity to create, to be part of the … process of life.[1]

This type of learning is not passive. You cannot simply soak up information. Instead, to learn you must continually question your beliefs, values, and goals. You must apply what you learn to your own life in order to change and grow. *Reaching Your Potential* will help you do this.

The Stages of the Mastery Approach

The process of reaching your potential takes place in stages. Each stage builds upon the previous stage to expand your ability to create your own success.

Stage 1: Developing Your Self-Belief   Self-belief is the foundation of success. It is your knowledge of and confidence in your own abilities. Self-belief underlies all your actions, both good and bad. You develop your self-belief little by little, by succeeding in small ways that eventually build up into a solid foundation.

Stage 2: Reframing Your Thoughts   By changing your beliefs and values, you can change the way you perceive and act. An example of reframing is the ugly duckling that was transformed into a beautiful swan. The ugly duckling's situation did not change, but he perceived it completely differently and acted accordingly. Another example of reframing is a student who gets an F on a math exam. At first, she perceives herself as a math "dummy," but then she reframes that F: She decides the failing grade is really a wake-up call, and she gets help from a math tutor. In order to change your behavior, you have to reframe your thoughts.

Stage 3: Setting Goals   Goals are the targets that we try to achieve. Without goals, we are aimless and confused. To establish goals, you must define your values and beliefs and examine the world around you in a realistic way. It is not helpful to be unrealistic about yourself or the world when you set goals. That is simply a way to excuse inaction and failure: *If there's no problem, I don't have to solve anything. If my parents were rich, I wouldn't be behind in my car payments. If I were smarter, I would pass that course.* Instead, goals should be realistic and achievable in a series of small steps.

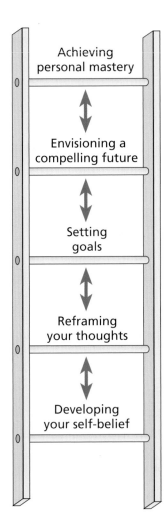

Achieving
personal mastery

↕

Envisioning a
compelling future

↕

Setting
goals

↕

Reframing
your thoughts

↕

Developing
your self-belief

The mastery approach is an ongoing, lifelong process of personal growth. It can be applied to any aspect of human achievement.

Stage 4: Envisioning a Compelling Future Envisioning a compelling future means you have a vivid picture of what the future can be. This creates a driving force that helps you move from your current reality toward your future reality. The gap between the present and the future creates the tension necessary to motivate you to act. If you take no action toward achieving a compelling future, the gap remains between the present and your vision of the future.

Stage 5: Achieving Personal Mastery The final stage in reaching your potential is achieving personal mastery. When you achieve this, you are able to get consistent results from your actions. You have a thorough understanding of yourself, the ability to reframe your thoughts when necessary, realistic and achievable goals, and a vision of the future.

Note that progress toward personal mastery is not a straight, unbroken line. Instead, we may achieve personal mastery in an area but then fall back to a previous stage. One way to think of the five stages is to compare them to the method used by mountain climbers to scale a high peak like Mt. Everest.[2] Climbers do not make straight for the top. Instead, they establish a base camp where plans are made and supplies are stored and where the climb begins. From the base camp, they climb a few thousand feet and establish a second camp, and so on up the mountain. During the ascent the climbers sometimes run into problems at a certain height and have to return to the base camp or a lower campsite for supplies, rest, or help before they resume the climb and reach the top. Similarly, in our quest for personal mastery we go from stage to stage, but when we get stuck we return to a previous stage and start again.

So the process of reaching your potential and achieving personal mastery does not end when you finish this book. Instead, it is a lifelong process. As you grow and change, your visions of a compelling future and your goals will also change. What you will get from working through *Reaching Your Potential* are the knowledge and skills you need to keep up the habits of self-examination, self-discovery, and self-management that will serve you all your life.

Before You Begin: Self-Assessment

Take a few minutes to assess yourself at this point in time, before you begin reading Chapter 1. Respond to the statements in the survey below. Later, when you have finished the book, you will reassess yourself by retaking the survey "After You're Done: Self-Assessment." We are confident that when you compare the two assessments, you will find that you have made real progress toward reaching your potential.

Directions: Read each of the following statements. Then circle *yes, maybe,* or *no* to indicate whether the statement is true of you at this time.

As a Lifelong Learner

1. I can name and describe the four areas of potential that each of us has.	Yes	Maybe	No
2. I have good self-belief, the foundation of success.	Yes	Maybe	No
3. I can learn new things and change my beliefs to change my behavior.	Yes	Maybe	No
4. I can set, pursue, and achieve realistic goals.	Yes	Maybe	No
5. I can envision a compelling future for myself.	Yes	Maybe	No
6. I have achieved personal mastery over at least some aspects of my life.	Yes	Maybe	No

UNIT 1 Developing Your Emotional Potential

Chapter 1 The Power of Self-Belief

7. I can explain my most important values and beliefs to another person.	Yes	Maybe	No
8. I usually think about things in a positive way.	Yes	Maybe	No
9. I recognize my good qualities and always make the most of them.	Yes	Maybe	No

Chapter 2 Setting Goals and Managing Time

10. I have a dream for my future.	Yes	Maybe	No
11. I have written personal, educational, professional, and community service goals.	Yes	Maybe	No

12. I have action plans for achieving my goals.	Yes	Maybe	No
13. I set priorities on the things I need to do.	Yes	Maybe	No
14. I use a planner to organize my time.	Yes	Maybe	No
15. I have the motivation needed to achieve my goals.	Yes	Maybe	No

UNIT 2   Developing Your Intellectual Potential

Chapter 3   Improving Your Thinking Skills

16. I use techniques to improve my memory.	Yes	Maybe	No
17. I am able to think critically.	Yes	Maybe	No
18. I try to solve problems in a systematic way.	Yes	Maybe	No
19. I use techniques to improve my creative thinking.	Yes	Maybe	No

Chapter 4   Improving Your Study Skills

20. I know my learning style and try to use it whenever possible.	Yes	Maybe	No
21. I have good study skills.	Yes	Maybe	No
22. I use special reading techniques when I read to learn.	Yes	Maybe	No
23. I take good notes on my readings and in class.	Yes	Maybe	No
24. I have good test-taking skills.	Yes	Maybe	No
25. I know how to use the resources of a library and the Internet.	Yes	Maybe	No

UNIT 3   Developing Your Physical Potential

Chapter 5   Eating Well

26. I can list the basic food groups and their nutrients.	Yes	Maybe	No
27. I eat a balanced diet.	Yes	Maybe	No
28. I maintain a healthy weight.	Yes	Maybe	No

Chapter 6   Staying Healthy

29. I am physically fit because I exercise regularly.	Yes	Maybe	No
30. I do not abuse drugs, including alcohol and tobacco.	Yes	Maybe	No
31. I understand how to prevent the spread of sexually transmitted diseases.	Yes	Maybe	No

UNIT 4   Developing Your Social Potential

Chapter 7   Communicating Effectively

32. I can explain the basic elements of communication.	Yes	Maybe	No
33. I know what my own communication style is.	Yes	Maybe	No
34. I use techniques to improve my communication with others.	Yes	Maybe	No

Chapter 8   Improving Your Listening Skills

35. I am an active listener, with respect for the speaker and comprehension of the message.	Yes	Maybe	No

Chapter 9   Improving Your Speaking Skills

36. I am a good speaker, with good voice qualities and a good command of Standard English.	Yes	Maybe	No
37. I am good at conversing with another person.	Yes	Maybe	No
38. I can prepare and deliver an oral presentation.	Yes	Maybe	No

Chapter 10   Getting Along with Others

39. I am assertive without being aggressive.	Yes	Maybe	No
40. I have ethical values that I try to live by.	Yes	Maybe	No
41. I am good at understanding the needs of other people.	Yes	Maybe	No
42. I give feedback tactfully and receive feedback openly.	Yes	Maybe	No
43. I use conflict resolution techniques to defuse angry situations.	Yes	Maybe	No

Chapter 11   Functioning in Groups

44. I can describe the basics of group dynamics.	Yes	Maybe	No
45. I function well as a member of a team or group.	Yes	Maybe	No
46. I can use different leadership styles in different situations.	Yes	Maybe	No

UNIT 5   Developing Your Action Plan

Chapter 12   Handling Change and Stress

47. I understand the causes of stress and the responses to stress.	Yes	Maybe	No
48. I know the signs of stress and watch out for them.	Yes	Maybe	No

49. I can reduce my feelings of stress by using coping techniques.   Yes   Maybe   No

Chapter 13   Managing Money

50. I know my values and goals and base short- and long-term financial decisions upon them.   Yes   Maybe   No
51. I have a written budget.   Yes   Maybe   No
52. I understand and use savings institutions, debit, credit, and insurance wisely.   Yes   Maybe   No
53. I know the factors that influence whether I should rent or buy a home.   Yes   Maybe   No
54. I invest now for large future expenses such as retirement.   Yes   Maybe   No

Chapter 14   Preparing for Your Career

55. I can match my skills and interests to one or more suitable occupations by using career resources.   Yes   Maybe   No
56. I have a good resume and career portfolio and can write a good cover letter.   Yes   Maybe   No
57. I know how to use various job-hunting resources.   Yes   Maybe   No
58. I am good at preparing for and undergoing employment interviews.   Yes   Maybe   No
59. I can evaluate whether a job fits into my long-term professional goals.   Yes   Maybe   No

Now look over your self-assessment. Underline the statements to which you replied *maybe* or *no*. These statements reflect areas in which you may not yet have reached your potential.

1. For the items to which you replied *maybe* or *no*, which five do you want to work on the most?

   _____

   _____

   _____

   _____

2. What do you hope to achieve by working on these areas of your life?

   _____

   _____

   _____

   _____

   _____

   _____

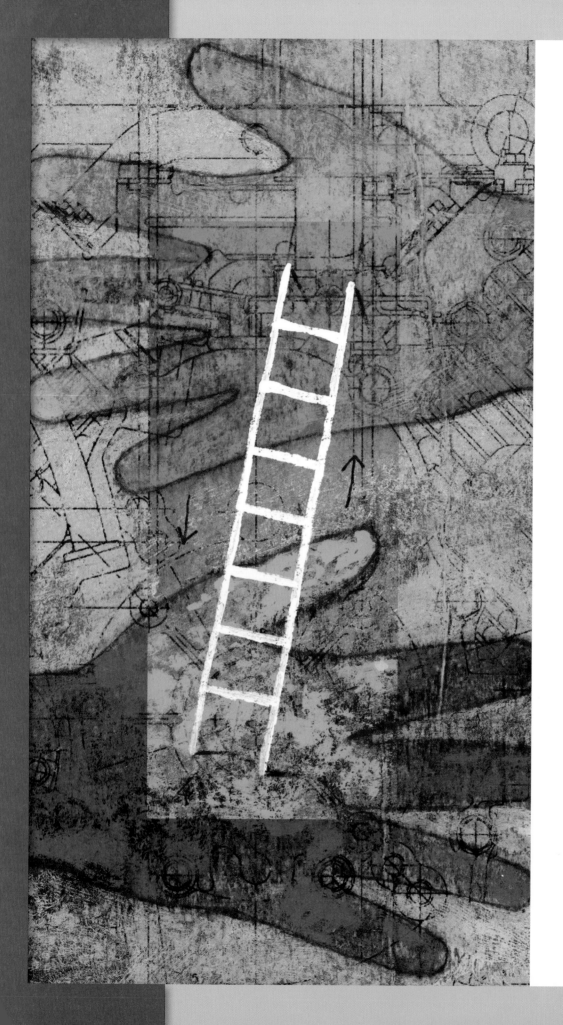

Developing Your Emotional Potential

Everything you think and do is colored by feelings and values. In the two chapters in this unit, you will develop your emotional potential by exploring your values and your self-belief. Then you will use your values and self-belief as the foundation for setting, planning, and achieving your goals.

CHAPTER 1
THE POWER OF SELF-BELIEF

In this chapter, you will be
. . . developing your self belief:

- I will explore my values and beliefs.
- I will learn how self-belief is the foundation of success.

. . . reframing your thoughts:

- I will compare my values to those of other people.
- I will change negative beliefs to positive beliefs through positive self-talk.

. . . setting goals:

- I will decide which values are most important to me.

. . . envisioning a compelling future:

- I will visualize success in my future.
- I will imagine myself having the traits needed for good self-belief.

. . . achieving personal mastery:

- I will view setbacks and failures as temporary.
- I will gain confidence to take action to achieve success.

CHAPTER 2
SETTING GOALS AND MANAGING TIME

In this chapter, you will be . . .
. . . developing your self belief:

- I will acknowledge my deepest wishes and dreams.
- I will accept my imperfections.

. . . reframing your thoughts:

- I will express my goals in positive language.
- I will maintain a hopeful outlook on the future.

. . . setting goals:

- I will set one personal, professional, educational, and community service goal.
- I will write action plans for three of my goals.
- I will use a planner to organize and schedule my course work.

. . . envisioning a compelling future:

- I will visualize what it will be like to achieve my goals.

. . . achieving personal mastery:

- I will get started on at least one of my long-term goals.
- I will keep working on my goals even when I experience setbacks.

1 The Power of Self-Belief

Success requires self-knowledge, motivation, and hard work. J. K. Rowling worked on the first Harry Potter novel for years while raising a daughter on her own.

When the last book of the Harry Potter series, *Harry Potter and the Deathly Hallows,* came out, it broke all records, selling 11 million copies on the first day of publication. By then its author, J. K. Rowling, was already well established as one of the best-selling writers of all time as well as one of the richest women in the world.

Rowling's success as a writer was not an overnight accomplishment. Born in England in 1965, Joanne Rowling often told fantasy stories to her younger sister Di. When she went to college, she wanted to study English, but her parents persuaded her to major in a foreign language, a more practical subject. After she graduated, she worked in London for several years. In 1990, the idea for the Harry Potter series came to her while she was stuck on a train for four hours. She started writing the first novel.

That same year Rowling's mother died after a 10-year battle with multiple sclerosis. Her mother's death affected Joanne Rowling deeply. Eager to get away, Rowling moved to Portugal to teach English with the unfinished manuscript in her luggage. There she married a Portuguese journalist and had a daughter, Jessica. When the marriage failed a year later, Rowling moved to Scotland with her daughter—and the still unfinished book.

The next couple of years were the bleakest of Rowling's life. She was depressed, unemployed, and living on welfare benefits. As a single mother, she had little time to write. Rowling would walk Jessica in her stroller until she fell asleep, and then she would go to a café, park the stroller beside a table, and work on her novel until Jessica awoke.

In 1995, Rowling finally finished the manuscript. During the next year, 12 publishers rejected the book. At last, a small company, Bloomsbury, agreed to publish it, giving her an advance of £1,500 (about $2,250). Her editor at Bloomsbury advised Rowling to get a day job, because writing children's books didn't pay well. In Rowling's case, he turned out to be spectacularly wrong, as the Harry Potter books and movies have been extremely successful worldwide.

Rowling's award-winning books have gained her fame and fortune. Yet there are many people whose success occurs in more private lives. These people—whether successful in athletics, personal relationships, business, community affairs, or other areas—share several characteristics. Successful people know who they are and what they want. In addition, they are committed to achieving their best.

The foundation of success in college and in life is a belief in yourself and your abilities. This is called self-belief. In this chapter, you will start developing your personal self-belief. You will:

- examine the meaning of success;
- explore your values;
- learn how values and beliefs affect behavior;
- gain insight into positive psychology;
- learn techniques for improving your self-belief; and
- use this knowledge to change your beliefs and behavior.

Finally, you will learn about the role of technology in college—an important tool for students to master to achieve success in school and beyond.

What Is Success?

Let's take a moment to think about success. In the United States, success is often equated with celebrity, glamor, and riches. Or it is thought of as a single achievement—winning an election or getting a good job. Yet leading a successful life is an ongoing process.

For example, Al Gore was a member of Congress, a U.S. senator, and vice president of the United States, surely a very successful political career. But when he lost his own bid to become president in 2000, he left politics and explored new tasks. Eventually Gore became an environmental activist, focusing on climate change. His film about global warming, *An Inconvenient Truth,* has been credited with raising public awareness worldwide about the dangers posed by global warming. In 2007, Gore received two major awards—an Academy Award for best documentary feature and the Nobel Peace Prize. These high honors were awarded to Gore for his work *after* he left U.S. politics.

"*Success doesn't come to you . . . you go to it.*"

MARVA COLLINS,
American educator

Fame and awards are not the only marks of a successful life. A feeling of worth and good relationships with others are often the basis of a successful life. As golf champion Chi Chi Rodriguez said, "The most successful human being I know was my dad and he never had anything financially."

So people who are truly successful are always trying to fulfill their **potential**. They focus on possibilities and work to turn them into realities. Furthermore, they see their potential as wide-ranging, from emotional to intellectual, from social to physical. They also see that their potential continues to change and grow as they gain experience. People who are trying to reach their potential know that the pursuit of success is a lifelong process.

Values

People who lead successful lives live by certain values. **Values** are your deepest feelings and thoughts about yourself and life. Values have three parts: (1) what you think; (2) how you feel; and (3) how you act, based on what you think and feel. For example, one of your values might be honesty. You think that telling a lie is wrong (thought). If someone you trust lies to you, you feel betrayed (feeling). When you make a mistake, you admit it rather than try to cover up or blame someone else (action).

Sometimes the three aspects of values do not always work in harmony. Let's take the value of honesty again. Even though you think telling a lie is wrong, there are times when you feel or act as though lying is okay. If someone asks you to do something you don't want to do, you might lie and say you're busy. Lying makes you feel uncomfortable because your actions and thoughts contradict one another. People are most comfortable in situations in which the thinking, feeling, and acting aspects of their values are working together.

It can be hard for families to teach their children what they value. Children learn values from many sources outside the family. Ratings systems help parents decide what movies, TV shows, CDs, and video games are appropriate for their children.

Where Do Values Come From?

You weren't born with a set of values. Rather, as you grew up, you were influenced by your family, friends, religion, culture, school, and society at large. For example, if your family expected each member to help with household chores, you may have learned the values of cooperation and helpfulness. When your friends became more of an influence, you may have learned the value of friendship.

Xernona Clayton, a broadcasting executive, says her basic values come from lessons her father taught her. Her father, a minister in a small Oklahoma town, often worked with people of various races and backgrounds. As a child, Xernona saw Native Americans, whites, and blacks

Your Turn 1-1

WHO ARE YOU?

Successful people usually have a clear sense of who they are and what they want from life. Take a few minutes to think about yourself and your life. Then answer these questions.

1. I like:

a. _____

_____

b. _____

_____

c. _____

_____

2. I respect:

a. _____

_____

b. _____

_____

c. _____

_____

3. I am good at:

a. _____

_____

b. _____

_____

c. _____

_____

4. Someday I would like to:

a. _____

_____

b. _____

_____

c. _____

_____

Your Turn 1-2

WHAT DO YOU VALUE?

Following is a list of 15 values arranged in alphabetical order. Study the list carefully. Then circle the five values that are most important to you. Rank these five by placing a 1 next to the value most important to you, a 2 next to the value that is second in importance, and so on until you have ranked the top five values.

When you have completed ranking your top five values, check your list. Feel free to make changes. Take all the time you need so that the end result truly reflects how you think and feel.

Value	Rank	Value	Rank
Affection	____	Honesty	____
Ambition	____	Logic	____
Bravery	____	Neatness	____
Cheerfulness	____	Obedience (duty, respect)	____
Competence (being capable)	____	Open-mindedness	____
Courtesy (being well-mannered)	____	Responsibility	____
Forgiveness	____	Self-control (commitment)	____
Helpfulness (working for others' welfare)	____		

"*The only place that success comes before work is in the dictionary.*"

VIDAL SASSOON,
salon professional

like herself consulting with her father. Her father's example taught her to look beyond race to see a person's inner qualities. He taught her to be kind to all people, regardless of race, and to focus on inner qualities and strength, not on outward appearances.

Our Society's Values

Although Americans come from many national, ethnic, and racial groups, we share many values. Polls have shown that adult Americans value honesty, ambition, responsibility, and broad-mindedness. We value peace, family security, and freedom. We may not always behave according to our values, but they are the standard against which we judge ourselves. Rank your values in Your Turn 1-2.

It's interesting to see how a large group of technical and business school graduates ranked the same values you ranked in Your Turn 1-2. Check this list to compare.

1. Competence (being capable)

2. Self-control (commitment)

3. Ambition

4. Open-mindedness

5. Honesty

6. Neatness

7. Forgiveness

8. Helpfulness (working for others' welfare)

9. Affection

10. Cheerfulness

11. Courtesy (being well-mannered)

12. Responsibility

13. Bravery

14. Obedience (duty, respect)

15. Logic

Apparently, these technical and business school graduates feel that being competent or capable (number 1), and self-controlled or committed

Your Turn 1-3

EXAMINE YOUR VALUES

Answer the following questions about the five values you chose and ranked.

1. Why is your top-ranked value so important to you?

_____

_____

2. Choose one of your top values and discuss (a) how you think about it; (b) how you feel about it; and (c) how it influences your behavior.

_____

_____

_____

3. How did your ranking of the values differ from those of the students who ranked them?

_____

_____

4. Now that you know how others ranked the values, how would you change your rankings, if at all?

_____

_____

News & Views

BENJAMIN FRANKLIN'S VALUES

Throughout history, people have been concerned about figuring out their values and trying to live by them. Benjamin Franklin (1706–1790), the American printer, author, diplomat, and scientist, was one of the writers of the Declaration of Independence. He also helped draft the U.S. Constitution. In his autobiography, Franklin explains how he tried to change his behavior by describing and then trying to live by his values, which he called "virtues." How are Franklin's values applicable today? Which of Franklin's values do you share?

The Thirteen Virtues

1. **Temperance:** Eat not to dullness. Drink not to elevation.
2. **Silence:** Speak not but what may benefit others or yourself. Avoid trifling conversation.
3. **Order:** Let all your things have their places. Let each part of your business have its time.
4. **Resolution:** Resolve to perform what you ought. Perform without fail what you resolve.
5. **Frugality:** Make no expense but to do good to others or yourself, i.e., waste nothing.
6. **Industry:** Lose no time. Be always employed in something useful. Cut off all unnecessary actions.
7. **Sincerity:** Use no hurtful deceit. Think innocently and justly; if you speak, speak accordingly.
8. **Justice:** Wrong none by doing injuries or omitting the benefits that are your duty.
9. **Moderation:** Avoid extremes. Forbear resenting injuries so much as you think they deserve.
10. **Cleanliness:** Tolerate no uncleanliness in body, clothes, or habitation.
11. **Tranquility:** Be not disturbed at trifles or at accidents common or unavoidable.
12. **Chastity:** Rarely use venery* but for health or offspring—never to dullness, weakness, or the injury of your own or another's peace or reputation.
13. **Humility:** Imitate Jesus and Socrates.†

Source: Franklin, Benjamin, *The Autobiography of Benjamin Franklin and Selections from His Other Writings*. New York: Random House, 1994, pp. 93–95.

*Sexual activity.

†Ancient Greek philosopher who taught about virtue and justice.

(number 2) were of greatest importance. They believe that competence and commitment are necessary for a successful life.

Research has supported the conclusions of these graduates. A five-year study to determine what 120 of the nation's top artists, athletes, and scholars had in common came up with surprising results. Researcher Benjamin Bloom, professor of education at the University of Chicago, said, "We expected to find tales of great natural gifts. We didn't find that at all. Their mothers often said it was their other child who had the greater gift." The study concluded that the key element common to these successful people was not talent but commitment.[1]

Changing Values

Our values can change as a result of experience. For example, after the terrorist attacks on the United States on September 11, 2001, a shift took place in Americans' values. According to a CBS News/*New York Times* poll taken a year later, 14 percent of Americans reevaluated their lives as a result of the attack. Although many felt the country had not changed, 17 percent thought that communities had become stronger, and 7 percent felt that Americans were more patriotic, had more pride in their country, and were nicer to one another than they had been before.[2]

Values can also change because of personal experience. For example, a young woman overcame a drug abuse problem with the help of her church's music director. As a result, she became aware of the importance of helping others. Today she is studying to become a psychotherapist so she can help others.

Beliefs

While values are your most deeply held general thoughts and feelings, beliefs are the specific opinions you have about yourself and particular people, situations, things, or ideas. In other words, beliefs are the specific attitudes that arise from your values. For example, if one of your values is ambition, you may have the belief that further education is important for success. If you value helpfulness, you may believe that you should do volunteer work in your community.

The Effects of Beliefs

Psychologists have shown that beliefs have a tremendous influence on behavior, and in turn, behavior can affect beliefs. Aesop's fable about the fox and the grapes shows how this can happen. When the fox first sees the grapes, he thinks they look delicious. This belief influences his behavior. He leaps up again and again, trying to reach the grapes. But the bunch of grapes is too high for him, and he gives up. Frustrated, the fox changes his belief: He decides the grapes must be sour.

This type of interplay between beliefs and behavior goes on all the time. Most of the time, you may not even be aware that it is happening. Yet your beliefs and other people's beliefs about you—both positive and negative—have a powerful influence on how you behave.

Negative Beliefs   Each person has the potential to live a successful and happy life. Yet most of us fall short of that ideal because we are carrying a bag of mental "garbage" that weighs us down. This

"They cannot take away our self-respect if we do not give it to them."

GANDHI (1869–1948),
Indian political and
spiritual leader

garbage is negative beliefs about ourselves. Some examples of negative beliefs are:

"I can't do algebra."

"I'm not smart enough to do that."

"Nobody cares about me."

"I'll never find a job."

Unfortunately, negative beliefs like these influence our behavior. The person who says she can't learn algebra in fact can't. The person who says he can't find a job doesn't find a job. Why? Because they don't try very hard. They think they will fail and so they do fail. A belief that comes true because it is believed is called a self-fulfilling prophecy.

Positive Beliefs   Self-fulfilling prophecies need not be negative, however. Sometimes they are positive; they enable you to take action and make progress. Some positive, or enabling, beliefs are:

"I will find the money to go to school."

"I will speak in class even though I'm nervous."

"I'm going to start my own business in five years."

"I will learn to swim."

The power of enabling beliefs is that they often come true. They come true not because of wishful thinking, however. Rather, enabling beliefs help you focus on what you need to do to accomplish something. They give you the self-confidence to persist and succeed.

Others Affect Your Beliefs   Your beliefs about yourself, both positive and negative, are influenced by the people around you. Family, friends, coworkers, and acquaintances all affect your beliefs. For example, many studies have shown the effect of teachers' beliefs on students' performance. In one experiment, 60 preschoolers were taught symbols. One group was taught by instructors who were told to expect good symbol learning. The other group was taught by instructors told to expect poor learning. The results? Nearly 77 percent of the first group of children learned five or more symbols. Only 13 percent of the second group of children learned five or more symbols.[3]

The power of other people's beliefs was dramatized in the movie *Stand and Deliver,* based on a Los Angeles mathematics teacher named Jaime Escalante. Escalante believed that his underachieving inner-city high school students could learn calculus. He also believed they could pass a national standardized calculus exam. After a year of intense effort on his part and theirs, *all* the students passed the exam. Such outstanding results were so unusual that the testing authority had the students retake the test. They passed again. Without the power of Escalante's belief in them and their belief in themselves, these students probably would not have learned calculus.

Beliefs can transform behavior. Jaime Escalante's students didn't believe they could learn calculus, much less pass a national calculus exam. Yet because he believed they could, they mastered calculus.

Your Turn 1-4

THE POWER OF OTHER PEOPLE'S BELIEFS

Think about a time when another person's opinion of you influenced your thoughts or actions. Then recall a time when your opinion of someone else changed what that person thought or did.

1. Describe a time when someone's opinion of you influenced your thoughts or actions.

_____

_____

_____

2. Describe a time when your opinion of someone changed that person's thoughts or actions.

_____

_____

_____

> "We need to internalize this idea of excellence. Not many folks spend a lot of time trying to be excellent."
>
> BARACK OBAMA,
> 44th President of the
> United States

> "No one can persuade another to change. Each of us guards a gate of change that can only be opened from the inside."
>
> MARILYN FERGUSON,
> American poet

Victims and Nonvictims If you allow yourself to be persuaded by negative beliefs, you will soon view yourself as a victim. Victims operate from a position of weakness. They feel that they are not smart enough or strong enough to take charge of their own lives. They live from day to day, allowing things to happen to them and others to control them.

Nonvictims, on the other hand, understand that negative beliefs can be crippling. Nonvictims have the ability to resist the negative beliefs of others because they believe in their own strengths. Because they have positive views of their abilities and goals, nonvictims often succeed where victims fail. The Reverend Jesse Jackson, for example, grew up in poverty and went on to become a political leader and Democratic presidential candidate. "My mother was a teenaged mother and her mother was a teenaged mother. With scholarships and other help, I managed to get an education. Success to me is being born in a poor or disadvantaged family and making something of yourself."

Changing Your Beliefs

We all suffer the effects of negative beliefs, some of us more than others. Sometimes events don't happen the way we expect. Or we fall into a pattern of negative behavior toward the people around us. Or a stressful event or change in our lives throws us off balance. When these situations happen, it's

The Three Doctors

In 1990, three Newark, New Jersey, high school seniors cut class and took refuge in their school library. There, representatives from Seton Hall University happened to be giving a talk on health and the sciences. One of the students, George Jenkins, was intrigued. By the end of the day, he had convinced his friends Sampson Davis and Rameck Hunt that they were all destined to become doctors.

Nothing in their backgrounds suggested that the three boys would succeed. All of them were being raised in broken homes in the poorest neighborhoods of Newark. Absentee fathers, drugs, gangs, and crime were part of their everyday lives. Their families didn't have the money to send them to college. None of them even knew a real doctor.

Still, the three students made an agreement that day in 1990: They would go to college and become doctors, and they would help each other along the way. And that's just what they did: All three attended Seton Hall University and the University of Medicine and Dentistry in New Jersey. They got financial aid to help with the costs. Davis and Hunt became doctors, and Jenkins became a dentist.

But that's not the end of their story. The three doctors decided they needed to reach out to others, and so they established the Three Doctors Foundation, whose mission is "to inspire and create opportunities for communities through education, mentoring and health awareness." They have written

The Three Doctors (left to right): Sampson Davis, George Jenkins, and Rameck Hunt

books about their experiences: *The Pact*, for adults; *We Beat the Street* (2005), for children; and *The Bond* (2007), a book about fathers.

On their Web site, www.threedoctors. com, Dr. Davis says, "Strength comes from knowing that the power to overcome adversity and prevail lies within one's self and you have to first realize that. Once realized, you have to accept accountability for your life and take the necessary steps to turn hopes and dreams into realities."

Sources: "Our Story," http://www.threedoctors. com/ourstory.php, accessed Jan. 4, 2008; Lornet Turnbull, "Three friends escaped streets to prosper as 'Three Doctors,'" *Seattle Times,* Oct. 4, 2004, http://seattletimes.nwsource.com/html/ education/2002051015_threedocs01m.html, accessed Jan. 4, 2008; Bob Minzeheimer, "Three Doctors," *USAToday,* Oct. 2, 2007, http://www. usatoday.com/life/books/news/2007-10-02-three-doctors_N.htm, accessed Jan. 4, 2008.

time to pay attention to your beliefs. If your beliefs are contributing to your difficulties, you can change them—and change your life for the better.

Why should you drop negative beliefs and adopt beliefs that will enable you to succeed? Because it works. You must:

1. understand the power that beliefs have in your life

2. realize that continuing to think in a negative way will harm the quality of your life

3. change your beliefs and how you feel about yourself

If you change your beliefs, you will change your behavior. If you change your behavior, you will change your life.

Using Positive Self-Talk   That negative inner voice that tells you how bad things are and how bad they always will be has to be silenced. Talking back to that negative voice can help you change your beliefs, attitudes, and behavior.

To change your beliefs and behavior, you needn't talk out loud in public, but you can use positive self-talk. Positive self-talk has three characteristics:

1. **Positive self-talk consists of "I" statements.** "I" statements show that you are taking charge of your life.

2. **Positive self-talk uses the present tense.** Using the present tense shows you are ready for action.

3. **Positive self-talk is positive and enthusiastic.** It focuses on *what is* rather than *what is not*.

For example, suppose that Jessica's longtime boyfriend Brian has broken off their relationship. Jessica wants to meet new people, but she makes no effort to do so. Instead, she gets more depressed and lonely. Jessica thinks, "Brian broke up with me so I must be boring and unattractive. Why should anyone want to go out with me?" It would be far more helpful if Jessica used positive self-talk. She could tell herself, "I am an interesting and attractive person. I am looking for chances to meet new people and form new relationships."[4]

Positive Psychology

Positive psychology is a branch of psychology that studies the positive aspects of human experience. It focuses on people's strengths instead of their weaknesses. It is concerned with mental health rather than mental illness.

At the level of the individual, positive psychology focuses on positive traits: the ability to love and work, courage, interpersonal skill, appreciation for beauty, perseverance, forgiveness, originality, future-mindedness, spirituality, talent, and wisdom. At the community level, positive psychology is about civics and citizenship: responsibility to the

"*Here's the challenge: This is the time, this is the place, and you are the person to do whatever it takes to succeed.*"

ROBERT K. THROOP,
educator

Your Turn 1-5

USE POSITIVE SELF-TALK

Each of the following is a negative belief. Rewrite each so that it is positive self-talk.

1. I'll never pass that exam. I missed too many classes.

_____

_____

2. That computer is too hard to operate.

_____

_____

3. I'll be ____ years old before I get my diploma (or degree or certificate).

_____

_____

Answer the following questions.

4. Describe a situation about which you had negative thoughts and feelings.

_____

_____

5. How could you have used positive self-talk to change your beliefs and behavior?

_____

_____

© 2011 Wadsworth, Cengage Learning

group, nurturance, generosity, civility, moderation, tolerance, and work ethic.

One aspect of positive psychology is prevention. How can problems like depression, substance abuse, and violence be prevented when society contributes to these problems? According to positive psychologists, improvements in prevention have come from building competencies in people, not from treating their weaknesses. There are human qualities that help prevent mental illness and antisocial behavior. Optimism, courage, hope, and perseverance are just a few.

Your Turn 1-6

To learn more about positive psychology, visit the Web site of the Positive Psychology Center at the University of Pennsylvania <http://www.positivepsychology.org>. It contains the latest information about the field and its findings, questionnaires to help you develop insights about your own outlook, and links to other positive psychology resources on the Internet. Then answer these questions:

1. What is the most interesting thing you learned about positive psychology?

_____

_____

_____

2. How might you apply the ideas of positive psychology to your own life?

_____

_____

_____

People who are optimistic tend to interpret their troubles as passing, controllable, and specific to one situation. In contrast, pessimistic people believe that troubles last forever, undermine everything that they do, and can't be controlled. Positive psychologists think that people can be taught to be more optimistic. Pessimistic people can distract and distance themselves from negative beliefs and reactions to failure. They can argue with themselves about the failure and discover it is not as bad as it could have been. By doing this, people can learn to turn pessimistic thought patterns into optimistic thought patterns. They can increase their sense of well-being.

Self-Belief

The net effect of your values and beliefs is your self-belief. Self-belief is your confidence in and respect for your own abilities. Self-belief is the part of us that is resilient in the face of difficulties. Bad things may happen and hurt us—physically, emotionally, or economically—but our positive self-belief does not need to be harmed. People with positive self-belief understand that outward circumstances do not change this inner belief.

> "Success is not final, failure is not fatal: it is the courage to continue that counts."
>
> WINSTON CHURCHILL (1874–1965), British prime minister

Your Turn 1-7

WHAT'S YOUR SELF-BELIEF?

Self-belief involves the way you think and feel about yourself. Use the following list of personality traits to describe your current self-belief.

aggressive	dishonest	irresponsible	quiet
ambitious	dumb	lonely	reserved
assertive	eager	loyal	responsible
bossy	fair	mature	sensitive
capable	funny	motivated	shy
caring	goal-oriented	neat	sincere
cheerful	gloomy	negative	sweet
confident	healthy	nervous	trusting
considerate	honest	open	unambitious
creative	humble	outgoing	understanding
daring	indecisive	passive	unhealthy
decisive	insensitive	polite	unmotivated
determined	intelligent	positive	warm

1. Current self-belief: I see myself as

_____

_____

_____

_____

Now imagine that you are at a banquet. Your family, friends, and colleagues are there to praise you. What qualities do you hope they talk about?

2. Future self-belief: I will be

_____

_____

_____

_____

Improving Your Self-Belief

Have you decided that your self-belief is not all it could be? There are ways to improve your self-belief.

1. **Accept yourself.** Recognize your own good qualities and don't expect to be perfect. Everyone has special talents and abilities. Work to discover and develop yours.

2. **Pay attention to yourself.** Try to discover what gives you inner satisfaction, and do things that give you pleasure. Successful people do what they enjoy.

3. **Use positive self-talk.** Encourage yourself to make the most of your abilities by developing a positive mental attitude. People who succeed tell themselves that they will succeed.

4. **Don't be afraid to try new things.** Remember that there is no such thing as failure—only results. If you don't try new things, you won't reach your potential.

5. **Remember that you are special.** No one else has your set of capabilities and talents. Your values, beliefs, and emotions, and the way you act upon them, make up your unique personality.

"*If you want a quality, act as if you already had it.*"

WILLIAM JAMES (1842–1910), psychologist and philosopher

"*If you want to succeed in life … you … need to know what you believe in…. Then you have to have the courage to act on those beliefs.*"

RUDOLPH GIULIANI, former mayor of New York City

The Foundation of Success

Positive self-belief is the foundation of success. When you believe in yourself, you can accomplish what you set your mind to. Self-belief allows you to use your emotional, intellectual, social, and physical potential to take action. Taking action means making progress toward achieving your dreams and goals. When you act, you get results. When you get results, your self-belief improves because you've succeeded at something. Improved self-belief gives you the confidence to take further action. The process of building self-belief is cyclical. The more you try, the more you accomplish and the greater your self-belief. Self-belief with commitment can create miracles.

Take the example of Mahatma Gandhi, a man with many exceptional traits, one of which was a strong belief in himself and his abilities. While the Indian power elites were trying to break England's colonial rule with speeches and infighting, Gandhi was working with the poor in the countryside of India. Gradually he gathered overwhelming support and trust from ordinary Indians. With no political office or military capability, he and his followers eventually defeated England. India won its independence as a nation.

Although Gandhi was clearly an exceptional person, successful people share some of his characteristics. They are willing to do whatever it takes to reach their potential without harming others. They are not necessarily the "best" or the "brightest," but they have positive self-belief and a strong commitment to their goals. You can be one of them.

Tech Tips

AN OVERVIEW OF COLLEGE TECHNOLOGY

One aspect of your success can be achieving your educational goals using computer technology. If you are not comfortable working with computers, now is the time for some positive self-talk. (Remind yourself that a computer is just a tool. But if that's not enough to ease your mind, look ahead to the section on dealing with "technostress" in Chapter 12, page 289.) Whatever your technology knowledge and skills, now is also the time to become familiar with what your campus has to offer.

At college you'll be using a computer every day to perform a variety of tasks. You'll need a computer for administrative tasks, like registering for classes and viewing your grades. You'll need a computer to access your school's online resources, like academic departments, course Web sites, and the library. And you'll need a computer for course assignments, like doing research and writing papers. If you're taking an online course, you'll need a computer for every aspect of the class.

Check Your College's Information Technology Resources

Today the use of computers and other technology on campus is so widespread that most schools have their own information technology departments. These departments run and maintain the college's public computers, campus network, communications, and other technology resources. They also provide training and help to students and faculty, and give out information about the types of computers and software that are most compatible with the school's systems.

Access Computers in a Variety of Places

If you have your own laptop computer to use at college, that is very convenient. But if you do not, there are several places you can find computers to use:

- On campus, you'll find public computers with campus network and Internet access in the computer labs, the library, and at scattered workstations in other buildings.
- In your neighborhood, you can find computers at the local public library.
- At home, you can use the family computer, if there is one, to access your college's network and do your course work.

Consider Technology beyond the Computer

Although it may seem that a computer can do just about everything you'll need to do, you may find some other technology useful as a student:

- **USB flash drive.** A portable memory device small enough to fit in your pocket, a flash drive is ideal for transporting files from computer to computer. If you use campus computers, a flash drive enables you to save and keep your files on your own storage device.
- **Printer.** It's convenient to have your own printer but not necessary, because printers are available on campus.
- **iPod or MP3 player.** Some course lectures and audio textbooks are available for download to iPods and MP3 players. You can listen at your own convenience.
- **Cable television.** Some colleges show course sessions on cable television stations. For students at a distance, these courses are ideal.

Your Turn 1-8

Search your college's Web site to learn specifics about computers and networks on your campus. If an information technology orientation session is available, take it. Then answer the following questions:

1. Where are the public computers on campus? When are they available?

_____

_____

2. What advice, if any, does the information technology staff give students about buying a computer that will be compatible with your school's systems?

_____

_____

3. What help does the information technology department offer to students?

_____

_____

4. What other tecnology-related resources are there on your school's Web site?

_____

_____

5. Where can you find an off-campus public computer in your area?

_____

_____

What's Up?

Name _____   Date _____

1. What are values?
_____

2. List the three aspects of values.
_____
_____
_____

3. What are beliefs?
_____

4. How do negative beliefs affect you?
_____

5. How do other people's beliefs affect you?
_____

6. How can positive self-talk be used to change your beliefs?
_____

7. What are the three characteristics of positive self-talk?
_____

8. What is positive psychology? What does it emphasize?
_____

9. What effect does changing your beliefs have?
_____

10. What is self-belief? Why is it important?
         Foundation of success
_____

Case Studies

The Case of the New Roommate

Elisa was discovering that her new roommate Pam had some unsettling habits. Although they had agreed to share chores, even listing who would do each task, Elisa felt that Pam was not doing her share. For example, when it was Pam's turn to clean, the apartment stayed messy for days. When Pam finally did clean up, Elisa thought she didn't do a good job. Elisa was very uncomfortable living in a dirty, disorderly apartment. She was starting to think she had made a mistake when she had asked Pam to share the apartment. Yet Elisa liked Pam because she was a cheerful, pleasant person.

1. Why is Elisa uncomfortable with her new roommate?

2. What does Elisa value?

3. Does Pam share these values? Explain.

4. What might Elisa do to improve the situation with her roommate?

The Case of the Gloomy Coworker

Lee and Dave were technicians who provided technology support for home and small business computer networks. Their boss was going to take a week's vacation, and she asked Lee to fill in for her. Instead of solving computer problems in the field, Lee would have to take customer calls, assign technicians to particular jobs, and make sure everything went smoothly. He was looking forward to the challenge. When Dave heard about Lee's temporary assignment, he began to discourage Lee. He told him all the things that could go wrong—angry customers, not enough technicians, system problems that couldn't be solved. Finally, Dave told Lee that Lee wouldn't get through the week without a major catastrophe. Lee started to feel very nervous about the assignment.

1. What was the effect of Dave's negative beliefs on Lee's attitude toward substituting for his boss?

2. What should Lee do to counteract the effect of Dave's beliefs?

Journal

Thinking about new ideas is helpful, but writing about them in a journal will help you understand them much better. You will be able to see how the ideas can relate to your own life. This journal focuses on what your ideal days would be like; a diary, in contrast, is about what your day actually was.[5]

Learn about success, values, beliefs, and behavior by answering the following journal questions.

1. Describe the most successful person you know. What makes this person successful, in your opinion?

_____

_____

_____

_____

_____

2. From whom did you learn your most important values? How were the values taught to you? How do your values relate to some aspect of your identity (as a man, woman, family member, member of a culture, or citizen)?

_____

_____

_____

_____

_____

3. Give a personal example of positive thoughts or beliefs that influenced your actions.

_____

_____

_____

_____

_____

4. Describe (a) a behavior that you would like to change and (b) how you might use positive self-talk to help you change the behavior.

_____

_____

_____

_____

_____

Setting Goals and Managing Time

Great accomplishments often start with a dream. Doug Blevins dreamed of a career in the National Football League, despite having a disabling disease, cerebral palsy. After coaching school teams, Blevins taught kicking skills and eventually was hired as a full-time kicking coach by the Miami Dolphins. He has coached some of the best kickers in the NFL, including Olindo Mare (shown here) and Adam Vinatieri. Today he runs his own kicking consulting business.

Have you ever set out for a walk or drive with no clear destination in mind? Or have you ever surfed the Internet when you had nothing better to do? You went from place to place at random, perhaps saw some interesting things, perhaps not. When you were finished, you couldn't really say whether you had accomplished anything or not.

People who can point to achievements and successes generally are those who don't wander all the time. Instead, they take charge of their lives. They realize that they are responsible for themselves. They understand their own values and abilities. They decide what they want, and they go after it. You too can take charge of your life and determine its direction. You have already started this process in Chapter 1.

The previous chapter prompted you to think about your values, beliefs, and self-beliefs. By now, you should have a good idea about who you are and what you do well. With this in mind, you can start thinking about what you want to accomplish. In this chapter, you will:

- identify and state your goals;
- create an action plan for three goals;
- learn some techniques for overcoming procrastination;
- discover how to manage time on a daily, weekly, and monthly basis;
- use time management tools to get organized; and
- discover how to keep yourself motivated to succeed.

Finally, you will learn how course management systems can help you organize your academic work and achieve your educational goals.

Identifying Your Goals

A good way to start identifying your goals is to think about your deepest wishes and dreams. Perhaps you've always longed to be a dancer, visit China, or own your own home. Maybe you want to have three children, be governor of your state, or start your own business.

Perhaps you haven't thought about your dreams in a long time. If that's the case, try asking yourself these questions: If you had only one year left to live, what would you do? If you were granted three wishes, what would they be? If you were guaranteed success in anything you chose to do, what would you do?[1]

Goals: Challenging and Realistic

Your dreams can be the source of many of your goals. People whose achievements are extraordinary often started with dreams that may have seemed out of their reach. By focusing on their dreams, they were able to concentrate their energies on achieving them, one step at a time.

However, it's important to be realistic. Suppose, for example, that Jon loves cars and wants to become a mechanic. Yet Jon has little aptitude for taking things apart and putting them together. He has trouble visualizing how things work. Jon's dream is not realistic. He can use up all his energy trying to become a master mechanic, or he can revise his dream. Perhaps another career involving cars would make better use of Jon's talents.

Being realistic doesn't necessarily mean giving up dreams that appear to be long shots. Your goals should be realistic, taking into account your unique talents and abilities. Yet they should also be challenging and require effort to achieve. If your goals are too easily achieved, you are not realizing your full potential. You can do more.

Types of Goals

Do you have dreams and goals for each aspect of your life? Goals can be thought of as personal, educational, professional, and community service.

Personal Goals   Personal goals relate to your family or private life. You may want to increase your strength, lose 10 pounds, or learn to play the electric guitar. Improving your relationships with family and friends and improving yourself in personal ways are the general objectives of personal goals.

Educational Goals   Educational goals relate to your efforts to learn more and improve your educational credentials. They may take the form of learning about something new, for example, learning how to use a spreadsheet program. Or the goals may relate to certificates, diplomas, and degrees that you want to earn.

Professional Goals   Your objectives for your work life are professional goals. Professional goals may be broad, for example, becoming a salesperson or earning $100,000 a year. Or the goals may be more specific. You may want to pass a licensing exam in a particular field or get a job at a specific company.

> "The tragedy in life doesn't lie in not reaching your goal. The tragedy lies in having no goal to reach."
>
> BENJAMIN MAYS (1895–1984), mentor to Martin Luther King, Jr.

> "People are not lazy. They simply have limited goals— that is, goals that do not inspire them."
>
> ANTHONY ROBBINS, motivational writer

> "Education is not preparation for life; education is life itself."
>
> JOHN DEWEY (1859–1952), philosopher and educator

Your Turn 2-1

WHAT ARE YOUR DREAMS?

Take a few minutes to write down what you've always dreamed of doing.

_____

_____

_____

_____

_____

_____

_____

_____

_____

_____

_____

> "*Service to others is the rent you pay for your room here on earth.*"
>
> MUHAMMAD ALI,
> boxing champion

Community Service Goals Community service goals are related to improving conditions in your neighborhood, town, or city. Examples are helping homeless people, giving kids the opportunity to play sports, participating in a parent–teacher organization, and bringing meals to housebound people. Achieving community service goals benefits the community, but it also gives you the satisfaction of accomplishing something yourself.

Length of Time to Achieve Goals

Some personal, educational, professional, and community service goals can be achieved in a month. Others might take a decade. When you are setting goals, it's helpful to think about how much time you will need to achieve them (see Figure 2–1).

FIGURE 2–1

Short-term goals take a year or less to achieve, intermediate-term goals take from one to five years, and long-term goals take more than five years to accomplish. (AP/Wide World Photos/Dennis Cook.)

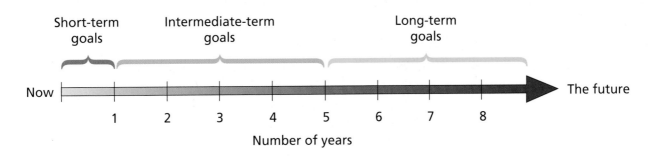

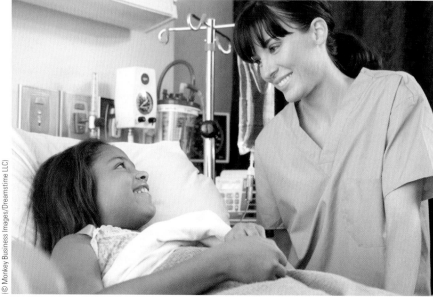

People have goals in many areas of life. Becoming physically fit, getting a college degree, becoming a health care worker, and helping to clean up the community are examples of personal, educational, professional, and community service goals.

- **Short-term goals** are those that can be achieved in a relatively brief period of time—a year or less.
- **Intermediate-term goals** can be achieved in one to five years.
- **Long-term goals** take at least five years to accomplish.

One of your short-term goals, for example, may be to pass a particular course. Achieving this goal will take only a couple of months. On the other hand, earning your degree, diploma, or certificate is an intermediate-term goal. It may take you several years to accomplish. For people who go to school part-time, earning a degree may be a long-term goal.

Note that long- and intermediate-term goals can often be thought of as a series of short-term goals. Earning an academic degree, diploma, or certificate is a long- or intermediate-term goal; each course you pass is a short-term goal that contributes to your objective.

Six Rules for Stating Goals

Thinking about your goals is not enough. It's important to write them down. Studies have shown that people who write down their goals are far more likely to achieve them than people who do not.

When you state your goals, you should keep the following six rules in mind:

1. **Express your goals in positive language.** For example, "I will get at least a C in English," rather than "I won't get a D or F in English." In goal-writing, positive language has the same beneficial effects as positive self-talk.

2. **Make your goals as specific as possible.** Avoid vague, general language like, "I would like to travel." Instead, be specific and say something like "I will vacation in Aruba." Making goals specific helps you focus on achieving them.

3. **Make your goals measurable.** For example, suppose you want to save some money. How will you know whether you've reached your goal? When you've saved $100? $1,000? You have to have some way to measure whether you've achieved your goal. If you say you want to save $1,000 of your part-time earnings, you have a measurable goal. When you state a goal, ask yourself, "What do I want to accomplish? How will I know that I have accomplished it?" Your goal will be measurable if you can respond to these questions.

4. **Set a deadline.** When do you want to achieve this goal? In two months? In two years? Whatever the answer, commit yourself to a time frame. Decide when you will start and when you will be done.

5. **Have a variety of goals.** It's important not to channel your efforts toward only one goal or one type of goal. If all your goals are professional, for example, you will find yourself neglecting other aspects of your life. Try to achieve a balance of personal, educational, professional, community service, short-term, and long-term goals.

> "If you are planning for a year, sow rice; if you are planning for a decade, plant trees; if you are planning for a lifetime, educate people."
>
> CHINESE PROVERB

News & Views

NEW YEAR'S RESOLUTIONS

New Year's Day is the traditional time for setting goals. After a holiday season in which people often eat, drink, and party too much, New Year's is the time when many people resolve to change something about their lives.

What do people resolve to do? MyGoals.com, a Web site devoted to goal-setting, issues annual statistics on New Year's resolutions. The people who run this Web site base their breakdown of types of resolutions on the site's goal-setting activity. According to their data, in 2009, health and fitness goals were the most common, followed by career and personal finance goals, as shown in this circle graph.

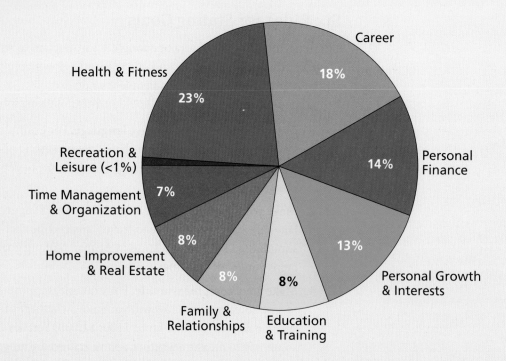

"All told, the data suggest a broader trend toward returning to basics—family, friends, and home," said Greg Helmstetter, CEO of myGoals.com, "because that's where people are finding security and fulfillment."

Source: "2009 New Year's Resolutions Reflect Tough Economy: Health & Travel Are Out, Nesting & Relationships Are In," <http://www.mygoals.com/about/pressRelease016.html>, accessed January 19, 2009.

> "A numerical goal without a method is nonsense."
>
> W. EDWARDS DEMING (1900–1993), statistician and quality-control expert

6. **Make your goals your own.** Having others set goals for you, even well-meaning people like parents, spouses, and friends, means that the goals are not truly your own. Your goals must be just that—yours. That way, you'll be committed to achieving them. Accomplishing your goals ought to give *you* pleasure and satisfaction.

Your Turn 2-2

WHAT ARE YOUR GOALS?

Use the chart below to record your personal, educational, professional, and community service goals. Remember to classify goals as either short-term (one year or less to accomplish), intermediate-term (one to five years), or long-term (more than five years to achieve). You may have more than one goal or no goals in a particular category.

Personal Goals

Short-term: _____

_____

_____

_____

Intermediate-term: _____

_____

_____

_____

Long-term: _____

_____

_____

_____

Educational Goals

Short-term: _____

_____

_____

_____

Intermediate-term: _____

_____

_____

_____

Long-term: _____

_____

_____

_____

Professional Goals

Short-term: _____

_____

_____

_____

Intermediate-term: _____

_____

_____

_____

Long-term: _____

_____

_____

_____

Community Service Goals

Short-term: _____

_____

_____

_____

Intermediate-term: _____

_____

_____

_____

Long-term: _____

_____

_____

_____

WHATEVER IT TAKES

Becky Zaheri and the Katrina Krewe

In September 2005, a week after Hurricane Katrina flooded New Orleans, Becky Zaheri visited the city to check on her house. She expected to see storm debris, water damage, and empty neighborhoods. What she didn't expect to see was trash all over the streets. Her family had planned to return to New Orleans in a few months. But Zaheri knew that something needed to be done about the garbage before her family could go home.

Zaheri couldn't pick up the large pieces of debris; the Army Corps of Engineers was doing that with their street sweepers. But lots of smaller trash was left behind. Zaheri decided to focus on trash that people could bag by hand.

In November 2005, Zaheri e-mailed about 100 friends and family, asking if they would help clean up the neighborhoods. About an hour later, she had 25 responses, some from people she didn't even know, who had been forwarded her message. That month, Zaheri organized two Saturday cleanups. Dozens of volunteers showed up to help.

Zaheri named her volunteers the Katrina Krewe (krewes are the groups that sponsor floats in the annual New Orleans Mardi Gras parade). Over the next several months, more than 10,000 local, national, and international volunteers participated in Katrina Krewe cleanups. They bagged about 250,000 pounds of trash, which the New Orleans Department of Sanitation hauled away.

Becky Zaheri (center)

(© Bill Haber/AP Photo)

By August 2006, the Katrina Krewe had accomplished their goal of removing storm-related trash, and they stopped organizing cleanups. Instead, the group began to run a "Keep It Klean" media campaign, which reminds New Orleans residents that it's now up to them to keep their neighborhoods clean.

Sources: "Katrina Krewe: Pitching In for a Cleaner New Orleans!" CleanNO.org, accessed Jan. 19, 2009. Maria Montoya, "Changemaker: A Mom Who Moves Mountains." Ladies Home Journal, Aug. 2006, at http://www.lhj.com/lhj/story.jhtml?storyid=/templatedata/lhj/story/data/1153841885160.xml, accessed Jan. 11, 2008. Steve Ritea, "Katrina Krewe Calls It A Day." The Times-Picayune, Aug. 25, 2006, at http://www.nola.com/news/t-p/frontpage/index.ssf?/base/news-16/1156486170218950.xml&coll=1, accessed Jan. 11, 2008. Becky Zaheri, "Katrina Anniversary." http://www.time.com/time/specials/2007/article/0,28804,1646611_1646683_1647789,00.html, accessed Jan. 11, 2008.

Creating an Action Plan

Once you've decided on your goals, you need to plan how you'll reach them. A written action plan will help you focus your efforts and reach your goals without getting lost along the way.

Running a marathon is an intermediate-term goal that requires a step-by-step action plan. Over the course of a year or more, these runners gradually increase the distance they can cover.

When preparing an action plan, think about your long-term goals first. In other words, start by knowing where you want to wind up. Let's say, for example, that Elena wants to open her own clothing boutique. First, she decides that she wants to accomplish this within seven years. With that target in mind, Elena plans the steps she must take to open the shop. First she plans to work in a large clothing store for five years to get experience. At the same time, she will take courses at night in fashion merchandising, accounting, and other business subjects. She will also save 10 percent of her income each year toward the expense of starting a business. At the end of five years, Elena plans to look for a job in a small specialty shop in order to get more experience. During the two years before she opens the shop, she will save 15 percent of her income.

Elena has created an action plan for one of her long-term goals. Essentially, the steps she took were:

1. stating a long-term goal in specific terms and giving it a time frame
2. breaking down the goal into short-term goals, or steps, that will lead to achieving the long-term goal
3. indicating specific results of the short-term goals in order to monitor progress
4. setting deadlines for the short-term goals

If you follow these steps for each of your intermediate- or long-term goals, you will have an action plan for each goal. A plan for a short-term goal would skip step 2. The plan should be written so you can monitor your progress toward achieving your goals.

Managing Your Time

Action plans for intermediate and long-term goals are big-picture plans. Whether you follow your plans and achieve your goals will depend on managing your time well on a daily, weekly, and monthly basis. Otherwise, time can easily slip away. Procrastinating, not having enough time, wasting time, and misusing time can add up to a life spent without reaching your goals and your potential. If you want to be in control of your life and achieve your goals, you will have to take charge of your time.

"Employ thy time well, if thou meanest to gain leisure."

BENJAMIN FRANKLIN (1706–1790), statesman, scientist, and writer

Your Turn 2-3

PREPARE AN ACTION PLAN

Refer to your goals statement on page 39 and select three of your most important intermediate- or long-term goals. Using the Action Plan form that follows, create an action plan for these goals.

ACTION PLAN: INTERMEDIATE- OR LONG-TERM GOALS

1. Intermediate- or long-term goal:

To be accomplished by: _____

Step 1: _____

  Results needed: _____

  _____

  To be accomplished by: _____

Step 2: _____

  Results needed: _____

  _____

  To be accomplished by: _____

Step 3: _____

  Results needed: _____

  _____

  To be accomplished by: _____

Step 4: _____

  Results needed: _____

  _____

  To be accomplished by: _____

2. Intermediate- or long-term goal:

To be accomplished by: _____

Step 1: _____

  Results needed: _____

  _____

  To be accomplished by: _____

Step 2: _____

  Results needed: _____

  _____

  To be accomplished by: _____

Step 3: _____

  Results needed: _____

  _____

  To be accomplished by: _____

Step 4: _____

  Results needed: _____

  _____

  To be accomplished by: _____

3. Intermediate- or long-term goal:

To be accomplished by: _____

Step 1: _____

  Results needed: _____

  _____

  To be accomplished by: _____

Step 2: _____

  Results needed: _____

  _____

  To be accomplished by: _____

Step 3: _____

  Results needed: _____

  _____

  To be accomplished by: _____

Step 4: _____

  Results needed: _____

  _____

  To be accomplished by: _____

Taking the First Step

Old habits and ways of living are powerful forces. Taking the first step toward a major goal can be hard. But procrastinating, or postponing a task that ought to be done now, is the sure way to fail to reach a goal. People who procrastinate usually have a "good" reason. Danielle may say, for example, that she will start studying for a course as soon as pressure eases up at work. In fact, Danielle knows she should start studying now, but she gives herself an excuse not to start.

Postponing a task will not make it easier. Rather, when you are tempted to put off something important, you should carefully think about what is holding you back. You may be feeling shy, indecisive, fearful, negative, or bad about yourself. You feel you can't do something, so you don't do it. The result is inaction.

To overcome procrastination, you can change your beliefs and you can change your behavior. In Chapter 1, we discussed the power of positive self-talk in improving your self-belief. If you are a procrastinator, now is the time for some serious conversation with yourself. Danielle, for example, should be telling herself, "Studying is important. I want to study to pass the course. I can start now despite pressures at work. When I'm at home I'll study from 8 to 10 each evening."

Tips for Getting Started   One approach for people who procrastinate is to start by doing a little bit. There are several techniques you can use to get yourself started on a task:

- **Set a deadline for getting started.** By focusing on a starting date, you will find the energy to begin because you have made a commitment to yourself.

- **List small tasks**—that will take only a minute or two—that can get you started. Then do the first one.

- **Do anything in connection with the goal.** If you have to write letters and can't get started, then ease into the task by looking up the addresses or preparing the envelopes first.

- **Assign a short period of time during which you will work on the goal.** For example, tell yourself that for the next five minutes you will do things that relate to the goal.

- **Do the worst thing first.** Sometimes tackling the hardest part and getting it done opens up the way to achieving the goal.

Any one of these approaches, in combination with positive self-talk, can help you get started.

Avoiding Wasted Time and Misused Time

Many people complain that they don't procrastinate, they just don't have enough time. They are beset by family, school, work, civic, and household responsibilities. Their spouses, children, parents, lovers, bosses, teachers, friends, and neighbors are making constant demands on their time. How can they ever get anything done?

> "The best way to get something done is to begin."
>
> ANONYMOUS

> "Those who make the worst use of their time are the first to complain of its shortness."
>
> JEAN DE LA BRUYÈRE (1645–1696), French writer

For some people, there is never enough time; they always seem to be rushing.

People who believe they don't have enough time to accomplish everything they want to accomplish may be facing two problems. First, they may be wasting time. They may be dawdling over meals, taking more time than necessary to finish a task, or doing nothing. (Of course, a certain amount of doing nothing is good for your mental health. But too much amounts to laziness.)

The second problem they may be facing is that they are misusing time. They are spending too much time on unimportant matters and too little time on what's important. Their days are eaten away by the trivial, and they never have time for the significant tasks that help them achieve their goals and for leisure activities.

Another way to misuse time is to drift mentally and lose focus. It's important to stay in the moment and make sure your attention doesn't wander. As the saying goes, "Pay attention to your attention."

Getting Organized

The key to using your time wisely is being organized. This means you must keep your goals and tasks in mind and learn to plan ahead.

Keeping Your Goals in Mind   Earlier in this chapter, you set long-, intermediate-, and short-term personal, educational, professional, and community service goals for yourself. How many of these goals have you already forgotten?

Setting goals is important, as we have learned. However, you will not reach your goals unless you learn to keep them in mind. Write them down and put them someplace where you'll see them, perhaps on your refrigerator or in your wallet.

Planning   You have already created action plans for your most important goals. No doubt you considered each goal separately and created plans for each. What happens, though, when your plan for one goal interferes with your plan for another goal?

Setting Priorities   Time management would be simple if you just had one goal to reach or one task to perform. But most of us have many goals and tasks on top of the dozens of routine activities we face each day. So every day, whether we're conscious of it or not, we make choices about how we will spend our time.

Part of planning is setting priorities—that is, deciding what tasks are the most important and must be done first. Setting priorities helps you decide which tasks are most pressing. You will find that you may have to postpone one or more tasks to achieve the others.

When you set priorities, you review everything you need to do and ask yourself:

1. What tasks must be done immediately (for example, getting your mother a birthday present when today is her birthday)?

> "Time is the scarcest resource, and unless it is managed, nothing else can be managed."
>
> PETER DRUCKER (1909–2005), management consultant

2. What tasks are important to do soon?

3. What tasks can safely be delayed for a short period?

4. What tasks can be delayed for a week, a month, or longer?

Assign each matter you must take care of to one of these four categories. That will establish your priorities. Tasks in the first two categories have the highest priority and deserve your immediate attention.

Scheduling Once you have your priorities set, you can schedule the tasks you need to accomplish. There are time management tools, discussed in the next section, that can help you set up a schedule. But before you get into the specifics of your schedule, remember these tips:

- **Be realistic about how long activities take.** Some people routinely underestimate the time needed for a particular task. For example, if you commute to school or work during rush hour, don't allow 20 minutes when it's really a 30-minute trip door to door.

- **Remember that some tasks have to be finished so that others may start.** For example, if you have to write a paper, you will need to schedule research time before writing time.

Your Turn 2-4

SET YOUR PRIORITIES

To give you practice in setting priorities, think about the most important things you want to do this week. Write each activity following, and assign it a priority number from 1 to 4.

1. highest priority, cannot be delayed

2. important, should be done as soon as possible

3. less important, can be done next week

4. least important, can be postponed more than a week if necessary

_____

_____

_____

_____

_____

Paper and electronic planners are excellent tools for time management. They come in different formats, sizes, and prices to suit different needs.

FIGURE 2–2

A daily "to do" list helps you plan and keep track of tasks. Crossing off items as you do them can give you a sense of accomplishment.

To Do
~~Read Ch. 12 of Stephenson~~
Do Ch. 12 of Stephenson study guide
Study for English quiz
~~Work 1:30~~
~~Return videos~~
Call Kaylee

- **Account for the time you spend on fixed daily activities** such as sleeping, eating, personal hygiene, work, and attending class. Then you can allocate the time left over to the tasks with the highest priority.

- **Remember that you have peak energy levels at certain times of day.** Try to schedule difficult or important tasks at those times.

Using Time Management Tools

To help you schedule your time, you can use a planner for intermediate- and long-term scheduling and "to do" lists for daily activities. You can go "low tech" by using paper, or "high tech" with an electronic planner.

Planners for Intermediate- and Long-Term Activities. Planners are basically calendars designed to be used for planning and scheduling. They take two basic forms:

1. Paper pocket calendars, weekly planners, and diaries

2. Electronic planners in the form of personal digital assistants (PDAs and some cell phones), computer-based calendars (Microsoft Outlook), and online time management tools (http://todoist.com)

Whichever planner you select, make sure that it is a convenient format to carry with you all the time. Your planner should be your single source of information about your time schedule. In other words, don't put goal schedules in one place, social appointments in another calendar, and school activities in a third. Use the planner to plan and record all commitments on your time. Keep it up to date.

"To Do" Lists for Daily Activities. In addition to using a planner for long-term scheduling, making a daily "to do" list can help you get things done. A paper or electronic "to do" list, prepared each morning or the night before, lists all the tasks you want to accomplish that day (see Figure 2–2). The act of creating the list helps you plan your day. Consulting the list during the day helps you remember what you need to do. And crossing off or deleting an item when you finish it will give you a sense of accomplishment.

Reaching Your Goals

Making an action plan to achieve your goals and managing your time are both important achievements. But to make real progress, you will have to work hard, keep your goals in view, and persevere, even when you run into problems.

Using the Personal Mastery Approach

Many people get off to a good start when they try to work on their goals, and then they get bogged down and give up. They experience a short burst of progress, followed by a period of being on a plateau, during

"You'll always miss
100 percent of the shots you
do not take."

WAYNE GRETZKY,
Canadian hockey player

which nothing seems to happen. A perfect example of this is a man whose goal is to learn a new sport. At first, he makes rapid progress. But then, instead of continuing to improve, he reaches a plateau. For weeks or even months, his skill level remains the same. Finally, another burst of progress occurs, and his mastery of the sport increases.

The secret of the mastery approach is to expect and accept that you will reach plateaus and stop progressing. When this happens, don't give up! Instead, persist, understanding that plateauing and backsliding are natural. Eventually you will make more progress and achieve your goal.

Motivating Yourself

How do you keep yourself moving toward a goal even when you've reached a plateau? How can you motivate yourself to act in ways that will keep you striving and trying?

Motivation is having the energy to work toward a goal. It is made up of the needs and incentives that make us act in particular ways. Motivation can be complex, but we will consider two aspects that are particularly relevant to achievement:

1. **Intrinsic motivation comes from within.** When you are intrinsically motivated, you do something because you want to and you enjoy it. Let's say you like to do aerobic exercises. They make you feel good. You are intrinsically motivated to exercise.

2. **Extrinsic motivation is an outside reward for behavior.** For example, you may want your sister to exercise for her health, so you offer her an exercise outfit and a ride to the gym. These extrinsic motivations may be enough to get your sister to come with you, at least for a while. Over time, though, the value of extrinsic motivation decreases. After a few weeks the extrinsic rewards may lose their power to get your sister to exercise.

In most situations, people have a combination of intrinsic and extrinsic motivations. Meg may enjoy learning how to use a new computer program (intrinsic), but she is also doing it to earn course credits (extrinsic). Psychologists have found that the best form of extrinsic motivation is praise. Unlike other extrinsic rewards, praise tends to increase a person's intrinsic motivation to do well.

"Fame or one's own self, which matters to one most? One's own self or things bought, which should count most?"

LAO-TZU,
ancient Chinese philosopher

Your Turn 2-5

USE A PLANNER

Practice using a planner by filling in your time commitments for the next week using the weekly planner on pages 48–49, or your own planner. Start by entering your routine commitments and any special appointments, whether school, work, or social. Then plan study time, goal time, and leisure time.

Weekly Planner			
Time	**Monday**	**Tuesday**	**Wednesday**
7 A.M.			
8			
9			
10			
11			
12 NOON			
1 P.M.			
2			
3			
4			
5			
6			
7			
8			
9			
10			
11			
12 MIDNIGHT			
1 A.M.			
2			
3			
4			
5			
6			

If you are intrinsically motivated to achieve a goal, your chances of achieving it are good. Working on the goal is something you enjoy, so you don't look for excuses to stop. If your intrinsic motivation needs a boost, you can use positive self-talk to keep your energy high. Congratulate yourself on what you've accomplished so far, and imagine what it's going to be like when you reach your goal.

If you need some extrinsic motivation to keep you going, you can do two things:

1. **Set up a system of rewards for yourself.** For example, when you accomplish one step toward a goal, reward yourself with something you enjoy. Just be careful not to let the reward become more important than doing the task.

Weekly Planner				
Time	Thursday	Friday	Saturday	Sunday
7 A.M.				
8				
9				
10				
11				
12 NOON				
1 P.M.				
2				
3				
4				
5				
6				
7				
8				
9				
10				
11				
12 MIDNIGHT				
1 A.M.				
2				
3				
4				
5				
6				

2. **Enlist the support of your family or friends.** If you communicate your goals and successes, the pride that others feel in your accomplishments will provide powerful motivation for you to persevere.

Using Visualization

Another technique you can use to help you achieve your goals is to visualize a compelling future. Visualization means imagining what it would be like to have already reached the goal. What scene do you picture? What sounds do you hear? How are the people around you reacting to you? Imagining the future can compel us to do things now, in order to create the kind of future we want. Visualizing your success gives you a powerful mental boost to get started and stay on course.

Your Turn 2-6

MAKE A "TO DO" LIST

In the space following, make a "to do" list of all the tasks you wish to accomplish tomorrow. Assign each one a priority number from 1 to 4 as follows:

1. highest priority, cannot be delayed

2. important, should be done as soon as possible

3. less important, can be done within a few days

4. least important, can be postponed a week or more if necessary

_____

_____

_____

_____

_____

_____

_____

_____

_____

_____

Tomorrow, as you finish each item, cross it off.

> "A failure is not always a mistake; it may simply be the best one can do under the circumstances. The real mistake is to stop trying."
>
> B. F. SKINNER (1904–1990), psychologist

Overcoming Fears

Fear often stands in the way of action. People are hampered by fear of many things. The two most important fears that can interfere with reaching a goal are fear of failure and fear of success.

You may think that fearing failure makes perfect sense. In a way, it does. No one likes to look stupid, incompetent, or ridiculous. Actually, it's our perception of failure that causes fear. Instead of seeing failure as a poor result or a temporary setback, we see failure as defeat and shame. If we remember that everyone fails at times, we can start putting failure in perspective. Out of failure can come valuable lessons for success.

However odd it sounds, people often fear success also. People who fear success are seldom aware of it. Yet they put obstacles in the way of

Your Turn 2-7

WHAT MOTIVATES YOU?

What motivates you to achieve your goals? Consider the three goals for which you prepared action plans. What will motivate you to accomplish these goals?

1. Goal 1:

Your intrinsic motivation: _____

Sources of extrinsic motivation: _____

2. Goal 2:

Your intrinsic motivation: _____

Sources of extrinsic motivation: _____

3. Goal 3:

Your intrinsic motivation: _____

Sources of extrinsic motivation: _____

Praise is a very effective form of extrinsic motivation. Receiving the approval and good wishes of others increases a person's intrinsic motivation to do well.

achieving their goals. Why? They fear that success will bring new situations and new responsibilities they can't handle. Some may believe that they don't deserve to succeed. In fact, they probably can succeed. Most people tend to underestimate their abilities.

If fear is preventing you from achieving your goals, tell yourself this: "Fear is natural. I feel afraid, but I'm going to do this anyway."

Being Flexible

Life means change, and people who don't change their goals accordingly run into trouble. Suppose your family moves to another state or you become interested in another career. It would be foolish to persist in trying to reach goals that are no longer relevant to you. Goals and action plans are not carved in stone. When your situation changes, be flexible and change your goals and action plans to suit your new circumstances.

Being Less Than Perfect

People who are perfectionists often get bogged down in trying to reach their goals. They demand perfection of themselves. Nothing they do is ever good enough.

On the other hand, people who reach their goals tend to be more relaxed about themselves. They acknowledge that they are human and have faults. They make mistakes, but they do as well as they can. They realize the importance of pleasing themselves. They are flexible and relaxed and open to new situations and people. These are the people who have the inner resources to succeed.

The Importance of Hope

Psychologists are finding that hope plays an important role in achieving success in life.

A study of 3,920 college freshmen showed that the level of hope at the start of school was a better predictor of their college grades than previous

Your Turn 2-8

ARE YOU A PERFECTIONIST?

Read the following pairs of sentences, and circle the letter of the sentence in each pair that is most like you.

1. a. I make mistakes occasionally.
   b. When I make a mistake, it's someone else's fault.

2. a. I do the best I can.
   b. It's hard, but I try.

3. a. My goals are pleasing to me.
   b. My goals are pleasing to my family and friends.

4. a. I take my time in getting things done.
   b. I'm always in a hurry to finish.

5. a. I'm open to sharing my feelings.
   b. I'd rather appear strong than show weakness.

If you circled three or more b's, you tend to be a perfectionist. Try to be easier on yourself!

performance on standardized tests or their high school grade-point average. Dr. Charles R. Snyder, a psychologist at the University of Kansas, says, "Students with high hope set themselves higher goals and know how to work to attain them."[2]

To Dr. Snyder, hope is more than the feeling that everything will be okay. Rather, he defines having hope as believing that you have both the will and the way to accomplish your goals. In other words, people with commitment and self-belief are hopeful people.

People who are naturally hopeful are fortunate. But others can learn hopeful ways of thinking. To imitate the mental habits of hopeful people, you can:

- turn to friends for help in achieving your goals
- use positive self-talk
- believe that things will get better
- be flexible enough to change your action plans when necessary
- be flexible enough to change your goals when necessary
- focus on the short-term goals you need to achieve in order to reach your long-term goal

Tech Tips

USING BLACKBOARD AND OTHER COURSE MANAGEMENT SYSTEMS TO GET ORGANIZED

Course management systems may at first seem to create extra work and waste time. But once you master their use, you will find that they help you organize your course work and time. They can contribute to your achieving your educational goals.

Your college's Internet home page is a portal through which you can access administrative offices, academic departments and the library. At many campuses, it is also the site through which you access a course management system like Blackboard, CourseCompass, or Web Tutor. **Course management systems** provide faculty and students with a convenient online tool for running a course. If your campus has one of these systems, you may be using it every day to manage your course work.

A course home page

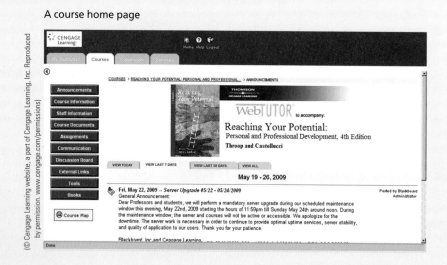

(© Cengage Learning website, a part of Cengage Learning, Inc. Reproduced by permission. www.cengage.com/permissions)

Explore the System Menus

If your college provides orientation sessions to learn the course management system, you should take one. If not, spend some time exploring the system on your own, going through the menus to see what is available and how the site might be used. In Blackboard, for example, when you log on you'll see a list of your courses. Choose a course and then explore the menu options. You'll find some or all of these features:

- Announcements from the instructor
- Course information including the syllabus
- Instructor information, including contact information and office hours
- Course documents, including readings in pdf format or links to readings on the Internet
- Assignments

continues

- Communication tools, including a discussion board, e-mail links to other course members, and group pages for large courses divided into sections
- Other tools, including an address book, calendar, digital drop box for submitting assignments, and your grades.

Assess Your Instructors' Online Style

You can see from the previous list that the course management system provides an array of features useful for taking (and giving) a course. However, you may find that your instructors use the system in different ways. Some professors will use the system for every aspect of the course. Others may use it only for posting the syllabus and readings. Still others won't use it at all. You will have to determine each instructor's "Blackboard style" and adjust accordingly.

Using the course management system in the first few days of a term can be confusing, especially if it's your first term. For example, you may be taking five courses, and getting online announcements about each course from five instructors. Furthermore, at the beginning of a term you don't yet know your instructors' preferences for using the system, so you have to check all your courses every day to make sure you don't miss anything.

After a week or two, you'll understand how each instructor expects you to use the course management system, and it will become easier for you to manage your course work.

Manage Your Courses Effectively

While course management systems like Blackboard provide a convenient online way to run or take a course, they do create some challenges. For example, you can't assume that nothing has happened in the course since the class met. Your instructor may have changed an assignment online, sent you an e-mail, or posted a reading since your last class meeting. As a result you need to develop an approach to the system that will ensure you don't miss anything:

- Check each course on the course management system daily, or at least before you start a homework assignment. That way you'll have the most up-to-date information.
- Check your campus e-mail every day as well, since many professors e-mail students rather than post announcements in the course management system.
- Use the course e-mail list, if one is posted, to get in touch with classmates if you've missed something.
- Use the calendar tool to keep track of your class schedule, assignment due dates, and exam dates.

With a little practice, you'll become so accustomed to using the course management system with a variety of instructors that you won't have to think about it. Instead, you'll be able to concentrate on your studies—which, after all, is the point of taking college courses.

Your Turn 2-9

If Blackboard or another course management is used at your school, take a few minutes to log on and explore each of your course sites. If necessary, ask your instructors how they plan to use the site and how they expect you to use it. Then for each of your courses, list (1) the type of information posted on the site and (2) describe how your instructor expects you to use the site.

Course 1: _____ **Instructor:** _____

    Information posted: _____

    _____

    How the course management site will be used: _____

    _____

Course 2: _____ **Instructor:** _____

    Information posted: _____

    _____

    How the course management site will be used: _____

    _____

Course 3: _____ **Instructor:** _____

    Information posted: _____

    _____

    How the course management site will be used: _____

    _____

Course 4: _____ **Instructor:** _____

    Information posted: _____

    _____

    How the course management site will be used: _____

    _____

Course 5: _____ **Instructor:** _____

    Information posted: _____

    _____

    How the course management site will be used: _____

    _____

What's Up?

Name _____   Date_____

1. Why is it important to have realistic and challenging goals?

_____

Match the specific goal in the second column to the type of goal in the first column. Write the letter of the goal in the space provided.

Type of Goal

2. _____personal

3. _____educational

4. _____professional

5. _____community service

Specific Goal

a. earning a degree, diploma, or certificate

b. becoming a manager

c. running a 5K race

d. becoming a hospital volunteer

6. List the six rules for stating goals.

37&38

_____

_____

_____

7. What is the purpose of a written action plan?

_____

_____

_____

8. What are three techniques that can be used to get started on a task?

Pg 43

_____

_____

_____

9. Why is it important to set priorities?

_____

_____

_____

10. Describe the difference between intrinsic and extrinsic motivation.

_____

_____

_____

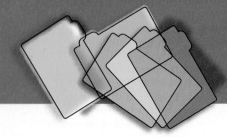

Case Studies

The Case of the Would-Be Nonsmoker

Will decided to stop smoking when he found himself out of breath on the basketball court after very little exertion. Since he loved to play basketball and wanted to feel fit again, he figured it would be easy to quit smoking. During the first week, Will did well. He was very pleased with himself for having the willpower not to smoke. He already felt healthier. During the second week, he went to a party and out of habit smoked a few cigarettes. By the third week, Will was regularly borrowing cigarettes from others. He felt disgusted with himself.

1. When Will first stopped smoking, what was his motivation? Was it intrinsic or extrinsic?

2. Will underestimated how hard it would be to achieve his goal. How can he get himself on track again?

The Case of the Harried Student

Barbara always complained to her friend Alyssa that she had no time. Alyssa found this hard to believe, since Barbara had a light course load at school and didn't have a part-time job. One day the two friends spent some time together, and Alyssa got to see what Barbara's day was like.

Barbara was late in meeting Alyssa, because she had gotten up late and spent too much time over breakfast. After Barbara's first class, which they barely got to in time, they had an hour's break. Barbara said she needed to get a book from the school library in order to complete an assignment that night. But instead of going to the library, they ran into some friends and had a latte. After the second class, they had an hour for lunch. Barbara was scheduled for an hour in the computer lab, which turned out to be only 45 minutes, since the friends got there late. Then Barbara had a doctor's appointment, and it was clear she would be late for that, too. When Alyssa left her friend, she realized they had never gotten to the library.

1. Describe three problems that Barbara has with time.

2. Do you think Barbara has enough time to do what she needs to do in the course of the day? Explain.

# Journal

Answer the following journal questions.

1. In Your Turn 2-2 (page 39), you listed your personal, professional, educational, and community service goals. Of all the goals you listed, which is most important to you? Why?

_____

_____

_____

_____

_____

2. Visualize yourself when you achieve your most important goal. Describe what your life will be like.

_____

_____

_____

_____

_____

3. Assess your current approach to time management. Are you a procrastinator? Are you organized? Do you meet all your deadlines? Do you use any time management tools?

_____

_____

_____

_____

_____

4. What activity do you consider your biggest time waster? What benefit do you get from this activity? Is it worth the amount of time you spend?

_____

_____

_____

_____

_____

5. How do you meet the demands of your family and friends, as well as the demands of school and work? What might make juggling these easier for you?

_____

_____

_____

_____

_____

Developing Your Intellectual Potential

The human brain is a powerful tool that helps us master our environment. As you work on developing your intellectual potential, the following two chapters will help you improve your thinking and learning skills. You will learn techniques to remember, think critically, and study that will help you reach your full potential in school and in all areas of life.

CHAPTER 3
IMPROVING YOUR THINKING SKILLS

In this chapter, you will be . . .
. . . developing your self belief:

- I will think critically in order to make good judgments.
- I will use thinking skills to work on good solutions to problems.

. . . reframing your thoughts:

- I will try different techniques to improve my memory.
- I will learn critical thinking skills to become a better problem solver.
- I will learn to approach challenges by using creative thinking methods.

. . . setting goals:

- I will use memory devices in one class to study for a test.
- I will apply the PrOACT approach to problem solving to make a decision.

. . . envisioning a compelling future:

- I will improve my performance as a student by using these thinking skills.
- I will do well in my career by using thinking and problem solving skills.

. . . achieving personal mastery:

- I will achieve higher test scores as a result of using new memory techniques.
- I will face challenges in college and beyond by thinking critically and creatively and solving problems.

CHAPTER 4
IMPROVING YOUR STUDY SKILLS

In this chapter, you will be . . .
. . . developing your self belief:

- I will set up a study area that works for me.
- I will take advantage of peak energy times to study more effectively.

. . . reframing your thoughts:

- I will use the learning style that works best for me whenever possible.
- I will reinforce what I am learning by using another learning style.

. . . setting goals:

- I will set study goals for at least one of my courses.
- I will use the P.Q.R. method to improve my understanding of assigned reading.
- I will improve my test scores by studying and preparing for tests.

. . . envisioning a compelling future:

- I will graduate from college because I will use effective study skills.
- I will have a better career because I have a good education.

. . . achieving personal mastery:

- I will acquire study habits that will help me as a lifelong learner.

Improving Your Thinking Skills

People in all walks of life solve problems and think creatively.

Have you ever done poorly on an exam because you had a cold? Have you ever been unable to solve a problem because you were too anxious about it? These common experiences show that our ability to think is affected by our physical and emotional well-being. When we feel good about ourselves, both emotionally and physically, our ability to think improves.

Studies have shown that all of us have far more brain power than we use. We can improve our ability to think by tapping into some of that unused power. If we understand how the brain works, we can sharpen our thinking skills. In this chapter, you will:

- learn about the brain;
- improve your ability to remember;
- develop your critical thinking skills;
- learn an effective approach to solving problems; and
- practice thinking creatively.

Finally, you will learn about the challenges and advantages of taking online and blended courses.

The Brain

Make two fists and place them together with your thumbs on top and your arms touching from wrist to elbow. You have just made a crude model of the human brain. The brain, a three-pound organ, is the complex director of all of your body's activities. It regulates basic life support systems such as breathing, controls all your movements, interprets your environment, and feels, remembers, thinks, reasons, and creates.

How does the brain do all this? Basically, the brain is made of billions of tiny cells called neurons. In fact, they are so tiny that 30,000 neurons would fit on the head of a pin. Neurons are shaped like trees, with roots, trunk, and branches. Networks of neurons provide communications pathways through the brain. Chemicals called neurotransmitters pass from one neuron to another, activating electrical impulses. The activation of a particular group of neurons produces a perception, feeling, thought, or memory. Each neuron's branches can make contact with between 5,000 and 50,000 other neurons, so you can imagine that billions of complex connections are possible. When you learn something new, you are making new connections among your neurons.

The human brain's ability to deal with complex perceptions, thoughts, and feelings is the key to our success as a species. We cannot run as fast as a cheetah or see our prey with eyes as sharp as an eagle's, but we use our brains to make up for our physical limitations. Humans survive because our brains are constantly filtering the information coming in from the environment. The brain tells us what is safe to ignore—most of what's around us. It tells us what we must pay attention to. Every encounter with something new means that the brain must try to fit the new information into an existing pattern of neurons or else change the pattern to make room for the new thing. Because humans learn and remember, we have thrived.

However, your brain can pay attention to only one train of conscious thought at a time. It is always getting rid of excess information through the process of forgetting. What does the brain pay attention to? It pays attention to things that have meaning to you (information that connects to an existing network of neurons) or things that arouse feelings (information that makes you afraid, happy, or angry).

We can use this very basic understanding of how the human brain works to improve our ability to remember, think logically, solve problems, and think creatively.

Remembering

One of the most basic functions of the brain is to remember. Without memory, other learning and thinking skills would be impossible. Imagine trying to solve a problem if you couldn't even remember what it was! Your brain stores a vast amount of information in memory. This ranges from

"*I will stuff your head with brains. I cannot tell you how to use them, however; you must find that out for yourself.*" *(The Wizard of Oz to the Scarecrow, who asked for brains.)*

L. FRANK BAUM (1856–1919), American writer

important information such as a friend's appearance to trivial information like the sound of the doorbell in your last apartment or house.

How does memory work? And why do we remember some things and not others? With the answers to these questions, we can actually improve our ability to remember.

How Does Memory Work?

Most psychologists think of memory as having three stages:(1) sensory memory; (2) short-term memory; and (3) long-term memory. Figure 3–1 is a diagram of the three-stage model of memory.[1]

Before you can remember anything, you have to **perceive** it. That means you must see, hear, smell, or become aware of it through some other sense. Everything you perceive is registered in **sensory memory,** the first stage of memory. The material in sensory memory lasts less than a couple of seconds while your brain processes it, looking for what's important. Then most of it disappears.

Some material in sensory memory reaches the second stage, **short-term memory,** where it lasts about 20 seconds. To make it into short-term memory, the new material is matched with information you already have stored, and a meaningful association or pattern is made. For example, when you see a T, you immediately recognize it as the letter *T*. You would recognize it whether it was a lowercase t, an italic *t*, an uppercase T, or a handwritten T. If you did not have these associations for the letter *T,* you would have much more difficulty placing it in short-term memory.

The material in short-term memory is the information we are currently using. The capacity of short-term memory is small—on average, about seven meaningful units of information. And short-term memory usually doesn't last more than 20 seconds. To make it last longer, repetition helps. For example, if you are lost and someone is giving you directions, you should repeat them to fix them in your memory. But if someone interrupts you, you will probably confuse or forget the directions.

FIGURE 3–1

The three stages of memory are sensory memory, short-term memory, and long-term memory. Our five senses perceive information from our environment, which is processed in sensory memory. Only the important information is sent on to short-term memory. There it is processed and used. Then the information is either forgotten or sent to long-term memory for storage. When the information is needed, it is retrieved from long-term memory, if it can be found.

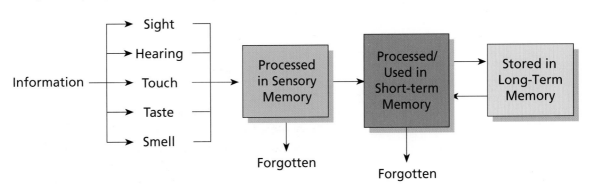

Some material in short-term memory makes it into the third stage, long-term memory, which lasts much longer than short-term memory. Long-term memories are those we don't need at the moment but have stored. In fact, long-term memory is often compared to a complicated filing system, index, or database. The way memories are stored affects the ease with which we can retrieve them. In general, we store new memories by associating them with old memories. For example, if we see a new shade of blue we may associate it with other shades of blue we know or with a blue object.

The capacity of long-term memory seems limitless. Even after a full life of remembering, people have room to store more information in long-term memory. Much of what we "forget" is still actually in long-term memory, but we have trouble getting it out.

Your Turn 3-1

HOW SOON WE FORGET...

Try this experiment on yourself to test your memory.

1. Look at the number below just once, cover it up, and then do something distracting such as singing a song.

   8519472

   Now write the number here: _____

   a. If you got the number right, which level of memory was it in?

   _____

   b. If you got the number wrong, which level of memory was it in?

   _____

2. Now look at the number below for a few seconds and repeat it to yourself several times. Then cover it up.

   461-8352

   Now write the number here: _____

   a. If you got the number right, which level of memory was it in?

   _____

   b. If you got the number wrong, which level of memory was it in?

   _____

   c. Why was this number easier to remember than the number in the first item?

   _____

   _____

Improving Your Memory

There are several techniques you can use to improve your short-term and long-term memory. Of course, one time-honored way to improve your memory is to write yourself lists and notes. However, you can learn other purely mental aids to memory that take advantage of how the brain works. These include repetition, organization, and mnemonics. They work best when you actually understand the material you are trying to memorize.

Repetition　Repetition is an effective way to improve your short-term memory. Going over something again and again in your head—or even better, out loud—will help you remember it.

Repetition is a memory technique used by actors and actresses when they are memorizing their parts.

Organization　Organizing material can help both your short-term and long-term memory. To help keep something in short-term memory, you can organize it into seven or fewer chunks. A grocery list of 20 items, for instance, can be "chunked" into produce, dairy, deli, meats, packaged foods, paper products, and cleaning products.

The way you organize material for long-term storage will help you when you need to retrieve it. One way is to make meaningful associations between the new information you are memorizing and other information you already know. For example, if you are trying to remember to buy fish at the supermarket, you can associate it with the meal you're planning to cook. Associations need not involve only words. You can associate new information with music, sounds, images, places, people, and so on. Another way to organize information for long-term memory is by rearranging or categorizing it. You can categorize by meaning, sound, familiarity, alphabetic order, size, or any other pattern that makes sense to you.

Mnemonics　"I before E except after C and when it sounds like A, as in *neighbor* or in *weigh*" has helped children learn one of the rules of English spelling for years. Devices that help people remember are called mnemonics. Mnemonics can work, but they require practice. Mnemonics can be poems, like this example, or they can be acronyms—the first letter of each item to be memorized. If you have ever studied music, you probably remember the acronym FACE, which stands for the notes associated with the spaces in the treble clef.

In addition to rhymes and acronyms, there are mnemonic systems that can be used to help memorize information. One system, called the peg word method, involves learning a jingle that contains words corresponding to the numbers 1 through 10:

1 is a bun; 2 is a shoe; 3 is a tree; 4 is a door; 5 is a hive; 6 is sticks; 7 is heaven; 8 is a gate; 9 is swine; 10 is a hen.

After repeating this jingle a few times, you will be able to count to 10 by peg words: bun, shoe, tree, door, and so on. Then you can visually associate items you need to remember with the peg words. For example,

Your Turn 3-2

Practice using the peg word method or the method of loci to memorize a list.

1. Make a list of the items you are carrying with you. There should be at least 10 items on your list.

_____

_____

_____

_____

_____

_____

_____

2. Describe or sketch your mental image for each item. Go over it a few times. Then cover the list and proceed to the next question.

_____

_____

_____

_____

_____

_____

_____

_____

3. Without referring to the original list, recall your mental images and write the 10 items here:

_____

_____

_____

_____

_____

_____

_____

_____

News & Views

THE NUN STUDY: THE IMPORTANCE OF MENTAL EXERCISE

"Use it or lose it" is a familiar saying that may turn out to be true in regard to the brain. A long-term study of 678 nuns has provided insights about why some people live to a great age with their minds lively and intact, while others suffer from Alzheimer's disease or other forms of dementia.

The School Sisters of Notre Dame are a good group to study from a scientific point of view. They do not smoke, drink very little, and get good health care. In addition, they live in similar communities all their lives. Many of them are teachers. The sisters keep mentally and physically active well into old age. The Nun Study, as it is known, has been conducted by Dr. David Snowdon of the University of Kentucky since 1986.

Each year, Dr. Snowdon and his colleagues test the nuns' memory, concentration, and language ability. For example, the nuns are asked to recall words they have seen on flash cards and to name as many items in a category as they can in one minute.

Dr. Snowdon also analyzed personal essays the nuns had written decades earlier when they entered the convent. These essays provided evidence of the young sisters' thinking and language abilities. The researchers measured the "idea density"—the number of ideas in 10 written words—and the grammatical complexity of the essays. They also looked for words that indicated a positive or a negative mental outlook. The essays gave Dr. Snowdon a way to compare the nuns' mental skills in their youth and in old age.

Much to his surprise, Dr. Snowdon found that the sisters who had shown a positive outlook in their essays lived longer than those whose essays showed a negative outlook. Furthermore, those whose essays had high idea density and grammatical complexity were far less likely than the others to develop symptoms of Alzheimer's disease in old age.

The results of the study suggest that people who exercise their minds may protect themselves from declining mental function as they age. Sisters who had taught school, for example, showed better mental health in old age than those who cooked and cleaned in the convent. Of course, Alzheimer's disease is partially caused by genetic factors, so in many cases it may not be possible to prevent the disease. Still, the educated nuns whose lives had been mentally active may have developed extra brain capacity—more connections among neurons. These extra connections gave them a surplus they could draw on, even as Alzheimer's disease may have been developing.

The results of the nun study suggest that the average person should choose new and stimulating things to do or study throughout life. A personal trainer could take up painting. A computer technician might learn a new language. Even activities like brain teasers, crossword puzzles, and video games can help expand the brain's capacity.

(© Steve Liss//Time Life Pictures/Getty Images)

Dr. David Snowdon plays cards with one of the Nun Study's oldest participants, Sister Esther, who is 106.

Sources: The Nun Study Web site, http://www.mc.uky.edu/nunnet/, accessed Jan. 13, 2008; Michael D. Lemonick and Alice Park, "The Nun Study: How One Scientist and 678 Sisters Are Helping Unlock the Secrets of Alzheimer's Disease, *Time Pacific,* May 14, 2001, http://www.time.com/tim/pacific/magazine/20010514/cover1.html, accessed January 28, 2003; Jay Copp, "This Is for the Benefit of Those Who Come after Us," *Our Sunday Visitor,* June 17, 2001, http://www.osv.com/periodicals/show-article.asp? pid=313, accessed January 28, 2003.

if the first item on your list is a notebook, you can imagine a notebook sandwiched on a bun. Later, when you need to remember the list, the 10 peg words will serve as clues to the items. The numbers will help you keep track of how many items you must remember.

Another mnemonic system that makes use of images is the **method of loci.** In this system, you associate items on a list with images of places along a route. (*Loci* means "places" in Latin.) First you must develop the stops along your route. You can use the path from your front door to the kitchen, from your home to school, or any other familiar route. When you want to memorize a list, you create an image of the item at the corresponding stop along your route. For example, if you must remember notebook, you could picture a notebook hanging on your front door. When you want to remember the list, you take a mental walk along your route, remembering the scene at each stop.

Thinking Critically

Memory is one form of thought, or **cognition,** as psychologists refer to mental processes. Another is critical thinking. When you think critically, you are evaluating what's true and making judgments. To do this, you must be able to reason, or think logically. You must also be able to distinguish fact from opinion.

Logic

Whether you are aware of it or not, you use logic hundreds of times a day. When you are hungry, you decide to eat. When you need to know the time, you look at a clock. When it's chilly, you put on a jacket. In all these cases, you have used a logical sequence of steps in thinking.

One type of logical thinking is called **deductive reasoning.** In deductive reasoning, the conclusion that is reached is true if the information it is based on, called the **premises,** is true. Let's consider an example of deductive reasoning:

> **Premise** When it rains, the street gets wet.
>
> **Premise** It is raining.
>
> **Conclusion** The street is wet.

You can see from this example that you use deductive reasoning all the time without even being aware of it. When you make a decision, however, you are often aware of your thought process. Let's say you must decide whether your car needs servicing. You might follow this train of thought:

> **Premise** If the car leaks oil, it needs servicing.
>
> **Premise** The car leaks oil.
>
> **Conclusion** The car needs servicing.

The conclusion in deductive reasoning is always true if the premises are true.

A type of thinking in which the conclusion is not always true is called **inductive reasoning.** In inductive reasoning, the conclusion drawn is probably true. Here's an example of inductive reasoning:

Premise Coworkers Francine and Devon have the same last name.

Premise Francine and Devon leave the office together every day.

Conclusion Francine and Devon are married.

While it is possible that Francine and Devon are married, this conclusion may not be true. Francine and Devon may be sister and brother, mother and son, daughter and father, or cousins. In fact, Francine and Devon may not be related at all—they may simply have the same last name.

Fact or Opinion?

An important part of critical thinking is the ability to distinguish between fact and opinion. A **fact** is something that can be shown to be true. The premises and conclusions of sound deductive reasoning are generally facts. **Opinions,** on the other hand, are beliefs based on values and assumptions. Opinions may or may not be true.

Your Turn 3-3

DRAW YOUR OWN CONCLUSIONS

Read each set of premises. If you can reach a logical or probable conclusion, write it down. Indicate whether you used deductive or inductive reasoning.

1. If a category 3 hurricane is predicted, the barrier islands are evacuated.
   A category 3 hurricane is predicted.
   Conclusion: _____
   Type of reasoning: _____

2. When I'm in love, I'm happy.
   I'm happy.
   Conclusion: _____
   Type of reasoning: _____

3. Dexter uses his computer to surf the Internet.
   Dexter used his computer yesterday.
   Conclusion: _____
   Type of reasoning: _____

Your Turn 3-4

Indicate whether each of the following is a fact or opinion by writing *fact* or *opinion* in the space provided.

1. Living in the suburbs is better than living in the city. _____

2. Mixing blue and yellow yields green. _____

3. On average, women live longer than men. _____

4. Modern fashions look better than those of 50 years ago. _____

5. Swimming is good exercise. _____

"*If everybody's thinking alike, somebody isn't thinking.*"

ANONYMOUS

To distinguish between fact and opinion, think logically. Evaluate the material and sort out the reasonable from the emotional or illogical. Look for inconsistencies and evidence. Above all, trust your own ability to distinguish logical facts and ideas from opinions and assumptions. One area in which Americans have had a lot of practice in sorting fact from opinion is advertising. Think of your favorite commercial and try to sort out the facts from the assumptions.

Solving Problems

Problem solving is another important thinking skill. To be a good problem solver, you must be able to think critically. In addition, recognize that problems often have an emotional component that affects your ability to deal with them.

Proactive versus Reactive Attitudes

Let's consider Steve, who is having trouble getting along with a coworker. Steve thinks, "It's unfair that I have to deal with him. He shouldn't be my problem. Anyway, it's his fault. I don't have the time to work things out." With this attitude, how likely is it that Steve will be able to solve the problem?

Now Steve pulls himself together and tells himself that he will take full responsibility for this problem. He will do what's necessary to solve it. Steve will even enlist the help of others, if necessary. Steve imagines that he has worked out the problem with his coworker. Since he believes that he can solve the problem, his chances of success are increased.

These two attitudes toward problem solving can be characterized as reactive or proactive. A reactive approach is essentially negative. A person

Your Turn 3-5

Think of a problem you have—personal, school-related, or job-related—and answer the following questions.

1. Describe your problem in one sentence.

   _____

   _____

2. Write down all the reasons why you can't solve this problem.

   _____

   _____

   _____

3. Now imagine that you can successfully solve the problem. Write down all the factors that are driving you to solve this problem.

   _____

   _____

   _____

4. Write a positive message to yourself about your commitment to solving the problem.

   _____

   _____

   _____

"*A problem is a chance for you to do your best.*"

DUKE ELLINGTON (1899–1974), composer and jazz musician

with a reactive attitude feels incapable of solving the problem and tries to blame someone else. In contrast, a person with a proactive attitude takes responsibility and is committed to solving the problem.[2]

So before we undertake the steps involved in thinking through and solving a problem, it's important to have a proactive attitude.

The PrOACT Approach to Problem Solving

Now that we've decided on a proactive attitude to problem solving, let's consider the elements involved in solving a problem or making a decision. Many people approach problem solving by using the trial-and-error method. This means they try out solutions at random and use the first one that works. It's not very efficient, and the results are often poor.

Lonnie G. Johnson

(© AP Photo)

You may never have heard of a flow-actuated pulsator, but you certainly know it by its more common name—the Super Soaker. Invented in 1982 by engineer Lonnie G. Johnson, the high-powered water gun has become one of the most popular summer toys ever made.

Johnson, who grew up in Mobile, Alabama, was the third of six children. Even though he was told he didn't have what it takes to become an engineer, Johnson persevered. When he was a high school senior, his science project, a remote-controlled robot, won first place at a University of Alabama science fair. "Back then, robots were unheard of, so I was one of only a few kids in the country who had his own robot," said Johnson. Johnson went to college on math and military scholarships. He earned a bachelor's degree in mechanical engineering and a master's degree in nuclear engineering.

Johnson worked for NASA's Jet Propulsion Laboratory, helping to fit an atomic battery into the space probe *Galileo*. He also worked on the stealth bomber for the Air Force. In his free time, Johnson fooled around with things at home. While trying to invent a cooling system that didn't use Freon gas, Johnson rigged up some tubing and a nozzle in his bathroom. When he pressed the nozzle, a blast of water shot into the bathtub. Johnson thought, "This would make a great water gun."

The Super Soaker sold so well that in 1991 Johnson was able to form his own company, Johnson Research and Development. Today he has more than a hundred patents to his name, and he is currently working on energy technology. When asked what the key to success is, Johnson said, "Perseverance! There is no short, easy route to success." And when asked why he invented things, he replied, "I have these ideas, and they keep on coming."

Sources: Logan Ward, "Supersoaker Inventor Aims to Cut Solar Costs in Half." *Popular Mechanics,* Jan. 8, 2008, <http://popularmechanics.com/science/earth/4243793.html>, accessed Jan. 16, 2008; "Yes, You Can Make a Million." *Kiplinger's Personal Finance*, Mar. 2007, <http://www.kiplinter.com/magazine/archives/2007/03/millionaire2.html>. Tracie Newton, "Inventor Encourages Audience to Persevere in Quest for Dreams, Holds Up Own Life as Example," *Athens Online,* February 28, 1999, <http://www.onlineathens.com/stories/022899/new_0228990002.shtml>, accessed January 13, 2003; Susan Fineman, "Sometimes It Does Take a Rocket Scientist," *Associated Press,* February 13, 1999, <http://www.invention-express.com/lonniejohnson.html>, accessed January 13, 2003; William J. Broad, "Rocket Science, Served Up Soggy," *New York Times,* July 31, 2001, pp. D1, D7.

TABLE 3–1 Decision Matrix for Buying a New Family Car			
	Alternatives		
Objectives	**Sedan**	**Minivan**	**SUV**
Seating	5	7	6
Gas mileage	28 mpg	25 mpg	14 mpg
Repair record	Excellent	Good	Good
Approximate cost	$20,000	$21,000	$30,000

A better approach has been devised by three business professors and decision-making consultants.[3] Essentially, they advise breaking down a problem and considering it one step at a time: **Pr**oblem, **O**bjectives, **A**lternatives, **C**onsequences, and **T**rade-offs. The acronym for these—PrOACT—serves as a reminder that the best attitude to problem solving is *proactive*.

In the PrOACT approach, you break a problem into the five PrOACT elements and think about each one separately. Then you put your thoughts back together and make a smart choice.

1. **Problem.** First, you have to figure out just what the problem is. Your ability to solve a problem depends on how you define it. For example, is your problem deciding whether or not to buy a car, or deciding which car to buy?

2. **Objectives.** Solving a problem or making a decision should bring you closer to achieving your goals. In a problem-solving situation, therefore, you need to know what your objectives are. For example, your objective could be to buy a vehicle that has room for your family of six, is reasonably priced, and gets good gas mileage.

3. **Alternatives.** What different courses of action can you think of? What solutions are there to your problem? Think of as many possible alternatives as you can.

4. **Consequences.** For each reasonable alternative you come up with, think through the possible consequences, or results. Which alternatives have consequences that match your objectives?

5. **Trade-offs.** Whatever solution you choose, there will be pros and cons. You need to evaluate the pros and cons and decide what trade-offs are acceptable. There is no perfect solution to a problem; even the best alternative has drawbacks.

Constructing a decision matrix, or grid, such as the one in Table 3–1, can help you frame the problem, explore alternatives, and make a good decision. Which new car would be best for a family of six?

Thinking Creatively

You may think of creativity as a characteristic of artists and writers rather than of ordinary people. Yet psychologists define creativity as the ability to see things in a new way and to come up with unusual and effective

Your Turn 3-6

Ramon has a problem. He volunteered to buy T-shirts for his son's baseball team. The shirts will cost about $150. Ramon doesn't have $150 to spare for the T-shirts. What should Ramon do? Use the PrOACT approach to solve Ramon's problem.

1. Problem. Define Ramon's problem.

_____

_____

2. Objectives. What objective(s) does Ramon need to achieve?

_____

3. Alternatives. What alternative solutions are there to Ramon's problem?

_____

_____

4. Consequences. What are the consequences of the different alternatives?

_____

_____

_____

5. Trade-offs. List any trade-offs Ramon needs to make.

_____

_____

6. In your opinion, what is the best solution to Ramon's problem?

_____

_____

> "To raise new questions, new possibilities, to regard old problems from a new angle requires creative imagination...."
>
> ALBERT EINSTEIN (1879–1955), physicist

solutions to problems. When we use this definition of creativity, it's apparent that anyone can be creative. A secretary who works out a new and efficient office procedure and a parent who helps a child overcome a problem are both being creative.

What makes people creative? Intelligence, you may be surprised to learn, has little relation to creativity. Many highly intelligent people do not think creatively. Rather, creative people tend to be those who are intrinsically motivated. They *choose* to do what they do. Often they live or work in an environment that is stimulating and brings them into contact

Your Turn 3-7

This is an ordinary brick. How many uses for a brick can you think of? Write these uses below.

_____

_____

_____

_____

_____

_____

_____

with other creative people. Creative people perform tasks without fear of being judged foolish. They are not afraid to make mistakes.

Improving Your Creativity

Creativity does not depend on talent or intelligence. Rather, creativity depends on how we use our brains. Most of the techniques associated with improving creativity are based on using neglected modes of thinking. Since analytic, verbal, and sequential modes of thinking dominate in our society, creative breakthroughs often come about when people tap into other modes of thinking. The techniques described here have one thing in common: They all focus on getting us to change our routine thought processes.

Associative Thinking   One thinking process that helps give you a jump start on creativity is associative thinking. Associative thinking is a method in which you let your mind wander from one thing to another, even seemingly unrelated matters, in order to get fresh insight on a problem. If you have ever used the Internet, wandering from Web site to Web site with the links provided, you have a good idea of how associative thinking works.

To use associative thinking, start with the problem or issue and think of a couple of key words. For example, if you must decide whether to go to school full-time or part-time, your key words might be *school* and *time*. Starting with those words, let your mind wander, and jot down words and thoughts as they come to you. Sometimes associative thinking triggers useful new connections in your mind.

Backburner Thinking Occasionally, when you think too much about a problem, you get stuck. No matter how you rack your brain, nothing useful occurs to you. So you put the problem out of your mind. Some time later, as if from nowhere, you have a great insight. The problem is solved.

What has happened? Essentially, although you've stopped thinking about the problem on a conscious level, your brain continues to work on it. You've put the problem on a "back burner." Backburner thinking involves knowing when to stop thinking about a problem and let your unconscious mind take over.

You can improve the chances that backburner thinking will help you solve a problem by following these tips:

■ Think about your problem, but if you are getting nowhere, stop.

■ Do something else, preferably something relaxing. If it's night, go to sleep.

■ Return to the problem after the break.

When you start thinking about the problem again, you may have gained a new perspective.

Mind-Mapping Mind-mapping is a creative technique that draws on the visual, intuitive thought processes that we often neglect when trying to solve a problem. In mind-mapping, you sketch your problem or topic and the thoughts that come to mind. The result is a drawing that represents your ideas (see Figure 3–2).

To draw a mind-map, follow these steps:

1. Draw a picture of the problem or issue in the center of a piece of paper.

2. Print key words and ideas, and connect these to the central drawing.

3. Use colors, images, symbols, and codes to emphasize important points.

4. Use associative thinking to come up with more ideas, and connect them with other parts of the mind-map.

When your mind-map is done, you can study it to find new relationships, insights, and ideas. Perhaps a pattern will emerge that can help you with the problem.

Brainstorming Someone once said that two heads are better than one. Taking this idea even further, brainstorming allows a group of people—preferably five to eight—to come up with as many ideas about a problem or issue as they can. To brainstorm effectively, people must not be critical of one another's ideas. Any idea, however farfetched, is considered. Evaluating and judging will come later. Brainstorming can be used effectively in business situations where groups of people share problems and goals.

Mindstorming Mindstorming is similar to brainstorming, but you do it alone. Take a piece of paper, and at the top write your problem or issue of

FIGURE 3–2

Visualizing the relationships among ideas and things can help you think creatively. You can draw a mind-map to show these connections.

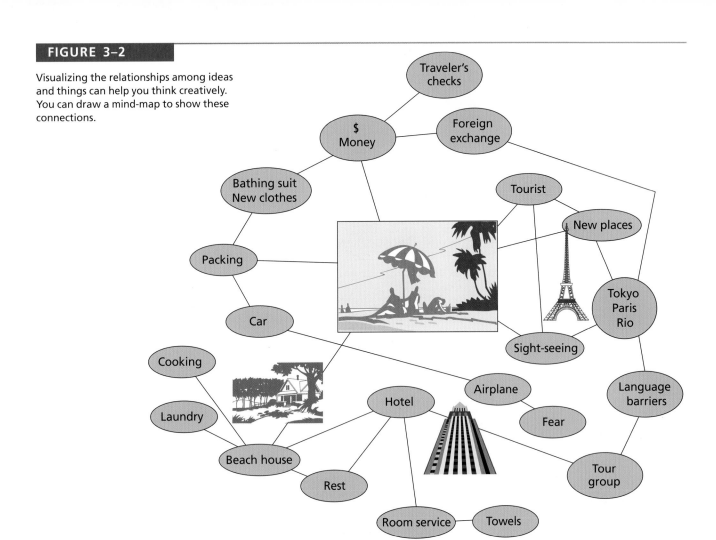

Your Turn 3-8

DRAW YOUR OWN MIND-MAP

Think of a problem you have or an issue that interests you.

1. On a separate sheet of paper, draw a mind-map with a picture related to this problem or issue in the center.

2. Write key words and phrases about the problem or issue around the central drawing, and draw lines to show the connections among these ideas.

3. Use colors, symbols, images, and codes to emphasize important ideas.

4. Use associative thinking to add related ideas to your mind-map.

5. Study your mind-map. What patterns or ideas might help you with solving this problem or dealing with this issue?

Your Turn 3-9

HAVE A BRAINSTORMING SESSION

With four or five other people in your class, have a five-minute brainstorming session on this issue: looking for a job in the computer industry.

One person should take notes on the ideas that come up. When the session is done, answer the following questions:

1. What did the group decide was important to do when looking for a job in the computer industry?

_____
_____
_____
_____

2. Did everyone contribute an idea? If not, why not?

_____
_____
_____
_____

3. Did you contribute an idea inspired by something someone else said?

_____
_____
_____
_____

4. Would you have come up with the same ideas the group did if you were thinking about this matter on your own? Explain.

_____
_____
_____
_____

great concern. Then list 20 ways you can solve the problem or approach the issue. The first 10 ideas will probably come easily and seem obvious. However, don't judge your ideas yet. Let your imagination take over and write down 10 more ideas, however odd, that come to mind. Then review the list and choose the ideas that are most likely to solve your problem.[4]

Tech Tips

TAKING ONLINE AND BLENDED COURSES

Millions of students are taking courses over the Internet. Online courses are those in which all—or almost all—of the content is delivered via the Internet. The technologies used in online courses can vary. For example, the instructor may record audio or video lectures or write lecture notes and post these online. You would "attend" these lectures on your computer. Written class "discussions" may take place in online forums or live chat rooms. Blended, or hybrid, courses are similar to online courses but include one or more face-to-face class meetings in addition to online work.

Both online and blended courses present students with special advantages and challenges.

The Advantages of Online and Blended Courses

The main advantage of an online or blended course is convenience. You can take a course without having to travel to campus several times a week. And, you can also do much of the course work at any time of the day or night. If you have work or family obligations, online courses may help you fit school into a busy life. You can even earn an entire degree online from many colleges and universities.

The Challenges of Online and Blended Courses

The convenience of online and blended courses is so great that many students overlook the challenges of learning via the Internet. Online courses have the same academic requirements and workload as traditional classes do. In addition, they have challenges unique to the online environment. These challenges can be broadly classified as technical and personal in nature.

Technical Challenges Access to a reliable, up-to-date computer with a fast Internet connection is a must for any online learner. Without this, the communications necessary for online courses will be impossible.

But the computer equipment and Internet access are just the beginning. To succeed in an online or blended course, you must have enough computer and Internet skills so that the technology doesn't become a barrier to learning. For example, you should be able to find things on the Internet, navigate the course Web site, communicate through e-mail, discussion forums, and bulletin boards, and manage and transfer computer files. If you are spending too much time learning how to perform these tasks during an online

Students who take courses online can work at their own convenience, but that means having the self-discipline to keep up with course work on their own.

(© Hola Images/Getty Images)

continues

course, you won't have time to learn the course material and you will quickly fall behind. To make the most of an online course, you should already be comfortable using a computer and the Internet.

Personal Challenges   Internet access and good computer skills are very important for online learning. Even more important are personal factors like internal motivation and self-discipline, as well as learning style.

Since online courses tend to be less structured than traditional courses, much of the responsibility for keeping up with the course rests with the student. You need to have the internal motivation and self-discipline to manage the course work on your own. For example, suppose there are no regular real-time online meetings, and you are expected watch or listen to lectures, do assignments, and post written contributions to class discussions on your own time. Under these circumstances, it's easy to let the work pile up unless you are self-disciplined enough to develop your own structure for the course.

Beyond having strong motivation and good organizational skills, you need to be comfortable with spending time by yourself, reading and writing on your computer and connecting to others via the Web. This way of learning works well for some students, but not for all. Some people prefer more social interaction when learning. We'll learn more about learning styles in the next chapter.

Your Turn 3-10

ASSESS WHETHER ONLINE OR BLENDED COURSES ARE FOR YOU

If you are seriously considering taking one or more courses online, you should assess your readiness for this form of learning. Ask yourself the following questions:

	Yes	No
1. Do I have access to a reliable, up-to-date computer and a fast Internet connection?	☐	☐
2. Do I have sufficient computer and Internet skills so that I can deal with computer and communication tasks without creating a barrier to learning?	☐	☐
3. Am I motivated to do the work involved in navigating the online environment as well as learning the course material?	☐	☐
4. Do I have the organizational and self-management skills necessary to keep up with an online course?	☐	☐
5. Will I be able to learn effectively in an environment that is based primarily on written communication instead of face-to-face class discussions and lectures?	☐	☐

If the answer to most or all of these questions is *yes*, then you are ready for online and blended courses. If possible, you might want to sign up for just one course to see whether this method of instruction works for you. Even if you are very computer savvy and organized, there is still a learning curve involved in taking an online course for the first time. Once you've mastered the technology and the format, online learning will greatly expand your access to education.

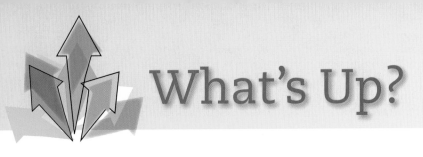

What's Up?

Name _____ Date _____

1. How has the brain contributed to our success as a species?

   _____
   _____

2. Describe the three stages of memory.

   _____
   _____

3. What are two mnemonic systems that are used to memorize lists of information?

   _____
   _____

4. What is the difference between deductive and inductive reasoning?

   _____
   _____

5. Describe the PrOACT approach to solving a problem.

   _____
   _____

6. Why are there no perfect solutions to problems?

   _____
   _____

7. How do psychologists define creativity?

   _____
   _____

8. What happens during associative thinking?

   _____
   _____

9. Describe what happens in backburner thinking.

   _____
   _____

10. In what situations is brainstorming particularly useful?

   _____
   _____

Case Studies

The Case of the Forgetful Counselor

Aneisha was a counselor at the day camp run by her local YMCA. Every two weeks, she met a new group of 10 campers for whom she was responsible. Aneisha found that she was terrible at remembering the campers' names. As soon as they introduced themselves, their names would vanish into thin air. Often she didn't get the kids in the group straight until the end of the two-week session. Then those kids left and she had to learn who was who in a new set of campers.

1. Why was Aneisha having trouble remembering the names of the kids in her group?

_____

_____

_____

_____

2. What suggestions do you have for Aneisha that would help her remember the campers' names?

_____

_____

_____

_____

The Case of the Unsold Bike

Arlen wanted to sell his old bike so he could buy a new, better model. He placed an ad on the Internet auction site eBay, offering the bike for $200. Arlen wanted at least $100 for his bike, but he got no bids. Arlen was discouraged. He can't afford a new bike unless he sells the old one for at least $100.

1. Using the PrOACT problem-solving method, indicate how Arlen might solve his problem.

_____

_____

_____

_____

2. Use associative thinking to help solve Arlen's problem. Write your associations in the space below.

_____

_____

_____

_____

Journal

Answer the following journal questions.

1. What is your earliest memory of school? Why do you think you remember this event or thing?

_____
_____
_____
_____
_____
_____
_____

2. If your memory was better, how would this affect your studies? Your job?

_____
_____
_____
_____
_____
_____

3. In Your Turn 3-5, you wrote about a problem you have. Describe how you might use the PrOACT approach to solve this problem.

_____
_____
_____
_____
_____
_____

4. Describe the most creative person you know. What makes this person creative, in your opinion?

_____
_____
_____
_____
_____
_____

4 Improving Your Study Skills

Oseola McCarty dropped out of school after sixth grade and earned her living as a laundress. Yet she valued education so much that she left her life savings of $150,000 to the University of Southern Mississippi to provide scholarships for deserving African-American students. Here she carries the Olympic torch in Columbia, Mississippi.

In Chapter 3, we learned that the brain is capable of far more than most people realize. Regardless of your age, sex, or background, your brain can remember phenomenal amounts of information, detect patterns, analyze information, and think creatively. These processes have a physiological basis in the structures of the brain. Therefore, your physical well-being can affect your ability to think and learn. We've all had the experience of performing poorly when we're feeling ill or tired.

In addition, your brain does not separate emotion from thinking. How you feel colors how you think. We saw a powerful example of this in self-belief, the connection between what you believe (your thoughts) and how you feel about yourself (your emotions). Your self-belief affects everything you do. More specific feelings have more specific effects. The feeling of stage fright can make an actress forget her lines. Someone who is in love may be unable to think rationally about his loved one.

In effect, physical and emotional well-being is the foundation upon which you can build specific learning skills. In this chapter, you will:

- identify your learning style preferences;
- discover what makes a good place and time for studying;
- learn a technique for reading books, articles, and Web sites that will help you remember what you read;
- improve your note-taking skills; and
- learn the best way to approach test taking.

Finally, you will discover the wealth of resources, both print and computer based, that school and community libraries provide to support your lifelong learning.

Just as no two people look alike, no two people learn in the same way. Some people like to get the big picture first and then fill in the details. Others prefer to start with examples and details, and from them develop an overarching concept. Many people are comfortable learning from books, and others prefer to participate in discussions. People have preferences for facts or feelings, analysis or intuition.

Some psychologists have attempted to categorize people's preferences for learning new material. Have you ever thought about how you prefer to learn? The chances are you will recognize yourself in one or two of the basic learning style preferences following.[1]

Some people learn best by using their eyes. In this photo, a visual learner reads some material on his laptop.

Visual Learning

The visual learner feels most comfortable learning through seeing. When learning a new subject, the visual learner prefers to read words and look at diagrams and pictures. Visual learners are most comfortable with reading print and online material, looking at images, reviewing notes, and using flashcards.

Auditory Learning

The auditory learner prefers sound. When learning, the auditory learner feels most comfortable listening to new material. Auditory learners prefer to hear lectures, participate in class discussions, and listen to recordings and podcasts.

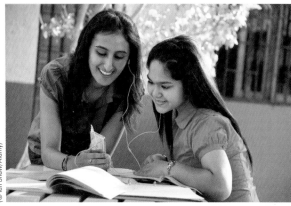

Auditory learners like to process information by listening. These students are listening to a lecture on an MP3 player.

Kinesthetic Learning

The kinesthetic learner prefers to learn by involving the whole body, not just the mind. He or she prefers to learn through real-life experience, role playing, designing and building things, interactive programs, and interviewing.

Tactile Learning

The tactile learner also prefers to learn by doing, but primarily by using the hands. Highlighting, note taking, and underlining, sketching, and diagramming are characteristic ways for the tactile learner to learn.

Using Learning Style Preferences

Do you recognize yourself in one or more of these learning styles? If so, you may already be aware of your preferred ways to learn new material; however, you shouldn't limit yourself to learning in one manner only. You can reinforce what you learn by combining two or more of the learning

Kinesthetic learners like to get their whole bodies involved in learning. This student is learning by making a model.

(© Corbis Premium RF/Alamy)

Some people learn best by taking notes. Tactile learners favor note-taking and highlighting when they study.

styles when trying to master a subject. For example, if you prefer auditory learning, you learn a lot just by listening to lectures. But you can reinforce this material by taking notes (tactile learning) and then by reviewing your notes (visual learning). Similarly, if you prefer visual learning, you may learn the most from your assigned readings but then you can reinforce this learning by listening to lectures (auditory) and by doing a related internship (kinesthetic).

Students with Special Needs

Although each of us has a preferred learning style, some people have disabilities that affect how they learn. The Americans with Disabilities Act (ADA) requires colleges and universities to help such students by making "reasonable accommodations" for their disabilities. Examples of reasonable accommodations include extra time on tests, a seat in the front of the class, sign language interpreters, alternative print formats for tests, tutoring, and so on.

There is a major difference in the way high schools and colleges treat special needs students. In high school, most of the procedures and accommodations are handled by the school. In contrast, once special needs students are enrolled in college, they must take the initiative to arrange their own accommodations with the administration. If you have special needs, you should contact your school's student services department to apply for accommodations. You will have to provide documentation that includes the diagnosis, your limitations, and your need for accommodations.

> "Whatever is received is received according to the nature of the recipient."
>
> ST. THOMAS AQUINAS (1225–1274), Italian philosopher and theologian

Your Turn 4-1

WHAT LEARNING STYLE(S) DO YOU PREFER?

Reread the descriptions of the learning style preferences on pages 88–89. Then answer the following questions:

1. If you had to choose one learning style to describe yourself, which would it be?

   _____

2. What other learning style preferences do you have?

   _____

3. Given your own assessment of your preferred learning style(s), describe how you would best learn a new subject.

   _____

News & Views

ARE THERE MANY TYPES OF INTELLIGENCE?

Scientists have struggled for centuries to define the idea of intelligence. Psychologist Howard Gardner proposed that intelligence is not one ability; instead, there are many forms of intelligence that people have in varying degrees. Gardner's ideas have influenced educators, because people benefit from being taught in ways that develop their particular combinations of intelligences. Following, briefly, is Gardner's theory of multiple intelligences.

The first two types of intelligence that Gardner proposes are those stressed in most schools and by most standardized tests such as IQ tests, MATs, and SATs. People who are strong in these types of intelligence tend to do well in school.

- **Linguistic intelligence** is the ability to use language well. Writers and journalists possess a high degree of this type of intelligence.
- **Logical-mathematical intelligence** is the ability to think logically, mathematically, and scientifically. Scientists, mathematicians, computer programmers, financial analysts, accountants, and others whose work involves logic and numbers have a high degree of this type of intelligence.

The next types of intelligence involve abilities to understand and use aspects of the environment.

- **Spatial intelligence** is the ability to form and use a mental model of a three-dimensional world. Sailors, engineers, mechanics, artists, architects, drafters, and surgeons have a high degree of spatial intelligence.
- **Musical intelligence** is the ability to hear musical sounds and make music. Singers, conductors, and other musicians have lots of musical intelligence.
- **Bodily-kinesthetic intelligence** is the ability to solve problems or make things using your body, or parts of your body. Athletes, dancers, and crafts people have high degrees of bodily-kinesthetic intelligence.

The last two types of intelligence that Gardner proposes are personal. Although they are not usually thought of as forms of intelligence, they are very important because they influence how well people do in life.

- **Interpersonal intelligence** is the ability to understand other people and to work cooperatively with them. Good salespeople, teachers, therapists, politicians, and parents possess this ability in a high degree.
- **Intrapersonal intelligence** is the ability to assess and understand yourself and use the knowledge to live an effective life. People with good self-belief and appropriate goals have considerable intrapersonal intelligence.

Looking at intelligence as a variety of different abilities opens up the way we evaluate ourselves and others. Each of us possesses some degree of each of these abilities, but most people have more of some than of others. What is your intelligence profile? How might it influence what you like to learn, the way you learn, and your professional goals?

Sources: Howard Gardner, *Multiple Intelligences: The Theory in Practice,* New York: Basic Books, 1993; Howard Gardner, *Frames of Mind: The Theory of Multiple Intelligences,* New York: Basic Books, 1983.

Preparing to Study

No matter what your preferred learning styles, you must set the stage for studying in order to learn productively. Establish a study area you can call your own, a study schedule that takes advantage of your peak learning times, and clear learning goals to focus your efforts.

Set Up a Study Area

The word *study* refers to the process of learning as well as the place where learning occurs. Many great learners have set up ideal spaces in which they can work and think. A good study area is a place where you can concentrate and learn with few distractions.

Setting aside space to study sends a message to yourself and others that you take studying seriously and have made a commitment to succeed. In addition, studying in the same place helps people learn. Psychologists have found that learning is often state specific. That means that what we learn is connected with the state and place in which we learn. The environment in which learning takes place provides cues associated with the learning, making things easier to recall when you're in the same location. That's why students who take a class and final exam in the same room generally do better than those who are tested in a different room.

You may be thinking that a good study area requires both space and cash. True, you can do a lot with these two resources. However, a study area can be set up in the corner of a bedroom or living room or on the kitchen table after dinner. If your home has too many distractions, you can find a quiet, temporary, portable study area in your school or local library. The most important consideration is that you find a study area, however small, that works for you.

Following is a list of questions to help you plan your ideal study or work area:

- Where will the study be located?
- What kind of furniture, if any, will you need?
- How will you decorate the area to make it functional, pleasant, and inspiring? What light, color, sound, pictures, and objects will you use?
- What access will you need to a computer and the Internet?
- What supplies will you need?
- What other resources will you need (for example, dictionaries, manuals, and calculators)?

Once you've got your study area set up, no doubt you will run into problems that will interfere with your ability to learn. Instead of thinking of these problems as inevitable, try making changes to improve your study environment. Some common problems include:

- **Too much noise from the environment.** People who need silence to concentrate can try earplugs to block out noise.
- **Too little noise from the environment.** Some people work better with background sounds. Use a computer and headphones

> *"Learning is not compulsory, but neither is survival."*
>
> W. EDWARDS DEMING (1900–1993), quality-control expert

© 2011 Wadsworth, Cengage Learning

CHAPTER 4 Improving Your Study Skills **91**

or an MP3 player for background music that won't disturb others.

- **Visual distractions.** Set up the work area so your back is to the source of distractions. You can also screen off the study area. If the visual distractions are coming from your own computer, close down all programs except the ones you need for studying.

- **Interruptions.** Ask people around you not to disturb you when you're studying. To avoid cell phone interruptions, turn off your phone or set it to send calls to voice mail and to store text messages. To avoid instant message (IM) interruptions when you are working online, post an "away" message. That way, friends and family will know you are not currently available for IMs.

- **Discomfort.** If you are uncomfortable, try adjusting your posture, chair, or work surface height.

Schedule Regular Study Time

Once your study area is set up, plan a study schedule. In other words, studying should be part of your everyday routine, not be left for occasional marathon sessions before exams.

Regular studying is much more effective than cramming because it takes advantage of the way your memory works. As you recall from Chapter 3, repetition and organization are two ways to improve your ability to remember. When you study each day, you organize what you've learned in class and from reading assignments. By reviewing this material, you commit it to your long-term memory.

If you think you are too busy to study every day, think again about your daily schedule. Can you study while commuting or between classes? Perhaps you have time after work or after dinner. You should plan your study time as carefully as you plan your work or class schedule. (We discuss scheduling your time more thoroughly in Chapter 2.) You can improve the effectiveness of your studying by taking advantage of your peak learning times. (See Figure 4–1.) People are mentally alert and motivated at different times

---

FIGURE 4–1

People learn best at different times of day. This person's peak study time is clearly the morning.

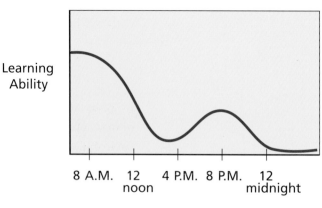

Your Turn 4-2

For each of the following statements, answer *true* or *false* to get a better sense of when your peak studying time occurs.

1. I would wake up early even if my alarm didn't go off. _____

2. When I have something to do that requires concentration, I do it first thing in the morning. _____

3. If I stay up late to get something done, I often fall asleep over it. _____

4. It usually takes all morning for me to get started. _____

5. I would rather go to school or work in the afternoon instead of the morning. _____

6. When I have to concentrate on something, it's best if I work on it after lunch. _____

7. I could stay up all night. _____

8. I usually start tasks that require concentration after dinner. _____

9. I wish I could relax during the day and go to work or school at night. _____

Here's how to figure out your peak learning time:

If you answered true to items 1–3, your best time is the morning.
If you answered true to items 4–6, your best time is the afternoon.
If you answered true to items 7–9, your best time is the evening.

of the day. Some people wake up early full of energy and purpose; others would sleep until noon each day if given the chance. If you can schedule studying for your peak times, you will learn faster and more easily.

Set Study Goals

Do you remember the educational and professional goals you set in Chapter 2? If you don't, now is a good time to review them. Keep your educational and professional goals in mind, because studying is part of any action plan to accomplish them. If you commit yourself to studying, you are committing yourself to doing well in your courses. Focusing on a short-term goal like studying helps you progress toward your intermediate- and long-term goals.

WHATEVER IT TAKES
Michael Hooks

Sometimes adopting a learning style is not a matter of preference, but of necessity. That was the case with Michael Hooks, who began to lose his eyesight as a child. Now in his 30s and legally blind, Hooks can only see things that are very close. But that hasn't stopped him from learning and working, and teaching others to do the same. Hooks has devoted his career to helping blind and visually impaired people succeed.

While still in school, Hooks learned to read Braille and use technology that helps people with poor vision. He went on to get a masters degree in assistive technology from Northern Illinois University. For seven years, Hook taught and was an assistive technology specialist at the Washington State School for the Blind.

In 1998 Hooks decided to form his own company, Next Level Assistive Technology, to provide products and services for people who are blind or visually impaired. One of his big successes was the development of software that would enable a blind medical student to access medical information on her hand-held computer. Hooks also

(© courtesy of Michael Hooks)

develops products that help aging adults compensate for vision loss. Hooks credits his teaching experience as well as his own experiences as a visually impaired student for much of his success. "You have to understand people and understand what they're going through before you can teach them," he says.

Sources: "PAC Mate Enables Blind Medical Student to Achieve Her Ultimate Goal," http://www.iinet. com, accessed Nov. 7, 2007; Amy McFall Prince, "Blind Ambition," *The Columbian* [Vancouver, WA], March 24, 2006; Next Level Assistive Technology web site, http: www.nextlevelat.com, accessed January 25, 2008.

Reading to Learn

One of the key study skills is the ability to read. When you were in elementary school, you learned how to read by reading stories. You may still enjoy reading novels and other books for your own pleasure. But reading in order to learn is a different process. It involves special techniques to help you understand and remember what you read. The basic steps in reading for information are (1) previewing, (2) questioning while reading, and (3) reviewing. This method is sometimes called the P.Q.R. system.

Previewing

When you first turn to a reading assignment, do you start at the first word and proceed until you get to the last? If you take this approach, you aren't getting as much out of the assignment as you could.

Experienced readers preview the material, before they start reading. Previewing means scanning the selection, looking for main points, and discovering how the material is organized. Previewing is like standing back from a new item of clothing and getting an idea of its style and fit rather than closely examining each button, thread, zipper, and piece of fabric.

Previewing a Book   To preview a book, you should look at the pages at the front. Skim the preface, which is a short essay that often summarizes the author's point of view (see page xix). Then turn to the table of contents and examine it. The table of contents is an outline of the main ideas of the book and how they relate to one another (see page vii). Finally, page through the book to get a feel for it.

Previewing a Chapter   To preview a chapter from a text, skim it first, looking at the headings. Like the table of contents, the headings provide an outline of the material. Many textbooks have other features to help you preview. These may include a list of what you will learn by reading the chapter and a chapter summary. Read these first to get an idea of the chapter's content and organization.

Previewing an Article   When previewing an article, scan any headings and look at charts, graphs, or other illustrations. These often highlight key ideas in the article. If the article has a summary, read it. If not, read the first and last paragraphs to get a general idea of what it is about.

Previewing a Web Site   Many Web sites are similar in size and complexity to books. However, since so much of a site is hidden "behind" the page you are currently viewing, they are a little harder to preview. To preview a Web site, start at the home page. (A home page's **URL,** or Web address, will end with .edu, .com, .org, or .net.) If there is an "About Us" link, click on it for background information about the site's sponsor. Back on the home page, look at the main links to other parts of the site. These links are often located in a banner at the top, or in a list at the bottom or side of the home page. If the home page has a link to a site index or site guide, click on it to see how information on the site is organized. If there is no site guide, you can click on each major link on the home page to see what type of material is located there.

Questioning while Reading

Only after you have previewed a reading assignment are you ready to start reading. To understand what you are reading, you must be an active reader. Take a questioning approach to the material. Ask yourself:

- Why am I reading this?
- How will this material meet my needs?
- What do I already know about this topic?

> "*Tell me, I'll forget. Show me, I may remember. But involve me and I'll understand.*"
>
> CHINESE PROVERB

> "*Hear them, read, mark, learn, and inwardly digest them.*"
>
> BOOK OF COMMON PRAYER

Your Turn 4-3

Preview the Web site of the Federal Emergency Management Agency, http://www.fema.gov, your college's Web site, or another site chosen by your instructor. You don't have to read the whole site. Just browse to get an overview of what is there.

1. List the main links on the site's home page—those at the top of the Web page.

_____

2. Read the "About Us" page. Who sponsors this site? What is its purpose?

_____

3. What could you use this Web site for?

_____

Your Turn 4-4

READ TO LEARN: USE THE P.Q.R. METHOD

1. Practice using the P.Q.R. method on the next main section of this chapter, Taking Notes, on pages 97–99.

P   Preview the section. In one sentence, describe what this section is about.

_____

Q   Question yourself while reading:

a.   What do you expect to learn by reading this section?

_____

b.   What do you already know about this topic?

_____

c.   Write down questions to ask yourself as you read:

_____

R   Review.

a.   **See** the material—go over the section again.

b.   **Say** the answers to your questions out loud.

c.   On a separate sheet of paper, **write** brief answers to the questions you posed in item 2c.

By answering these questions, you will begin to make associations between the new material you are reading and what you already know.

As you are reading, continue to question yourself, using the words *who, what, where, when, why,* and *how.* One way to do this is to turn every heading into a question that you must answer. For example, if the heading in an accounting text is "Balance Sheet," ask yourself, What is a balance sheet? Then read the section with your question in mind. If you own the book, after you read a section you can underline or highlight key ideas and words that help answer the question. Asking and answering questions as you read helps.

Reviewing: Seeing, Saying, Writing

When you are studying, reading something once is not enough. You must review what you read to fix it in your long-term memory. You do this by using three processes: seeing, saying, and writing.

First, go back over the material, skimming each section of the chapter or article. As you *see* the material, *say* the main points out loud. Then *write* brief study notes that outline the main ideas. This review method helps you remember by organizing and repeating the material using three different processes: seeing, saying, and writing.

Taking Notes

When you are learning a subject, it's important to take notes during class sessions and reading assignments for two reasons. First, taking notes forces you to be an active learner. Writing down important facts and ideas helps you understand and remember them. Second, a good set of notes provides you with a concise summary of the course content—a valuable resource when you're preparing for an exam.

You should use a spiral notebook or loose-leaf binder with ruled paper for your notes. Set up sections or separate notebooks for each course. When you go to class, make sure you have the right notebook and a couple of pens with you.

If you prefer to take notes on a laptop computer, be sure the battery is charged. Set up a note-taking document template that you can use in all your classes. Bring a paper notebook, too. You may need to draw sketches, diagrams, or flowcharts as part of your note taking.

Choose a seat near the front of the room so you will be able to see and hear clearly. You'll find that taking classroom notes is easier if you keep up with reading assignments and come to class prepared.

Taking good notes on your readings is less difficult than taking good classroom notes. If you miss something in class, you can't go back over it to fill it in. You have to wait until the class is over and ask your instructor or another student for help. On the other hand, when you miss something in a reading, you can reread it as many times as you need to in order to understand it.

Several techniques can help you get the most out of note taking. Formatting your notes, outlining, and diagramming are basic techniques. In addition, there are special techniques you can use for building your vocabulary.

When you read to learn, you should take notes. By taking notes, you repeat the important material, making it easier to remember.

Using a Two-Column Format for Notes

Many students find that a two-column format, with one narrow and one wide column, is the best setup for notes (see Figure 4–2). The narrow column is used for **recall words,** important words that provide cues for the main ideas. These are filled in when you review your notes, not when you first take them. The wide column is used for main ideas and important facts.

FIGURE 4–2

These notes were taken using a two-column format and outlining. Note the recall words in the narrow column.

	Evaluating Software　　　　　　Oct. 10
Hardware requirements	Check that computer system meets or exceeds hardware requirements:
	• PC or Macintosh
	• processor speed
	• which operating system
	• amount of memory needed to run the program (RAM)
	• amount of free space on hard drive
Documentation/Help	"How to" manual (documentation) and/or help system:
	• complete
	• organized
	• easy to find what you need (good index)
	• tech. support hours
Installation	Installation
	• clear instructions
	• fast & easy
	• Internet download or CD ROM

Outlining and Diagramming

When you take notes, you should not be writing every word the instructor says or copying a whole reading. Rather, you should write main ideas and important facts. Generally, definitions, lists, formulas, and solutions are important enough to write down. To save time, use phrases and abbreviations rather than full sentences.

Using an outline format will help you take down the important material and organize it at the same time. In an outline, indentions are used to show the relationship of main ideas to secondary ideas or supporting details. For example:

I. Three stages of memory

   A. Sensory memory—perceptions of senses

   B. Short-term memory—information brain is using

   C. Long-term memory—permanent storage

Your outline need not be numbered. More important than letters and numbers are the indentions that show the relation of one idea to another.

In addition to outlining your notes, you should use diagrams and drawings whenever possible to simplify the ideas (see Figure 4–3).

- **Time lines** are good for showing the sequence of historical events.
- **Flowcharts** can be used to show the steps in a process or procedure.
- **Pie charts** show the relationship of parts to a whole.
- An **idea diagram** is like a mind-map; it shows the relationship of secondary ideas to a main idea and to one another.
- A **drawing** gives an instant description of something visual.

© 2011 Wadsworth, Cengage Learning

FIGURE 4–3

Diagrams and drawings can be helpful when you are taking notes. An image can summarize facts and ideas that would take many words to describe.

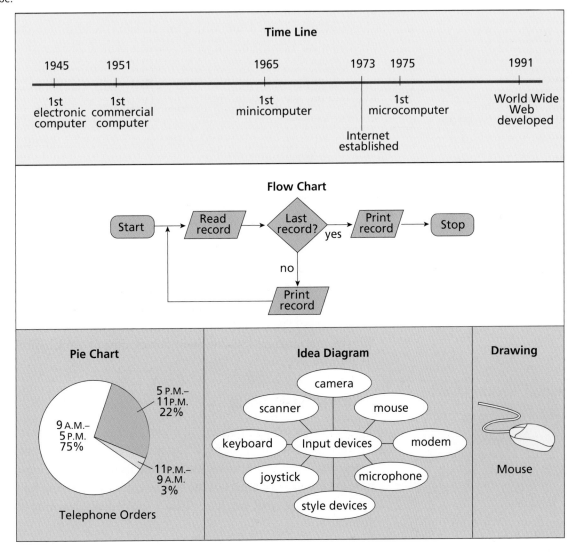

Your Turn 4-5

Use the techniques described in the sections on reading and taking notes to prepare notes on this chapter. Use your own notebook or laptop.

Building Your Vocabulary

You may hear words you don't understand from your instructor and find unfamiliar words in your textbooks. Don't skip over them! Building a good vocabulary is important for educational and career success. Particularly important are the specialized words, called jargon, that are used in every field.

When you hear an unfamiliar word in class, write it down as best you can and look it up in a dictionary after class. In your readings, you will find that many words are defined for you in the text or at the end of the book in a glossary (see page 000). When you look up a new word, write it down, along with its definition. Some students prefer to record vocabulary words for each course on a separate page in their course notebook. They write the word in the narrow column and the definition in the wide column. Other students prefer to make flash cards with the word on one side and the definition on the other (see Figure 4–4).

Having written notes of all new vocabulary words associated with a subject will help you master the subject and prepare for exams.

FIGURE 4–4

Flash cards are useful for learning technical and course-related vocabulary.

laser printer

a printer that uses laser light to make an image on a rotating drum before transferring the image to paper using toner

Taking Tests

Many students think that a long cramming session—even an "all nighter"—is the best way to prepare for an exam. Unfortunately, this method doesn't work well. Learning is more effective when done in short sessions of no more than two hours. Longer study sessions are tiring, and a tired brain doesn't think, memorize, or recall things effectively.

The keys to doing well on exams are good study habits; preparation, both mental and physical; and an understanding of some basic test-taking techniques.

Studying for Tests

You will never need to pull an "all nighter" if you have made studying a regular part of your routine. If you attend class regularly, take class notes, read your assignments, and take notes on your readings, you will have absorbed a good part of the course content. Studying for a test will mean reviewing what you have already learned, not learning it from scratch.

"Forewarned, forearmed; to be prepared is half the victory."

CERVANTES (1547–1616),
Spanish writer

Your notes are your primary resource when you are preparing for an exam. A complete set of course notes, on class discussions and readings, provides an outline of the course content. By studying your notes, you can refresh your memory.

Now is the time that the two-column format for note taking will pay off. If you have not already done so, *read* the material in the wide column and *write* corresponding recall words and questions in the narrow column. Then cover the wide column and answer *out loud* the questions you have written in the narrow column. Uncover the wide column to check each answer. If you did not answer correctly, review the material and ask yourself the question again. This time *write* your answer and check it. Repeat this process until you have mastered the material.

You can use the memory techniques discussed in Chapter 3 to help you remember. Repeating material, organizing facts and ideas into small groups, and using associations, acronyms, rhymes, the pegword method, and the method of loci are useful ways to improve your ability to recall what you are studying.

However, don't try to memorize material without understanding it first. If you need help understanding some of the course concepts, ask your instructor or fellow students to work with you. Some colleges offer learning centers or tutors to help students study. If your college has such resources, use them.

Preparing to Take a Test

If you have studied thoroughly, you have done 90 percent of the preparation needed for taking an exam. But don't stop now—the other 10 percent is also important.

First, check your emotional state. Are you feeling prepared, relaxed, and capable? Do you feel you will do well on the exam? Or do you feel uneasy, anxious, and sure to fail? A certain amount of anxiety is normal; it will even sharpen your performance. But excessive anxiety can cause you to "blank out" during an exam. If you tend to be anxious before exams, don't tank up on coffee, energy drinks, or cola. The caffeine and other substances in these beverages will make you feel even more stressed. Instead, have a complex carbohydrate snack (grains, fruits, or vegetables) to calm yourself and help you focus.

If you are feeling very anxious, ask yourself whether you have studied enough. Perhaps you need to review your notes one more time. Or perhaps you need a positive self-talk session to boost your confidence. Tell yourself it's normal to feel anxious but that you are prepared and will do well anyway. Remember, a positive attitude will improve your performance.

You can give your feelings of preparedness a boost by making sure that you are physically ready—not just mentally and emotionally ready. Gather all the materials you will need to take the exam—pens, pencils, calculator, watch, books, and so on—and pack them the night before. Then get a good night's sleep and eat breakfast so you will be well rested and have plenty of energy.

Test taking can be stressful. Thoroughly prepared students who are well rested and have good test-taking habits generally do well.

Your Turn 4-6

Use the following checklist to evaluate your study habits.

	Yes	No
1. I have a separate notebook, section, or computer folder for each class.	☐	☐
2. I attend class regularly.	☐	☐
3. I check my campus e-mail and course management system (Blackboard) regularly for updates from my instructors.	☐	☐
4. I take notes on class lectures and discussions.	☐	☐
5. When I miss class, I borrow another student's notes to learn what was covered.	☐	☐
6. I keep up with reading assignments and special projects.	☐	☐
7. If I have trouble understanding course material, I ask for help.	☐	☐
8. I take notes on readings.	☐	☐
9. I review my notes regularly.	☐	☐
10. I use my notes to study for exams.	☐	☐

If you answered *yes* to all these items, congratulations! You have excellent study habits.
If you answered *no* to any items, you should concentrate on improving these aspects of your study routine.

Basic Test-Taking Techniques

Successful students also improve their test-taking performance by using some basic test-taking techniques. Of course, no technique can substitute for thorough preparation. But understanding the best way to approach a test can improve your score. Following are some suggestions:

- **Skim the whole test first.** Just as you preview a reading to get an idea of what it's about, you should preview the test to see what's on it.

- **Pace yourself.** Know how much each question is worth and budget your time accordingly. For example, if the test is an hour, don't spend half an hour on a question worth only 10 points. Check your watch or a clock every few minutes to make sure you are not wasting time.

- **Answer the easy questions first.** Put a check in the margin next to difficult questions, and return to these questions last. That way you won't spend too much time trying to answer the hard questions and miss answering the easy ones.

- **Make sure you understand each question.** Underline key words and ideas. If you think a question is vague or unclear, ask your instructor for help.

■ **Look for clues to the answer in the question itself.** For example, if you get stuck on a multiple-choice item, eliminate the choices that are clearly wrong, then choose from the two or three remaining possibilities. When answering true-false questions, look for the words *always* or *never*. These words often signal a false statement.

Approaching test taking in this methodical way will help you minimize feelings of anxiety.

Tech Tips

USING LIBRARY RESOURCES

Your school and community libraries are among the most useful resources to help you succeed at college. Not only do libraries provide material when you need to prepare a research paper or project for school but also they have information that can help you in your professional and personal life. It pays, therefore, to become acquainted with your libraries, because as a lifelong learner, you can benefit from these resources over the years. If you have never used a particular library before, sign up for an orientation session, if these are given, or take a tour on your own. Since access to so many library resources is available online, be sure to explore your library's Web site. Take a virtual tour or browse links on your own.

A modern library has books, periodicals, reference works, online or CD-ROM indexes and reference materials, and access to the **World Wide Web.** Doing research in such a library can be confusing because there are so many possible sources of information. When you are looking for information, it helps to narrow the topic you need to research; the more specific you can be, the better the quality of information you will find. It also helps to know what type of source material is likely to have the information you need, whether books, magazines, newspapers, academic journals, or Web sites. Above all, do not hesitate to ask a librarian for help if you get stuck, either in person or via e-mail or chat links on the library's Web site. Librarians, because they know where to find different types of information, are still the most valuable resource of the library.

USING THE ONLINE CATALOG

You can find books, and nonbook items such as tapes and DVDs, by searching the library's catalog. Most library catalogs can be accessed from any computer, anywhere, although you may need a user name and password to do this.

You can search the online catalog in several ways: by the author's last name, the title, the subject, or by **key words.** If you are looking for a specific book or item, look under the author's name or the title. If you are looking for books on a particular topic, look under the subject. In addition to searching by general subject headings, you may be able to search an online catalog by specific key words. Once you find material that looks promising, you can find related works with a keystroke. An online catalog may also tell you whether the item is checked out and, if so, when it is due back. It may tell you which other libraries in your area have the item.

Once you find an item that interests you, save the item or copy its **call number,** an identification number that shows where it is shelved in the library.

continues

Specific methods for using online catalogs vary from library to library. You'll need to learn how to use your own library catalog by direct experience. Ask a librarian for help if you need it.

USING REFERENCE WORKS

Most libraries have collections of basic reference works that cannot be borrowed. Reference works include dictionaries, encyclopedias, atlases, biographical directories, indexes, handbooks, telephone books, and almanacs. Many of these are in book form, but an increasing number are on CD-ROMs or in online databases and are accessed by computer.

In addition, many school libraries put copies of texts and other course readings in the print reference collection during the term so that students can use them in the library.

FINDING ARTICLES IN ONLINE DATABASES

Periodicals are publications that appear at regular intervals, such as newspapers, magazines, and scholarly journals. Newspapers and magazines contain articles geared to the general public. Scholarly journals contain articles written by experts and geared to students, teachers, and professionals in a particular field. Since the information in periodicals is more up to date than the information in books, you may need to consult periodicals when doing research.

Articles are not indexed in the library's main online catalog. Instead, you must search for articles in online databases compiled by various companies. Following are just a few examples:

- **EBSCOhost.** A database covering most academic subject areas and containing full-text articles from more than 3,000 periodicals.
- **ProQuest.** A database covering many academic areas, as well as articles from newspapers.
- **ERIC.** A specialized database that contains articles from education journals.
- **Medline.** A specialized database that covers health-related and medical journals.

You can access online databases at a computer terminal in the library or from your own computer by using a password. Note that these databases of periodical articles cannot be searched by Web search engines like Google or Yahoo!. Your library must subscribe to a particular database for you to access it.

Each database has its own search engine. You can search the articles by author, title, subject, key words, date, type of periodical, and other characteristics. The database usually contains citation information as well as an abstract, or summary, of each article. In many cases it also contains the full text of the article (but often no illustrations). You can download the article, print it, or e-mail it to yourself.

The database also tells you whether the library owns a paper copy of the periodical in which the article appears. If it does, you should locate the paper copy, even if it seems easier just to download the article's text from the database. That's because seeing the paper copy will give you a better idea of what type of publication the article appears in. The paper copy also includes illustrations, which may be very important in your research.

Your Turn 4-7

CHECK OUT YOUR LIBRARY

Get to know your library better by taking a tour and answering the following questions. Use your school or local library.

1. What types of searches can you do on the online catalog?

   _____

2. List four books in the library's reference section.

   _____

   _____

   _____

3. What periodicals' databases does your library subscribe to? Which of them is used for general searches?

   _____

   _____

4. How can you get back issues of periodicals?

   _____

   _____

5. How can you get items that your own library does not own or subscribe to?

   _____

   _____

What's Up?

Name _____ Date _____

1. Why are physical and emotional well-being important for effective learning?

   _____

   _____

   _____

2. Briefly describe each of the four basic learning styles. Circle the name of the style(s) you prefer.

   Visual learning: _____

   Auditory learning: _____

   Kinesthetic learning: _____

   Tactile learning: _____

3. Why it is important to have a study area?

   _____

   _____

   _____

4. How can you take advantage of your peak learning times?

   _____

   _____

   _____

   _____

5. Describe each step in the P.Q.R. system of reading.

   _____

   _____

   _____

   _____

Name _____ Date _____

6. Give two reasons for taking notes on class sessions and readings.

_____

_____

_____

_____

_____

7. Why should you outline and diagram your notes?

_____

_____

_____

8. How can the two-column format for note taking be used when you are studying for an exam?

_____

_____

9. Describe two techniques for taking tests.

_____

_____

_____

_____

10. How would you find each of the following items in your school library?

(a) a book by Colin Powell, former secretary of state

_____

(b) an article in an education journal about methods of teaching freshman composition

_____

(c) a DVD of the first Harry Potter movie

_____

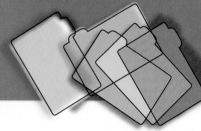

Case Studies

The Case of the Unhappy Learner

When Arianne transferred from a small rural school to a large urban school, she found her studies suffering. In the country, classes had been small and group discussions encouraged. Arianne had done very well and had always enjoyed her courses. Now Arianne found herself in large classes with little opportunity for discussion and lots of assigned readings. The subjects were not harder, but Arianne's marks were slipping and she wasn't happy about her studies.

1. What learning style does Arianne prefer? How do you know?

_____
_____
_____
_____

2. How can Arianne make up for the fact that her new school does not offer instruction tailored to her preferred learning style?

_____
_____
_____
_____

The Case of the Disorganized Student

Michael had always managed to get by on the strength of his cleverness, but when he got to college he found that cleverness was not enough. He had several hard courses and lots of reading to do for each one. In addition, there were quizzes plus midterms and finals. Michael liked the freedom of college, and often he skipped class. Since no one checked whether he was keeping up with the readings, he let them slide. Michael had always depended on cramming to pass exams. When he tried this during his first semester, he was dismayed to find he had failed two of his midterms.

1. What poor study habits has Michael fallen into?

_____
_____
_____
_____

2. What can Michael do to improve his school performance?

_____
_____

Journal

Answer the following journal questions.

1. Now that you understand your own learning style preferences, what will you do to change the way you study and learn?

2. Describe your ideal study location.

3. If you suffer from anxiety before tests, what can you do to reduce this? How can you improve your approach to taking tests?

4. What do you use the library for? If you don't regularly use the library now, what uses might it have for you in the future?

Developing Your Physical Potential

A strong and healthy body provides the foundation for all your activities—as well as your state of mind. A feeling of well-being will help you reach your potential in all areas of your life. In the following two chapters, you will learn how to eat well and stay healthy.

CHAPTER 5: EATING WELL

In this chapter, you will be . . .

. . . developing your self belief:
- I will remember that "you are what you eat."

. . . reframing your thoughts:
- I will think about the nutrients provided by the foods I usually eat.
- I will keep the five basic food groups in mind when planning meals.

. . . setting goals:
- I will eat more fruits, vegetables, and whole grains.
- I will consume less fat, sugar, salt, and alcohol.
- I will maintain a healthy weight by eating well and exercising.

. . . envisioning a compelling future:
- I will look and feel great as a result of eating well.

. . . achieving personal mastery:
- I will reach my physical potential in part by eating a healthy diet.

CHAPTER 6: STAYING HEALTHY

In this chapter, you will be . . .

. . . developing your self belief:
- I will exercise and get enough rest to improve the way I feel about myself.
- I will recognize the damage that drug abuse does to self-belief and relationships.

. . . reframing your thoughts:
- I will assess my level of physical activity and adjust my exercise habits if needed.
- If I am dependent on alcohol or other drugs, I will develop the motivation to change.

. . . setting goals:
- I will make an exercise agreement with a friend or family member.
- If I use alcohol or other drugs, I will moderate or give up their use.
- If I am sexually active, I will take steps to prevent the spread of disease.

. . . envisioning a compelling future:
- I will look and feel great as a result of living a healthy lifestyle.

. . . achieving personal mastery:
- I will reach my physical potential so I can meet life's challenges with energy.

Eating Well

Lorena Garcia always loved to cook, but cooking wasn't considered a career option in her native Venezuela. Trained as a lawyer, Garcia spent time in restaurant kitchens until attending culinary school. She opened, operated and sold two successful restaurants until starring in her own cooking show on Telemundo. Today she is a successful entrepreneur with three cooking shows and a complete kitchenware product line.

© 2011 Wadsworth, Cengage Learning

Over the years, the media have warned us about eating too much salt, sugar, and fat, smoking cigarettes, drinking alcohol, failing to exercise, practicing unsafe sex—the list goes on and on. As the headlines come and go, people try to adjust their habits to the latest round of advice. The result is often confusion about what's healthy and what's not.

Anyone who has been ill doesn't doubt the value of good health. People who don't feel well simply don't perform up to their potential. As we've seen, our ability to reach our potential as human beings depends on our emotional and intellectual well-being. Add physical well-being to that list, and you have the foundation for all your achievements. The better your physical health, the greater your chances of reaching your potential.

You may think you're in great shape, and perhaps you are. Yet studies have shown that most Americans have poor eating habits, don't get enough exercise and rest, and abuse their bodies with substances like alcohol and tobacco. These people may think they feel well, but in reality they are functioning below their potential.

On the other hand, people who eat healthy diets and are physically active are rewarded by increased well-being and self-confidence. They feel full of health and energy and mentally alert. As a result, they look good, too. To reach this level of physical potential, you must have a well-balanced approach to maintaining good health.

In this chapter, the focus is on eating a healthy diet. You will:

- learn about the major nutrients and how they affect your health;
- understand how to classify foods into the basic food groups;
- discover how to eat a balanced diet;
- figure out your body mass index to see if your weight is healthy; and
- determine your calorie needs based on your level of activity.

Finally, you will use various Internet tools to find out more about food and healthy eating.

Nutrients

Food provides nutrients, the substances your body uses for growth, maintenance, and repair, as well as for energy. Diets with too much or too little of a nutrient can be harmful to your health. In addition, the nutrients in foods affect your mind, mood, and energy level. To look, feel, and act your best, you have to eat your best, and that means a diet with foods rich in nutrients.

All foods contain one or more nutrients. The major types of nutrients are protein, carbohydrates, fats, water, vitamins, and minerals.

Protein

Protein is a chemical substance that is part of all body cells. It has many functions, including growth and the maintenance and repair of tissue. Meat, fish, poultry, eggs, dairy products, nuts, and tofu are all sources of protein. In addition, beans can be sources of protein if they are eaten with grains.

Carbohydrates

There are two basic types of carbohydrates: simple and complex. Simple carbohydrates are sugar, corn syrup, and other sweets. Complex carbohydrates are starches (like potatoes) and grains (like whole wheat). Starches and grains also contain dietary fiber that aids digestion.

In general, the more that a complex carbohydrate food has been processed, the less fiber it has. So, for example, white bread has less fiber than whole wheat bread, which is made from the whole grain.

Flour, cereal, bread, rice, noodles, grits, fruits, and vegetables all contain carbohydrates and varying amounts of dietary fiber. The healthiest choices are made from whole grains and contain complex carbohydrates.

WHATEVER IT TAKES
Michele Hoskins

In 1983, Michele Hoskins was a recently divorced mother of three with no business experience. However, she did have determination—and a secret recipe for honey crème syrup passed down through the third daughter of each generation from her great-great-grandmother America, who was a slave.

When Hoskins got the recipe from her mother, she served the syrup, a blend of honey, churned butter, and cream, at Sunday family breakfasts. Rather than passing down the recipe to her own daughter, she decided to pass down a business instead.

To finance the business, Hoskins sold everything she owned and moved into her parents' attic to save on living expenses. She and her daughters bottled syrup by hand in the basement. It took them an hour to fill 12 bottles, and their feet stuck to the spilled syrup on the floor.

At first, Hoskins made some bad deals and lost money. She and her girls moved to a public housing project and went on welfare for 18 months. But she continued to make and sell syrup. First she sold syrup to her neighborhood grocers in Chicago. Then she sold syrup to local and regional grocery and restaurant chains. She added butter pecan and maple crème syrups to her inventory. Finally, in 1993, Hoskins got her big break. She landed a $3 million contract with Denny's, the national restaurant chain. How did she do that? She phoned them to promote her syrup every Monday morning for two years.

(© Courtesy of Michelle Hoskins)

Today, Hoskins's business, Michele's Foods Inc., sells syrup to 10,000 stores nationwide. To help others achieve the success she has, Hoskins started Recipes to Retail, a group that mentors women who want to start food service businesses. She has also written an autobiography called *Sweet Expectations: The Michele Hoskins Success Bible* (2004), in which she describes how family, faith, and determination contributed to her success.

Sources: Ting Yu and Barbara Sandler, "Topping o' the Morning: Ex-Welfare Mom Michele Hoskins Finds a Rich New Life in a Family Recipe," *People*, July 29, 2000, pp. 121–122; "The History of Michele's Foods," and "Welcome to Michele Foods" [video] on the Michele's Foods Inc. Web site, <http://www.michelefoods.com>, accessed March 15, 2008; Charlotte Mulhern, "Through Thick and Thin: Cashing In on an Age-Old Family Recipe," *Entrepreneur*, June 1998.

Fats

Fats provide concentrated storage of energy for the body. They also provide insulation and dissolve certain vitamins. There are several types of fat:

- **Saturated fats** are those that are solid at room temperature; they are found in meat, lard, dairy products, and palm and coconut oils. Saturated fats increase the body's own production of cholesterol and have been linked to heart disease.

- **Trans fats** are a type of saturated fat. Most are produced during the manufacture of processed foods such as baked goods, chips, vegetable shortening, margarine, and fried foods. Trans fats have also been linked to heart disease.

- **Cholesterol,** a fatty acid, is found in animal products like meat, cheese, shellfish, and eggs. High levels of cholesterol in the blood are associated with heart disease.

- **Unsaturated fats** are liquid at room temperature. Polyunsaturated fats are found in corn, safflower, and soybean oil. Monounsaturated fats are found in peanut and olive oils. Unsaturated fats are healthier than saturated or trans fats.

- **Omega-3,** a fatty acid needed for proper brain functioning, is found in fish such as tuna, salmon, trout, and sardines. Fish also has the benefit of being low in saturated and unsaturated fats.

All fats have the same number of calories, but some are healthier than others. When you have a choice, opt for fats that come from plants and fish—the unsaturated fats and omega-3. Keep animal-based fats—saturated and trans fats—to a minimum.

Water

Water is an extremely important nutrient; it is found in every cell of the body. It transports nutrients throughout the body and removes waste products. Water cushions and lubricates parts of the body, and it is an essential part of many chemical reactions. It also helps regulate the body's temperature. Water is present in most foods, as well as in the liquids we drink.

Most healthy people get enough water by drinking a beverage with meals and from the water content of the food they eat. Only if you are thirsty, experiencing heat stress, or performing sustained physical activity do you need to drink extra water.

Vitamins and Minerals

Protein, carbohydrates, fats, and water are the major nutrients by weight in most food. However, foods also contain trace amounts of other chemicals, called vitamins and minerals, that are essential for life and growth. Each vitamin and mineral has specific functions in the body. For example, the mineral calcium is needed for strong bones, and Vitamin D is needed to help the body absorb calcium. Sodium (salt) is needed for fluid balance, but excess amounts contribute to high blood pressure (hypertension).

Your Turn 5-1

(© John Wynn/Shutterstock.com)

Fast food is popular, because it is convenient and inexpensive. But it's also popular because it contains a lot of fat and sodium (salt). These nutrients tend to satisfy our appetites and our taste buds; however, they have been associated with heart disease and hypertension.

Take the following quiz to see if you can identify the "healthier" choice—the one with fewer calories and less fat and sodium—from these pairs of fast food menu offerings. Note that we say "healthier" in quotation marks because none of these offerings is really healthy, as you'll discover as you read the rest of this chapter.

1. *The "healthier" choice from KFC:*

   ☐ Crispy Caesar salad with ranch dressing   OR   ☐ one fried chicken breast

2. *The "healthier" choice from McDonald's:*

   ☐ Big Mac sandwich   OR   ☐ premium grilled chicken classic sandwich

3. *The "healthier" choice from Subway:*

   ☐ Six-inch steak and cheese sandwich   OR
   ☐ six-inch tuna sandwich (both with lettuce, tomatoes, onions, green peppers, pickles, olives, and cheese)

Note that if you are interested in finding out the nutrients in your favorite fast foods, the restaurants post nutrition guides for their menus on their Web sites, and sometimes in the restaurants, too. Following is partial nutrition information for the menu items above.[1]

continues

Item	Calories	Fat (grams)	Sodium (milligrams)	Better choice	Comments
KFC crispy caesar salad with ranch dressing	550	39	1550		The ranch dressing accounts for more than 1/3 of the calories and fat. Without the dressing, the salad is the better choice.
KFC fried chicken breast	440	27	970	√	
McDonald's Big Mac	540	29	1040		
McDonald's premium grilled chicken classic sandwich	420	10	1190	√	Less fat but a little more sodium. Still, this is the better choice.
Subway six-inch steak and cheese sandwich	400	12	1110	√	
Subway six-inch tuna sandwich	530	31	1010		This Sandwich mart have a lot of mayonnaise or other oils to raise fat and calories. Usually, tuna is a healthier choice than steak.

Finding Information about Nutrients

How can you tell what nutrients are in the foods you eat at home? You can look up the foods you eat in dieters' booklets containing tables of nutrition information, or search the Internet for such tables (see page 129). For packaged foods, you can check the nutrition facts chart on the label. This chart, which is required by law on all packaged foods, tells you the amount of each nutrient a serving of that food contains. It also tells you what percentage of the daily requirement for that nutrient one serving provides. For example, the Nutrition Facts chart shown in Figure 5–1 is from a package of macaroni and cheese.

If you make a habit of checking the nutrition facts charts on the packaged foods you eat, you will have a pretty good idea of the nutrient content of your diet. You may be surprised to discover how much fat, sodium, and carbohydrates there are in most packaged foods, including this macaroni and cheese.

FIGURE 5-1

All packaged foods must have a nutrition facts chart showing the nutrients in one serving. This chart is from a package of macaroni and cheese.

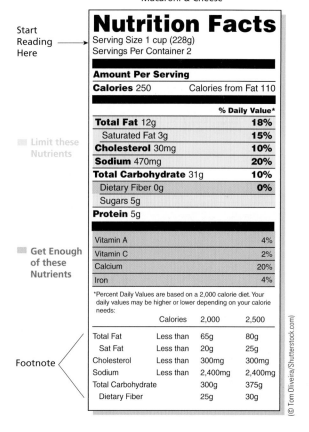

Macaroni & Cheese

Start Reading Here →

Nutrition Facts

Serving Size 1 cup (228g)
Servings Per Container 2

Amount Per Serving

Calories 250   Calories from Fat 110

% Daily Value*

Total Fat 12g	**18%**
Saturated Fat 3g	**15%**
Cholesterol 30mg	**10%**
Sodium 470mg	**20%**
Total Carbohydrate 31g	**10%**
Dietary Fiber 0g	**0%**
Sugars 5g	
Protein 5g	

Limit these Nutrients

Vitamin A	4%
Vitamin C	2%
Calcium	20%
Iron	4%

Get Enough of these Nutrients

*Percent Daily Values are based on a 2,000 calorie diet. Your daily values may be higher or lower depending on your calorie needs:

	Calories	2,000	2,500
Total Fat	Less than	65g	80g
Sat Fat	Less than	20g	25g
Cholesterol	Less than	300mg	300mg
Sodium	Less than	2,400mg	2,400mg
Total Carbohydrate		300g	375g
Dietary Fiber		25g	30g

Footnote

(© Tom Oliveira/Shutterstock.com)

Eating From the Basic Food Groups

Watching the fat and sodium in your diet is important, but it's not the only factor in good eating. The key to making sure you get all the necessary nutrients is to eat a wide variety of healthy foods from different food groups. According to the U.S. Department of Agriculture, the basic food groups include fruits, vegetables, grains, meats and beans, milk and dairy products, and oils, as shown in Table 5–1.

TABLE 5-1   The Basic Food Groups

Food Group	Some Examples	How Much Each Day?
Fruits Provide essential nutrients and fiber, which helps digestion. (© Simage/Alamy)	■ citrus fruits like oranges, grapefruit, and pineapple ■ melons such as cantaloupe, honeydew, and watermelon ■ berries such as strawberries and blueberries ■ stone fruits such as peaches, plums, and apricots ■ other fruits like apples and pears	One or two pieces (or 1 or 2 cups) of fresh or frozen fruit; half that if eating dried fruit

TABLE 5-1 **The Basic Food Groups** (*Continued*)

Vegetables Provide essential nutrients and fiber, which helps digestion. (© Gleb Semenjuk/Shutterstock.com)	■ dark green vegetables like broccoli, spinach, and kale ■ orange vegetables like carrots, winter squash, sweet potatoes, and pumpkin ■ legumes such as dry beans, chickpeas, and tofu ■ starchy vegetables like corn, white potatoes, and green peas ■ other vegetables such as tomatoes, cabbage, lettuce, onions, peppers, mushrooms, and summer squash.	2 to 2.5 cups
Grains, especially whole grains Provide carbohydrates for energy and fiber for digestion. (© Denise Kappa/Shutterstock.com)	■ bread, preferably whole grain bread ■ pasta, preferably whole grain pasta ■ rice, preferably brown rice ■ bulgur (cracked wheat), as in tabouli ■ oatmeal and oat bran ■ other breakfast cereals, preferably whole grain	3 to 6 slices of bread or 1.5 to 3 cups; half should be whole grains
Meats and beans Provide protein and fat. (© Jeffrey Coolidge/Getty Images)	■ cooked lean meats, poultry, and fish ■ eggs ■ beans, tofu, peanut butter, nuts, seeds	6 ounces or less
Milk and dairy products Provide protein and calcium. (© Daniel Hurst/Dreamstime LLC)	■ milk, preferably skim or 1 percent ■ yogurt, preferably low-fat ■ cheese, preferably low-fat	2 to 3 cups of milk or yogurt OR 1.5 ounces of cheese Note that people who do not eat dairy products can find the necessary calcium in soy milk, tofu, dark leafy vegetables, and some fish.
Oils Help growth and development and provide energy. (© Maram/Shutterstock.com)	■ Margarine or butter ■ Mayonnaise, preferably low-fat ■ Salad dressing, preferably low-fat ■ Cooking oil	2 to 6 teaspoons Limit saturated fat, which is found in animal products like butter, cheese, and meat. Also limit trans fat, found in processed foods.

Source: Adapted from U.S. Department of Health and Human Services and U.S. Department of Agriculture, *Dietary Guidelines for Americans, 2005*, Table 1, Sample USDA Food Guide and the DASH Eating Plan at the 2,000-Calorie Level, p. 10.

Your Turn 5-2

WHAT ARE YOU EATING?

Use the food diary form below to keep track of what you eat or drink for three days. Be honest! Then review your diet. Use the information in this chapter and the nutrition facts charts on the foods you've eaten to answer the following questions:

Three-Day Food Diary

Meal	Day 1	Day 2	Day 3
Breakfast			
Lunch			
Dinner			
Snacks			
Beverages			

1. What fruits did you eat?

_____

2. What vegetables did you eat?

_____

3. What grain products did you eat?

_____

4. What meat and beans did you eat?

_____

5. What dairy products did you eat?

_____

6. What oils did you eat?

_____

7. What else did you eat (for example, soda, candy, and alcohol)?

_____

Eating a Healthy Diet

Many vitamins and minerals are essential to prevent certain diseases. For example, rickets, a disease that affects bone development in children, can be prevented with vitamin D and calcium, both found in fortified milk. Goiter, an enlargement of the thyroid gland, can be prevented with iodine, a mineral in iodized salt. The relationship between diet and health in these types of disease is clear-cut.

The more general relationship between diet and health is not as clear cut. Many things influence health, and diet is just one of them. Still, nutritionists and scientists at the U.S. Department of Health and Human Services and the U.S. Department of Agriculture study the eating habits of Americans, and every few years they issue *Dietary Guidelines for Americans*.[2] This publication provides advice on healthy eating for Americans. Among the current guidelines are the following:

- Get adequate nutrients by eating a variety of healthy foods from all the food groups.
- Engage in regular physical activity.
- Balance calories from food with physical activity to maintain a healthy weight.
- Eat a lot of fruits, vegetables, and whole-grain products.
- Consume three cups of skim or low-fat milk daily, or its equivalent.
- Limit fats, especially saturated fats, trans fats, and cholesterol. Fats should make up between 20 and 35 percent of your daily calories.
- Limit sodium to less than 2,300 milligrams (about one teaspoon) per day.
- Limit your consumption of foods and beverages with lots of sugar and few other nutrients (for example, candy, soda, and sweetened fruit drinks)
- If you drink alcohol, do so in moderation. This means one drink per day for women, and two for men.

Changing Your Eating Habits

If your diet falls short of these guidelines, you can change it. There are several steps you can take to improve the way you eat.

1. **Find out what you are really eating** by keeping a food diary for a few days, as you are doing (or did) in Your Turn 5–2. It's easy to deceive yourself, so be sure to record everything, even sodas and snacks.

2. **Analyze the foods you eat and decide what changes are necessary.** If you are like most Americans, you will find you need to cut down on fats, processed foods, sweets, and soft drinks, and eat more whole grains, fruits, and vegetables.

"*Food is our common ground, a universal experience.*"

JAMES BEARD (1903–1985),
chef and cookbook author

"*Eat breakfast like a king, lunch like a prince, and dinner like a pauper.*"

ADELLE DAVIS (1903–1974),
nutritionist

MyPyramid.gov
STEPS TO A HEALTHIER YOU

BMI	Weight Category
18.5 to 25	Healthy weight
25 to 30	Overweight
Over 30	Obese

3. **Evaluate your meal patterns.** Do you skip breakfast? That's a bad habit, because breakfast fuels the start of your day and helps spread your eating into smaller meals. Studies have shown that eating several small meals each day rather than one or two large meals helps prevent the storage of fat.

4. **Evaluate your snacks.** Do you always eat a high-calorie sweet when doing a particular activity like studying? If you do, try to substitute a healthy snack like fruit.

5. **Limit the number of restaurant meals you eat.** It's much harder to control what you eat when you dine out. First, portion sizes in restaurants are often very large. Second, you may have to look hard to find restaurants whose foods are not full of fat, sodium, and sugar, as you saw in Your Turn 5-1.

6. **Consider your weight.** If you have a healthy weight, changing your eating habits may simply mean adjusting your diet so it has a better balance of foods. If you need to lose or gain weight, you will have to make further changes to increase or decrease the number of calories you take in every day.

In addition to issuing the *Dietary Guidelines* described on page 119, the U.S. Department of Agriculture offers an interactive Web site to help Americans plan and maintain a healthy, balanced diet. The site, www.MyPyramid.gov, enables you to personalize your diet, create menus and exercise plans, and determine your calorie needs. Its centerpiece is the Food Guide Pyramid, a graphic guide to healthy eating that can be modified to suit your needs.

Are You a Healthy Weight?

Only one-third of American adults are at healthy weights. Almost two-thirds are overweight or obese, and fewer than 2 percent are underweight.[3] Being underweight, overweight, or obese is not simply an appearance issue. It's a health issue. Overweight and obese people have a higher risk of developing hypertension, heart disease, stroke, certain types of diabetes, and some cancers. Underweight people have a higher risk of health problems as well. Underweight women have a greater chance of developing osteoporosis, a bone disease, and underweight men and women, on average, do not live as long as people whose weight is healthy.

Measuring Body Mass Index

Is your weight healthy? Your body mass index (BMI) will tell you. BMI is a measure of weight in relation to height. It's the relationship that is important, not the weight alone. For example, someone who is 5 feet 5 inches tall and weighs 200 pounds has a higher BMI than someone who is 6 feet tall and weighs 200 pounds. Your BMI will put you in one of three categories: (1) healthy weight, (2) overweight, or (3) obese.

FIGURE 5-2

This chart shows the BMI ranges for healthy, overweight, and obese people. A healthy BMI ranges from 18.5 to 25.

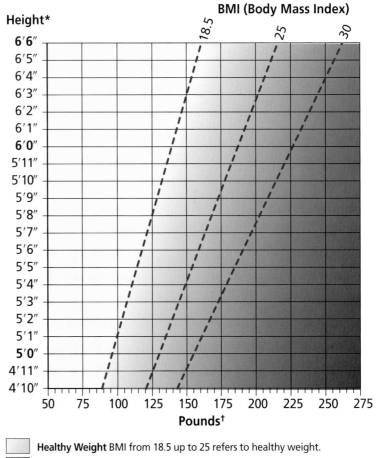

Healthy Weight BMI from 18.5 up to 25 refers to healthy weight.

Overweight BMI from 25 up to 30 refers to overweight.

Obese BMI 30 or higher refers to obesity. Obese persons are also overweight.

*Without shoes
†Without clothes

Your Turn 5-3

WHAT IS YOUR BODY MASS INDEX?

1. In the BMI chart shown in Figure 5–2, find your weight along the horizontal axis. Go straight up from that point to the line that matches your height. What is your BMI? _____

2. Which weight group do you fall into? Are you a healthy weight, overweight, or obese?

_____

Counting Calories

It's easier to control your weight if you understand what a calorie is. A **calorie** is the amount of heat needed to raise the temperature of one kilogram of water one degree Centigrade. Think of a calorie as a unit of energy. If you are active, the calorie is used to produce energy. If you are inactive, the calorie is stored as fat.

The number of calories you need each day just to maintain your present weight varies according to your sex, age, and activity level (see Figure 5–3). If you want to lose weight, you will have to consume

"Glutton: one who digs his grave with his teeth."

French proverb

FIGURE 5–3

Calorie requirements to maintain your current weight.

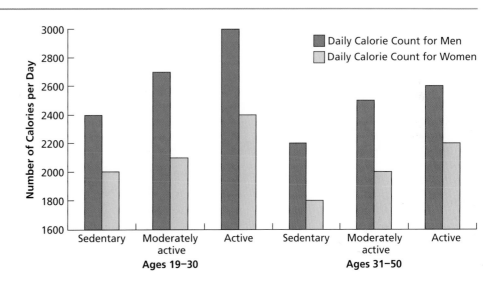

fewer calories and increase your level of activity. If you want to gain weight, you will have to consume more calories.

Of course, women who are pregnant or breast-feeding need more than their normal number of calories and are advised to consult with their doctors before changing their diets.

Losing Weight

Most Americans who are overweight weigh too much because of their lifestyles. Today, we drive instead of walk, work at computers instead of on farms, watch television or surf the Internet instead of exercise, and eat as if we were still very active. Losing weight means changing this lifestyle with two goals in mind: (1) cut the number of calories you eat each day, and (2) increase your activity level to burn more calories. For most people, these changes result in gradual weight loss.

To maintain the weight loss, you must change the way you live— not simply diet for a month or two and then resume your old habits. You must get in the habit of cutting down on foods and beverages rich in calories. You must get used to eating lean meat, fruits, vegetables, and whole grains. And you must exercise regularly. An exercise program is an important part of any serious plan to maintain a healthy weight (see Chapter 6).

For people whose weight problem has a genetic or medical cause, weight loss is more difficult and needs to be medically supervised. And for those who are inclined to try quick weight-loss diet programs, fads, and pills, a word of warning: Diets that rely on eating one food—like grapefruit—or on fewer than 1,000 calories a day are dangerous to your health. That's because one food—or too little food—cannot possibly provide the range of nutrients your body needs to function. Losing weight rapidly is hazardous; it can cause faintness, changes in blood pressure, and heart trouble, as well as malnutrition. In addition, avoid diet pills unless you are using them under a doctor's supervision. These can cause nausea, rapid heartbeat, nervousness, irritability, sleeplessness, and more serious side effects.

Neither diet fads nor diet pills get at the root of most people's weight problem—changing eating and exercising habits over the long term. If

Your Turn 5-4

HOW MANY CALORIES DO YOU NEED EACH DAY?

1. Read the descriptions of physical activity in this chart, and check the level that applies to you.

Key to Level of Physical Activity	
Level	**Description**
Sedentary	Only the light physical activity associated with daily life
Moderately active	Physical activity that includes the equivalent of walking 1.5 to 3 miles daily at 3 to 4 miles per hour
Active	Physical activity that includes the equivalent of walking more than 3 miles daily at 3 to 4 miles per hour

2. Now check your daily calorie count by finding the bar that represents your sex, age, and activity level in the graphs shown in Figure 5–3. How many calories per day should you be eating if you want to maintain your current weight? _____

3. If your BMI is below 18.5, you will probably want to increase your calorie intake. If your BMI is above 25, you will probably want to decrease your calorie intake and/or increase your physical activity.

you need support to change your diet permanently, consider joining a diet club or group such as Weight Watchers.

Gaining Weight

If you are underweight, you must increase your intake of calories to gain weight. You can do this by eating larger portions or by adding some fat-rich foods to your diet. It's not recommended that you cut your level of exercise unless it is extremely high. Remember, as you get older and your level of activity decreases, it's easier to put on weight and keep it on.

Tech Tips

USING THE INTERNET

The Internet has many elements, some of which you may use all the time; others you may never use. Here is a brief overview of some important aspects of the Internet.

1. **E-mail.** E-mail allows you to exchange messages via computer with anyone else who has an e-mail address, anywhere in the world. You can attach files with documents, sounds, pictures, or software to your e-mail messages. If you don't have a personal e-mail address, you can get one through Web sites such as <http://www.hotmail.com> or <http://www.yahoo.com>.

2. **The World Wide Web.** The World Wide Web consists of millions of Web pages— interlinked documents containing text, pictures, sounds, and video. When you click on a link, which usually appears as underlined text or a picture, you are taken to a related Web page. Surfing the Net refers to the process of clicking on links to go from one page to another, following topics that interest you. A collection of related Web pages maintained by an individual or group is called a Web site.

3. **Blogs.** Web logs, or blogs, are online diaries on a wide range of subjects, from the personal to the political. Many blogs are maintained by individuals and reflect their personal interests and points of view. Other blogs are maintained by corporations using them for marketing purposes. Still others are run by organizations with a political agenda.

4. **Online social networks.** The Internet has created a new way of associating with people and keeping in touch with them—the online social network. MySpace and Facebook are the most popular of these. Anyone can join and post information about themselves and maintain links to others. For this reason, these sites have to be used with caution. If you belong to an online social network, don't post anything you wouldn't want your mother to see, and be careful about giving out personal information.

5. **Groups or forums.** There are a huge number of Internet forums, or groups, on almost any subject you can think of, from horror movies to college to entrepreneurs. These forums are global bulletin boards where you can read and post messages. Keep in mind that in most groups no one is keeping an eye on the content or the users. You may find silly, boring, repetitive, or obscene material. On the other hand, you may also find something useful or brilliant.

continues

FINDING INFORMATION ON THE INTERNET

There are two main ways of finding information on the Internet: by its address and by using a search engine.

By Address

If you know the Internet address of what you are looking for, you can use it to locate the information. Different types of Internet addresses look different:

Type	Example	Description
E-mail	Jsmith@abc.net	Janelle Smith's e-mail address
World Wide Web	www.foodnetwork.com [note that www stands for World Wide Web]	The Web site of the Food Network
Group	rec.food.veg	A group devoted to vegetarian diets

By Using a Search Engine

If you do not know the Internet address of what you are looking for, you can use a **search engine,** which is a computerized index such as Google <http://www.google.com>, Yahoo <http://www.yahoo.com>, or Alta Vista <http://www.altavista.com>. Or you can use Metacrawler, which is a search engine that searches the search engines <http://www.metacrawler.com>. Once you have accessed a search engine, you enter a key word or phrase, and the search engine provides a list of Internet locations where they appear. If you are searching for a phrase like *unsaturated fat,* enclose it in quotation marks ("unsaturated fat") so the search engine will look for the whole phrase rather than each word separately. The more specific you can be with key words and phrases, the better the results of your search.

For example, using Google we did a search on "fats" and got more than 18 million "hits," or Web pages, with a reference to fats. To narrow the search, we added the words "unsaturated fats" to "fats." This time we got 302,000 hits. To narrow it even further, we added the words "trans fats" and got 53,800 hits. So, the more, and the more specific, the key words, the fewer the results and the more on target they are.

Evaluating What You Find

Remember that anyone can post anything on the Web. The quality of the material you will find ranges from the full text of authoritative encyclopedias to "get rich quick" schemes to biased opinions and rants. Be very skeptical of what you find. Ask yourself:

- Who is running this Web site?
- What is its purpose?
- Is it a commercial, educational, nonprofit, or government site?
- How credible is the site?

Your Turn 5-5

EXPLORING THE INTERNET

1. Find some information related to the topics in this chapter. Visit these Web sites:

   ■ <www.mypyramid.gov/guidelines/index.html>

   A Web site run by the U.S. Departments of Health and Human Services and the U.S. Department of Agriculture includes links to the Dietary Guidelines for Americans. It also allows you to tailor your own diet based on your sex, age, and level of physical activity using an interactive Food Guide Pyramid.

   ■ <www.americanheart.org>

   The American Heart Association provides lots of information on food and nutrition, including recipes.

   ■ http://nutrition.tufts.edu/
   Tufts University provides links to research and publications on nutrition.

2. If you have e-mail, send a message to one of the authors. We'd love to get your suggestions for improving this text.

   ■ rthroop@ec.rr.com
   ■ marioncastellucci@verizon.net

3. Find an Internet group on a particular food-related topic that interests you, such as cooking or chocolate. You can search in the Groups section of Google or ask this group:

   ■ http://www.faqs.org

4. Use a search engine and try searching for these key words: *nutrition, food groups, dietary guidelines, body mass index, eating disorders, anorexia nervosa, bulimia.*

News & Views

EATING DISORDERS

"You can never be too rich or too thin." So said the Duchess of Windsor, but she was wrong. You *can* be too thin if you suffer from an eating disorder.

In anorexia nervosa, a person loses weight until she is 15 percent or more under her ideal weight. In spite of being thin, she thinks she is fat and continues to eat very little. Some people with anorexia nervosa are so worried about food intake that they won't even lick an envelope flap because the glue may have a fraction of a calorie. Between 5 and 10 percent of individuals with anorexia nervosa die of starvation or complications of severe weight loss.

Another eating disorder is bulimia. A person with bulimia secretly binges, eating huge amounts of high-calorie foods, and then purges, either by vomiting or by using laxatives. People with bulimia may or may not be underweight. Because they binge and purge in private, their condition is easy to hide.

Both anorexia nervosa and bulimia are disorders whose victims are almost all adolescent girls and young women. Some people with the disorders may have a genetic predisposition to the disorders. However, the incidence of these disorders is highest in weight-conscious cultures such as those of the United States and Europe. In these cultures, the ideal of female beauty is the ultra-thin high-fashion model. Images of thin, glamorous women are everywhere. Adolescent girls, especially those with low self-belief, feel enormous pressure to look like the ideal. As a result, many go on diets. Eventually, some lose control of their diets and develop anorexia nervosa or bulimia.

It's important to realize that people who have eating disorders cannot consciously control their eating habits. Instead, they need professional help. Both psychotherapy and drugs are used to treat the disorders.

(© WWD/Conde Nast/Corbis)

Actress Mary-Kate Olsen has suffered from an eating disorder.

What's Up?

Name _____   Date _____

Match the letter of the nutrient with the food that provides the *best* source of the nutrient.

1. Yogurt

2. Orange juice

3. Chicken

4. Whole wheat bread

5. Vegetable oil

a. Water

b. Fat

c. Complex carbohydrates

d. Protein

e. Calcium and Vitamin D

Answer the following questions in the space provided.

6. Name the basic food groups and give an example of a food from each.

_____

_____

_____

7. What types of foods do nutritionists think Americans should eat more of?

_____

_____

_____

8. What types of foods do nutritionists think Americans should eat less of?

_____

_____

_____

9. What does BMI stand for? What does it measure?

_____

_____

_____

10. What two lifestyle changes would enable most Americans to lose weight?

_____

_____

_____

Case Studies

The Case of the Man Who Dined Out

Since his work demands that he travel, Matt dines out regularly. When given a choice between a bagel and scrambled eggs for breakfast, Matt chooses the eggs. At lunchtime, he orders a cheeseburger instead of a salad. In the evening, he often chooses a steak and french fries instead of pasta with tomato sauce. Since he does not snack between meals, Matt can't understand why he is putting on weight.

1. What is wrong with Matt's diet?

_____

_____

_____

_____

2. What can Matt do to lose the weight he has gained?

_____

_____

_____

_____

The Case of the Dinnerless Diet

Luisa wanted to lose about 10 pounds, and she decided the best way to do it was to skip dinner every day. For breakfast she had a doughnut or muffin, and for lunch she ate a salad with dressing. At dinnertime she fed her family but did not eat. By 8 or 9 P.M., however, Luisa was so hungry that she had a snack of microwave popcorn or chips. Luisa maintained her level of physical activity—she went dancing one evening a week. After a month, she found she had lost only one pound. Even worse, she didn't feel very well.

1. What is wrong with Luisa's diet and eating patterns?

_____

_____

_____

_____

2. How can Luisa lose 10 pounds and still feel well?

_____

_____

_____

_____

Journal

Answer the following journal questions.

1. What does food mean to you and your family? What foods reflect your family's heritage?

_____
_____
_____
_____
_____
_____
_____

2. Describe a food or beverage you love that's not very healthy. How can you enjoy this food and still have a healthy diet?

_____
_____
_____
_____
_____
_____
_____

3. In this society, the ideal beautiful woman is slim and tall. Is this ideal healthy? How do you think this ideal affects you?

_____
_____
_____
_____
_____
_____
_____

4. What changes do you plan to make to your diet after reading this chapter?

_____
_____
_____
_____
_____
_____
_____

Staying Healthy

When she was born, Shawn Johnson flunked the Apgar, a test of newborns' vitality, with a score of 0. She quickly rebounded, however, and channeled her energy into gymnastics. At age 15, Johnson was the All-Around World Champion gymnast, and in 2008 she won a gold medal and three silver medals at the Beijing Olympics.

Take a look in a mirror. Do you see a person with bright clear eyes and skin, fit and attractive, with lots of energy? If you do, you are probably already working hard at reaching your physical potential. But if that person in the mirror looks less than glowing, don't worry! There are many things you can do to improve your health and feel better mentally as well as physically.

If you have ever felt sick, you know the value of good health. When you are not feeling healthy, all aspects of your life suffer. You become unable to live up to your emotional, intellectual, and social potential. All of you suffers—not just your body.

What does it take to feel healthy and energetic? You have already learned about the importance of eating a balanced diet in maintaining good health and preventing disease (see Chapter 5). In this chapter, the focus shifts to other aspects of health, and you will:

- learn about the health benefits of different types of exercise and make an exercise plan to improve your fitness;
- learn about the importance of adequate and regular sleep;
- discover the negative physical, emotional, and intellectual consequences of abusing drugs; and
- learn about preventing and treating sexually transmitted diseases.

Finally, you will explore health issues that interest you by reading and responding to blogs on the Internet.

Exercise

"*When you enjoy what you do, you never get tired.*"

DONALD TRUMP,
real estate developer

Modern life, with cars, office work, computers, and TV, tends to make "couch potatoes" of us all. For most of us, physical activity is not a natural part of the daily routine. To be active, we must make a conscious decision to exercise or play sports.

Why take the time to exercise? First, exercise increases the number of calories we burn and helps us keep our weight under control. People who exercise regularly look better because they have more muscle than fat. They are stronger, more energetic, and more flexible. And perhaps most important, people who are fit feel better about themselves, both physically and mentally.

Becoming Fit

What is physical fitness? The President's Council on Physical Fitness and Sports suggests that physical fitness is the ability to carry out daily tasks without tiring and with enough energy left to enjoy leisure activities and to handle an emergency requiring physical exertion. Your own level of fitness is determined to a great extent by your daily routine—your work or schooling, your chores, your sports activities, and how much you walk in the course of the day. To improve your normal level of fitness or to lose weight, you must add physical activities, exercise, or sports to your daily life (see Figure 6–1).

There are several aspects to physical fitness. For example, a woman who jogs regularly may have a heart and lungs in great condition, but she's not strong enough to carry a heavy suitcase more than five feet. That's because she lacks muscular strength and endurance in her upper body. A person who is truly physically fit has good:

- **cardiorespiratory endurance**—the ability to do moderately strenuous activity over a period of time without overtaxing the heart and lungs

- **muscular strength**—the ability to exert force in a single try

---

FIGURE 6–1

How much energy are you using? This graph shows the average number of calories burned during an hour of various activities. Note that the data are averages for a 154-pound person. People who weigh less will burn fewer calories, and people who weigh more will burn more calories.
Source: Data from U.S. Department of Health and Human Services and U.S. Department of Agriculture, *Dietary Guidelines for Americans, 2005,* Table 4, Calories/Hour Expended in Common Physical Activities, p. 16.

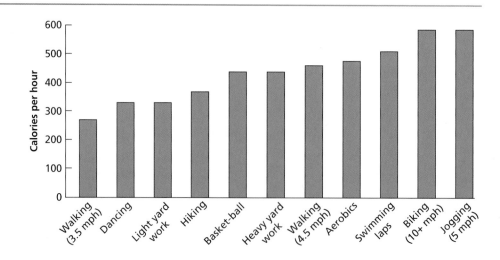

- **muscular endurance**—the ability to repeat movements or to hold a position for a long time without tiring
- **flexibility**—the ability to move a joint through its full range of motion
- **body composition**—the proportion of the body made of muscle compared with fat

Different types of physical activities improve different aspects of fitness. In general, activities involving continuous movement, such as running, basketball, aerobic routines, and tennis, are best for cardiorespiratory endurance and body composition (burning calories and losing fat). Activities such as calisthenics, weight training, karate, yoga, and stretching improve strength, endurance, and/or flexibility.

Aerobic Exercises Exercises that improve cardiorespiratory endurance are called aerobic exercise. They work by gradually increasing the ability of the heart and lungs to supply the body's increased need for oxygen during the activity. When you first start doing aerobic exercise, you may find yourself out of breath and unable to continue. However, if you keep exercising, gradually your body will adapt and your heart will become stronger, increasing your body's oxygen supply without greater effort. Aerobic exercises, because they use large parts of the body, have the added advantage of turning fat to muscle, which improves body composition.

Any type of exercise that involves continuous movement is aerobic.

© 2011 Wadsworth, Cengage Learning
(© Eliza Snow/istockphoto.com)

Aerobic exercise strengthens the heart and lungs. An aerobics class is a good place to work out, but walking, running, swimming, and biking are also good aerobic exercises.

- **Aerobic exercise routines** consist of 20 or more minutes of running, skipping, hopping, stepping, boxing, jumping, sliding, stretching, and bending, usually set to music. Low-impact aerobics are designed for people who need to minimize jarring their joints. Aerobic routines can be done in exercise classes or at home using exercise videos.
- **Fitness walking**—walking at a brisk pace—is an excellent aerobic activity. It has the advantage of requiring no special equipment or skill, and it can be done almost anywhere.
- **Jogging** is a very popular aerobic exercise requiring just a pair of good jogging sneakers. Joggers sometimes develop leg problems because jogging is a high-impact activity.
- **Swimming** is often considered the best aerobic activity because it exercises all the major muscle groups in an environment— water—that cushions impact.
- **Bicycling** has aerobic benefits when done at a brisk pace for long distances. In addition, it provides good exercise for the lower body.

Your Turn 6-1

RATE YOUR LEVEL OF ACTIVITY

You can check your level of physical activity by rating how hard, how long, and how often you exercise. Circle your score for each question.

1. How hard do you exercise in a typical session?   **Score**

no change in pulse	0
little change in heart rate (slow walking, bowling, yoga)	1
small increase in heart rate and breathing (table tennis, active golf)	2
moderate increase in heart rate and breathing (rapid walking, dancing, easy swimming)	3
occasional heavy breathing and sweating (tennis, basketball, squash)	4
sustained heavy breathing and sweating (jogging, aerobics)	5

2. How long do you exercise at one session?   **Score**

less than 5 minutes	0
5 to 14 minutes	1
15 to 29 minutes	2
30 to 44 minutes	3
45 to 59 minutes	4
60 minutes or more	5

3. How often do you exercise?   **Score**

less than once a week	0
once a week	1
2 times a week	2
3 times a week	3
4 times a week	4
5 or more times a week	5

4. Now take your scores from each question above and multiply them: _____ × _____ × _____ × = _____ Activity level Rate your activity level as follows:

Score	Activity Level
less than 15	inactive
15–24	somewhat active
25–40	moderately active
41–60	active
over 60	very active

If your score is 41 or higher, you are active enough to enjoy a wide variety of physical activities. If your score is less than 41, you should approach a change in your physical fitness program gradually and with caution. Anyone who is starting a new or increased fitness program should check with his or her doctor first.

- **Cross-country skiing** provides excellent aerobic benefits. It is ideal for those who live in areas with lots of snow for several months a year.
- **Rowing a boat, paddling a canoe, or kayaking** at a steady, brisk speed provides good aerobic benefits.
- **Jumping rope** for extended periods is an excellent aerobic activity, although it can be hard on the joints.

Strength, Endurance, and Flexibility Exercises   Although aerobic exercise improves cardiorespiratory endurance and body composition, it is not enough to promote all-around fitness. To improve muscle strength, endurance, and flexibility, you need to do other forms of exercise as well. Weight training and calisthenics are good for increasing muscle strength, endurance, and flexibility, and yoga and stretching are good for flexibility.

Weight training is an exercise program in which you use weights or resistance machines to improve strength, endurance, and flexibility. As your body becomes stronger, you gradually increase the number of pounds you are using and the number of repetitions. Weight training improves muscle tone, bone density, and appearance. Older women, who are at risk for osteoporosis, a weakening of the bones, can benefit from the increased bone strength that results from weight lifting. And contrary to popular belief, women can do weight training without developing "bulging" muscles. (The muscles of male weight trainers and weight lifters are the result primarily of a male hormone.) Weight training can be done with barbells, dumbbells, or even household objects such as canned foods. Many fitness centers have exercise machines that can be used for weight training.

Calisthenics—exercises such as pushups and situps—are especially good for increasing muscular endurance. Because the exercises are repeated many times, the muscles become more able to hold a position for a length of time or to repeat the same motion many times. Calisthenics can be done at home or in an exercise class.

For those seeking to promote flexibility, yoga is ideal. The movements of yoga are slow and emphasize joint flexibility and stretching, as well as mental relaxation. Yoga can be done at home once the movements are learned or in an exercise class under an instructor's guidance.

Sports and Recreational Activities   For those who can't bring themselves to exercise regularly—and for others as well—many sports and recreational activities provide fitness benefits. And sports and recreational activities have additional advantages. We play them because they are fun. Many activities involve interacting with people who share our interest. So the social advantages of sports and activities can be as great as the fitness advantages.

© 2011 Wadsworth, Cengage Learning

(© Steve Bonini/Getty Images)

Weight training improves the strength of muscles. It also strengthens bones, an important benefit for women, who lose bone mass as they age.

News & Views

WHERE ARE U.S. RESIDENTS PHYSICALLY ACTIVE?

We all know we should be physically active, but how many of us really are? The U.S. Centers for Disease Control and state health departments wanted to know the answer to this question, so they conducted a telephone survey to find out. People were asked about their leisure activities (such as sports and exercise), their household chores (like gardening and vacuuming), and their transportation (for example, did they drive, bike, or walk places). Those who reported moderate activity at least five days a week for 30 minutes a day, or intense activity at least three days a week for 20 minutes a day, were considered physically active. The results showed that the states vary considerably in the percentage of people who are physically active, as shown in this map.

If you are interested in finding out more about physical activity statistics where you live, go to <http://apps.nccd.cdc.gov/PASurveillance/StateSumV.asp> and click on your state in the drop-down menu.

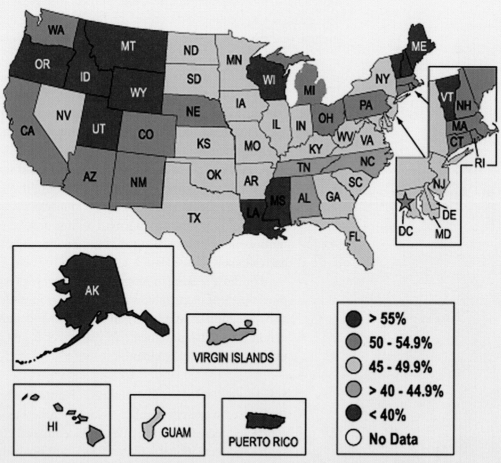

Legend:
- > 55%
- 50 – 54.9%
- 45 – 49.9%
- > 40 – 44.9%
- < 40%
- No Data

Source: U.S. Centers for Disease Control, Physical Activity Statistics, http://apps.nccd.cdc.gov/PASurveillance/StateSumV.asp, accessed April 9, 2008.

When you select a sport or activity, keep two things in mind. First, choose activities you will enjoy and to which you have easy access. And second, choose activities that will give you a range of fitness benefits. For example, bowling and golf may be fun, but they won't improve your physical fitness. On the other hand, continuous-action sports like basketball and handball provide excellent aerobic benefits.

Sticking to an Exercise Program

Many people start an exercise program with the best intentions, and within several months they quit. To avoid this fate and to make physical activity part of your routine, follow these guidelines:

1. Choose a friend or relative, and make an agreement with them to exercise. Be sure to write it down.

2. Be specific. Write down the days you will exercise, what you will do, and the number of months you will do it.

3. Include rewards and punishments. Specify what you'll do to earn a reward and what will result in punishment—doing an unpleasant chore, for example.

4. Get the person with whom you made the agreement to support you. This will make it harder to skip sessions or quit.

For people who think exercise is boring or too much work, playing recreational sports is a way to stay fit.

"He who has health, has hope; and he who has hope, has everything."

Arabian proverb

Rest

Eating well and exercising are two components of maintaining good health. A third essential component is adequate rest. More than 100 years ago, Thomas Edison invented the lightbulb and radically changed people's sleeping habits. Whereas people used to sleep at night because doing anything else was impractical, now it's possible to ignore the body's natural rhythms and stay awake. The result? We sometimes get less rest than we need.

Your Turn 6-2

MAKE AN EXERCISE AGREEMENT

Use the four exercise program guidelines to draw up an exercise agreement with a friend or relative.

Sleeping at different times of the day can make people tired and irritable. Shift workers with irregular schedules often have sleep problems.

Scientists have found that our bodies operate according to **circadian rhythms,** an inner time clock that roughly matches the 24-hour cycle of night and day. Left to their own devices, most people go to sleep when their body temperature is falling and sleep seven to eight hours. If you go to bed when your body temperature is at its peak, you tend to sleep much longer—as much as 15 hours. So the time of day you go to sleep, not how long you've been awake, generally determines how long you sleep.

As a consequence, people with irregular schedules often suffer from sleep problems. Airline pilots, for example, who work long shifts and cross time zones, often suffer fatigue. People whose sleep is irregular tend to be fatigued, inefficient, and irritable.

To feel good and perform at your peak, regular sleep habits are essential. If you are a poor sleeper, consider these suggestions to improve your sleep habits:

- Follow a regular schedule for sleeping and waking up, even on weekends.
- Exercise regularly.
- Don't eat or drink anything with caffeine after midday. Caffeine, a stimulant found in coffee, tea, chocolate, cola, and energy drinks, can keep you awake.
- Before bedtime, do whatever relaxes you. Read, watch TV, listen to music, or take a hot bath.
- Avoid alcoholic beverages before bed. They may help you fall asleep, but they interfere with your staying asleep.
- Don't worry about not sleeping. If you can't sleep, get up and do something boring until you feel sleepy.

> " [Sleep is] the golden chain that ties health and our bodies together. "
>
> THOMAS DEKKER (1572–1632),
> English writer

> " The basic thing nobody asks is, why do people take drugs of any sort? "
>
> JOHN LENNON (1940–1980),
> one of the Beatles

Drug Abuse

In this unit, we've discussed things that help maintain your health: good food, exercise, and rest, all of which contribute to your physical and mental well-being. Unfortunately, many Americans misuse **drugs,** which are chemical substances that create a physical, mental, emotional, or behavioral change in the user. Some drugs, of course, are used properly as prescription medicines under the care of a doctor. But others, such as alcohol, nicotine, cocaine, and methamphetamine, are misused. **Drug abuse** is the nonmedicinal use of a drug, which results in physical, emotional, or mental harm to the user.

Why do people take drugs? People try drugs for the pleasure they bring, to feel better, to escape from problems, to experience

Your Turn 6-3

WHAT KIND OF SLEEPER ARE YOU?

People have different sleep patterns. Answer the following questions to establish your sleep profile.

1. How long do you normally sleep each night?_____

   If you regularly sleep less than six hours a night, you are a short sleeper. If you regularly sleep more than nine hours a night, you're a long sleeper. People who sleep between six and nine hours a night are average sleepers.

2. Some people need different amounts of sleep for weeks at a time during different periods of their lives. Moving, ending a relationship, other stressful events, illness, or pregnancy may cause them to sleep more. Do you need more sleep at different periods in your life?_____

   If you answered yes, you are variable sleeper.

3. Do you sleep through disturbances such as loud music, thunderstorms, babies crying, car alarms, and slammed doors?_____

   If you said yes, you are a sound sleeper. If you said no, you are a light sleeper.

something new, or to be sociable. The reasons people try a drug are usually very different from the reasons they continue to use it. Most drug abusers suffer from poor self-belief and lack of confidence. They use drugs to bolster their feelings about themselves. Unfortunately, drug abusers become dependent on the drugs they take. The dependence may be physical: The body needs the drug to function. Or it may be psychological: The user believes he or she needs the drug to function or even to survive. Often the dependence is both physical and psychological, and breaking the habit is extremely difficult.

Unfortunately, the harm done by drug abusers is not limited to themselves. Because they are unable to function well in daily life, drug abusers often damage their relationships with family, friends, coworkers, and employers. Drug abuse does social and economic harm, as well as physical and psychological harm.

You may think of drug abusers as those who use illegal drugs. But many drug abusers misuse legal substances such as alcohol, nicotine (in cigarettes), and prescription drugs.

Alcohol

One of the most abused drugs in the United States is alcohol. About 9.6 percent of American adults are heavy drinkers.[1] (For men, "heavy drinking" means more than two drinks per day; for women, more than one drink per day.) More than 30 percent of heavy drinkers admit to binge drinking— having five or more drinks in a row, four or more for women—at least once in the previous year. Among college students, binge drinking is even more widespread—44 percent of college students overall.[2]

Alcohol is a depressant, a drug that decreases brain activity and lowers blood pressure. The effects of alcohol vary. Some people become outgoing, silly, or aggressive. Others become quiet. But large amounts of alcohol dull sensation and harm judgment, memory, and coordination, eventually causing unconsciousness. When alcohol is taken in large quantities or mixed with other drugs, it can be deadly.

Alcohol is a leading cause of traffic accidents and deaths. A police officer is giving a driver a Breathalyzer test to see whether he has more than the legal limit of alcohol in his blood.

Moderate social drinking, like having a glass of wine or beer with a meal, is not a problem for most people. But alcohol consumption becomes a problem when it interferes with a person's functioning in school, on the job, or in relationships.

For students, heavy alcohol use, especially binge drinking, is linked to poor academic performance and lower grades. In addition, heavy alcohol use is associated with other problems: death and injury from drunk driving, sexual assaults, unplanned and unsafe sex, and vandalism. About 1,700 college students die each year from alcohol-related causes, including alcohol poisoning and car crashes.[3]

Considering all these dangers, why do people drink? In part, the answer is that the use of alcohol is deeply ingrained in our society. Alcohol has been part of many cultures and religions for years. It is served at social occasions, and many people can enjoy it in moderation. On college campuses, drinking alcohol is a large part of the social scene. Since alcohol is everywhere, each of us needs to monitor our own consumption. Some people should not drink at all, and everyone should be moderate.

Alcohol abusers who have tried to stop drinking have found the most success with support groups like Alcoholics Anonymous. AA, as it is known, gets drinkers to focus on their problems, abstain totally from alcohol, and draw on the support of other recovering alcoholics, using a 12-step program.

Nicotine

Cigarettes, cigars, and other forms of tobacco contain nicotine, a stimulant. A stimulant is a drug that increases brain activity and other body functions. Stimulants (like nicotine and caffeine) make the user feel more awake. Nicotine stimulates the heart and nervous system,

Your Turn 6-4

DO YOU HAVE A PROBLEM WITH ALCOHOL?

You can take this self-test[4] to see if you have a problem with alcohol.

1. Have you missed classes because of a hangover? _____

2. Have you gotten into fights or other trouble because of your drinking? _____

3. Do you routinely binge drink? _____

4. Have you ever been unable to account for a period of time after you had been drinking? _____

5. Have you had sexual experiences after drinking that you later felt bad about? _____

6. Have you decided to cut down on your drinking and found out that you could not? _____

7. Have you been angered by the criticism of others about your drinking? _____

   If you answered *yes* to any one of these questions, you should evaluate how much you are drinking, how often, and the effect that drinking is having on you. One *yes* also indicates that you should probably reduce the quantity of alcohol you consume. Two or more *yes* answers indicate you should reduce or stop your alcohol consumption; if you can't do this on your own, you may need counseling or other help to do so.

raising blood pressure and making the heart beat faster. People who smoke become addicted to nicotine. Studies have shown that, on average, teenage girls become addicted in about three weeks; teenage boys in less than six months. Adults who have not previously smoked become addicted in about two years.[5] When smokers try to give up smoking, they experience irritability, headaches, anxiety, depression, and nicotine cravings.

People who smoke for years may experience even worse effects. The life expectancy of smokers is shorter than that of nonsmokers. On average, adults who smoke live 14 fewer years than those who don't smoke. Smoking is the major cause of death from cancer of the lungs, throat, and mouth. It contributes to heart disease and respiratory problems. And breathing the smoke of others can affect the health of nonsmokers. According to the Centers for Disease Control and Prevention, each year about 438,000 Americans die prematurely as a result of smoking.[6]

The health risks associated with smoking have caused a gradual change in the public's attitude toward smoking. Smoking was once

THE MORE YOU SMOKE THE MORE
COOL GEAR
YOU'LL EARN.

ALL EXPENSE PAID TRIP TO
CANCER CLINIC OF YOUR CHOICE
2000 POINTS

DELUXE
CARRYING CASE
10,000 POINTS

SPORT DEFIBRILLATOR
5000 POINTS

PORTABLE
RESPIRATOR
1000 POINTS

truth

Ads linking smoking to respiratory diseases and death have helped reduce the percentage of Americans who smoke.

"If we burn ourselves out with drugs or alcohol, we won't have long to go in this business."

JOHN BELUSHI (1949–1982), comedian and actor who died of a drug overdose

widely accepted socially and considered to be a mark of adulthood. In fact, about 42 percent of Americans smoked in 1965. Today, smoking is banned in many government buildings, business offices, schools, and airplanes. Restaurants often ban smoking altogether or have smoking sections to accommodate smokers. As a result, smoking is on the decline, except among teenagers, although about 21.8 percent of adult Americans still smoke.[7]

Most people who quit smoking do it on their own. Others try counseling, behavior modification programs like Smoke Enders, nicotine patches, or hypnosis. The success rate of such programs is low. Health professionals emphasize that not starting to smoke is far easier than stopping.

Other Drugs

Misusing any drug, including prescription and over-the-counter drugs, can cause problems. For example, a side effect of taking anti-histamines for allergies is sleepiness. Thus driving a car or operating machinery while taking antihistamines is dangerous. Prescription medicines and over-the-counter preparations should be taken as directed.

When you take illegal drugs, your exposure to risk increases. First, you don't know what you're actually buying when you buy drugs on the street. Second, you are subject to arrest for possession of illegal substances. And third, the long-term effects of some drugs are still unknown. Some of the more common abused drugs are briefly discussed following.

Marijuana   Marijuana is the most widely used illegal drug. Street terms for marijuana include "grass," "pot," "weed," "ganja," and "herb." In some states, it is legal for doctors to prescribe marijuana to relieve symptoms such as the nausea of chemotherapy; however, the medicinal use of marijuana is highly controversial.

Marijuana creates mild feelings of pleasure, slows thinking and reaction time, distorts perceptions, and upsets balance and coordination. Like alcohol, it harms the coordination and reaction time needed to drive a car or operate machinery. Long-term use of marijuana has many negative effects. Because it is usually smoked, it harms the lungs and causes respiratory problems. Marijuana interferes with the process of forming memories, an effect that continues beyond the period of smoking; therefore, using marijuana interferes with a person's ability to learn.

Cocaine   Cocaine, a stimulant, acts on the brain to produce a brief rush of happiness and excitement. As the dose wears off, feelings of panic, depression, and anxiety set in. Cocaine can be sniffed, injected, or smoked,

WHATEVER IT TAKES
Tom Coderre

By the time he was 30, Tom Coderre seemed to have everything. He had a supportive family and many friends. He had a good job heading a nonprofit agency. He had a love of politics and an elected seat in the Rhode Island State Senate. As he has said, "On the outside, everything about this man's life looked perfect."

However, all was not as it seemed, as his friends and family were well aware and his colleagues were soon to find out. For years, Coderre had been drinking heavily to cope with stress. His friends thought he had a problem with alcohol, but Coderre thought he could handle it. Then a friend gave him some crack cocaine, and he began to smoke it regularly. Still, he thought he could smoke crack and continue his normal life, just as he had done with alcohol. Instead, his craving for crack intensified until everything else became secondary.

Within three years, Coderre's life fell apart. He pushed his family and friends away when they tried to help him overcome his addiction. He lost his job, his seat in the senate, and his apartment. He lost his love of life and became hopeless.

Eventually, Coderre tried overcoming his addiction at several treatment centers, but he failed at all of them. He tried shaking his addiction at his parents' house with outpatient therapy, but that didn't work, either. Finally, he was arrested for possession of cocaine and ordered into yet another treatment center. When he skipped out on that and was rearrested, the judge put him in jail until a bed opened up at a treatment center that he would not be able to leave. "If I hadn't been arrested for possession of a controlled substance in my home city, I don't know if I'd be here today," says Coderre.

Coderre spent more than five months at the treatment center, and then moved into a long-term recovery house with other former drug abusers. He lived there for two years, went back to college to finish his degree, started working again, all the while attending support meetings with other recovering people. Coderre attributes his recovery to the help he received from friends, family, and social service organizations like Faces and Voices of Recovery. "When people get the help they need, they recover," Coderre explains. Today, as the national field director for Faces and Voices of Recovery, Coderre's job is to help build recovery resources around the country to give others the opportunity to overcome addiction, as he did.

Sources: Testimony of Tom Coderre before the California Select Committee on Alcohol and Drug Abuse, Jan. 10, 2008, <http://democrats.assembly. ca.gov/members/a24/pdf/AgendaItem3b.pdf>, accessed April 8, 2008; Jennifer Levitz, "Out of Darkness," *Providence Journal*, Dec. 11, 2005, <http:// www.projo.com/news/content/projo_20051211_ coderre.32c16b4.html>, accessed April 6, 2008; "About Tom Coderre," Faces & Voices of Recovery Web site, <http://www.facesandvoicesofrecovery. org/about/trainings_events/coderre/php>, accessed April 9, 2008.

and is also called "coke," "blow," and "nose candy." Crack, sometimes called "tornado," is a powerful form of cocaine. Because crack is smoked, it enters the bloodstream quickly and in higher concentrations. It is difficult to estimate a dose of crack, so users sometimes overdose, suffering convulsions, cardiac arrest, coma, and death.

Users of cocaine become extremely dependent on it. Some experts call it the most addictive drug of all. The long-term use of cocaine often leads to emotional disturbances, paranoia, fear, nervousness, insomnia, and weight loss. Many people become unable to function normally at work or with their families. Their lives are focused on getting and using the drug.

Methamphetamine Methamphetamine, known popularly as "crystal meth," "meth," "ice," and "Tina," is a highly addictive stimulant. It can be smoked, snorted, injected, or taken orally. In the short term, meth users feel a brief intense rush, increased energy, and decreased appetite. In the long term, people addicted to meth can develop many problems, including anxiety, insomnia, and mood disturbances. Some develop psychotic symptoms such as paranoia (a feeling that others are out to get you), hallucinations (seeing and hearing things that aren't there), and delusions (sensations such as insects crawling under the skin).

Barbiturates and Benzodiazepines Barbiturates (barbs, reds, and yellows) and benzodiazepines (tranquilizers, tranks, downers, sleeping pills, Valium) are depressants. They slow the activity of the nervous and cardiovascular systems, making people calm down and feel relaxed and sleepy. When barbiturates and tranquilizers are taken with alcohol, they can cause death.

Different types of barbiturates and benzodiazepines create different levels of physical and psychological dependence. Users who stop taking them experience tremors, nausea, cramps, and vomiting.

Club Drugs The phrase club drugs refers to a variety of drugs used by young adults at parties, clubs, raves, and bars. The most common club drugs are MDMA (ecstasy, X); GHB (G, grievous bodily harm); Rohypnol (roofies); and ketamine (K, special K). These drugs have a variety of effects, which are summarized in Table 6–1. The club drugs are even more harmful when taken in combination with alcohol.

Some club drugs are colorless, odorless, and tasteless. They can easily be slipped into a drink in order to intoxicate or sedate other people. In recent years there have been reports of club drugs being used to commit date rapes and other sexual assaults. Women should get their own drinks at parties and keep an eye on them so they can't be tampered with.

Steroids Anabolic steroid is a synthetic form of the male hormone, testosterone. Because the drug increases the body's ability to turn protein into muscle, steroids are popular among athletes and others who wish to improve their athletic performance and appearance.

TABLE 6–1   The Most Common Club Drugs

Drug	Form	Short-Term Effects	Potential Health Effects
MDMA *Ecstasy, XTC, E, X, go, hug drug, disco biscuit*	Tablet or capsule	■ Stimulant: increased heart rate, blood pressure; feelings of alertness and energy; mild hallucinogenic effects ■ In high doses, can lead to high body temperature, dehydration, and death	Depression, sleep problems, anxiety, impaired memory and learning
GHB G, *grievous bodily harm, goop, max, soap, juice, liquid ecstasy, fantasy*	■ Clear liquid, white powder, tablet, or capsule ■ Often made in home laboratories	■ Depressant: reduced heart rate, blood pressure; reduced pain and anxiety; feeling of relaxation and well-being; reduced inhibitions ■ In high doses, can lead to drowsiness, loss of consciousness, coma, and death ■ Used as a date rape drug	Unknown
Ketamine *K, special K, kettle mine, cat Valium, jet, super acid*	■ Liquid for injection, powder for snorting or smoking ■ Used legally as an anesthetic, usually for animals	■ Depressant: hallucinations; poor judgment; poor coordination ■ In high doses, can cause delirium, amnesia, depression, respiratory problems, heart rate abnormalities, and death	Memory loss; numbness; nausea and vomiting
Rohypnol *Roofies, roaches, forget-me drug, Mexican valium*	■ Pill or powder ■ Used legally in Europe as a sleeping pill	■ Depressant: reduced heart rate, blood pressure; reduced pain and anxiety; feeling of relaxation and well-being; reduced inhibitions ■ Visual and digestive disturbances; urine retention ■ Used as a date rape drug	Loss of memory for period while under the effects of the drug

Experts say that steroid users face side effects and risks that are not fully understood. Women risk changes in their sexual characteristics, including shrinking of the breasts, growth of body hair, baldness, and a deepened voice. Some men suffer high blood pressure, lowered sperm counts, and acute acne. In addition, steroids seem to be as addictive as alcohol or nicotine.

Heroin   **Heroin** is a depressant that makes its user feel happy, safe, and peaceful. It is physically addictive, and users need greater amounts of it as they become tolerant of its effects. An overdose of heroin is deadly. In addition, since addicts inject the drug, they are at risk of contracting diseases such as hepatitis and HIV from shared needles.

When users stop taking heroin, they experience agonizing symptoms including nausea, shaking, chills, vomiting, and pain. Stopping the psychological dependence on heroin is even more difficult, because addicts have poor self-belief and rely on the drug to escape from reality.

Treating Drug Abuse

Although weaning drug abusers from their physical dependence on drugs can be difficult, it is easier than overcoming their psychological dependence. Typical drug abusers have negative self-belief, low self-confidence, and a feeling of helplessness. Drugs are a way to escape this bleak outlook on life. *Unless the underlying attitudes of the abuser change, he or she is likely to return to the use of the drug.* Recovering from drug addiction is a long-term process with three stages (see Figure 6–2):

Stage 1: Wanting to stop. Motivation is the key during stage 1. People wanting to stop drug use must learn to trust, love, and respect themselves.

Stage 2: Stopping. During this stage it is critical for users to distance themselves from the drug. That may mean distancing themselves from the people and circumstances associated with drug use.

Stage 3: Staying stopped. During the recovery period, a support group is essential. Support groups meet all over the country to help recovered drug users stay off drugs.

If you or someone you know needs treatment for drug or alcohol abuse, you can call the Center for Substance Abuse Treatment (CSAT), a division of the U.S. Department of Health and Human Services. Their hotline number is 1-800-662-HELP, and they offer assistance in English and Spanish. The CSAT hotline will refer you to drug treatment programs and counselors in your area. You can also find local treatment programs on their Web site, <http://csat.samhsa.gov>.

FIGURE 6–2

Recovering from drug abuse is a three-stage process: (1) wanting to stop, (2) stopping, and (3) staying stopped. The third stage is often the most difficult.

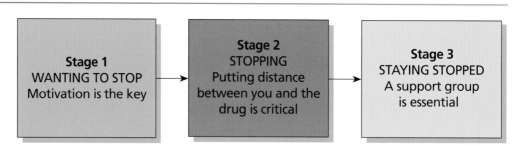

Stage 1
WANTING TO STOP
Motivation is the key

Stage 2
STOPPING
Putting distance between you and the drug is critical

Stage 3
STAYING STOPPED
A support group is essential

Sexually Transmitted Diseases

Protecting yourself against sexually transmitted diseases (STDs) is a commonsense way to maintain your good health. These diseases are widespread; they are not limited to specific groups in the population. By one estimate, there are 19 million new infections each year, almost half of them among young adults.[8] The most common STDs are gonorrhea, chlamydia, and genital herpes.

Gonorrhea is an infection of the genital mucous membranes. In men, symptoms are painful urination with a discharge of pus. In women, the symptoms are often mild or undetectable. Untreated gonorrhea can lead to sterility in both sexes. Fortunately, gonorrhea can be cured with antibiotics.

Chlamydia is an infection of the genital and urinary tracts. It is the most common of the STDs, and its symptoms are similar to those of gonorrhea, although milder. Three-quarters of infected women and half of infected men have no symptoms. Chlamydia can be treated with antibiotics. If it is left untreated, it can cause severe pelvic inflammatory disease in women and sterility in both women and men.

Genital herpes is caused by a virus similar to the one that causes cold sores and fever blisters. The first symptoms are a tingling in the genital area and small, sometimes itchy, blisters. Genital herpes flares up and dies down periodically, and stress seems to aggravate the condition. Although it cannot be cured, there are drugs that can control the symptoms and reduce the number of relapses.

Syphilis is a highly infectious STD caused by a bacterium. The first symptom is a small hard sore in the genital area, mouth, or anus. By the time this symptom has appeared, the syphilis infection has already spread to the blood. If left untreated, early-stage syphilis causes fever, sore throat, headache, and sores. The disease then seems to disappear, sometimes for years. In the final stage, blindness, paralysis, insanity, and death can result. Syphilis can be treated with antibiotics, but any damage that has already occurred cannot be reversed.

HIV-AIDS (acquired immune deficiency syndrome) is a group of diseases or conditions resulting from the gradual destruction of a person's immune system. A person infected with the human immuno-deficiency virus (HIV) gradually loses immune system cells and so becomes unable to fight off infection and disease. The time between infection with HIV and the onset of AIDS can vary considerably, from one or two years to over two decades, with the average being seven years. Drugs now enable people with HIV to keep their immune cell counts high for years. Although AIDS is usually transmitted sexually, it can also be transmitted through contact with blood (by sharing needles among drug abusers or by accident) or passed from an infected mother to her baby.

If you think you have a sexually transmitted disease, see a doctor or go to a clinic immediately. Pregnant women with a history of sexually transmitted disease should inform their doctor, since some diseases are passed from mother to child. The best strategy for dealing with sexually transmitted disease is prevention. The spread of these diseases can be prevented through celibacy or by practicing "safe sex" using latex condoms. Note that condoms do not provide complete protection from all STDs.

"Don't blog what you don't own."

LISA WILLIAMS,
author of *Bloggers in Love*

Tech Tips

EXPLORING BLOGS

A **blog** is a Web site on which people post items of information or opinion—the online equivalent of a journal. On a blog, which is short for "Web log," items are usually displayed in reverse chronological order, the most recent posting first. The items posted to a blog can be text, images, videos, links to other Web pages, or any combination of material. On most blogs, readers can respond by leaving postings of their own.

There are several broad categories of blogs.

- **Personal blogs** are about the blogger's private life or interests. They are essentially online diaries or commentaries that anyone can read. Very few personal blogs are widely read or become widely known.

- **Topic blogs** focus on a subject or issue, such as politics, sports, travel, health, music, technology, entertainment, or law. Some topic blogs have become very well known and influential. For example, TechCrunch focuses on Internet products and companies; the Huffington Post is a political blog with a liberal slant; Red State is another political blog, but with a conservative point of view; and Boing Boing is a cultural oddities blog.

- **Corporate blogs** are blogs run by businesses. Their purpose is to market the business's products, provide good public relations, and increase customer loyalty. Many large corporations, including McDonald's and Dell, operate their own blogs.

Occasionally, bloggers have gotten in trouble for items they have posted. For example, flight attendant Ellen Simonetti was fired by Delta Air Lines for "inappropriate" comments and photographs of herself in her Delta uniform. Mark Cuban, who owns the Dallas Mavericks, was fined by the NBA for criticizing NBA officials on his blog. In other nations with limits on free speech, bloggers have been imprisoned for their comments.

However, these incidents are the exceptions; there are more than 100 million blogs on the Web today. To find a blog on a topic that interests you, you can use a blog search engine such as Technorati (www.technorati.com).

Your Turn 6-5

Using a blog search engine such as Technorati (www.technorati.com), search for and read blogs on the following topics. Add your own comments to each blog, if you wish. Record each blog's name and URL and briefly describe it in the space provided.

1. Health and fitness

   Name of blog_____URL_____

   Description _____

2. Sleep and/or dreams

   Name of blog_____URL_____

   Description _____

3. Substance abuse and recovery

   Name of blog_____URL_____

   Description _____

4. Sexually transmitted diseases

   Name of blog_____URL_____

   Description _____

5. A topic of your own choice

   Name of blog_____URL_____

   Description _____

What's Up?

Name _____   Date_____

1. List and briefly describe five aspects of physical fitness.

_____

_____

_____

2. What are the benefits of aerobic exercise?

_____

_____

_____

3. What are the benefits of weight training, calisthenics, and stretching?

_____

_____

_____

4. What are the results of irregular sleep habits?

_____

_____

_____

5. What is drug abuse?

_____

_____

_____

continues

Name _____   Date_____

6. What is the difference between a stimulant and a depressant? Give an example of each.

_____

_____

_____

7. Describe some of the long-term effects of nicotine.

_____

_____

_____

8. What are the effects of drinking alcohol?

_____

_____

_____

9. Describe the three stages in the process of recovering from drug abuse.

_____

_____

_____

10. How can sexually transmitted diseases be prevented?

_____

_____

_____

Case Studies

The Case of the Breathless Weight Trainer

Gabe worked out with weights and was proud of the way he looked. He felt strong and able to take on anything. One weekend, his friend Sula asked him to help her move. Sula's new apartment was in a building with no elevator, and Gabe had to carry Sula's furniture and other things up three flights of stairs. He was up and down the stairs all morning, and to his surprise, he was out of breath and needed frequent rests. Lifting the furniture was no problem, but the stairs were wearing him out.

1. How would you rate Gabe on the five aspects of physical fitness?

_____

_____

_____

2. Suggest an exercise program that would help Gabe develop all-around physical fitness.

_____

_____

The Case of the "Social" Drinker

Each weekend, Tessa goes out with friends and has four or five drinks. Although she binge drinks, she never feels sick or hungover. After a while, Tessa starts to have a drink each evening before dinner, just enough to make her feel relaxed. One day when she ran out of wine and beer, she became anxious—so anxious she immediately went out to buy more. Tessa thinks of herself as a "social" drinker—someone who drinks a little with friends to relax.

1. Do you agree with Tessa that she is a social drinker? Why or why not?

_____

_____

_____

2. Does Tessa have a problem with alcohol? Explain your answer.

_____

_____

_____

# Journal

Answer the following journal questions.

1. What sport or type of exercise do you enjoy the most? What fitness benefits do you gain as a result of this activity?

_____

_____

_____

2. How can you improve your sleep habits to get more rest?

_____

_____

_____

3. Describe someone you know who abuses drugs. What problems does this person—and the people around him or her—have as a result? What approach might help this person get off drugs?

_____

_____

_____

4. Describe your ideal of perfect fitness and health.

_____

_____

_____

5. Does the idea of having your own blog appeal to you? Why or why not? If you did start a blog, what would it be about?

_____

_____

_____

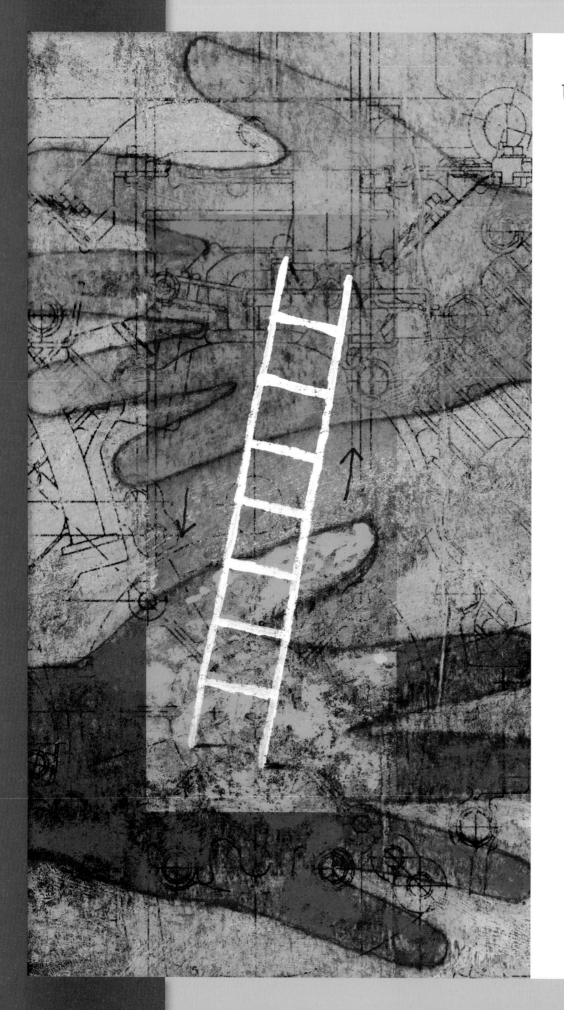

Developing Your Social Potential

So far you have explored your emotional, intellectual, and physical potential—all aspects of the inner you. In the next five chapters, you will turn your attention outward and work on your social potential. You will learn how to be a more effective communicator, improve your listening and speaking skills, and develop your ability to get along with other people, both one-on-one and in groups.

CHAPTER 7 COMMUNICATING EFFECTIVELY

In this chapter, you will be . . .

. . . developing your self belief:
- I will remember that "the quality of your life is the quality of your communication."

. . . reframing your thoughts:
- I will become more aware of the meaning of nonverbal communication in various cultures.
- I will overcome mental and emotional barriers to good communication.
- I will analyze my communications with others in terms of communication styles.

. . . setting goals:
- I will improve my rapport with at least one fellow student or colleague.

. . . envisioning a compelling future:
- I will enjoy better relationships with others.

. . . achieving personal mastery:
- I will succeed in my personal and professional life by being a more effective communicator.

CHAPTER 8 IMPROVING YOUR LISTENING SKILLS

In this chapter, you will be . . .

. . . developing your self belief:
- I will be open to changing my beliefs, attitudes, and feelings by carefully listening to others.

. . . reframing your thoughts:
- I will pay attention to what others are saying rather than to my own thoughts.
- I will interpret nonverbal cues in order to better understand spoken messages.

. . . setting goals:
- I will sit up front in classes so I can better see and hear classroom discussions.

. . . envisioning a compelling future:
- I will do better in my courses by listening and responding more effectively in class.

. . . achieving personal mastery:
- I will improve all my relationships by actively listening to others.

CHAPTER 9 IMPROVING YOUR SPEAKING SKILLS

In this chapter, you will be . . .

. . . developing your self belief:
- I will be aware that the way I speak is an expression of my personality.

. . . reframing your thoughts:
- I will pay attention to other people when I converse with them.
- I will establish a positive atmosphere by mirroring the communication style of others.

. . . setting goals:
- I will use Standard English in academic, business, and other public speaking situations.
- I will improve at least one of my voice qualities.

. . . envisioning a compelling future:
- I will become an effective public speaker.

. . . achieving personal mastery:
- I will be able to express myself effectively in conversations and in groups.

CHAPTER 10 GETTING ALONG WITH OTHERS

In this chapter, you will be . . .

. . . developing your self belief:
- I will remember that when I believe in myself, it is easy to believe in other people.

. . . reframing your thoughts:
- I will balance my own needs with those of others.
- I will be open rather than defensive in order to be able to change and grow.

. . . setting goals:
- I will use anger management techniques to defuse my next conflict with a friend.
- I will resolve the conflict rather than let it continue.

. . . envisioning a compelling future:
- I will have happier, more satisfying relationships in all areas of my life.

. . . achieving personal mastery:
- I will more easily reach my goals by getting along well with others.

CHAPTER 11 FUNCTIONING IN GROUPS

In this chapter, you will be . . .

. . . developing your self belief:
- I will improve my self-belief by contributing to the efforts of worthwhile groups.

. . . reframing your thoughts:
- I will resist conforming when doing so runs counter to my beliefs and values.
- I will analyze the goals, roles, and norms of the groups to which I belong.

. . . setting goals:
- I will participate more actively in at least one group.
- I will take a leadership role in at least one group.

. . . envisioning a compelling future:
- I will imagine what an effective group of people can accomplish when they work together on a common goal.

. . . achieving personal mastery:
- I will reach my social potential in part by functioning well as a group member and leader.

Communicating Effectively

(© Trinity Mirror/Mirrorpix/Alamy)

Oprah Winfrey's communication skills have played a large role in her success. Early in her career, she became the host of a morning TV talk show in Chicago. A year later, the show was renamed for her and went national. *The Oprah Winfrey Show* is now just part of the Oprah media empire, which also includes magazines, films, and other TV shows.

© 2011 Wadsworth, Cengage Learning

At six months, a baby cries, laughs, smiles, makes faces, and waves his or her arms and legs to communicate. As babies grow into children, they acquire more communication skills. They speak and listen, they learn to read and write, and the quality of their communication improves. As children mature and become adults, they become even more effective communicators, and their ability to get along with others, as well as their own sense of well-being, improves.

Even though most of us developed communication skills without giving them a thought, we should not take communication for granted. Good communication is the basis of our social potential. Without it, each of us would live dreary lives in isolation. It's no accident that solitary confinement is one of the harshest punishments in prison. We need other people, and our connections to others are forged by communication.

Yet because we learned how to communicate gradually, as we grew up, most of us have never thought much about this valuable skill. For example, have you ever considered the difference between communicating in your private life and communicating on the job? When you communicate at home, the communications belong to you. However, when you communicate on the job, your communications belong only partly to you. Your communications also belong to your employer. On the job, the written and oral messages you create represent not only you but also your employer. Thus you can see that although communication is an everyday matter, the quality of your communication is extremely important for your success in all areas of life. In fact, good communication skills are so important for reaching your potential that there are three chapters on communication in this book. In this chapter you will:

- learn the basic components and processes of communication;
- discover that nonverbal communication varies from culture to culture;
- learn about the problems we face when we communicate;
- explore different communication styles; and
- improve the effectiveness of your communication skills by improving your rapport with other people.

Finally, you'll learn how to use e-mail as an effective communication tool.

> "The level of success that you experience in life, the happiness, joy, love, external rewards, and impact that you create is the direct result of how you communicate to yourself and to others. The quality of your life is the quality of your communication."
>
> ANTHONY ROBBINS,
> motivational writer

What Is Communication?

Communication is the exchange of messages. Messages can be verbal, using spoken or written words, or they can be nonverbal, using symbols, gestures, expressions, and body language. For communication to take place, there must be a sender, a person who transmits the message. There must also be a receiver, a person who receives the message. Effective communication occurs when the sender and the receiver have the same understanding of the message (see Figure 7–1).

FIGURE 7–1

The communication process: The sender transmits a message, the receiver gets the message, and the receiver sends another message—the feedback—to the sender, and the process starts again.

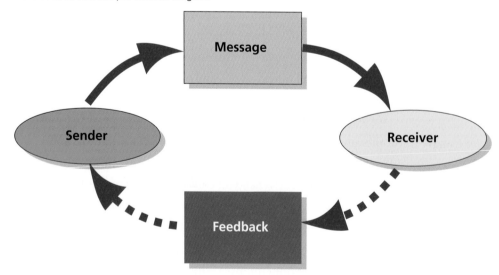

In one-way communication, the speaker speaks and the receiver doesn't get a chance to respond.

In two-way communication, both the sender and the receiver get and give feedback.

The three basic components of communication—sender, receiver, and message—can be combined in two basic patterns for the communication process. The first is one-way communication, and the second is two-way communication.

■ **In one-way communication, the sender transmits a message, the receiver gets it, and the process is complete.** When a company sends you a product catalog, and you look at it and throw it away, one-way communication has taken place. Another example of one-way communication occurs when your instructor tells you the next assignment and you write it down and leave the classroom.

■ **In two-way communication, the sender transmits a message, the receiver gets it, and the receiver responds with another message.** Sender and receiver alternate roles, giving one another feedback. Conversations and correspondence are examples of two-way communication.

One-way communication has the advantage of being fast. It also maintains the speaker's authority, since no feedback—either negative or positive—is expected of the listener. For example, in the armed forces, one-way communication is used to transmit orders and maintain the authority of rank. But one-way communication is far less effective than two-way communication. In one-way communication, the speaker has no way of determining whether the receiver has received the correct message, because there is no feedback. In contrast, two-way communication provides an opportunity for both parties to correct mistakes and misunderstandings.

Both one-way and two-way communication can take place in many types of situations and between different types of senders and receivers. Both patterns can take place between two people, between one person and a small group, between one person and a large group, and even between groups. Table 7–1 shows examples of one-way and two-way communication between different types of senders and receivers.

Nonverbal Communication and Culture

Most people think of words as the chief means by which we communicate. Being clear, concise, and courteous in your choice of words is important.

		Example of Two-Way Communication
Sender and Receiver	**Example of One-Way Communication**	
Two individuals	A manager forwards a vacation policy e-mail to her assistant.	A manager and her assistant discuss their vacation plans.
An individual and a small group	An instructor gives a lecture on social psychology to a small class.	An instructor leads a class discussion about social psychology.
An individual and a large group	The President of the United States delivers the State of the Union address to all U.S. citizens (and the world).	The President of the United States has a press conference to answer questions from journalists.
A group and an individual	The Internal Revenue Service mails a tax refund check to a taxpayer.	The Internal Revenue Service notifies a taxpayer that his tax return is being audited, and the taxpayer replies.
Two groups	A student activities group puts posters advertising a rock concert all over campus, and the student body reads them.	A student group negotiates an agreement with a rock group to perform on campus.

TABLE 7–1   Examples of One-Way and Two-Way Communications

However, studies of face-to-face communication have shown that 80 to 90 percent of the impact of a message comes from nonverbal elements—facial expressions, eye contact, body language, and tone of voice. Nonverbal communication can be far more revealing of the content of a message than its words. The speaker usually has more control over choice of words than over facial expressions, eye contact, body language, and tone of voice. The expression, "It wasn't what he said, it was how he said it," reflects this truth. Words may say one thing while the body communicates another message.

Nonverbal communication varies from culture to culture. Because the United States is a multicultural society, it's important to be sensitive to cultural differences in communication. Sometimes it may be necessary to change your interactions with others based on your perception of cultural differences in nonverbal communication.

Facial Expressions

Smiling, frowning, and raising your eyebrows are just a few of the thousands of movements of which your face is capable. These movements communicate feelings. Researchers have found that many facial expressions are universal. A frown means the same thing in Detroit, Michigan, as it does in Beijing, China. The intensity and frequency of facial expressions vary from culture to culture.

"The face is the mirror of the mind, and eyes without speaking confess the secrets of the heart."

SAINT JEROME (C. 347–419), translator of the Bible

A smile communicates good feeling among people all over the world.

"Most people are good at judging a speaker's feelings from his or her expressions. Sadness, anger, hostility, excitement, and happiness are easily conveyed by expressions. But people are less accurate when it comes to judging character from facial expressions. For example, many people think that a person who nods and smiles a lot is warm and agreeable, but studies have shown no such correlation.

Eye Contact

Smiles and frowns may have a common meaning throughout the world, but eye contact does not. In some cultures, looking downward while speaking to someone is a sign of respect. In mainstream U.S. culture,

News & Views

GESTURES: ONE CULTURE'S "GOOD LUCK" IS ANOTHER CULTURE'S INSULT

Some gestures do not need words to have meaning. Gestures such as a salute and a shake of the head have meaning without words. Each culture has its own gestures that people use to communicate. However, sometimes the same gesture has different meanings in different cultures. When that happens, people from different cultures can unintentionally confuse or offend one another.

In most parts of the world, for example, "victory" is conveyed by an upraised palm with the second and third fingers in a V-shape. If you make that gesture in Great Britain, however, you will be giving someone a sexual insult (similar in meaning to the middle-finger upward jerk of the United States).

All may be well in the United States, but in some other countries, this gesture is an insult.

The thumbs-up gesture means that all is well in much of Europe and North America. But in Greece, Turkey, and Iran, the thumbs-up sign is a sexual insult. Another insult in Greece and Turkey is called "the hand of Moutza." It is an open palm with the fingers extended, held facing the person being insulted. The origin of the palm of Moutza goes back 1,500 years. At that time, ordinary citizens helped punish prisoners by pressing handfuls of dung into their faces. So be careful not to signal "five things" using your hand when in Greece or Turkey!

Another gesture that can cause misunderstanding is the sign of the University of Texas football team, the Longhorns. At a college football game, extending the second finger and the pinkie is a sign of encouragement and victory to the Longhorns. However, the same gesture in Italy and other parts of Europe means that a man's wife has been unfaithful—a terrible insult.

Similarly, crossing your fingers means luck in the United States. But in some Asian countries, crossing your fingers means you are making a sexual offer.

So be aware when you are communicating with people from another culture. The gestures whose meanings you take for granted may not mean what you think they mean to a person from another culture.

Sources: Peter Marsh, ed., *Eye to Eye: How People Interact*, Topsfield, Mass., Salem House, 1988, p. 54; Carole Wade and Carol Tavris, *Psychology*, 4th ed, New York, HarperCollins, 1996, p. 670. "Exploring Nonverbal Communication," <http://nonverbal.ucsc.edu/>, accessed April 13, 2008.

however, a person who doesn't meet your eyes during conversation is thought to be hiding something. Making eye contact with someone when speaking to them is considered desirable in the United States.

In mainstream American culture, eye contact is used to establish communication. For example, if you want salespeople to help you, you try to make eye contact with them. If you don't want your instructors to call on you in class, you avoid their eyes in the hope that they will not notice you.

Body Language

Try to speak for two minutes and hold your head, arms, and legs completely still. Impossible? Probably. Without being aware of it, people move their bodies constantly while they talk. They nod, shrug, gesture with their hands, and shift their weight. Body language can indicate a wide range of emotion from boredom (yawning) to impatience (tapping your fingers or feet) to enthusiasm (gesturing with your hands).

In addition to communicating meaning by moving the body, people communicate by the distance they leave between themselves. In mainstream U.S. culture, people who are lovers, close family members, or good friends are comfortable standing about a foot apart. Acquaintances or colleagues, on the other hand, usually stand four-to-twelve feet apart when communicating. The tone of an interaction can be changed just by changing the distance between two people.

The meaning of body language and distance varies from one culture to another. In some cultures, gestures are expansive and expressive. In other cultures, body language is controlled to avoid showing too much emotion. Each culture has extensive unwritten rules about body language. For example, if a stranger walked up to you and stopped one foot away, you would feel threatened. That's because a person you don't know has entered space that's reserved for people you know intimately.

Voice Qualities

A voice can be loud or soft, high or low pitched, fast or slow. Its tone can be pleasant, harsh, or monotonous. Voice qualities can convey whether you are interested, bored, tired, or happy.

It's sometimes risky to make generalizations about what voice qualities mean. For example, a New Yorker may speak faster than someone from Atlanta. When they speak to one another, the New Yorker may feel the Southerner is slow to understand and the Southerner may perceive the New Yorker as rude. Neither one of them would necessarily be right. On the other hand, people who know one another well are very good at picking up meaningful changes in voice quality. You probably have had the experience of knowing that something was bothering a friend because of the tone of voice you heard.

Barriers to Communication

Effective communication means that both sender and receiver have the same understanding of the message. The first prerequisite is that the message, both verbal and nonverbal, should be clear. But beyond the message itself are factors that influence both the sender and the receiver. Each person brings a distinct set of abilities, knowledge, experience, attitudes, and feelings to the communication process. Miscommunication may occur because of physical, mental, or emotional barriers on the part of the communicators.

> "If his lips are silent, he chatters with his fingertips; betrayal oozes out of him at every pore."
>
> SIGMUND FREUD (1856–1939), Austrian founder of psychoanalysis

Your Turn 7-1

OBSERVING NONVERBAL COMMUNICATION

Following is an activity that will improve your awareness of nonverbal communication. Observe a conversation at a supermarket or mall. Pay particular attention to nonverbal communication. Write what you observed in the space provided.

1. What facial expressions did you notice?

   _____

   _____

2. Did the people maintain eye contact throughout the conversation? If not, when was eye contact broken?

   _____

   _____

3. What body postures, head movements, and gestures did they use?

   _____

   _____

4. Describe the voices.
   Volume _____
   Pitch _____
   Speed _____
   Tone _____

When you communicate, you can take responsibility for your share of the process. You can try to overcome barriers to communication by making the message you send clear. If you receive a negative or unexpected response, examine yourself first to see if your message is the cause. You may have to overcome communication barriers by revising your message.

Physical Barriers

Any disturbing factor in the physical environment or your body can prevent full communication. If the room is noisy, you may not be able to hear or make yourself heard. If there is a lot of other activity, you may find yourself distracted. If you are sitting or standing in an awkward

Too much activity and noise can interfere with effective communication.

position, your discomfort may act as a barrier to communication. In some cases, hearing loss makes it difficult to understand what's being communicated.

Mental Barriers

Every person has a unique set of knowledge and experience that influences what he or she does. When you communicate, for example, you tend to interpret what's being said in light of your previous knowledge and experience. People make assumptions all the time, and frequently they are wrong. For example, a teenager may ask to borrow the family car on Saturday night to see his friend. He may assume that his destination doesn't matter to his parents. At the same time, his parents may assume their teen is going to his friend's house, as he frequently does, and say yes. However, when the parents find out their son intends to drive to a distant late-night rock concert instead of staying in the neighborhood, they may take back the car keys.

Another type of mental barrier that prevents good communication is selective attention. People tend to focus on what interests them and pay little or no attention to the rest. Or we pay attention to positive matters and ignore unpleasant ones. During a performance evaluation, for example, an employee may remember each word of praise, while his boss's criticisms don't even register!

Another mental barrier to good communication is choice of words. In some cases, communication breaks down because one person simply doesn't understand the vocabulary of the other. When someone uses technical, specialized words to explain how a machine works, for example, a nontechnical person may not understand. Or communication may break down because one person "talks down" to another, and the second person becomes resentful. In other cases, the words being used are emotionally charged. Discussions about politics, for example, frequently go nowhere because people have long-standing emotional associations with words such as *conservative, liberal, left, right, Republican,* and *Democrat.*

Emotional Barriers

Feelings and emotions can also create barriers to communication. Stress, fear, happiness, anger, and love can all prevent effective communication. A person who is worried about something, for example, finds it hard to pay attention to a class lecture. Someone who just won the lottery may have trouble focusing on ordinary conversation.

People's long-held feelings and attitudes can also cause communication problems. Prejudice, which is a negative attitude toward people because of their membership in a group, is a communication barrier. It prevents people from communicating effectively as individuals because their attitudes can cloud the sending and receiving of messages.

> "When we talk about understanding, surely it takes place only when the mind listens completely— the mind being your heart, your nerves, your ears—when you give your whole attention to it."
>
> JIDDU KRISHNAMURTI (1895–1986), Indian writer

> "Hating people because of their color is wrong, and it doesn't matter which color does the hating. It's just plain wrong."
>
> MUHAMMAD ALI, boxing champion

Shyness is another emotional barrier to effective communication. Shy people are afraid to communicate with others because they think they will be judged negatively. They lack confidence in themselves, so they tend to withdraw and be quiet.

Lack of Rapport

The physical, mental, and emotional barriers to communication all have the same basic effect: They drive a wedge between the two communicators. In essence, the two communicators lack rapport, or harmony. This situation is so common that there are several expressions to describe it: "They're not on the same wavelength," "They're out of sync," "There's no chemistry between them," and "They're not in tune."

Without rapport, people who try to communicate have a difficult time. Misunderstandings, hard feelings, and mistakes are the consequences. How can you establish rapport and communicate effectively? We'll try to answer that question in the rest of this chapter.

Communication Styles

The key to effective communication is awareness—of yourself but, more important, of the people with whom you communicate. You must be conscious of the feelings, needs, and personalities of the people around you. Once you become sensitive to others, you will find that their response to you is more positive. You will be on the way to establishing rapport, the foundation of effective communication.

Naturally, both people and the communication process are extremely complex. No two people or communication situations are alike. So how can you even begin to improve your awareness of others as communicators? The answer lies in using a model that simplifies a complex process and gives you insight into what's really going on.

There are many communication models, but the model we use in this chapter is based on the work of David Merrill and Roger Reid. They proposed that people show two major forms of behavior when they communicate: responsiveness and assertiveness.[1] Responsiveness is the degree to which a person is closed or open in his or her dealings with others. Someone with a low degree of responsiveness hides emotion and is very self-controlled. On the other hand, a person with a high degree of responsiveness shows emotion and seems friendly. Reid defines assertiveness as behavior ranging from asking questions (low assertiveness) to telling others what's expected (high assertiveness).

The two communication behaviors can be combined in a diagram, as shown in Figure 7–2. You can see that placing the two behaviors of responsiveness and assertiveness at right angles to each other results in a model with four boxes. When you plot a person's degree of responsiveness and assertiveness, the intersection of the two lines falls in one of the boxes. Each box represents a communication style: Thinker, Achiever, Seller, and Relater.

FIGURE 7-2

A person's communication style can be characterized by the assertiveness and responsiveness he or she shows. By plotting these characteristics on a grid, you can determine the person's communication style.

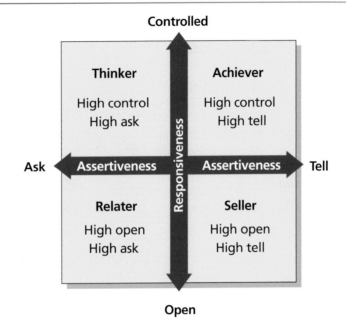

The Thinker

Thinkers are people who tend to be guarded in their interactions with others. Self-control is very important to them. Thinkers don't reveal much of themselves. Rather, they deflect attention from themselves by asking questions of the other person.

The Achiever

Like Thinkers, Achievers are self-controlled and guarded about revealing their inner selves. Achievers are very assertive, however. They express their expectations clearly.

The Seller

Sellers tend to be warm and outgoing in their dealings with others. Like Achievers, they are assertive and express themselves forcefully.

The Relater

Relaters are usually warm and friendly in their interactions. They are less concerned about themselves than about others. Relaters ask questions that are sometimes personal in nature.

Understanding the Communication Styles

At one time or another, each of us has used aspects of each communication style. For example, when you communicate with a close friend or spouse, you may be very open and personal (Relater). But when you communicate with your boss, you may be very self-controlled and unassertive (Thinker). In general, over time, each of us tends to favor one style in most of our interactions with others.

Your Turn 7-2

You can find out what your dominant communication style is by checking each of the communication characteristics that apply to you. The box with the most check marks represents your preferred communication style.

Thinker

_____ Quiet, level tone of voice

___•___ Leans back or away

___•___ Limited eye contact

_____ Stiff posture

_____ Uses big words

Achiever

___•___ Factual speech

_____ Leans forward and faces others

_____ Limited facial expressions

___•___ Limited body movements

___•___ Fast-paced speech

Relater

_____ Little emphasis on detail

___•___ Touches others

___•___ Smiles, nods

___•___ Casual posture

___•___ Talks about relationships

Seller

_____ Dramatic or loud tone of voice

___•___ Animated facial expressions

_____ Direct eye contact

___•___ Lots of body and hand movement

___•___ Uses voice to emphasize points

You can use your knowledge of communication styles to improve the quality of your communication. By identifying your own style and the style of the person with whom you are communicating, you can identify potential communication problems. Once you understand the problems, you can take action to improve your rapport, and consequently your communication, with the other person.

Effective Communication

Why is effective communication so important? Imagine visiting a place whose language you do not speak and whose people don't speak your language. Every message you send will probably be misunderstood or, at best, only partially understood. Everything you try to do will be difficult. Every relationship you try to establish will be based on very limited understanding. Now imagine that your communications with your friends, family, and peers suffer similar problems. The messages you send are partially misunderstood, and the feedback you receive is not what you need or understand. Not only is your communication with others affected, but your relationships with them suffer as well. If you improve the quality of your communication with others, you will improve your relationships with them. And that, in turn, will improve the quality of your life.

WHATEVER IT TAKES
Elizabeth Vargas

(© Nancy Kaszerman/ZUMA/Corbis)

The one constant in Elizabeth Vargas's childhood was her family. Vargas's father, who was in the Army, took his family with him as he was posted to military bases all over the world. Vargas was born in Paterson, New Jersey. By the time she graduated from high school in Stuttgart, Germany, she had lived in Heidelberg, Brussels, Okinawa, Kansas, and San Francisco.

A childhood of frequent moves prepared Vargas for the life of a journalist—ready to travel at a moment's notice to the latest story. Vargas studied journalism at the University of Missouri and got her first job there at KOMU-TV. She spent several years as a broadcast journalist at various local TV stations.

In 1993, Vargas made the big move in TV journalism—from local to national broadcasting for NBC News. Later she became a correspondent for ABC's news magazine show *20/20,* and was also the show's coanchor. In 2006, Vargas became the first Latina to co-anchor a major network evening news program, *ABC World News Tonight.* After the birth of her second son that year, Vargas returned to *20/20* instead of the evening news in order to have more time with her family.

Vargas recalls that early in her TV career, when Hispanic journalists were rare, she received mail suggesting that she go back to Mexico. She was very surprised by the letters, not only because of their rudeness but also because her family was originally from Puerto Rico. In her early years in the business, says Vargas, "There were no Latina or Latino role models." Instead of focusing on being Hispanic, Vargas concentrated on being a good journalist. Her advice to aspiring journalists is to "read, read, read." Interestingly, given her career, Vargas grew up in a home with no TV.

Sources: Elinor J. Brecher, "Elizabeth Vargas: Tuning In at the Top," *Hispanic,* June 2002, pp. 24–25; Luis Fernando Llosa, "Elizabeth's Reign," *Latina Magazine,* February 1999 <http:// www.latina.com/new/magazine/books/99/feb/triunfos.html>, accessed March 6, 2003; "Elizabeth Vargas" <http:// www.abcnews.com>, accessed March 6, 2003; "Elizabeth Vargas: Biography," <http://tvguide.com/celebrities/elizabeth-vargas/bio/216823>, accessed April 13, 2008.

Identifying Communication Problems

You've already identified your own preferred communication style in Your Turn 7–2. By listening and observing, you can identify the preferred communication styles of others. Do they look you in the eye or turn away? Do they ask personal questions or do they tell you just what's on their mind? Are they friendly or aloof? Are their voices loud or soft? By noticing such aspects of their behavior, you can use the chart in Your Turn 7–2 on page 172 to determine other people's preferred communication style.

If a person shows four to five characteristics of a style, he or she has a high preference for it. Two to three characteristics of a style reveal a moderate preference for that style. One characteristic is not significant.

Now let's use the information we have gathered. Let us suppose that Kelly has a moderate preference for the Seller style, that is, she has checked two or three characteristics in the Seller box. After observation, Kelly has decided that the person with whom she is communicating, Adam, shows a high preference for the Thinker style, with four or five characteristics of that style.

We can plot this style information by using a communication effectiveness map as shown in Figure 7–3.[2] You can see that a communication effectiveness map uses the same four boxes as the communication style model. In each box there are two circles. The outer circle represents the style of people who show four to five indicators of the style's behavior. The inner circle represents the style of people who show two to three indicators of the style's behavior.

In the example we've been discussing, Kelly's style is Seller with two or three indicators, and Adam's style is Thinker with four or five indicators. This is shown by the colored circles in the communication effectiveness map. You'll notice that Kelly's circle and Adam's circle do not touch. There is a gap between their communication styles. What does the gap mean? It means that Kelly and Adam are likely to have communication problems. The difference in their styles indicates they lack rapport.

FIGURE 7–3

A communication effectiveness map is a way to plot the communication styles of two people. Each person's style is represented by a circle. The closer the circles, the more similar their styles, and the fewer communication problems they are likely to have.

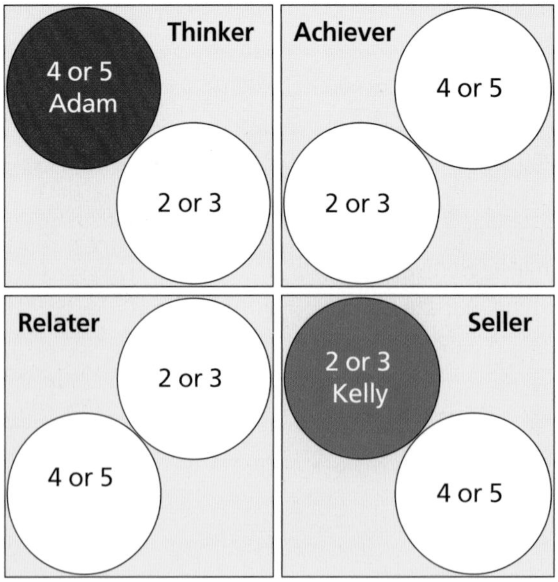
Thinker
4 or 5
Adam
2 or 3
Achiever
4 or 5
2 or 3
Relater
2 or 3
4 or 5
Seller
2 or 3
Kelly
4 or 5

Improving Rapport

How can Kelly, a Seller, and Adam, a Thinker, improve the quality of their communication? The answer is they must improve their rapport. In other words, they must become more alike in their communication styles. The way people do this is by imitating one another's behavior, or mirroring.[3]

People do a certain amount of mirroring without being aware of it. If you have ever observed people deep in conversation, you may have noticed that their postures were similar or they both spoke softly. You can take this unconscious process further by paying attention to the other person's behavior and mirroring it. Mirroring does not mean imitation so obvious that the other person notices it. Rather, mirroring consists of subtle, small adjustments in your communication behavior to more closely match your companion. When you mirror successfully, the other person feels that you are in harmony. People are most comfortable with those they feel are like themselves.

Mirroring does not always improve rapport, so there are times it should not be used. For example, mirroring the behavior of someone who is angry or verbally aggressive will only make the interaction escalate. Instead, to calm the tone of the interaction, you can respond by acknowledging the other person's anger in a quiet, evenhanded way.

Mirroring the Body and Voice You can make people with whom you are communicating more comfortable by gradually mirroring some of their body movements and voice qualities. For example, suppose you are talking to someone who is slouching in his or her chair. Without taking the same position, you can relax your posture to more closely match his or her position. Or perhaps the person you are talking with occasionally smiles or nods; you can respond in kind.

There are many aspects of nonverbal communication that can be mirrored: facial expressions, eye contact, posture, gestures, rate of speech, and pitch, volume, and tone of voice. The important thing is to match the other person's behavior in such a way that it is not noticeable. In addition, select just a couple of aspects of the person's style to mirror. Trying to mirror too much is distracting.

Mirroring Words Another useful way to mirror others' communication style is to match their use of words. People tend to use words that reflect how they perceive the world. As you recall from Chapter 3, we perceive through our senses of sight, hearing, touch, taste, and smell. Each person has a

People often mirror one another's body language while communicating, even though they may not be aware of it.

Your Turn 7-3

Choose a friend or classmate and observe him or her communicating. Use the indicators in Your Turn 7–2 to decide which communication style he or she favors and how many indicators he or she shows. Then plot your style and your friend's or classmate's style in the communication effectiveness map below.

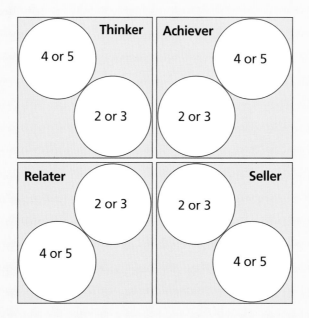

1. What is your style?

   _____

2. What is your friend or classmate's style?

   _____

3. Do your styles overlap or touch?
   If yes, describe the quality of your communication with this person.

   _____

   _____

4. Is there a gap between your styles?
   If yes, describe any communication problems you may be having.

   _____

   _____

preferred sense, and you can often tell which it is by listening to them talk. Most people prefer the senses of sight, hearing, or touch:

- Visual people say things such as, "I'll watch out for that," "It's clear to me," and "I can see that."
- People who rely on the sense of hearing use phrases such as, "That rings a bell," "I hear what you're saying," and "That sounds good to me."
- People who favor the sense of touch say things such as, "This feels right," "I can't get a hold on it," or "I grasp the meaning of that."

A few people rely on the sense of taste or smell:

- Those who rely on the sense of taste use phrases such as, "Let me chew on that a while," "That leaves a bad taste in my mouth," or "He's so delectable."
- People who favor the sense of smell say things such as, "That idea stinks," "It seems fishy to me," or "She came out of it smelling like a rose."

When you've determined a person's preferred sense, you can increase your rapport by speaking the same language. For example, if the person is visual, you can ask, "Do you see what I mean?" If the person relies on hearing, you can phrase your question, "Does that sound right to you?"

Your Turn 7-4

SAY IT AGAIN

How could you say the same thing to three different people who prefer different senses for perception? Rewrite the question, "What do you think it means?" using words that each person might choose.

1. Visual person:

_____

_____

2. Auditory (hearing) person:

_____

_____

3. Feeling (touching) person:

_____

_____

Overcoming Shyness Bernardo Carducci, a psychology professor at Indiana University Southwest, has some suggestions to help people overcome shyness with small talk.[4]

- Before a gathering, think about the people who will be there and what they may discuss.

- Arrive early. It's easier to start a new conversation than to break into a conversation that's in progress.

- Start a conversation by talking about something you and the other person share—the place, the weather, the host, and so on. Then introduce yourself.

- When the other person introduces a topic, support his or her remark. Make a comment on the topic, or throw out another topic.

These small talk pointers show that you need not be brilliant to be an effective communicator. You simply need to be responsive to other people.

Tech Tips

USING E-MAIL

In the past, you might have written a letter, made a phone call, or sent a memo. Today you are more likely to communicate by e-mail, or with friends, by text message. E-mail and text messages are so fast and convenient that people often dash them off without much thought or care. The result can be ineffective communication or, worse, miscommunication.

Since text messaging should be used only among friends and family, it can be casual and informal, full of abbreviations and shortcuts. But e-mail, especially e-mail in a business or academic setting, needs to have a courteous, professional tone and presentation.

Writing an E-Mail Message

Following are some pointers for writing effective e-mail:

- Use an informative subject line. That way the recipient can easily see the topic of your message.

- Start your message with a salutation (*Dear Professor Brenner* or *Hi Mom*), just as you would a written or typed letter.

- Keep your intended receiver in mind, and write your message accordingly. If you are writing to your professor or your boss, for example, use more formal language than if you are writing to your best friend or your sister.

- Keep your message short and to the point. People don't like to do lots of reading on a computer or hand-held device.

- Don't write anything you wouldn't want the whole world to see, because e-mail is not private. Your recipient may decide to forward your message to a large group of people. In addition, many companies routinely review and save employee e-mails, whether business or personal.

- Don't include sensitive information like social security numbers, credit card numbers, user names, and passwords in an e-mail in order to prevent identity theft.

- Don't use all capital letters because they are hard to read. they are also considered bad manners, like shouting.

- Don't write "flame" e-mails, messages that are insulting and meant to hurt. Wait until you cool down to send any e-mail message.

- As a courtesy, put your name at the end of your message. To make this easier, create signature blocks you can insert automatically.

- Check and proofread your message. Use a spell-checker, too.

Sending E-Mail

Once your message is written and checked, review the transmission options before you hit the "Send" key.

- Check the "To" line, and make sure it contains only the person or persons from whom you expect a response.

- Send CC copies of the message to those who need to see it but don't necessarily need to respond. (The abbreviation CC means "carbon copy" and dates back to typewriter days.)

- If your message is a reply, be sure you used "Reply" or "Reply All" appropriately. In general, you should reply only to those who need to see your response. Double-check the "To" and "CC" lines to make sure your message is going to the right people.

- Use BCC copies when you are sending a message to a group of people who don't know one another and who might not want their e-mail addresses seen by strangers. (BCC means "blind carbon copy.") With BCC copies, recipients see only their own e-mail address and yours.

- Don't spam—send impersonal e-mail messages to large groups.

- Don't forward chain e-mails—they are inappropriate for business or college e-mail.

Using Smilies in Personal Messages

When you talk to someone face to face, you see the other person's facial expression and gestures. These supplement the message in the words. E-mail users have a group of keyboard symbols that add visual cues to e-mail messages. Called "smilies," they usually appear at the end of a sentence and refer back to the sentence.

continues

Following are some of the common smilies and their meanings. Tilt your head to the left to see the faces.

: -) Smiley face; happiness

; -) Wink; light sarcasm

: - | Indifference

: - > Wicked grin; heavy sarcasm

: - D Shock or surprise

: - / Perplexity; puzzlement

: - (Frown; anger or displeasure

: - e Disappointment

Note that smilies are used only in personal e-mails to friends or family. They are *not* considered appropriate for academic or business e-mail.

Your Turn 7-5

WRITING E-MAIL

Imagine that you've gotten sick and have to reschedule your next day's activities. On a separate sheet of paper, write two e-mail messages, using appropriate tone and language for each.

1. A message to your professor, asking to postpone a presentation you were due to give the class tomorrow.

2. A message to your older sister, telling her you may not be able to come for dinner with her family tomorrow night but that you'll call her later to let her know for sure.

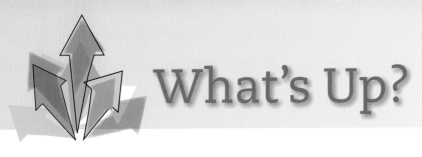
What's Up?

Name _____   Date_____

1. What is communication?

    _____

    _____

    _____

    _____

2. What is effective communication?

    _____

    _____

    _____

    _____

    _____

3. Why is two-way communication generally more effective than one-way communication?

    _feedback._____

    _____

    _____

    _____

4. What is nonverbal communication?

    _____

    _____

    _____

    _____

5. Describe the three types of barriers to communication and give an example of each.

    _____

    _____

    _____

    _____

continues

Name _____ Date _____

6. How can a knowledge of communication styles be helpful in improving communication?

_____
_____
_____
_____

7. What is the purpose of mirroring?

_____
_____
_____
_____

8. Give two examples of mirroring a person's body movements or voice during communication.

_____
_____
_____
_____

9. Describe how you can mirror a person's preferred way of perceiving the world.

_____
_____
_____
_____

10. Why does mirroring aspects of a person's communication style lead to more effective communication?

_____
_____
_____
_____

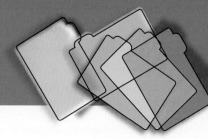

Case Studies

The Case of the Irritable Ex-Smoker

It was Bob's third day without cigarettes, and he was beginning to feel the effects of quitting. He awoke with a headache, feeling grouchy, and during breakfast he snapped at each person in his family. He found it harder than he had expected to have his coffee without smoking. By the time he got to the office, he felt anxious and somewhat ill.

When Bob walked in, his assistant greeted him with a cheery "Good morning." "What's good about it?" Bob growled in reply.

1. What barriers to effective communication is Bob experiencing because he has quit smoking?

_____

_____

_____

_____

2. What can Bob and the people around him do to prevent the communication situation from getting worse?

_____

_____

_____

_____

The Case of the Odd Couple

Rajiv and Barb were paired off by their instructor to work on a marketing problem together. As soon as they were seated in a corner of the room, Rajiv leaned forward, facing Barb, and started listing the facts of the case. Barb was a little taken aback by his desire to get right down to work. She smiled at him and nodded in appropriate places, but her attention was still partly on the rest of the class. "Rajiv," she said, tapping his arm lightly, "Why do you suppose Mrs. Valk picked us to be a team?" Rajiv looked at her in surprise, his train of thought completely thrown off.

continues

1. What communication style does Rajiv prefer? Describe the behavior that supports your conclusion.

_____

_____

_____

_____

_____

2. What communication style does Barb prefer? How can you tell?

_____

_____

_____

_____

_____

3. What would Rajiv have to do to improve his rapport with Barb?

_____

_____

_____

_____

_____

4. What would Barb have to do to improve her rapport with Rajiv?

_____

_____

_____

_____

_____

Journal

Answer the following journal questions.

1. Describe your family's use of nonverbal communication. What facial expressions, eye contact, and body language are used to communicate in your home?

_____

_____

_____

_____

2. Which of the barriers to communication—physical, mental, or emotional—poses the greatest problem for you? How can you overcome this barrier?

_____

_____

_____

_____

3. Use the communication effectiveness grid and map in Your Turn 7–2 and 7–3 to plot your communication style and that of your spouse, significant other, or close friend. Are your communication styles similar or different? How does this affect your relationship?

_____

_____

_____

_____

4. Think about the various ways you communicate—in person, on the phone, by text messages, by e-mail, by instant messages, via Facebook, and so on. With whom do you use each type of communication, and why? Which are your favorites? Why?

_____

_____

_____

Improving Your Listening Skills

Listening is an important skill, particularly for people who do interviews on the job, such as social workers, psychotherapists, and journalists. This student journalist is conducting an interview for her campus newspaper.

Tanisha was explaining to her friend Joanna why she had decided to quit her job. As Tanisha talked, Joanna nodded and said, "Uh-huh." When Tanisha finished her story she paused, waiting for Joanna to say something. Startled by the silence, Joanna said, "Oh, sorry, Tanisha, what did you say?"

At one time or another, all of us have been in Tanisha's position—exasperated because someone with whom we thought we were communicating was not listening. And we all have been guilty of behaving as Joanna did—seeming to pay attention while our minds were elsewhere. Failing to listen to a friend can damage the friendship. Failing to listen to instructors, bosses, and coworkers has repercussions, too. It can lead to misunderstandings, poor performance, and hard feelings. For example, poor listening skill is associated with low academic performance, and effective listening is associated with success in school. Interestingly, listening skill is not associated with any particular personality style,[1] which suggests that with a little effort, anyone can improve their listening skill.

Since most communication—personal, academic, and professional—involves listening, it's important to have good listening skills. In this chapter, you will:

- identify barriers to listening;
- evaluate your own listening skills; and
- learn techniques you can use to become a more effective listener.

Finally, you will learn how iPods and MP3 players can be used as study aids.

(Hard because requires concintration.)

Listening is more than hearing

└ears   *└Brain.*

Why Is Listening so Hard?

Listening means concentrating on what's being said. The napping student is clearly not paying attention to what's happening in the classroom.

Listening seems like such an easy thing to do. After all, you just have to keep your ears open. But listening is more than hearing. You hear with your ears, but you listen with your brain. Imagine talking with an interesting person at a party. You can hear many conversations in the room, but you are listening to just one.

So why is listening so hard? Listening requires concentration. That means ignoring the hundreds of other things going on around you as well as in your head. Distractions, preconceptions, self-absorption, and daydreaming can all interfere with your ability to listen.

Distractions

It's easy to be distracted when you're listening to someone. Perhaps there's other activity in the room that draws your attention. Perhaps the person with whom you are speaking has piercings that you can't stop looking at. Or another individual may pace or gesture or exhibit a mannerism that's hard to ignore. Whatever the distraction, it competes with the communication for your attention. And once your attention is divided, it's hard to listen well.

Preconceptions

Preconceptions about the speakers or what they have to say are barriers to effective listening. If you think that the speaker is a fool or has opinions that are the opposite of yours, you may close down your brain and pay no attention. What you lose is an opportunity to learn something—even if your preconceptions turn out to be true. You may even be surprised to hear something of interest if you decide to listen in spite of your presumptions about the speaker or the message.

Self-Absorption

Another cause of poor listening is when you focus on yourself rather than on the person who is talking. Instead of listening carefully to the other person, you are busy thinking about your own agenda. While the individual talks, you are planning and rehearsing your response. In effect, you are just waiting for the other person to be quiet so you can jump in with your contribution to the conversation.

Daydreaming

Have you ever fallen into a mental "black hole" during a conversation? Your body is there, but your eyes are glassy, and anyone looking closely at you can tell your mind is miles away. Unfortunately, it's easy to fall into the trap of daydreaming while you are supposed to be listening. That's because your brain can process words much faster than the speaker can say them. What does your brain do with this down time? It fills it with daydreams.

Listening Effectively

Many people listen with just one ear. They understand just enough of what the speaker is saying to keep the conversation going with nods, smiles, and a well-placed "Uh-huh." With these responses, the listener is trying to convince the speaker that he or she is paying attention. In reality, the listener is listening passively. He or she is paying just enough attention to avoid seeming rude. This type of passive listening may be sufficient for some types of casual conversations, but it will not do for important personal and professional communications.

Instead, active listening is required when you communicate in most situations. Active listening means that your mind is engaged with the message and the speaker. You are concentrating on the speaker, and you are participating in the communication.

There are many techniques you can use to practice active listening. These techniques include being physically prepared, being open to the other person, being curious, asking questions, and listening for the meaning of the words and the unspoken message.

Be Physically Prepared

Listening is both a physical and a mental activity. If you cannot hear properly, you will have trouble listening. So the first prerequisite for effective listening is the ability to hear. If you always have trouble hearing, you should have your hearing checked to make sure it's normal. Don't assume that hearing problems are confined to older people; young people sometimes have damaged hearing because of overexposure to loud music or noisy machinery.

You can maximize your ability to hear by making sure the environment is free of noise and other distractions. In classrooms, lectures, and meetings, make sure you sit close to the speaker so you can hear well. You should also be able to see the speaker, because your sense of sight helps you listen. Watching the speaker's nonverbal cues helps you understand the message.

Be Open

The Japanese symbol for the word *listen* shows the character for "ear" placed within the character for "gate." When we listen to someone, we are in effect passing through the other person's gate and entering his or her world. When we listen effectively, we are receiving the speaker's message in an open, nonjudging way.[2]

This is not always easy. Being open to another person means you risk having to change your feelings, ideas, or attitudes. Yet listening in an open, nonjudging way does not necessarily mean you must agree with everything the speaker says. You must just be willing to accept their right to say it and to listen.

Being willing to accept the speaker's message means that you stop focusing on finding contradictions and errors. Instead, you let the message

News & Views

(© Rif Spahni/age fotostock/PhotoLibrary)

NOISE AND HEALTH

Heavy traffic, rock concerts, jet engines, leaf blowers, jack hammers—these are just a few of the sounds that make modern life so noisy. If you live, work, or study in a noisy environment, you may think you are used to the high level of sound. However, studies have shown that loud noise affects us. It can damage hearing, increase blood pressure, disrupt digestion, raise anxiety levels, and decrease performance.

The intensity of a sound is measured in decibels (dB). The higher the decibel level of a sound, the louder it is. The table following shows the decibel levels of some common sounds.

Level of Sound	Decibel Level	Example
Quiet	15 dB	A whisper
	30 dB	A quiet library
Moderate	50 dB	A medium rainfall
	60 dB	A conversation
Loud	80 dB	Busy street
	90 dB	Lawnmower
Extremely loud	110 dB	Car horn
	120 dB	Rock concert
Painful	130 dB	Jack hammer
	140 db	Jet engine

Sounds in the shaded portion of the chart—over 80 decibels—are considered hazardous. The cells of the inner ear and hearing nerve can be damaged by prolonged exposure to loud noise, or by a single exposure to a painfully loud noise like a gun shot, explosion, or jet engine taking off. You can tell if the noise around you is more than 80 dB if you can't hear someone two feet away or you have to raise your own voice to be heard.

Workplace noise is regulated in the United States. If a workplace has an average decibel level or 85 or more, it must have a hearing protection program that includes noise monitoring, hearing tests, and hearing protection devices for employees.

But what about the ordinary noise of daily life? Traffic, power tools, loud appliances, stereo headsets, loud clubs—these sounds are common today. In fact, researchers estimate that children living in industrial nations today will start losing their hearing thirty years earlier than their parents did—just because of continued exposure to increasingly loud noise.

How can you protect your hearing and your health? There are several things you can do:

■ **Be aware of the noise around you.** If you have to shout to be heard, the noise is too loud and can damage your hearing.

- **Limit your exposure to noise.** If you like to go to rock concerts or noisy clubs, don't sit or stand near the speakers, and go outside occasionally to give your ears a break.
- **Turn down the volume if possible.** You can't muffle a jack hammer, but you can turn down the volume on stereo headsets and car stereo systems.
- **Wear hearing protectors if you must regularly be in a noisy environment.** Rock musicians, and workers exposed to loud sounds, should wear ear protectors. You can buy ear muffs and ear plugs at drug stores and sporting goods stores.

Sources: Nick Moore, "British Campaign Against Tinnitus." The Deafened People Page, <http://www.deafened.org/timestin.htm>, accessed April 17, 2008; "Noise and Hearing Loss." American Speech-Language-Hearing Association, <www.asha.org/public/hearing/disorders/noise.htm>, accessed April 17, 2008; "What Is a Decibel, and How Is It Measured?" How Stuff Works, <http://science.howstuffworks.com/question124.htm> accessed April 17, 2008.

> "He heard it, but he heeded not—his eyes were with his heart, and that was far away."
>
> LORD BYRON (1788–1824),
> English poet

> "It is the province of knowledge to speak and the privilege of wisdom to listen."
>
> OLIVER WENDELL HOLMES
> (1809–1894),
> writer and physician

get through. Then you can evaluate the message—after you've actually listened to it.

If you can listen openly, you will communicate to the speaker that you think he or she is important and has ideas worth hearing. You communicate an attitude of respect for the other person. The bonus of open listening is that the speaker will feel less defensive and more open to you.

Be Curious

Part of being an open listener is being curious about other people. If you can really listen to what another person has to say, you will find that you can learn a lot. Try to be observant and objective about listening, and you will be able to gather a great deal of information.

To do this, you must let your curiosity overcome your need to judge the other person and justify your own position.

Ask Questions

You can express your curiosity about the speaker as well as clarify your understanding of the message by asking questions. Effective listeners ask questions in a way that will elicit informative answers.

In general, the most effective questions are open-ended questions. Open-ended questions cannot be answered with just a *yes* or a *no*; they require an explanation as a response. Questions that begin with *what*, *how*, and *why* are generally open-ended questions. For example, "What happened at the meeting?" "How do you feel about that?" and "Why did he leave?" are questions that require an informative response. Open-ended questions are used to get more detail and to clarify messages.

Effective listeners ask questions in a way that will elicit information.

© 2011 Wadsworth, Cengage Learning

(© martin purmensky/istockphoto.com)

Your Turn 8-1

HOW GOOD A LISTENER ARE YOU?

Take a moment to think about your own qualities as a listener. Then answer the following questions to see what your strengths and weaknesses are.

		Yes	No
1.	Is your hearing normal?	☑	☐
2.	Do you look at the person who is speaking?	☑	☐
3.	Do you try to ignore other sights and sounds when you listen to someone speak?	☑	☐
4.	While listening, do you avoid doing something else at the same time (like texting or watching TV)?	☐	☑
5.	When someone is talking to you, do you concentrate on him or her rather than on your own thoughts?	☑	☐
6.	Do you think that other people can teach you something?	☑	☐
7.	If you don't understand something, do you ask the speaker to repeat it?	☑	☐
8.	Do you listen even when you disagree with what the speaker is saying?	☑	☐
9.	If you think the subject is dull or too hard, do you tune out?	☑	☐
10.	Do you frequently have to ask people to repeat themselves because you've forgotten what they have said?	☒	☑
11.	If the speaker's appearance or manner is poor, do you pay less attention?	☐	☑
12.	Do you pretend to pay attention even when you are not listening?	☐	☑

If you answered *yes* to the first eight questions and *no* to the last four questions, your listening skills are good. Even if you got a perfect score, the tips and techniques that follow will help you improve your listening skills.

On the other hand, closed-ended questions can be answered with a simple *yes* or *no*. "Did you agree with her?" and "Do you like it?" are examples of closed-ended questions. Closed-ended questions tend to limit the exchange of information, especially when the speaker is shy or reserved. Effective listeners can use closed-ended questions, however, when information needs to be checked. "Do you mean you'll be a day late?" is a closed-ended question that verifies the listener's understanding of the message.

Remember, good questions, both open- and closed-ended, arise out of the conversation. That means that you, the listener, must be paying attention. The next time you watch someone doing an interview, notice whether they stick to a script of questions, no matter what the response, or whether they allow their questions to arise from the content of the interview. Good interviewers are good listeners, and their questions are relevant to the conversation.

Your Turn 8-2

ASKING GOOD QUESTIONS

For each of the following items, write a question that will elicit the response indicated. Then say whether the question is open-ended or closed-ended.

1. **Question:**

   _____

   Response: The jacket is black leather with a faux fur collar.
   Type of question: _____

2. **Question:**

   _____

   Response: I feel uncomfortable, because he tells me what to do instead of asking me to do something.
   Type of question: _____

3. **Question:**

   _____

   Response: I like the red one better._____
   Type of question: _____

4. **Question:**

   _____

   Response: First we decided what type of playground we wanted, then we made a plan, and finally we got people to help us build it.
   Type of question: _____

5. **Question:**

   _____

   Response: No, I don't like it.
   Type of question: _____

Listen for Meaning and Verbal Cues

We mentioned earlier that listeners can understand verbal messages far faster than speakers can say them. Rather than using the brain's down time for daydreaming, effective listeners use it to think about the meaning of what they hear.

As you listen to the speaker's words, use your critical thinking skills (see Chapter 3). Try to identify the ideas and facts and the relationships between them. Ask yourself, What is the most important thing being said? What facts or ideas support the main idea? Does one thing cause another? Is sequence or time involved? Does this represent a fact or an opinion? Thinking critically about the message will help you understand it and keep your attention focused on the communication.

In addition, thinking about the meaning of the speaker's message can give you cues about your own responses. For example, if you are being interviewed for a job, you should listen carefully to what the interviewer is saying. If the interviewer talks a lot about the company's reputation for high-quality service, you can describe your own commitment to high quality in some aspect of your life. If the interviewer asks an open-ended question, give a full response.

Listen between the Lines

Effective listening requires more than just paying attention to the words. An active listener also focuses on nonverbal cues. As we learned in Chapter 7, voice qualities, eye contact, facial expressions, and body

Your Turn 8-3

FACT OR OPINION?

Distinguishing between fact and opinion is important for effective listening. Indicate whether each of the following statements is a fact or an opinion.

1. You don't need reservations to eat dinner at that restaurant. _____

2. The food there is delicious. _____

3. The last time we had dinner there, the waiter spilled water all over the table. _____

4. I thought the chocolate sundae was too sweet. _____

5. The bill came to $32 without the tip. _____

There are no visual cues when you listen on the phone, and when you encounter a voice mail system, you can't even ask questions. Instead, you must rely on your ears to pick up the message.

"*When you talk, you repeat what you already know; when you listen, you often learn something.*"

JARED SPARKS (1789–1866),
historian and educator

language all contribute to the meaning of a message. By paying attention to the nonverbal aspects of communication, you can improve your ability to listen.

Most nonverbal communication cues are visual, so it's important for the listener to be able to see the speaker. You can get a sense of how sight contributes to effective listening by comparing the experiences of talking face to face and by phone. When you talk face to face, you can perceive the person's feelings and unstated messages by looking at the other person's face, eyes, and gestures. In contrast, when you listen on a phone, you rely on your ears to pick up both the words and the voice cues. Your ability to detect the unstated message is reduced, because you cannot see the speaker. When you communicate by e-mail, texting, or instant messaging, you lose both sight and voice cues and depend entirely on words and symbols for meaning.

Take Notes

Another way to ensure that you listen actively is to take notes. Taking notes forces you to pay attention to the message and decide what's important enough to write down. As we discussed in Chapter 4, taking and reviewing notes also helps you remember what you hear.

Although you may be used to taking notes in class, there are other situations in which note taking is a good way to ensure effective listening. When you are listening to directions, for example, it's helpful to write them down. When you are doing business on the phone, take notes about the details. That way you'll be sure to get the message accurately and completely.

Tech Tips

USING IPODS AND MP3 PLAYERS TO STUDY AND LEARN

Apple's iPod and other MP3 portable media players started out as entertainment-only devices. But now you can study and learn on the go by downloading education-related podcasts (digital media files) onto your iPod, MP3 player, or computer. Podcasts are being used by many college students and instructors as study aids. If you favor the auditory style of learning, this technology may be particularly effective for you (see Chapter 4, page 88). If you favor the visual learning style, an iPod or MP3 player with a video display may be a more useful study aid.

But no matter your preferred learning style, you are likely to find something helpful in the wide variety of study material that can be downloaded from the Internet to an iPod, MP3 player, or computer:

- Audio study guides for popular college courses like psychology and business and for frequently assigned works of literature like Shakespeare's plays

- Test preparation materials for exams like the SAT

- Audio books so you can listen to reading assignments

- Self-guided tours of historic sites, architecture, or art

- Foreign language instruction and practice, including English as a second language

This student looks like she's listening to music, but she's actually studying on the way to class.

In addition to these commercial offerings available on Apple's iTunes and other Web sites, individual colleges and instructors are making their own podcasts for student use. For example, some instructors record all their lectures and class sessions and post them on the Internet as podcasts that students can download. If you missed a class or simply want to hear parts of it again, you can do so at your own convenience.

At some schools, the use of iPods is required in certain courses. The college lends an iPod to each student registered for the course. During the term, the student uses the iPod to download lectures and other audiovisual material. Instead of writing a paper for the course, the student may produce a podcast to share with the class. At the end of the term, the student returns the iPod.

Some colleges and universities have even partnered with Apple and created their own sections on the iTunes U Web site. There students and others can download podcasts that range from campus tours to academic course content to student life.

Your Turn 8-4

USING PODCASTS

Search your college's Web site, Itunes U (at www.iTunes.com) or the Internet for free podcasts. (Universities, radio stations, and cable and broadcast network sites are good sources of podcasts.) If you have the technology to do so, download a podcast and listen to it.

1. What types of podcasts did you find during your search?

   _____

   _____

2. How would you use a digital media player and/or podcasts in your own studies?

   _____

   _____

3. How could using podcasts improve your listening skill?

   _____

   _____

WHATEVER IT TAKES
Chan Ho Yun

(© Courtesy of Tannery Hill Studios)

When Kika Keith looked for music lessons for her daughter, she found that Colburn, a famous performing arts school in downtown Los Angeles, was too far away from her neighborhood. Private violin lessons there were too expensive as well. But she also found Chan Ho Yun at Colburn. Yun, who was born in Korea and has lived in Australia as well as the United States, is a violinist and teacher there. He offered Keith a deal. If Keith would find space in her neighborhood and more kids to take lessons, he would teach them free of charge.

So began Sweet Strings, a classical music program for the kids of South Central Los Angeles. For Keith, the way Sweet Strings took off was a complete surprise. South Central, better known for its rap fans, turned out to have a lot of classical music lovers, too. When word of free violin lessons got around the neighborhood, people flocked to join the program. The first class had 25 children and no instruments. A year later, there were 60 students and 50 donated violins. Soon the program was giving free violin, viola, cello, and bass lessons to over 100 African American, Latino, and Asian kids, with a waiting list of more than 300.

As the children learn music, the community has also benefited in other ways. Yun required that parents accompany their children to lessons. So parents learned to read music, too. In addition, they got to know their neighbors. People of different backgrounds found that stereotypes were breaking down and friendships were forming because of the shared interest in children and music. Says Yun, "No matter where we come from or what color we are, the only color I recognize is the color of the sound of the music we make."

Sources: Amy Reeves, "Sweet Strings in South Central L.A.," *Strings*, January 2001, No. 91 <http://www.stringsmagazine.com/issues/strings91/Newsprof.shtml>, accessed February 28, 2003; Christina Cheakalos and Caren Grigsby Bates, "Strings of His Heart," *People*, March 19, 2001, pp. 69–70; "Chan Ho Yun, Violin Teacher and Performer, Co-founder, Sweet Strings" <http:// www.digitalheroes. org/dhc/bios/bio_yun.html>, accessed February 28, 2003; "Chan Ho Yun," 2008 Idyllwild Arts Summer Programm, <http://www.artegemini. com/iamffaculty.htm#Chan%20Ho%20Yun>, accessed April 19, 2008.

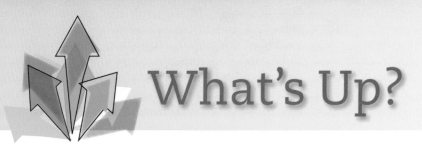

What's Up?

Name _____   Date_____

1. What is the difference between hearing and listening?
   _____
   _____

2. Why is effective listening so hard?
   _____
   _____

3. Why is it easy to daydream while listening?
   _____
   _____

4. What is the difference between passive and active listening?
   _____
   _____

5. Describe two things you can do to make sure you are physically prepared to listen.
   _____
   _____

6. Why it is important to listen in an open, nonjudging way?
   _____
   _____

7. What is an open-ended question? Give an example.
   _____
   _____

8. What is a closed-ended question? Give an example.
   _____
   _____

9. When you are listening, your brain has down time. What should you use this down time for?
   _____
   _____

10. How do nonverbal cues help the listener understand the message?
    _____
    _____

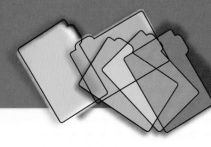

Case Studies

The Case of the Absent-Minded Employee

Julio was the night manager at a fast food restaurant. Each night, he gave instructions to the staff about what needed to be done. One of the employees, Rick, was always interrupting, chatting about other topics, and daydreaming. He made a lot of mistakes, and he had to be told what to do again and again.

1. Why does Rick make so many mistakes at work?

_____

_____

_____

_____

2. What might Julio do to get Rick to listen attentively?

_____

_____

_____

_____

The Case of the Mistaken Messages

Jill had just started a part-time job as a receptionist for a medical office. Part of her job was to answer the phone, make appointments, and take messages for the doctors and nurses. The phone was constantly ringing, people told her messages to pass on, and she had to make appointments and greet visitors, too. Jill had a good memory, and she usually remembered to tell the doctors and nurses about their calls. But at the end of the first week, a couple of doctors complained that they weren't getting all their messages. Some of the messages they did get were wrong.

1. What is wrong with Jill's approach to taking phone messages?

_____

_____

_____

_____

2. What can Jill do to improve her listening skill and make sure she is passing messages on correctly?

_____

_____

_____

_____

 Journal

Answer the following journal questions.

1. What barriers to listening interfere with your ability to listen effectively? How can you overcome these barriers?

_____
_____
_____
_____
_____
_____
_____

2. In what situations do you find yourself not paying attention to a speaker? How can you be more open to hearing the messages of others?

_____
_____
_____
_____
_____
_____
_____

3. What role does listening play in your life at home? At school? At work? In which situation is your listening most effective? Why?

_____
_____
_____
_____
_____
_____
_____

4. If you improved your listening skill at school, how would this benefit you?

_____
_____
_____
_____
_____
_____

Listening is learned.

Improving Your Speaking Skills

It's considered an honor to deliver a commencement speech. Preparation and rehearsal helped this graduate's address go well.

From the time you get up in the morning until you go to sleep at night, you use your voice to communicate. At home, you converse with your family about the events of the day. With your friends, you talk about whatever concerns you. You use your phone to speak about business and personal matters. At school, you ask and answer questions in class and talk with other students. At work, you give directions, explain things, ask and answer questions, participate in meetings, and talk with customers and coworkers. You may occasionally give oral presentations at school or work.

Since talking is the basic form of human communication, you are judged to a great extent by your ability to speak. People recognize you by your speech. The words you choose, your gestures, the expressions on your face, the sound of your voice, and the way you pronounce words add up to an instantly recognizable person. The way you speak is an expression of your personality. In this chapter, you will:

- discover the importance of first impressions;
- compare standard and nonstandard forms of English;
- learn that your voice qualities and how you say things have a great impact on the people around you;
- practice techniques for effective face-to-face conversations; and
- improve your ability to speak to groups, both informally and formally.

Finally, you will learn about the many hidden features of cell phones, as well as etiquette tips for their use.

FIGURE 9–1

Your appearance and voice have far more impact on your listeners than what you actually say.

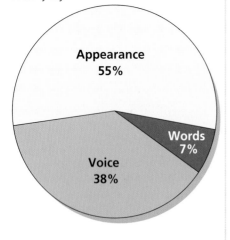

First Impressions

Speaking is not limited to the words you say. In addition to the words of your message, listeners perceive the way you look and the way you sound. In studies of face-to-face communication, Dr. Albert Mehrabian has found that a speaker's appearance and voice has a far greater impact than his or her words (see Figure 9–1). In fact, because listeners see you before they hear you, your appearance has a great effect on your ability to get your message across. You have 7 to 10 seconds to make a good first impression!

If people's visual impression of you is poor, they are less likely to listen to what you have to say. Most people are put off by bad posture, lack of cleanliness, and sloppiness. Good posture, hygiene, and grooming are essential to forming a favorable first impression.

Also important in creating a good first impression is the way you dress. In recent years, dress standards have changed considerably. It's no longer possible to prescribe appropriate dress for every situation. Rather, you should think of your listeners. If their opinions are important to you, then you should dress in a way that is acceptable to them. So ask yourself: On what basis will my listeners judge the way I dress? Do I want to wear a navy blue suit or casual clothes? Should I look conservative or fashionable? Whatever type of clothing you decide on, it should be clean and neat. Your clothes should not distract your listeners from your message.

Speech Qualities

Once your listeners have gotten a first impression of you from your appearance, they get their second impression from your speech. Forgetting for a moment the specific words of your message, what do you want to communicate with your speech? Most people want to be perceived as attractive, smart, and competent. To be perceived this way, you must speak well. In business and academic situations, that means using standard American English. It also means controlling the qualities of your voice—volume, pitch, rate, and tone. You must pronounce words accurately; enunciate, or speak clearly; and use correct grammar and appropriate vocabulary.

Spoken American English

In the United States, there are four basic varieties of spoken American English: standard English, dialects, accented English, and substandard English.

- **Standard English** is the English spoken by national news broadcasters, actors, and others.

National news broadcasters are trained to speak standard English. Many people learn standard English by listening to them on TV.

- **Dialects** are variations of American English that are spoken in particular areas or by particular social groups. The most familiar regional dialects are those of the South, New York City, Boston, and the Midwest. Black English, a dialect spoken by many African Americans, is found in all regions of the United States. It is sometimes called African American English or Ebonics.
- **Accented English** is spoken by the many Americans for whom English is a second language.
- **Substandard English** is English spoken with poor pronunciation, enunciation, grammar, and vocabulary.

Largely through the influence of television, standard English is understood easily throughout the United States. It has therefore become the norm against which people's public speech is judged. In business, academic, and other public speaking situations, you should aim to speak standard English, no matter what variety of English (or other language) you speak with your friends and family. Since the purpose of speaking is to communicate, it makes sense to communicate in language that people from all social groups and regions of the country understand.

So if you are trying to improve your speech, you should be imitating the standard English you hear on national news broadcasts. As you practice improving various aspects of your speech, try to record your voice so you can hear what you sound like.

Your Turn 9-1

EXPLORING SPOKEN ENGLISH

There are many Web sites related to spoken English. Choose one of the following sites and explore its offerings and links to other resources. Then write a paragraph about what you found.

- **The Columbia Guide to Standard American English** is a reference work available on Bartleby.com <http://bartleby.com>. (On the home page, choose "American English" in the drop-down References menu.) You can check the meaning, pronunciation, and usage of words and phrases in standard American English as well as American dialects.
- **The Language Samples Project** at the University of Arizona maintains a site, called "Varieties of English," containing information about and samples of American dialects, including Black English, <http://www.ic.arizona.edu/~lsp/index.html>.
- **Dave's ESL Café on the Web** is a comprehensive site of interest to speakers of English as a second language. Their search engine provides links to ESL resources on the Internet, including speaking skills resources <http://www.eslcafe.com>.

Volume

The **volume** of your voice refers to its intensity or loudness. In most situations, a moderate volume is appropriate for standard English and will enable listeners to hear you. Of course, if you are addressing a large group, you will have to raise the volume of your voice or use a microphone. In addition, a good speaker uses changes in volume to emphasize parts of the message.

If you are having trouble speaking loudly enough, you should practice breathing properly. If you take quick, shallow breaths, your lungs do not have enough air to produce sounds loud enough to be heard easily. Instead, you should breathe deeply and control your breath as singers and actors do.

Pitch

Pitch refers to the level of sound on a musical scale. People who speak with a high-pitched voice sound shrill and unpleasant. On the other hand, people whose voices are pitched too low can be hard to hear. And people whose pitch never varies speak in a monotone, which is boring for listeners. A moderate pitch with variations is best for standard English.

Pitch carries different meanings in standard English and regional dialects. For example, when you ask a question in standard English, the pitch of your voice rises toward the end of the sentence. The rising pitch at the end of the sentence conveys a question, doubt, or hesitation. Since a rising pitch at the end of a sentence means uncertainty in standard English, many Northerners are confused when they listen to people speaking a Southern dialect. Southerners have a slight rise in pitch at the ends of most sentences. This rise doesn't mean uncertainty; rather it's meant to convey courtesy, a meaning that's lost on the Northerners. You can see from this small example that using standard English can prevent the miscommunication that results when dialect differences are not understood.

Rate

Standard English is spoken at a moderate rate. Indeed, because of the long vowel sounds in English, it's hard to speak the language very fast. As with pitch, there are regional differences in the rate of speech. Northerners tend to speak faster than Southerners, and people from the Northeast speak faster than those from the Midwest.

To avoid sounding boring, you can vary the rate of your speech. You can slow down to emphasize important facts or ideas or to accommodate a listener who can't keep up with you. You can also pause to emphasize major points. A moment of silence has the power to refocus your listener's attention. Avoid filling your pauses with sounds like "um" and "uh." These fillers are distracting to your listeners.

> "Words mean more than what is set down on paper. It takes the human voice to infuse them with shades of deeper meaning."
>
> MAYA ANGELOU, poet and writer

Tone

As you know, **tone** of voice reveals the speaker's feelings and attitudes. A voice can be depressed, cheerful, angry, or neutral. Because tone of voice is so revealing, you should be aware of what you sound like. Sometimes it's appropriate to convey your emotions through the tone of your voice. For example, you may want to communicate your happiness that your friend is getting married. At other times you may want to change your tone to avoid communicating a feeling you would rather hide. You may wish to sound neutral rather than angry, for instance, when you are disagreeing with your boss.

Enunciation

Enunciation refers to the clarity with which you say words. Saying "didja" for "did you" or "talkin'" for "talking" are examples of poor enunciation. Poor enunciation is the result of leaving out sounds, adding sounds, and running sounds together. Poor enunciation in standard English may be the result of speaking a regional dialect.

Commonly left out sounds are the final *t, g,* and *d* when they follow another consonant. For example, many people say "stric" rather than "strict," "goin" rather than "going," and "pon" rather than "pond." Some vowels are frequently swallowed as well. When two vowel sounds occur together, one is often lost. For example, many people say "pome" rather than "poem" and "crule" rather than "cruel." Sometimes entire syllables are lost, as in "praps" for "perhaps" and "lil" for "little."

Another type of poor enunciation is the addition of unnecessary sounds. "Umberella" for "umbrella," "disasterous" for "disastrous," and "exshtra" for "extra" are some examples.

Finally, slurring words—saying them indistinctly and running them together—makes you difficult to understand. "C'mere, I wancha t'gimmee a hand" is an example of slurred speech. Unless you enunciate clearly, your listeners may pay more attention to decoding your speech than to interpreting its meaning.

Most speech pathologists work with children who have speech problems. However, some of them help people improve their accents, learn new dialects, and change their speech patterns.

Pronunciation

Pronunciation is closely related to enunciation. Whereas enunciation refers to the clarity with which you say words, **pronunciation** refers to the correctness with which you say words. A person who says "Febyuary" instead of "February" or stresses the wrong syllable in "harassment" is mispronouncing words. Many pronunciation errors in English arise from the quirks of spelling. The *t* in "often," for example, is not pronounced. The letters *ea* sound different in "break" and "beak." In addition, some

TABLE 9–1	Commonly Mispronounced Words		
Incorrect	**Correct**	**Incorrect**	**Correct**
omost	almost	liberry	library
irrevelant	irrelevant	fas*t*en	fas(t)en
probly	probably	nucular	nuclear
akst	asked	idear	idea
oways	always	sophmore	sophomore
famly	family	drownded	drowned
mischievious	mischievous	burgular	burglar
corps	cor(ps)	often	of(t)en
'po-lice	po-' lice	'di-rect	di-'rect
jest	just	preventative	preventive

words have more than one acceptable pronunciation. When in doubt about the pronunciation of a word, look it up in the dictionary. Generally, the preferred pronunciation is listed first. Table 9–1 shows some commonly mispronounced words.

Grammar and Vocabulary

You may enunciate clearly and pronounce words correctly, but if you've chosen the wrong words or put them together incorrectly, you will not be considered a good communicator. A good vocabulary allows you to present your thoughts with precision. You don't need to use fancy words, just have a wide enough vocabulary to express yourself clearly.

Good grammar is also essential. However, the rules of grammar are not necessarily the same in a dialect as in standard English. For example, "He runnin" is a grammatical Black English sentence, but the same sentence in grammatical standard English would be "He is running." If you are used to speaking a dialect informally, pay closer attention to the rules of grammar when speaking standard English. Justly or not, people who constantly make grammatical errors when speaking standard English are considered poorly educated and unprofessional. If you think your grammar could use improvement, try reading more. By reading you will absorb many of the rules of standard English grammar. If you think you need more help than that, you can enroll in a course at your school or an adult education center.

Effective Conversations

An attractive appearance and good speech contribute to your effectiveness as a communicator, but they are not enough to ensure good communication. In face-to-face communication, it's important to think as much of the person with whom you are conversing as you do about

Your Turn 9-2

RATE YOUR SPEECH QUALITIES

Answer the following questions to evaluate your speech qualities. You may have to ask a friend to help you if you're not sure how you sound.

		Yes	No
1.	I usually speak standard English.	☐	☐
2.	I speak at a moderate volume, neither too loud nor too soft.	☐	☐
3.	I speak at a moderate pitch and vary the pitch to convey different meanings.	☐	☐
4.	I speak at a moderate rate, neither too fast nor too slow.	☐	☐
5.	I use pauses to emphasize major points.	☐	☐
6.	I control the tone of my voice in order to better communicate my messages.	☐	☐
7.	I usually enunciate clearly and distinctly.	☐	☐
8.	When I'm not sure of the pronunciation of a word, I look it up in a dictionary.	☐	☐
9.	I use a wide range of words when speaking.	☐	☐
10.	When I speak, I use correct grammar.	☐	☐

A *no* answer to any of these questions indicates that you can improve your speech.

yourself and your message. So in addition to knowing what you want to communicate, you must make others feel comfortable by establishing a positive atmosphere, using appropriate body language, listening, letting others speak, and mirroring their speech.

Know What You Want to Say

If a conversation has a purpose other than social chitchat, you should be mentally prepared for it. That means you know beforehand what message you want to communicate. You have decided what points you need to cover and what your approach will be. When you are mentally prepared, instead of floundering, you will be able to direct the conversation where you want it to go.

Know What You Don't Want to Say

There's another side to knowing what you want to say, and that's knowing what you *don't* want to say. It's important to respect confidences and to

"*A rumor goes in one ear and out many mouths.*"

Chinese proverb

News & Views

WANTED: BILINGUAL WORKERS

"What is an extra language worth?" That question is being asked all over the country by workers who are bilingual. As Americans do more business with non-English speakers, both here and overseas, the demand for employees who can speak more than one language is rising. Bilingual workers are needed in marketing, finance, health care, technology, social work, teaching, public safety, and administrative jobs.

Steffi Jones is the president of the organizing committee for the 2011 Women's World Cup in soccer. Formerly an international "football" player, Jones has found that her bilingual English-German skills are a big plus in her new job.

In some places, the need for extra languages is so great that local governments have mandated the hiring of bilingual workers. For example, the city of Oakland, California, requires that bilingual workers be hired, whenever possible, for positions involving contact with the public. Candidates who are bilingual in Spanish, Chinese, or Vietnamese are sought for positions including police officer, firefighter, sanitation worker, and recreation worker. In 2007, the city hired 295 new workers in jobs that involve dealing with the public, and almost half of them were bilingual.

But are bilingual employees paid more for their language skills? Some bilingual employees are paid more, especially those with higher-level jobs. Bilingual financial analysts, merchant bankers, stockbrokers, and middle- and upper-level managers are often paid extra for their relevant language skills. For lower-level jobs, the situation varies considerably, although the trend is toward extra pay. For example, Oakland, California, and Lubbock, Texas, pay some bilingual workers extra if their language skills are critical to job performance.

Whether bilingual employees are paid more also depends on the regional job market. For example, in Miami and south Florida, so many people speak both English and Spanish that companies don't need to pay extra to attract bilingual employees.

Even if there is no bonus pay, being bilingual in today's job market is a plus for applicants. Many employers want to hire employees who are bilingual and bicultural as well, meaning that they understand the language, customs, and traditions of immigrant and international customers. A survey conducted by Hispanic Times Enterprises revealed that, when two people with equal qualifications apply for a job and one of them is bilingual, most companies will hire the bilingual applicant.

If you are bilingual and want to use your language skills, the Internet will make your job search easier. In addition to checking general-purpose jobs sites, you can check job sites that specialize in placing bilingual applicants. There are also job fairs that specialize in career opportunities for bilingual workers.

Sources: City of Oakland, "Revised Follow-Up Status Report on the Implementation of the Equal Access Ordinance for Fiscal Year 2006-2007," Sept. 11, 2007, <http://clerkwebsvr1.oaklandnet.com/attachments/17245.pdf>, accessed April 22, 2008; Rich Heinz, "Employers Eager to Buy Lingual Skills," *California Job Journal,* September 2, 2001 <http://www.jobjournal.com/ article_printer.asp?artid=333>, accessed March 4, 2003; Kendall King and Alison Mackey, *The Bilingual Edge.* New York: Collins, 2007.

Friends can achieve greater rapport when they treat one another as equals.

be discreet and tactful. Communicating private matters to people who are not directly concerned will eventually result in your being perceived as untrustworthy and rude. To avoid this, make sure you keep confidences and speak to others with tact and discretion.

Establish a Positive Atmosphere

The environment of a conversation has a great effect on the quality of the communication that takes place. No one would expect to have a mutually satisfying conversation, for example, in a brightly lit police interrogation room. Sitting behind a large desk or in an imposing chair or standing over the person with whom you're conversing sends a similar message: You are in control. Any setup that makes the speaker appear dominant has the effect of stifling the free flow of communication.

So if you want to converse openly and honestly with someone, be sure that the environment contributes to a relaxed atmosphere. Make sure there are no physical barriers between you and your listener. Move out from behind a table or desk, sit if the listener is sitting, and move the furniture to get comfortable seating if necessary.

Use Body Language

You are already aware of how much facial expressions, eye contact, posture, and gestures can communicate. When you speak, try to use the vocabulary of body language to add to the meaning of your verbal message. Smiling, looking people in the eye, holding yourself tall but relaxed, and gesturing for emphasis will help hold the attention of your listeners. On the other hand, do not exaggerate your use of body language, because that is distracting. It's also important to control any mannerisms you may have, such as biting the end of a pen or playing with objects in your hands.

Listen

Nothing conveys your interest in the other person as much as listening carefully to what he or she has to say. Your success as a speaker is dependent on your effectiveness as a listener. Only if you listen carefully will you get feedback to your message. And good feedback is necessary to keep a conversation effective. Listening is so important that we devoted a whole chapter to it. If you need to brush up on your listening techniques, review Chapter 8.

Let Others Talk

A conversation is a dialogue, not a monologue. If you monopolize the conversation, you will find that effective communication is not taking

> "Bore: one who has the power of speech but not the capacity for conversation."
>
> BENJAMIN DISRAELI (1804–1881), British statesman

> "Silent? Ah, he is silent! He can keep silence well. That man's silence is wonderful to listen to."
>
> THOMAS HARDY (1840–1928), English novelist

place. Part of being a good speaker is knowing when to let the other person talk. Be attentive to your listener so you will know when he or she wants to say something. Then be silent and listen.

Mirror the Speech of Others

As you recall, people are most comfortable communicating with those who are like themselves. Part of establishing rapport with another person is to mirror aspects of their communication style (see Chapter 7). When you have a conversation, you can mirror the speech of the other person. You can match the pace, pitch, tone, or volume of others' speech, the words they use, and their body language. Mirroring aspects of the other person's communication style will help the person relax and be more open with you.

In addition to reacting to the other person's communication style, you can affect that style by your actions. For example, suppose you are talking to someone who speaks very slowly. You can try to speed him up by mirroring his pace, then gradually speaking faster. Without even being aware of it, he will speed up a bit to match *you*. If you want someone to relax, make sure your own posture is relaxed, your voice is calm, and your facial expression interested and pleasant. Changing aspects of other people's communication style by getting them to mirror you is called leading.

Speaking to Groups

Many people are perfectly comfortable speaking to one person but find speaking to groups very difficult. Yet since so many of our activities are accomplished in groups—social, educational, and business—it's important to learn to speak well in group situations. Most of the time you will find yourself speaking informally as you participate in a group activity. Occasionally, you may be asked to make a formal presentation to a group.

Speaking Informally in a Group

Whether it's a class, club, committee, or meeting of coworkers, the chances are that at least once a day you will find yourself communicating in a group. People who are good at speaking in groups have a great deal of influence over the actions of the group. Good speakers are generally well prepared, assertive, and courteous.

Be Prepared Preparation is the first prerequisite of effective participation in groups. You cannot speak well unless you know something about the topic under discussion. To prepare for classroom

(© Andrea Gingerich/istockphoto.com)

People who work in teams spend a lot of time speaking informally in a group.

Your Turn 9-3

CAN YOU IMPROVE THIS CONVERSATION?

For each of the following scenarios, make a suggestion that will improve the quality of the conversation.

1. Carl went to his instructor's office to discuss his term project. They sat together and Carl outlined his ideas. As Carl got more involved in the details of the project, the instructor stood up and began to pace.

   _____

   _____

   _____

2. Kiyoko and Tamara ran into one another in the cafeteria and sat down to eat together. They had just met in their English class the previous week. Tamara chatted on about this and that, never running out of things to say. By the end of the meal, Kiyoko was bored and restless. She had barely gotten a word in.

   _____

   _____

   _____

3. Jessica was a bit upset about work when she ran into a coworker, Carlos. She told Carlos about the problem. Carlos tried to offer some suggestions, but Jessica didn't seem to hear them. She went right on with her own thoughts.

   _____

   _____

   _____

discussions, you should keep up with the assigned readings. To prepare for other types of group discussions, you must keep abreast of the subjects that are likely to come up by paying attention to the news and reading trade or professional publications.

Before some meetings, the person leading the meeting distributes an **agenda**, a list of topics to be discussed. If you have an agenda, study it before the meeting and learn more about things with which you are unfamiliar. If you don't have an agenda, try to find out before the meeting what subjects are to be covered.

Be Assertive   You may be thoroughly prepared, but unless you speak up you will not contribute to a group's efforts. Speaking up in a group requires **assertiveness**, the self-belief and determination to make your opinions heard. To be assertive, you must believe that you have something

Bobby Jindal

To say that Bobby Jindal's career has been on a fast track is an understatement. At 24, he was appointed to head Louisiana's Department of Health and Hospitals. At 26, he served on a national commission about Medicare. At 27, he became the president of the University of Louisiana. At 29, he became a U.S. secretary of health and human services.

(© Tim Mueller/AP Photo)

Finally, at age 32, Jindal suffered his first real professional setback—he ran for governor of Louisiana as the Republican candidate and was defeated. But after a stint representing Louisiana in the U.S. Congress, a 36-year-old Jindal ran for governor again—and won. In 2008, Jindal became the nation's youngest governor, and its only Indian-American governor.

Just who is Bobby Jindal? Jindal was born in Baton Rouge, Louisiana, in 1971, to parents who immigrated from India. At age 4, he stopped using his given name, Priyush, and adopted the name "Bobby" after a character on the TV show *The Brady Bunch*. He graduated from Baton Rouge High School and Brown University, where he converted to Catholicism. After earning a master's degree as a Rhodes Scholar in England, he returned to Louisiana. His academic background in healthcare administration caught the eye of the state's governor, who appointed him to his first government post.

Jindal's success in politics has surprised many people who thought his ethnic background would be a disadvantage at the polls. Jindal himself treats his ethnic background as a plus, but does not emphasize it. In government documents he leaves the line for "race" blank. He says, "America is the greatest....Here anyone can succeed."

Jindal has a lot of plans for Louisiana, which is still trying to recover from Hurricane Katrina and the flooding of New Orleans. In his inaugural speech, Jindal declared, "Under the spotlight of the world, with generosity from many and a clear call to common purpose...we have the opportunity to make lasting and positive change." To watch a video of his speech, go to the American Rhetoric Web site, <www.americanrhetoric.com>.

Sources: John Fund, "Bayou Boy Wonder," *Wall Street Journal,* October 22, 2007; John Fund, "Bobby Jindal's Rise," *Wall Street Journal,* October 9, 2003; Piyush "Bobby" Jindal, "Louisiana Gubernatorial Election Victory Speech," <http://www.americanrhetoric. com/speeches/bobbyjindallouisianagovvictory. htm>, accessed April 25, 2008; Roopa Nemi and Amala Nath, "South Asian Americans in U.S. Politics," *The Modern American,* Spring 2005, p. 16, <http://www.wcl.american.edu/ modernamerican/01/1rnemi.pdf>, accessed April 24, 2008; "About Bobby Jindal," <http:// bobbyjindal.com> accessed Feb. 4, 2009.

worth saying. You must have confidence in your own ability to contribute to the group.

Being assertive also means you must achieve a balance between your own right to be heard and the rights of others to express themselves. A good communicator speaks up but also yields the floor to someone else who wants to speak. Being assertive does *not* mean that you monopolize the discussion.

Be Courteous   There are often as many opinions as there are people in a group. So it is important, when you express an opinion, to speak tactfully. Even when you think someone else is wrong, you should acknowledge others' right to their opinions before you express your own ideas.

When you speak in a group, respect the rights of others. That means that you must not interrupt, fidget, daydream, or carry on side conversations. You should listen carefully to what others say and express yourself firmly but politely.

Making a Presentation

When you make a presentation, you are the featured speaker and your listeners are your audience. People who are normally relaxed and open when communicating may experience great anxiety when making an oral presentation. Fearful of making mistakes, they appear rigid and wooden. A person who makes effective presentations, however, has learned to project the same personality on stage as in one-to-one conversations.

It's normal to feel anxious about making presentations. However, you can minimize your anxiety by following several basic suggestions for making a good presentation. You can prepare your presentation in advance, relate to your audience, and be yourself.

Prepare Your Presentation   The most effective speakers are prepared. No matter what the subject or the audience, effective presenters have planned their presentations in advance. They know what information they want to communicate and how they will deliver it. Effective presenters follow these basic steps when preparing presentations.[2]

A good presenter is well prepared, makes the message meaningful for the audience, and communicates some of his or her own personality.

- **Think about the audience and the setting.** Is the audience young or old, experienced or inexperienced, male or female? Is the setting formal or informal? The answers to these questions will help you tailor your presentation.

- **Outline your message.** Think about your objective and include only information that supports your objective. Remember, people can't absorb too much information at once, so keep the presentation simple. Three or fewer main points are usually enough.

Your Turn 9-4

Spend a day keeping track of the number of groups you interact with and the number of times, if any, you speak in each group situation. You can record this information in the chart following.

Description of Group   **Number of Times You Spoke**

_____

_____

_____

_____

_____

Once you've recorded a day's participation in groups, answer the following questions:

1. Did you speak in each group of which you were a part?

_____

_____

_____

If not, why not?

_____

_____

_____

2. Did you find it easier to speak up in some groups than in others?

_____

_____

_____

If yes, why?

_____

_____

_____

- **Prepare supporting materials.** You can reinforce the impact of your message by preparing audio or visual material that supports your message. Presentation software packages like Powerpoint make it easy to produce and present professional-quality supporting materials.
- **Rehearse.** Run through your presentation a few times. Then find an audience, even if it's only one person. Give your presentation and ask for feedback.

Relate to Your Audience   Presenters who rely primarily on the weight of facts and figures to engage their audiences usually fail. That's because people relate to speakers who relate to them. A good speaker gives a presentation that is relevant and meaningful to the audience, in terms of both its message and how the message is delivered.

If you have considered your audience and setting before you prepare your presentation, the chances are your message will be meaningful to your listeners. For example, suppose you are giving a talk on one of your company's new products. Is your audience made up of your coworkers or your customers? Your presentation will be very different to each of these audiences.

Your presentation will also be more effective if you can relate to your audience in the way you deliver your message. Address yourself to the audience. Talk *to* them rather than *at* them. Get them to participate by asking questions, recalling well-known events or people, and having them use their imaginations. If the group is small, the audience can actively participate. If the group is large, you can persuade them as they participate silently.

Be Yourself   Truly effective presenters take these suggestions one step further by communicating something of themselves as individuals. They take off the formal mask and let people see the real person beneath. To be an effective presenter, you must be willing to be open and disclose parts of yourself to the audience.

GETTING THE MOST OUT OF YOUR CELL PHONE

Almost everyone has a cell phone these days, from kids in middle school to senior citizens. Cell phones are handy for conversations and text messaging as well as for other tasks. They have given rise a whole new set of etiquette do's and don'ts.

Cell Phone Functions

Most people use their phones to talk, to text, and perhaps to take pictures, but did you know there were many other uses for an ordinary cell phone? (You don't need a smartphone to perform these functions.) Here are a some other uses:

- **Emergency help.** The emergency number for cell phones is 112. You can call this number even if you are outside your network and even if the phone is locked.

- **Remote car key.** If you lock your key inside the car, use a cell phone to call the person who has your spare key. You must call him on his cell, not a land line. Ask him to press the "unlock" button on the spare key into his cell phone while you hold your phone within a foot of the car door. The signal should unlock the door. This doesn't work with all phones, but it's worth a try.

- **Alarm clock.** Use the alarm clock feature to wake yourself or just to keep track of the time.

- **Calendar.** Use the calendar as a time management tool (see Chapter 2). You can enter appointments, deadlines, and exam dates.

- **Calculator.** Use the calculator to figure out tips, add up how much you're spending in a store, and so on.

- **Portable phone book.** You can store all your contact information in the phone.

- **Three-way communication.** If your phone has three-way calling, you can call one person, establish the connection, then call another person for a conference call.

- **Call forwarding.** You can set your calls to be forwarded to your land line or another number. This feature is especially handy if you've used up your minutes.

- **Internet search via text message.** Even if you do not have a smartphone, you can do a limited Google search via text message. Enter your key words or search question, and send it to GOOGLE (46645). You'll get a text message back.

(© Martin Diebel/fStop/Getty Images)

Cell Phone Etiquette

The cell phone functions that annoy other people when you use your phone in public are the ones that involve sound, like the ringer and talking. It makes sense to use a cell phone in public places without disturbing others. Here are some suggestions:

- Don't set your ringer to a loud or annoying tune.

- Never take or make a personal call or text message in class or during a business meeting, including interviews. If you are expecting an *emergency* call, set the ringer to vibrate and excuse yourself to answer the phone.

- Don't talk on a cell phone in classrooms, lecture halls, elevators, libraries, museums, restaurants, theaters, waiting rooms, places of worship, buses, trains, or other indoor public spaces.

- Don't talk on the phone while conducting personal business, such as banking.

- If you must use your phone in public, make your conversation brief or use texting instead.

Your Turn 9-5

USING A CELL PHONE

1. If you still have your cell phone's instruction booklet, check to see what functions your phone offers. (If you don't have the manual, scroll through the phone's menus to explore its features, or log on to the manufacturer's Web site to locate instructions.) List five things your phone can do and how you would use each function:

_____

_____

_____

_____

_____

2. How should cell phones be used on campus? Make a list of "Campus Cell Phone Rules."

_____

_____

_____

_____

What's Up?

Name _____   Date_____

1. On what basis are people's first impressions of you formed?

   _____
   _____
   _____
   _____

2. Define the following terms:

   Standard English: _____

   _____

   Dialect: _____

   _____

   Accented English: _____

   _____

   Substandard English: _____

   _____

3. Why do people switch from dialects to standard English when they are speaking in public?

   _____
   _____
   _____
   _____

4. What does your tone of voice communicate?

   _____
   _____
   _____
   _____

5. What is enunciation?

   _____
   _____
   _____
   _____

continues

Name _____   Date_____

6. What is pronunciation?

_____

_____

_____

_____

7. What are the essentials of effective conversation?

_____

_____

_____

_____

8. How can you improve rapport with another person while conversing?

_____

_____

_____

_____

9. Why is it important to be assertive when speaking in groups?

_____

_____

_____

_____

10. List the four basic steps of preparing a presentation.

_____

_____

_____

_____

Case Studies

The Case of the Clashing Speakers

Brenda, who lived in Boston, had a part-time job as a telemarketer, selling over the phone to people in New England. She was good at her job, and some evenings she made as much as $17 an hour in commissions. When her firm got a major new client in Georgia, she started calling potential customers in the Southeast. Within two weeks, her average hourly rate had dropped to $9.

1. What speech qualities may have contributed to Brenda's success in selling to customers in the Northeast?

_____

_____

_____

2. Why might Brenda have trouble selling to southern customers?

_____

_____

_____

3. How can Brenda improve her ability to sell to Southerners?

_____

_____

The Case of the Interrupted Job Interview

Tyson dressed in his only suit for a job interview with a recruiter from a large consumer goods corporation. A college senior, Tyson was anxious to have a job lined up by the time he graduated. During the interview, the recruiter asked him what he would like to be doing in five years. In the middle of his response, Tyson's cell phone rang. He said, "Excuse me" to the recruiter and took the call.

1. What did Tyson do wrong during his interview?

_____

_____

_____

2. After the interview, Tyson never heard from the company again. What should he do in the future to improve the impression he makes at job interviews?

_____

_____

_____

Journal

Answer the following journal questions.

1. If you could hire a dialect or speech coach, what aspect of your speech would you change or improve? How would this change in speech benefit you?

_____

_____

_____

_____

_____

_____

2. Describe someone you know who is a good conversationalist. What makes this person so skillful?

_____

_____

_____

_____

_____

_____

3. What role does the telephone play in your life? If you use a cell phone, how does it affect your behavior?

_____

_____

_____

_____

_____

4. In polls, fear of making a speech ranks high, along with fear of snakes. If you get very anxious before you have to speak in public, what can you do to reduce the stress you feel? Given what you have learned in the chapter, what strategies might you try in the future?

_____

_____

_____

_____

_____

_____

CHAPTER 10
Getting Along with Others

On the International Space Station, diverse groups of people work together in close quarters for long periods. There's nowhere to go when conflict arises, so astronauts have to learn to resolve their problems and get along.

Have you ever watched actors, directors, and other movie people accept Oscars for their work? Nine times out of ten, Oscar winners thank the people—parents, spouses, friends, or colleagues—who made it possible for them to succeed. People who lead full, successful lives have a tremendous respect for and appreciation of others. They understand that good relationships with the people around them are important to their well-being. People who reach their potential are able to form and maintain good relationships with family, friends, classmates, coworkers, customers, and neighbors.

This is especially important in the United States, a diverse society with people of all races and ethnic backgrounds. Here it is not possible to associate only with people you like, or who are like you. Instead, you must get along with all sorts of people from all sorts of backgrounds. To do this, you need to understand and apply some basic principles of interpersonal relations. In this chapter, you will:

- discover that the foundation of good relationships is self-belief combined with trust, respect, and empathy for others;
- learn how to express your own needs while acknowledging the needs of others;
- commit yourself to ethical values;
- learn how culture influences how you relate to others;
- improve your interactions with others by evaluating their needs as well as your relationships with them;
- learn how to give and get feedback; and
- handle anger and conflict in a productive way.

Finally, you will explore how online social networks have extended the way we relate to friends, family, colleagues, and acquaintances.

Stop&think
mom

When you believe in yourself its easy to believe in others.

Begin with Yourself

When you believe in yourself its easy to believe in others.

"If you don't look out for others, who will look out for you?"

WHOOPI GOLDBERG,
actress

"Trust you? Sure I trust you! (I wonder what he's after now.) Be open with you? Of course I'm open with you! (I'm as open as I can be with a guy like you.) Level with you? You know I level with you! (I'd like to [level] more, but you can't take it.) Accept you? Naturally I accept you—like you do me. (And when you learn to accept me, I might accept you more.) What's the hang-up? What could ever hang up two open, trusting, leveling, and accepting guys like us?"

LYMAN K. RANDALL

What kind of person are you? How do other people see you? Your values, attitudes, beliefs, and emotions are the foundation of your uniqueness. How you act upon these states of mind determines how other people react to you. We have already discussed, in Chapter 1, how certain values and beliefs can contribute to your success in life. Now let's reexamine some beliefs and values—those that are essential for good human relations.

Self-Belief

As you recall, people with good self-belief are convinced of their own worth. They believe in their ability to influence events, and they approach new people and new challenges with self-confidence. When you believe in yourself, it's easy to believe in others. You recognize that other people are as important and unique as you are. The inner confidence of self-belief means that you don't feel threatened by everyone around you.

Trust, Respect, and Empathy

Whether you get along well with people depends on you. A good relationship with another person is built on the values of trust, respect, and empathy.

- **Trust** means that you can rely on someone else, and he or she can rely on you.
- **Respect** means that you value the other person, and he or she values you.
- **Empathy** means you can experience another person's feelings or ideas as if they were your own.

When there is trust, respect, and empathy between two people, there is rapport. Rapport is the essence of good human relations. As you learned in Chapter 7, rapport is achieved through effective communication. Good communication can establish and improve the rapport between two people, and poor communication can just as easily break down rapport. People who value trust, respect, and empathy are careful communicators. They avoid SAD comments—*s*arcastic, *a*ccusing, and *d*emeaning messages that destroy rapport.

Assertiveness

Trust, respect, and empathy show a concern for the feelings and rights of others. Assertiveness shows that you understand the importance of your own feelings and rights as well. Let's suppose, for example, that someone asks you to chair a fund-raising committee for a

Some people are naturally assertive, but others can learn. Assertiveness training workshops teach people how to speak up for themselves and how to achieve a good balance between their own rights and those of others.

(© Tetra Images/Jupiter Images)

Good relationship impossible w/o trust.

neighborhood group. You really don't feel comfortable asking for money, and you have no time to spare. If you are passive, you will agree to chair the committee even though it will be an uncomfortable and inconvenient chore. If you are aggressive, you'll reply that you have too much to do to deal with such nonsense. You'll be standing up for your rights but trampling on the feelings of others. If you are assertive, you will refuse the assignment politely.

Framing an Assertive Communication   How can you be assertive and tell people *no* or disagree with them—and still be polite? You can try framing your response as a three-part communication using these key phrases:

1. I feel …

2. I want …

3. I will. …

Following is an example:

1. *I feel* uncomfortable asking people for money, but …

2. *I want* to support your efforts even though I don't have time to spare.

3. *I will* be glad to help with a different fund-raiser later in the year.

Notice that these responses focus on the speaker's thoughts and feelings but also show trust, empathy, and respect for the receiver. They give as much due to the speaker's feelings as to the receiver's needs.

Achieving a Balance between Passivity and Aggression   Achieving a good balance between your own needs and those of others is hard for many people to do. For some people, the problem is not being assertive enough. They feel they are not important enough, or they don't have rights, or their feelings don't matter. The truth is that being passive often leads to resentment and unhappiness. Failing to acknowledge that you have important rights and feelings means you're shortchanging yourself. In these situations, others win, but you lose.

Other people have trouble distinguishing assertive behavior from aggressive behavior. They assert themselves in such hostile, angry ways that they create problems for themselves. Aggressive people tend to alienate those around them. In these situations, everyone loses.

Assertiveness is somewhere between passivity and aggression. It takes thought and practice to be assertive. When you are assertive, you share your feelings in a clear, positive, and courteous way. You are not so polite that people misunderstand your message, and you're not so rude that people feel attacked. In these situations, you win, but others win, too.

Assertiveness is a skill that can be learned. Many companies think it is such an important interpersonal skill that they give employees training in assertiveness techniques.

"*Precision of communication is important … in our era of hair-trigger balances when a false or misunderstood word may create as much disorder as a sudden thoughtless act.*"

JAMES THURBER (1894–1961), humorist and cartoonist

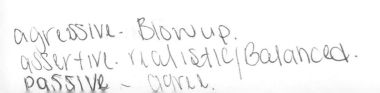

Your Turn 10-1

THE FINE LINE BETWEEN ASSERTIVENESS AND AGGRESSION

Think for a moment about a situation in which you reacted passively and found yourself doing something you really didn't want to do, or in which you reacted aggressively and found yourself involved in an argument.

1. What was the situation?

_____

_____

2. How did you react?

_____

_____

3. What do you think you could have done to protect your rights and feelings without harming the other person?

_____

_____

_____

4. Reframe your response using the "I feel ... , I want ... , I will ..." model.

_____

_____

_____

_____

> "Watch your thoughts; they become words. Watch your words; they become actions. Watch your actions; they become habits. Watch your habits; they become character. Watch your character; it becomes your destiny."
>
> ATTRIBUTED TO FRANK OUTLAW, actor

Consider Your Ethical Values

Many of the ethical values you hold are shared by society in general, and much behavior that our society views as wrong is also against the law. If people break the law, they are punished. Stealing, for example, is both unethical and illegal.

But people also have beliefs about what is right and what is wrong that are not dealt with by the law. For example, lying is unethical, but it is not usually illegal. Still, if you value honesty, you don't lie, your conscience is clear, and you feel comfortable with yourself.

Each of us has a set of ethical values by which we try to live. You may value honesty, trustworthiness, and loyalty, for example. You do your best to behave in a way that reflects these values, and your ethical conduct becomes part of your character.

Schools and employers have expectations about the ethical conduct of students and employees. For example, students are expected to do their own work and not to cheat on exams or to plagiarize papers. In a work situation, employers expect workers to put in an honest day's work in return for their pay. Beyond that basic contract, employers expect employees to behave honestly in the dozens of day-to-day situations that arise in the workplace. Taking merchandise home, stealing supplies, using the telephone for personal or long-distance calls, and using a company computer to surf the Internet are examples of unethical behavior.

The argument that "everyone does it" is no excuse for unethical conduct. Unethical behavior has the effect of diminishing self-belief, because the person behaving this way is compromising his or her values. Beyond its negative effect on self-belief and character, unethical behavior in the workplace usually means that employees are stealing from their employers. If they are caught, they may be fired or even prosecuted under the law. Unethical behavior in school—such as cheating and plagiarism—is also a form of stealing, except you are stealing other peoples' ideas and work instead of their things. Such behavior also has consequences. When you cheat or plagiarize, you are undermining your own effort to educate yourself. In addition, such behavior can lead to a failing grade, suspension, or expulsion from college.

When it comes to ethical issues, you can behave according to your values fairly easily when the situation involves only yourself. For example, you can easily refrain from taking office supplies home with you. But your sense of what's right may not be the same as your friend's, your instructor's, or your boss's. In fact, most people don't give much thought to questions of right and wrong until there is a conflict between their values and other people's values. When an ethical conflict involving others arises, you must decide what to do.

In some situations, you may be able to ignore what you consider wrong behavior on the part of others. For example, if a coworker is making lots of personal phone calls, you may feel it's better to tolerate the situation than to upset it. In other circumstances, you may feel it's necessary for you to act to prevent the unethical behavior or to stop yourself from becoming part of it. An example of this type of situation might be when the behavior has the potential to harm others, such as when an ambulance driver turns off the communication device in order to run an errand and thus doesn't respond in time to an emergency call.

When you have an ethical problem that involves others, think about the situation. Before doing anything, ask yourself what effect your action will have on others and on yourself. It sometimes takes courage to stand up for what you believe is right.

"He is most cheated who cheats himself."

Danish Proverb

"Upon the conduct of each depends the fate of all."

ALEXANDER THE GREAT
(356–323 BCE), king and military
leader

Your Turn 10-2

DO THE RIGHT THING

What would you do in each of the following situations? Explain your response.

1. You've been put in charge of ordering supplies. Someone in the office tells you to order some extra supplies, because everybody helps themselves to what they need for personal use.

   _____

   _____

2. You're about to take an important exam whose outcome will affect your future. Although you've studied quite a bit, you're so anxious that you're considering cheating if the opportunity arises.

   _____

   _____

3. You have to submit a paper on Shakespeare's *King Lear* tomorrow morning, and although you've read the play, you haven't yet written a word. You do an Internet search of "King Lear" and "paper" and find several sites that offer free, downloadable essays.

   _____

   _____

Consider Cultural Influences

Many basic ethical values are universal, but culture also plays a role in shaping your attitudes and behavior. Some of these influences are very apparent—for example, the holidays you celebrate. But other influences are harder to see because they involve the way you think about yourself and relate to others. One example of culture influencing the way people think and behave is the idea of the self (see Figure 10–1).

Some cultures define the self primarily as an individual. In these cultures, the individual is thought of as being an independent entity. The individual is emotionally separate from groups, including family groups. Individual-centered cultures place a high value on self-reliance and competitiveness. Does this sound familiar? It should, because mainstream culture in the United States is individual-centered.

Other cultures define the self in relation to a group. In these cultures, the individual's core identity is closely embedded in that of the group. These cultures place a high value on solidarity, concern for others, and

FIGURE 10-1

People from an individual-centered culture like that of the United States see themselves as independent, with clear boundaries between themselves and others. People from a group-centered culture like those of Japan and China see themselves as interdependent with others.

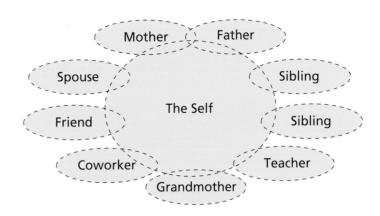

The Self in an Individual-Centered Culture

The Self in a Group-Centered Culture

"The Golden Rule" by Norman Rockwell depicts one of the fundamental principles of all major religions. The mosaic is located in the United Nations building in New York City.

cooperation. Group-centered cultures include those of Japan and other East Asian nations, as well as Mexico and other Latin American countries.

You can see that the way you think of yourself influences how you relate to others. Keep these ideas of the self in mind when you are thinking about your relationships with others, especially those whose view of the self may differ from yours.

Reach Out to Others

Do you like to be treated with courtesy and respect? Of course you do. And so does everyone else. The key to getting along with other people is to treat them with the same courtesy and respect with which you would like to be treated. Of course, doing this is not always easy.

As we have seen, people have different assumptions about the role of the individual in society. People may also have difficulty communicating with people of other races or ethnic backgrounds. The meanings people attach to the use of language, facial expressions, and gestures differ from culture to culture, and misunderstandings may be frequent (see Chapter 7). To overcome cultural barriers, it's important to be open to different ways of life and to communicate carefully. Don't assume you have been understood completely, and don't assume you have understood the other person completely, either.

While acknowledging that each person may have a different background and unique characteristics, keep in mind that people do have many things in common. There are basic hopes, fears, and emotions that we all experience. Understanding these human feelings and empathizing with others form the basis for good relationships with people.

For most people, their family provides the shelter, food, security, and love they need.

What Do People Need?

The quality of empathy is the basis for good human relations skills. Being able to imagine what another person feels, thinks, and needs means that you are able to interact with him or her in an intelligent and caring way. When people sense that you are attuned to their needs, they react positively to you.

In the course of a day, you may encounter many people, all of them unique, with whom you must interact—preferably in a positive way. How can you make sense of the bewildering variety of emotions, thoughts, feelings, and needs of each person you meet? You may find it helpful to think of people's needs in terms of a hierarchy, as shown in Figure 10–2. Abraham Maslow, a psychologist, proposed that people are motivated by different levels of needs depending on their circumstances. Homeless people, for example, have basic survival needs: They must find food or starve. Once hunger is satisfied, they can attend to their personal safety. If security needs are satisfied, people can think about meeting the need for love and relationships with others. Once feeling secure in their ties to others, people can focus on meeting their needs for achievement, competence, and self-respect.

When people feel healthy, safe, loved, and competent, they can pursue the highest level of needs—what Maslow called self-actualization (and what we have been calling "reaching your potential"). Self-actualization is reached when people are fulfilled in every aspect of their being. Not many of us experience complete and lasting self-actualization. Occasionally, we may have peak experiences in which we feel moments of perfect happiness or fulfillment. These feelings might come from creating a work of art, falling in love, running a race, or having a baby. Unfortunately, the peak experiences do not last long.

Maslow did not view his hierarchy of needs as rigid. In other words, people do not always focus on their needs in sequential order. They sometimes focus on higher-level needs even when lower-level needs remain only partly fulfilled. Parents, for example, may neglect their own

Maslow's hierarchy of needs provides a way to think about human needs. In general, people try to satisfy lower-level needs before higher-level needs.

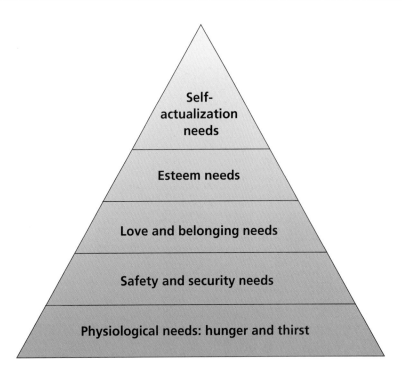

Self-actualization needs

Esteem needs

Love and belonging needs

Safety and security needs

Physiological needs: hunger and thirst

Your Turn 10-3

UNDERSTANDING THE NEEDS OF OTHERS

1. According to Maslow's hierarchy of needs, which need would be your focus in the following situations?
   a. You want to get an A on your term project.

   _____

   b. You've moved to a new town or neighborhood and have no friends in the area.

   _____

   c. You're hiking in the mountains and get lost for three days.

   _____

   d. You're walking home alone one night, and someone tries to mug you.

   _____

   e. You have just thought of a great idea for starting your own business.

   _____

2. Where would you place yourself on Maslow's hierarchy? Which level of needs are you trying to satisfy most? List three ways you try to satisfy this need.

   _____

   _____

Community Cousins

In 1992, Diane Bock watched the Watts riots on television from her home in San Diego, California. She was horrified by what she saw: white, black, Asian, and Hispanic people fighting one another in the streets of Los Angeles. For months, Bock wondered what she could do to combat the hatred she saw. Then she had an idea: introduce people of different backgrounds to one another to break down barriers and foster understanding, one person at a time.

Bock took her idea to several community agencies and organizations, but no one was interested in her idea. So in 1995, she founded Community Cousins, an organization that matches up families with similar interests but different racial and ethnic backgrounds.

This is how it works: A family who joins is paired with another family of a different background, according to their common interests. The families first meet at a Community Cousins gathering and then decide on their own how much they want to socialize. Some paired families have become so friendly that they share birthday and holiday celebrations with each other. They also attend the occasional Community Cousins potluck, barbeque, or ball game.

(© Ariel Skelley/Getty images)

Since the organization started, hundreds of families in California and Idaho have participated. According to Bock, the "cousins" don't necessarily discuss race during their get-togethers. Rather, they gradually get to know one another. Bock says, "What I'm trying to do is stir the pot enough so that everyone has a friend who's different."

Sources: Paul Bush, "Community Cousins Builds New Ethnic Relationships," *American News Service,* July 7, 1997, <http://www.villagelife.org/news/archives/CS_gettingalong/comm_cousins.html>, accessed April 27, 2008; Betty Cortina, "She Found the Courage to Fight Racism," Oprah, July/August 2000; "Who We Are," Community Cousins Web site, <http://www.cuzz.org/who_we_are.php>, accessed April 27, 2008.

needs to give loved children something extra, or good Samaritans may neglect their need for personal safety to come to the aid of someone in trouble. Even though people may not always attend to their needs in hierarchial order, Maslow's model is helpful when you're trying to figure out a person's motivations. It's also helpful to use the model when you are setting goals (see Chapter 2).

How Do You Relate to Others?

Another way of thinking about human relations is to focus on the dynamics of the relationship itself, rather than on your needs or the needs of the other person. When you first meet someone, you tend to be cautious and guarded about revealing yourself. As you reveal more about yourself to the other person, trust and empathy develop. The other person also lets her or his guard down and reveals more to you. Gradually, the relationship deepens and becomes more intimate. The quality of a relationship depends on the degree of mutual trust and openness.

The Johari Window   One way of diagramming the effect of mutual understanding and knowledge on a relationship is to use the **Johari window** (see Figure 10–3).[1] The Johari window is named after its inventors, Joseph Luft and Harry Ingham. It is a square with four sections, each section representing information known or unknown to yourself and to others.

The Known.   The first section of the Johari window represents the part of the relationship characterized by openness, shared information, and mutual understanding. In this section are matters known to yourself and to the other person as well. The more intimate and productive the relationship, the larger this section grows. If you sketched a Johari window representing your relationship with a

---

FIGURE 10–3

The Johari window is a way of diagramming the amount of shared and unshared knowledge in a relationship. The more shared knowledge there is between people (Box 1), the more openness and trust in the relationship.

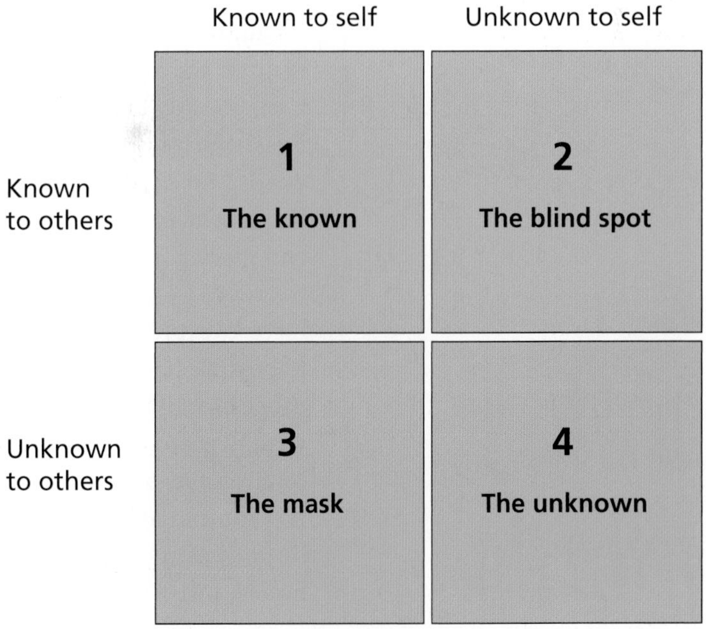

	Known to self	Unknown to self
Known to others	**1** The known	**2** The blind spot
Unknown to others	**3** The mask	**4** The unknown

close friend, this section would be large. It might be small, however, if you sketched your relationship with an instructor or manager. If you are shy and reserved, this section might be small in most of your relationships.

The Blind Spot. The second section of the Johari window consists of feelings, behaviors, and information that are known to the other person but not to you. This section is sometimes called the blind spot. The unknown matters may include your annoying mannerisms (of which you are unaware) or the other person's hidden motivations. Whatever is unknown to you in the relationship is a handicap. Therefore, the larger this section, the less effective you are in the relationship.

The Mask. The third section of the Johari window also limits your effectiveness in a relationship, but in a different way. It is everything that you know but the other person doesn't. This information, unknown to the other person, provides you with a protective mask. At first glance, it might seem that the more you know that the other person doesn't, the better off you are. If power is your object, this may be true. But if the mask becomes so large that it crowds out openness (the first section of the Johari window), the relationship suffers from a lack of trust and rapport. So, for example, if you are asked to show a classmate how to do something, and you withhold critical information, the classmate may fail and you may look competent. But in the long run, you have set the tone for a relationship in which there is little trust or cooperation.

The Unknown. The fourth section of the Johari window consists of matters that are unknown to both people. These matters include information about the context of the relationship, each person's psychological makeup, personality traits, creative potential, and so on. As a relationship develops, the size of this section of the Johari window may decrease.

Using the Johari Window to Improve Relationships. As you may have realized, the four sections of the Johari window are not fixed in size. As a relationship develops and changes, the internal vertical and horizontal lines, which separate the known from the unknown, can move. In other words, you can take actions that will increase the size of the first section, the known, to make a more effective relationship. By being open, trusting, and sharing information, you can decrease the size of your mask (section 3). Doing this is not always easy, especially for shy people. It involves expressing your feelings and knowledge in a way that exposes you to possible harm. As anyone who has ever asked another person for a first date can attest, disclosing your feelings and needs may be hard. Yet if you want to get to know another person, self-disclosure is necessary, and its rewards may be great.

You can also increase the size of the first section, the known, by decreasing your blind spot. One way to do this is through honest introspection. That is, you must examine your feelings and

Your Turn 10-4

DIAGRAM TWO RELATIONSHIPS

Use the Johari windows below to diagram two relationships. Use the first window to model a relationship with a spouse, lover, or friend. Use the second window to model a relationship with a fellow student, coworker, or acquaintance.

	Known to self	Unknown to self
Known to others	**1** **The known**	**2** **The blind spot**
Unknown to others	**3** **The mask**	**4** **The unknown**

	Known to self	Unknown to self
Known to others	**1** **The known**	**2** **The blind spot**
Unknown to others	**3** **The mask**	**4** **The unknown**

behavior to understand your needs and motivations. Another way to decrease your blind spot is to ask another person for feedback. What information does the other person have that will help you in the relationship? Using feedback to decrease your blind spot requires the cooperation of the other person. And the amount of cooperation you get will depend in part on your own willingness to be open and to share. You can see that you can exercise a lot of control over the quality of your relationships.

Feedback in Relationships

Giving and getting feedback makes relationships grow and develop. Whether the growth is healthy or stunted depends in large part on our ability to give feedback in a nonthreatening way and to receive feedback without being crushed by it. Of course, some feedback is positive. Praise and affirmation are good to give and to receive, and most of us thrive on it. Dealing with negative feedback is much more difficult.

Giving Feedback

Why is giving feedback a necessary part of every relationship? Feedback is part of a communication loop that helps create the knowledge, openness, and mutual trust necessary for effective relationships. As we saw from the Johari window, the larger the area of mutual knowledge, the more effective the relationship. Giving feedback is one way to increase what is known about a relationship.

However, it takes skill to give negative feedback in a way that helps the other person. The person who is being helped must feel respected and valued, not demeaned. If those being helped are made to feel defensive, they will not be receptive to feedback. So it's important when giving feedback to be calm, concerned, and encouraging. You must accept the other person without judging him or her, and direct the criticism at behaviors, not at personality. For example, if a parent criticizes children's behavior by telling them they are bad, the children feel demeaned and worthless. If, on the other hand, the parent gives specific feedback about behavior—such as it's rude to interrupt—the children's self-esteem is intact and they have some idea how to behave in the future.

When you give feedback in a relationship, keep these things in mind:

- Understand your own feelings and motivations.
- Be accepting and nonjudgmental about the other person.
- Be sensitive to the other person's resistance. Pressure doesn't work in the long run.

Most companies have regular performance appraisals to ensure that their managers give employees feedback about their work.

(© Chabruken/Getty Images)

News & Views

MY SPACE IS NOT YOUR SPACE

Did you know that social scientists can predict where you will sit at a library table? Videos have shown that the first person to arrive takes a corner seat. The second person takes the seat diagonally opposite the first. Why? Because the two opposite corner seats are farthest from each other, and each person is intent on preserving his personal space.

Our concern for personal boundaries operates everywhere. In elevators, we stand in opposite corners and look straight ahead. On park benches and low walls, we sit spaced at equal distances. In buses and trains we choose seats so no one is next to us. Even in the online alternate universe Second Life, game players' avatars, or online characters, observe the rules of personal space.

What are these unspoken rules? Edward T. Hall, an anthropologist who pioneered the study of personal space, or proxemics, observed that we have different "zones of interaction." We are comfortable at these distances:

- **Intimate space,** up to 18 inches—close family and intimate friends only
- **Personal space,** 18 inches to 4 feet—family and friends
- **Social space,** 4 feet to 12 feet—coworkers, classmates, acquaintances, and strangers using public areas
- **Public space,** 12 feet and up—strangers, audiences.

When these personal boundaries are invaded, we feel threatened and move away, avoiding eye contact. However, Hall's distances are averages for North Americans, who like their space. In contrast, people from Latin America, Russia, and the Middle East are comfortable at closer distances—8 to 12 inches less for intimate and personal space.

It's possible to use a knowledge of proxemics to make yourself, and others, more comfortable. First, in public, be aware of the people around you and the space between you. If you think you may be too close, move away slightly if you can. In your home and work space, consider the furniture—are the distances and angles such that visitors will feel comfortable? If not, you can make changes that will put people at ease.

Sources: Edward T. Hall, *The Hidden Dimension.* New York: Doubleday, 1963; Paul Preston, "Proxemics in Clinical and Administrative Settings," *Journal of Healthcare Management,* Vol. 50, No. 3, May/June 2005, pp. 151–4; Stephanie Rosenbloom, "In Certain Circles, Two Is a Crowd," *New York Times,* November 16, 2006, p. E1, E10.

- Criticize specific behavior, not personality.
- Give feedback only on matters that the other person can change. If something can't be changed, there's little value in discussing it.
- Don't tell others what to do.

Receiving Feedback

Even harder than giving productive criticism is being on the receiving end of negative feedback. Even though on one level we know we are not perfect, still, no one likes to be told he or she is in some way inadequate. In fact, our first reaction to criticism is often defensive. Rather than being open to the criticism, we react by protecting our self-belief.

Protecting Your Self-Belief   Our self-belief is so important to our well-being that people have evolved many ways to defend it. These processes, which reduce anxiety and protect our self-belief, are called defense mechanisms. Some common defense mechanisms are withdrawal, rationalization, substitution, fantasy, and projection. The defense mechanisms are not unhealthy unless they come to dominate our interactions with others.

1. **Withdrawal.** People who feel threatened sometimes deal with their anxiety by trying to avoid the situation that caused the stress. Trying to escape from negative feedback is called withdrawal. People who have difficulty with the give and take of close relationships often withdraw. Separation, divorce, quitting a job—all may be examples of withdrawal.

2. **Rationalization.** Another way to defend your self-belief is to rationalize, that is, to explain or excuse an unacceptable situation in terms that make it acceptable to yourself. Rationalizing involves distorting the truth to make it more acceptable. For example, if you are criticized for missing an important course deadline, you may rationalize that it was your instructor's responsibility to remind you, whereas in truth it was your responsibility.

3. **Displacement.** Displacement is a defense mechanism in which you react to a negative situation by substituting another person for the person who aroused your anxiety or anger. For example, if your instructor criticizes you in front of the class, you may go home and yell at your sister. In general, the person you choose as the substitute is less likely to harm your self-belief.

4. **Fantasy.** Fantasy is a form of withdrawal in which daydreams provide a boost to self-belief when reality threatens. For example, if you've been told that you'll be off the team unless your grades improve, you may fantasize about being indispensable to your team and leading it to victory. Everyone fantasizes to a degree; fantasy becomes a problem only when it is a substitute for reality.

5. **Projection.** Projection is a defense mechanism in which you attribute your own unacceptable behaviors and feelings to another person. If you are criticized for treating a coworker discourteously, for example, you may project that the coworker was being rude to *you*.

Handling Feedback Positively   All the defense mechanisms can help us maintain our self-belief. But at what cost? People who are always on

Your Turn 10-5

DEFENDING YOURSELF

1. Identify which defense mechanism is being used in each situation.

   a. A person having difficulty in school drops out.

   _____

   b. A person criticized for poor judgment goes home and picks a fight with her husband.

   _____

   c. A person who is told he needs training decides that his manager doesn't know what he's doing.

   _____

2. Most people consistently use one or two defense mechanisms when they feel threatened. Which defense mechanism(s) do you use? Give an example of a situation in which you reacted defensively.

   _____

   _____

   _____

the defensive find it hard to change and grow. Their relationships with others are characterized by a lack of openness and trust. On the other hand, people who can handle negative feedback constructively have an opportunity to develop and grow. Their relationships with others become more, not less, effective.

How can you handle negative feedback in a positive way? Learning to accept feedback means paying less attention to how criticism makes you feel and more attention to what's actually being said. If you remember that criticism is information that can help you, you will be able to deal with it more effectively. Try these tips for handling negative feedback:

- **Consider who is criticizing you.** Is the person in a position to know what he or she is talking about? If not, the criticism may not be valid. If so, it's worth listening to.
- **Decide whether the person criticizing you is upset about something else.** If so, he or she may just be venting. If he or she is calm, though, you should pay more attention.
- **Ask for specific information.** Many people who offer criticism do so in the most general terms, which is not helpful.
- **Think about what you've heard.** Give yourself time to react.
- **Decide whether the criticism is appropriate.** If it is, think about what you will do to change your behavior.

Conflict

Throw any two people together for any length of time and they are sure to disagree about something. The conflict may be over what time they go to the movies or whether a war can be morally justified. If they cannot settle the disagreement, they may become frustrated and angry. This scenario is so common that you may think conflict is always a negative experience. Yet if handled properly, conflict can have healthy and productive results.

What Causes Conflict?

Differences over facts, ideas, goals, needs, attitudes, beliefs, and personalities all cause conflict. Some conflicts are simple and easy to resolve. A difference of opinion about a fact, for example, usually does not escalate into an emotional battle. If you and a friend disagree about who holds the world's record for the 100-meter dash, you can easily resolve the conflict by checking a sports almanac.

But conflicts about personalities, values, needs, beliefs, and ideas can be more serious. Such conflicts often cause frustration and anger. The issues are more fundamental, and they can have an emotional component that makes disagreement threatening. Unless the anger is dealt with properly, the conflict is not resolved.

In addition, when people feel that the outcome of a conflict is a reflection of their self-belief, conflict can be damaging. For example, Brian and Anya disagreed about how to do a course project, and their group adopted Anya's plan. Instead of thinking that his plan had been rejected, Brian felt that his self-belief had been attacked. Such a conflict is not easily resolved.

Anger

Anger, the result of unresolved conflict, is a powerful emotion. Think about the last time you got angry. What did you do? Did you tell the other person why you were angry? Did you snap at them about something else? Or did you keep your feelings to yourself? People express anger in different ways.

Expressing Anger Directly   People often express their anger directly. If someone annoys you, you tell them so, or you glare at them, or you shove them, or you tailgate them on the road. Obviously, the direct expression of anger can run the gamut from assertiveness to aggression to violence. How people express anger directly depends on their personalities and the extent to which they are provoked. People with negative self-belief often have an underlying attitude of hostility that is easily triggered by even minor events. Others,

(© Jupiter Images/Workbook Stock/Getty Images)

Conflict is part of everyday life. People who can control their anger have a better chance to resolve their conflicts than people who lose control.

more secure in their self-belief, can express anger more calmly without being aggressive. (See the discussion of assertiveness on page 226.)

Expressing Anger Indirectly   Another way to express anger is indirect. Instead of confronting the person with whom you are angry, you direct your anger at a third party, who is less threatening. Since this process is similar to the defense mechanism of displacement, it is often called displacement.

In many situations it is inappropriate to express anger at the person with whom you are angry. Suppose you've just started your own business and one of your clients keeps changing his mind about what he wants you to do. You are angry because he's wasting your time. Yet expressing anger directly will cause you to lose a customer. In this case your anger may find an outlet when you snap at your child or a friend. This is certainly unfair to the person at the receiving end of your wrath!

Internalizing Anger   The third way to deal with anger is to keep it bottled up inside you. Many people consider the expression of anger to be threatening, bad, or rude, and so they internalize it. Unfortunately, the result of internalizing anger is that you feel a growing resentment. Since your anger is not expressed, there is no way for the conflict to be resolved, and it festers. Internalized anger can cause stress and harm your emotional and physical health.

Controlling Anger   You can minimize the destructiveness of anger by trying to control it. There are several approaches that you can take.

- Don't say or do anything immediately. It's usually best to cool off and give yourself a chance to think. Counting to 10 may help.
- Figure out why you are angry. Sometimes the cause of the anger is something you can easily change or avoid.
- Channel your anger into physical exercise. Even a walk can relieve the tensions of anger.
- Use relaxation techniques such as deep breathing to calm yourself.
- Find a friend who will listen to why you are angry and offer constructive suggestions.

Resolving Conflicts

Once your anger is under control, you can try to resolve the conflict that caused it. The energy created by your anger can be channeled into solving the problem. Here are a few suggestions.

- **Commit yourself to resolving the problem.** Don't just decide to keep the peace.
- **Ask yourself what you hope to achieve by resolving the conflict.** Is it critical to get your way, or is your relationship with the other person more important? Your priorities will influence how you settle the conflict.

"*It is hidden wrath that harms.*"

SENECA (4 BCE–65 CE), ancient Roman philosopher, dramatist, and statesman

Your Turn 10-6

TAKE AN ANGER INVENTORY

Some people get angry easily, and others remain calm. Where are you in this spectrum? Raymond W. Novaco of the University of California devised an anger inventory upon which the following questionnaire is based.

For each item, indicate whether you would be very angry, somewhat angry, or not angry by circling the numbers 1, 2, or 3.

	Very Angry	Somewhat Angry	Not Angry
1. Your coworker makes a mistake and blames it on you.	1	2	3
2. You are talking to a friend, and she doesn't answer.	1	2	3
3. You lose a game.	1	2	3
4. An acquaintance always brags about himself.	1	2	3
5. Your instructor tells you your work is poor.	1	2	3
6. You are driving on a highway and someone cuts in front of you.	1	2	3
7. At a store, a salesperson keeps following you and offering help.	1	2	3
8. A car drives through a puddle and splashes you.	1	2	3
9. Someone turns off the TV while you are watching a program.	1	2	3
10. You are studying and someone is talking on her cell phone.	1	2	3

Add the numbers you circled in each column. Then add the subtotals to get your grant total.

_____ + _____ + _____

Grand Total _____

If your score was:
10–15 You get angry quickly.
16–20 You get angry fairly easily.
21–25 You have a moderate level of anger.
26–30 You are slow to get angry.

- **Make sure you and the other person have the same understanding of the reason for conflict.** Ask questions and really listen. You may be surprised: Some conflicts are the result of misunderstanding.

- **Be assertive, not aggressive.** Remember that the other person has rights and feelings, too.

■ **Try to keep to the facts.** When discussing the issue, make sure you understand the difference between facts and feelings. The more you can keep feelings out of it, the better your chance for resolving the conflict.

At first, you may find it difficult to control your anger and to approach conflicts in a more thoughtful, rational way. With practice, you will become more comfortable in dealing with conflict. You may find that effectively resolving conflict is a way to learn more about yourself and to grow, as well as to improve the quality of your relationships with the people around you.

Tech Tips

USING ONLINE SOCIAL NETWORKS

About 200 million people worldwide use Facebook, the most popular online social network. Millions more use MySpace. On these sites, people post profiles of themselves, exchange information with others, share photos and videos, use blogs and messaging to communicate, and play games. Online social networks have dramatically changed the way many people relate to one another.

If you join a site like Facebook and MySpace, you post a profile giving information about yourself, and then connect with "friends." In order to establish an online "friend" link, both you and the other person must confirm that you are, indeed, friends. You can search for "friends" in categories—those who live in your area, are connected with your high school or college, work for the same organization you do, or are the friends of your friends. After you've been a member for a while, you may have hundreds of "friends" from various parts of your life. Because of this, you may find that formerly separate parts of your life are colliding. For example, your mother, your co-worker, and your best friend may all be online "friends" with access to lots of information about you.

How can you control your personal flow of information? The first step, of course, is to post only information that you are willing to share with others. The second step is to use the site's privacy settings to control who has access to your profile and its updates. For example, on Facebook you can set your profile and updates to be viewed by everyone, by only your "friends," or by specifically selected "friends." That does not solve the problem entirely, however, because others can post information about you over which you have no control. For example, many people have been embarrassed to find compromising information or photos of themselves posted on someone else's profile for many to see.

As online social networking sites grow, they are being used for various purposes besides socializing. Corporations market their products and services. Employers check out the profiles of potential employees. Law enforcement agencies look for crime, and college security departments look for underage drinking and drug use on campus. Criminals, imposters, sexual predators, identity thieves, and bullies all exploit these sites for their own ends.

On the other hand, the sites are wonderful for keeping friends and family in touch and for networking. The key is to balance the display of information with common sense privacy rules in order to enjoy the best these sites have to offer without experiencing their down side.

Your Turn 10-7

Check out either of two most popular social networks, MySpace (www.myspace.com) or Facebook (www.facebook.com). On the home page, click on the link "About" for an overview of the site. Briefly summarize the site's purpose in the space below.

_____

_____

_____

_____

_____

_____

What's Up?

Name _____   Date_____

1. How do trust, respect, and empathy affect good human relations?
   _____
   _____

2. What is the difference between aggressiveness and assertiveness?
   _____
   _____

3. Describe the different levels of needs in Maslow's hierarchy.
   _____
   _____

4. What is self-actualization?
   _____
   _____

5. What does the Johari window show? How can it be used?
   _____
   _____

6. Why is it important to give specific, behavior-related feedback?
   _____
   _____

7. What is the purpose of a defense mechanism?
   _____
   _____

8. What causes conflict between two people?
   _____
   _____

9. Why should you try to control your anger before resolving a conflict with someone else?
   _____
   _____

10. Name one advantage and one disadvantage of belonging to an online social network.
    _____
    _____

Case Studies

The Case of the Worried Man

Paul attends college part-time and works for an electronics firm that has just been acquired by a large multinational corporation. Since the takeover, there have been rumors that his company will be downsized or closed. Paul has had trouble concentrating on his studies, and his grades are falling. He worries about whether he'll have a job tomorrow.

1. Before the takeover, what needs were uppermost in Paul's mind?

2. After the takeover, Paul's needs changed. What was his new need?

3. According to Maslow, why did Paul's needs change?

The Case of the "Sick" Employee

Julie was hired to help Mary run her small housewares shop by doing record keeping and accounting. On the last day of each month, Julie had to balance the accounts, pay vendors, and send statements to customers with account balances. She wasn't very good at this task, and she made quite a few mistakes the first two months. Mary criticized her sharply about the errors. On the last day of the third month, Julie called in sick.

Mary was annoyed, because in addition to helping customers she had to do the end-of-month accounting. Mary became really angry when Julie called in sick on the last day of the fourth month as well. But she said nothing, and the next day it was business as usual.

1. Why is Julie calling in sick on the last day of each month?

2. Describe the conflict between Julie and Mary.

3. How did Mary deal with her anger?

4. How might Mary and Julie resolve this problem?

 Journal

Answer the following journal questions.

1. How good are you at getting along with others? What aspects of your relationships with others would you like to improve?

2. Explain your code of ethics. What ethical values are most important to you? Least important? Why?

3. Describe a conflict you've recently experienced. How was the conflict resolved? In your view, was the resolution successful? Explain.

4. If you belong to an online social network, how do you use it? What advantages and disadvantages does it have?

Functioning in Groups

One of the purposes of basic training is to forge group bonds. As soldiers gain experience, some will demonstrate leadership skills and be promoted up the ranks.

From the time you were born into a family until this moment, when you are reading these words for a class, you have belonged to hundreds of groups. Psychologists define a **group** as the conscious interaction of two or more people. This means that the members of a group must be aware of one another. So, for example, people shopping at Target are not a group unless an incident takes place that makes them pay attention to one another. If a security guard starts chasing a shoplifter and people stop to watch, they become members of a group.

The group at Target lasts just a few minutes and breaks up. Other groups, such as the U.S. Senate or the *American Idol* judges, last for years. And some groups, like the one in Target, are informal. **Informal groups** are loose associations of people without stated rules. Passengers on a bus, a group of friends, or people at a party are all part of informal groups. Other groups are **formal**; that is, they have clear goals and established rules. Political parties, businesses, schools, labor unions, orchestras, baseball teams, and other such associations are all formal groups.

In this chapter, you will:

- learn that all groups have goals, roles for members to play, and standards of behavior;
- discover that different groups have different patterns of communication;
- learn how people behave as members of groups;
- improve your ability to interact in groups;
- list the norms for classroom behavior as well as for online course discussion boards; and
- discover the qualities of a good leader and the basic leadership styles.

Understanding how groups work will help you be an effective group member or leader— vital skills in all areas of life.

The swimmers on this team have a cooperative goal: to beat the opposing swim team. But they also have a competitive goal: Each swimmer wants to have the best time in the freestyle event, beating her teammates as well.

"*Man is a social animal.*"

SENECA (4 BCE-65 CE),
Roman philosopher, dramatist,
and statesman

(© Dimitri Iundt/TempSport/Corbis)

Group Dynamics

Group dynamics is the study of how people interact in groups. All groups have goals they try to achieve; roles for members to play; norms, or standards of behavior; communication patterns; and a degree of cohesiveness.

Goals

All groups have goals, whether they are explicitly stated or taken for granted, short-term or long-term. People at a party, for example, are there to have a good time. A business's goal may be to make a profit by serving a particular market. A hockey team's goal is to win as many games as possible.

In groups, the goals can be cooperative or competitive. When the goals are cooperative, people in the group work together to achieve an objective. A group putting on a play, for example, has a cooperative goal. When group goals are competitive, people in the group work against one another to achieve their objectives. Four people playing Monopoly have competitive goals; only one can win the game.

Of course, in real life things are seldom so clear-cut. In most groups, there are both cooperative and competitive goals at the same time. Take the example of a theater group: Clearly, the cooperative goal is to have the play ready to perform on opening night. Yet the actors in the group may have competitive goals. Each may be trying to win the most applause or the best reviews.

Most of the groups you will encounter, both at school and at work, will have both cooperative and competitive goals. Today, for example, many businesses organize their workers into project teams. Members of the team cooperate with one another to achieve the goals of the team. At the same time they compete with other teams in the organization. They may even compete with each other. Consider a corporation that creates teams of workers to develop new products. People on the widget team cooperate with one another to design, produce, and market the best and most profitable widget. At the same time, they compete with people on the gadget team, who are trying to design, produce, and market the best and most profitable gadget. The widget people are also competing among themselves for recognition, promotion, raises, and power.

Studies have shown that groups with cooperative goals have better communication and are more productive. In groups with competitive goals, members tend to spend too much energy on rivalry. However, competitive goals can be positive forces. They can create a feeling of challenge and excitement that motivates people to do their best.

Roles and Norms

If you pitch for a baseball team, you are expected to stand on the pitcher's mound, try to strike out the opposing batter, catch any fly balls that come your way, and so on. On the team, your role is pitcher, and your norms are the rules of baseball. In a group, a **role** is a set of expected behaviors for a particular position. **Norms** are the rules by which people in particular roles are expected to behave.

Norms cover almost all aspects of our interactions with other people, although they vary from one culture to another. For example, when in public, many Muslim women cover their hair. In contrast, most women cover their heads only when it is cold. Norms change gradually over time and through the influence of one culture on another. For example, 75 years ago blue jeans were considered appropriate wear only for people who did manual labor or farm work. Today blue jeans are acceptable on a wide range of people in all but the most formal or conservative settings.

There are many roles that have a substantial number of norms associated with them. Mother, father, wife, husband, child, friend, boss, employee, teacher, and student are common roles with dozens of norms. Teachers, for example, are expected to be hardworking and knowledgeable. Friends are expected to be supportive and loyal. The norms for these roles are deeply ingrained in our society, and they help make it function smoothly.

One person can have many roles in life.

Your Turn 11–1

Think about the class for which you are reading this book. Then answer the following questions.

1. What are the cooperative goals of the class, if any?

   _____

2. What are the competitive goals of the class, if any?

   _____

3. What class roles can you identify? What role do you play?

   _____

4. What norms do you associate with each role you identify?

   _____

In many formal groups, explicit roles are assigned to members. In a committee a chairperson leads and a secretary records the minutes. In a band, there may be a singer, guitarist, keyboard player, and drummer. In a college, there may be faculty, administration, support staff, and students.

Communication

Communication is key to the success of any group. As you participate in various groups, observe the communication patterns. Does one person dominate, telling everyone else what to do? Do two or three people talk among themselves while the rest observe? Is communication like a chain, with messages passed from one person to another? Or do all members communicate with all other members?

Communication patterns can tell you a great deal about groups. In formal groups, communication patterns may be rigid. For example, in the armed services, the communication pattern looks like a chain (see Figure 11–1). Messages are passed down the **chain** from the higher ranks to the lower ranks and occasionally in the other direction. Skipping a link of the chain is a serious breach of group norms in the armed services.

Another example of a formal communication pattern is called the **wheel**. One person at the hub communicates with each group member on the spokes, but the members do not communicate with each other.

FIGURE 11–1

There are three basic communication patterns in groups: (1) In the chain pattern, a message is passed from one person to the next. (2) In the wheel pattern, the person at the hub communicates with each person on the spokes, but the people on the spokes don't communicate with each other. (3) In the all-channel pattern, all members communicate with each other.

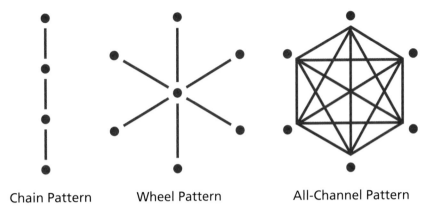

Chain Pattern   Wheel Pattern   All-Channel Pattern

An example of this is a dispatcher directing the activity of police officers on patrol, or a store manager supervising a group of cashiers.

In smaller, less formal groups, such as a project team, social group, or small business, members communicate more freely with one another in the all-channel pattern. In theory, each group member communicates with every other group member, although in practice the pattern may be more random.

Your Turn 11–2

DRAW A COMMUNICATION PATTERN

In the space following, draw the typical communication pattern of your class and your family.

Your Class   **Your Family**

Cohesiveness

All groups have a certain amount of cohesiveness, that is, the degree to which members stick together. Very cohesive groups have a strong identity and clear goals and norms, and their members are very loyal to one another. Families usually have a high degree of cohesiveness, as do some religious congregations and social groups.

A certain amount of cohesiveness is good; it keeps the group from falling apart and it keeps members cooperating to achieve group goals. One of the jobs of a coach or manager, for example, is to encourage the cohesiveness of the team or department. But too much cohesiveness can cause problems, as we shall see.

How People Behave in Groups

Have you ever found yourself doing something you wouldn't ordinarily do because "everyone else is doing it"? You might have cheated on an exam, gotten your navel pierced, or spent too much money on something trendy. The cohesiveness of your group caused you to behave in a way that was contrary to your beliefs or values. You found yourself conforming or complying with the group's norms.

Conformity

Changing your opinion or behavior in response to pressure from a group is called conformity. The urge to conform can be extremely powerful, as was shown in a famous experiment conducted by psychologist Solomon Asch.[1] Groups of seven students were told they were participating in an experiment about perception. They were shown these cards and asked to select the line on the right-hand card that matches the line on the left-hand card (see Figure 11–2).

No doubt you picked the correct line without any trouble. But how would you do in the following situation? In Asch's study, six of the seven students were "in" on the true nature of the experiment. The group was given the same task: to match the sticks. The six were instructed to answer unanimously, out loud in front of the group. The seventh, the true subject, answered last, also out loud. At first, the six answered correctly, and so did the true subject. But then the six started to unanimously select the incorrect line, contradicting what the seventh subject could see perfectly well. In one out of three groups, the true subjects conformed—that is, they gave the wrong answer to go along with the group.

In follow-up interviews, it became apparent that both the conformers and the ones who stuck to the evidence of their senses were disturbed by what happened. The conformers reported that their feelings of self-confidence had been eroded by the unanimous judgments of the other group members. Those who remained independent of the group reported feeling embarrassed and uneasy at being the odd one out.

FIGURE 11–2

Which of the lines on the right-hand card matches the line on the left-hand card?

Why do some people conform and others do not? Psychologists think that people who conform to group behavior that is contrary to their beliefs and values suffer from poor self-belief. They lack the confidence necessary to act independently. Those who act independently when group values contradict their own values tend to have good self-belief.

In addition, the size of the unanimous majority influences the degree of conformity in a group. When confronted with one or two people who hold a different opinion, a person is not so likely to conform. But when three or more people hold a differing belief, others are more likely to go along with the majority.

Of course, it's important to realize that conformity is not always bad. In common social situations such as waiting in line, entering an elevator, or taking a class, conformity is simply convenient behavior. It means that these situations will take place in a way that everyone expects. It relieves people of the necessity of making a decision about what to do all day long.

The important thing about conformity is to know when it is appropriate. In most circumstances, it probably is appropriate. But when the beliefs, values, and behavior of a group run counter to your own beliefs, values, and codes of behavior, then whether to conform becomes an important decision. Do you go along to get along, or do you act independently? This can be a hard question to answer.

Groupthink

When a group is very cohesive and its members very loyal to one another, a special type of conformity sometimes arises. Called groupthink, it is an uncritical acceptance of a group's beliefs and behaviors in order to preserve its unanimity. When loyalty to the group becomes more important than anything else, the members are suffering from groupthink.

When a group is suffering from groupthink, its members lose their ability to think critically and independently. They lose sight of their own values and of moral consequences. Some political groups suffer from groupthink. Loyalty to a leader, party, or ideology creates an atmosphere in which the group makes poor decisions.

Participating in Groups

You can use your knowledge about how groups work to improve the way you interact with others. By analyzing the goals, roles, and norms of the groups you belong to, you will be able to understand the nature of each group. You can also get the most out of groups by learning to be an active participant.

Analyzing Group Goals, Roles, and Norms

When you first join a group, are you quiet? Do you keep to yourself, observing how people interact? Most people behave this way when they

Your Turn 11–3

Think about your class again, and answer the following questions.

1. Give two examples of conformity in the classroom.

   _____

2. Describe a situation in which a member of the class did not conform to group norms.

   _____

3. Does the class suffer from groupthink? Give evidence to support your answer.

   _____

join a new group. Unconsciously, they are trying to understand the group's goals, roles, and norms. A good example of this is your first few days in a new school or on a new job, when you are figuring out who's who and how things work.

You can sharpen your powers of analysis by asking yourself some questions when you first encounter a group. As you observe, try to answer the following questions:

- What are the objectives of the group?
- Are the group's goals cooperative or competitive?
- Does the group function as a team, or are there rivalries among members?
- Are some members pursuing individual goals rather than group goals?
- Does the group have a leader? Who is the leader?
- What other roles are apparent in the group?
- What are the norms of the group? Is it formal or informal?
- What communication patterns are being used?

By answering these questions, you will better understand the nature of the group and your role in it. As you begin to feel comfortable with the norms of the group, you can start to participate more actively.

News & Views

PREJUDICE, STEREOTYPES, AND DISCRIMINATION

In 1902, Takuji Yamashita, a Japanese immigrant, graduated from the University of Washington law school. He passed the bar exam with honors, but the State of Washington said that Yamashita could not be a lawyer. At the time, Japanese immigrants could not apply for American citizenship, and a person had to be a citizen in order to be a lawyer. Yamashita argued his own case in court, saying that laws excluding people based on race were unworthy of "the most enlightened and liberty-loving nation of them all." The court agreed that Yamashita was "intellectually and morally" qualified to be a lawyer; however, he lost his case because the prejudices of the time were built into the legal system.

(© Courtesy of the descendants of Takuji Yamashita)

As a young man, Takuji Yamashita was denied the right to practice law based on his ethnicity.

Ninety-nine years later, the laws excluding nonwhites from citizenship were no longer on the books. So in 2001, 42 years after Yamashita's death, the State of Washington finally admitted him to the bar. In a special ceremony attended by his descendants, Yamashita was awarded the honor for which he had studied and fought.

Like all victims of prejudice, Yamashita was prejudged because of his background. Prejudice is a negative attitude about people based on their belonging to a particular group, without any regard for their individuality. Stereotypes are the simplified beliefs that people have about the characteristics of members of a particular group. And discrimination is action taken against someone we are prejudiced against.

Where does prejudice come from? Psychologists have different ideas about the origins of prejudice. Some think that prejudice is the result of competition between groups. When blacks and whites, or Americans and Mexicans, for example, compete for jobs, members of both groups become prejudiced against the other group.

Other psychologists believe that prejudice is learned behavior. In this view, children acquire the prejudices of the adults around them, much as they learn any other type of behavior.

Another theory holds that people with certain personality traits are more likely to be prejudiced. People who are rigid and conventional, and who have poor self-belief, are prone toward prejudice. They feel better about themselves when they can feel better than others.

Still another point of view is that prejudice is a result of lazy thinking. Because the world is so complex and hard to understand, people resort to stereotypes to simplify their thinking and to categorize people.

Most people have prejudices, and most people are either unaware of them or won't admit to them. Prejudice that results in unfair discrimination harms the people discriminated against, like Yamashita. Today legislation makes discrimination based on sex, age, race, ethnicity, or religion illegal. Yet discrimination still persists in the attitudes and behavior of individuals.

FIGURE 11–3

An agenda can be used to prepare for a meeting and to make sure the group covers all the necessary topics and tasks in an organized way.

> College Council Meeting
> December 11, _____
> 4 p.m.
>
> Agenda
>
> 1. Minutes of November 7 meeting
> 2. Proposal to add a new section to English 101, Expository Writing
> 3. Proposal for new teaching award, Innovative Educator of the Year
> 4. Middle States accreditation process

Participating Actively

Groups tend to accept those who adopt their norms and reject those who ignore them. So once you figure out the norms of a group, you will have better success if you behave accordingly. If the group is formal, with rules of order, then you too will have to be formal. If the group is informal, you can behave in a more casual manner.

If the group is formal—perhaps at work or school—you may be given an agenda before the group meets. An agenda is a list of matters to be discussed or decided at the group's meeting (see Figure 11–3). Read the agenda and make sure you are prepared to discuss the subjects that will come up at the meeting. Preparation may involve thinking, reading, or researching. You should bring the agenda and any relevant information to the meeting.

Whether the group is informal or formal, you will get more out of it if you participate actively. In addition to being prepared, active participation requires that you:

- **Pay attention.** Use your listening skills to follow what's going on. In some situations, it may be appropriate to take notes.

- **Acknowledge what other people think and feel.** Even if you disagree with them, you should not tear down others' ideas.

- **Be assertive.** Speak up when you have something to say.

- **Contribute your own ideas.** Realize that what you think may have value for the group.

- **Be courteous.** Remember that groups are more productive when members cooperate with one another.

WHATEVER IT TAKES

Luma Mufleh and the Fugees

(© Bill Frakes /Sports Illustrated/Getty Images)

One day on her way to the store in Clarkston, Georgia, Luma Mufleh stopped to watch a group of boys playing pickup soccer in the street. None of the boys had uniforms or cleats, and many spoke with foreign accents. The sight reminded Mufleh of home. She had grown up in Amman, Jordan, playing soccer with her cousins in her grandfather's yard.

Like Mufleh, most of the boys were immigrants to the United States. But unlike her, most of them were refugees from countries in Africa, the Middle East, and Eastern Europe. Many had experienced wartime atrocities, witnessed the deaths of loved ones, and spent years living in refugee camps. The boys had little in common except their refugee status and their love of soccer. Inspired by their joy at playing ball, in 2004 Mufleh started a YMCA soccer program for them, naming the team the Fugees, short for "refugees."

During the first few years, the Fugees struggled to establish themselves. The team had many good players, but they also had many problems. The players couldn't afford cleats and uniforms. They had no way to get to practice or games except by walking. Their parents, struggling to establish themselves in a strange country, couldn't afford the time or money to help them. The town, more accustomed to baseball than soccer, couldn't find them a permanent field to practice. Basically, the Fugees had to help themselves.

And that's what they did. Coach Mufleh and team manager Tracy Ediger drove the boys everywhere, translated when their families had to deal with landlords and government bureaucrats, and helped people find jobs. In turn, the boys signed contracts to behave properly, avoid alcohol and drugs, and do well in school. They also helped raise funds for equipment, uniforms, and travel expenses. Slowly, the boys became a team, and they began to win games.

In 2007, the story of the Fugees appeared in *The New York Times,* and people all over the country were inspired. Contributions poured in from individuals and organizations, and the team sold the movie rights to its story to Universal Pictures. Mufleh started a foundation called Fugees Family to help run the soccer program and manage all its related activities. Today there are four boys' teams and one girls' team, with players from 24 different countries. In addition to soccer, the Fugees Family has a broad mission to help refugee families make the transition to life as Americans. The organization focuses on soccer and education for the children, and community resources for the adults.

Adjusting to life in a new country is difficult enough for ordinary immigrants, according to Mufleh. For refugees, it's even harder. "I just want them to feel there is a place for everyone here," she says. For refugees in Clarkston, Georgia, Fugees Family is that place.

Sources: Steve Amoia, "Interview with Luma Mufleh, Youth Coach and Founder of the Fugees Family," Soccerlens. com, Mar. 21, 2008, <http://soccerlens.com/interview-with-Luma-Mufleh/6652>, accessed May 11, 2008; Kate Kelly, "Heartwarming Soccer Story Kicks Off Hollywood Fight," Wall Street Journal, Jan. 30, 2007, <http://onlinewsj.com>, accessed Jan. 30, 2007; Warren St. John, "Refugees Find Hostility and Hope on Soccer Field," *New York Times,* Jan. 21, 2007, <http://www.newyorktimes.com>, accessed May 9, 2008; Kimberly Winston, "Luma Mufleh," Beliefnet, 2008. <http://www.beliefnet.com/story/225/story_22556.html>, accessed May 9, 2008.

Norms for Classroom Behavior

In a classroom, there are norms for both teachers and students. Here a student waits to speak until she is called on.

"*Eighty percent of life is just showing up.*"

WOODY ALLEN,
film director and actor

If you had a class in which the instructor often came late, was poorly prepared, and took phone calls during lectures, you would probably drop it as soon as possible. Instructors, however, can't drop a class when students come late, are poorly prepared, and pay no attention. For a class to function smoothly, everyone should have the same expectations about the class's norms—how students and teachers will behave. In some classes, the instructor is very explicit about the behavior expected. But most often, instructors simply assume that students will adapt to acceptable group norms. The following shows some norms of good classroom etiquette.

- **Attend class.** Just as you expect the instructor to be present at every class, you should plan to attend every course session. Students who attend class usually get better grades than students who skip class. An occasional absence due to illness or emergency may be necessary, but beyond that, absences show a lack of commitment to your education.

- **Arrive on time.** Make sure you arrive on time and are seated and ready to begin before the class starts. It's disruptive to everyone when a student walks in late. If your schedule means you can't make it to a particular class on time, then drop the class.

- **Stay until the end.** Plan to stay in class until it's over. Don't schedule appointments, jobs, or other personal business to interfere with class sessions. If you must leave early on occasion, inform the instructor before class that you have to leave early.

- **Respect the instructor's or school's policies about eating and drinking.** Some teachers tolerate an early-morning cup of coffee, but others don't want any food or drink in their classrooms. The smells are distracting, food winds up on the desk and floor, and trash accumulates. If you do bring something to eat or drink to class, be sure to clean up after yourself.

- **Turn off cell phones during class.** We've already discussed cell phone etiquette in Chapter 9, but in case a reminder is necessary, cell phones and pagers should be turned off during class. If you are expecting an extremely important emergency call, inform the teacher beforehand. Then set the ringer on vibrate, and take the call outside in the hall.

- **Listen to others during discussions and presentations.** Be courteous and pay attention to your fellow students. You might even learn something. At the very least, you will be helping to ensure that people pay attention to you when you speak up during discussions or give an oral report.

- **Treat others with respect when you speak.** A classroom contains many people who may have attitudes very different from yours. Whatever your private opinions are about people, respond to them with respect, even when you are disagreeing with them. Don't interrupt, don't dominate a discussion, and don't make personal comments about anyone, including the instructor.

- ■ **Use a computer appropriately.** If you bring a laptop or handheld electronic device to class, use it only for class business. Do not surf the Web, do your on-line shopping, catch up on your e-mail, play games, or keyboard an assignment for the next class. Use the device for taking notes or accessing course-related materials on line.

- ■ **Resolve issues with the instructor.** If you have a disagreement with the instructor or are upset by something you think is unfair, don't bring up the issue in class. Instead, discuss the problem after class or during a scheduled appointment.

These are just some common norms to help people get along in class groups and thus get more out of their courses.

Your Turn 11–4

RATE YOURSELF AS A MEMBER OF YOUR CLASS

How well do you function as a member of your class? Think about the last few class sessions you've attended, and then answer these questions:

1. What do you do, if anything, to prepare for class meetings?

    _____

2. Do you take notes in class?

    _____

3. What do you do if you disagree with something that's said?

    _____

4. How frequently do you participate in class discussions?

    _____

5. Are you courteous to other group members?

    _____

6. Compare your class's norms to the classroom norms listed on page 262. How are they similar? How are they different?

    _____

Tech Tips

NORMS FOR COURSE DISCUSSION BOARDS

Traditional classes have one set of norms, and online classes have another. When you take an online or hybrid course, most of your interactions with instructor and classmates will take place on course discussion boards. These are Internet sites where people write and post messages to one another. Even in traditional courses, you may use online discussion boards for some communications. Following are some Internet etiquette norms (also called netiquette) to follow in online discussion boards:

- **Treat your instructor and classmates with courtesy and respect.** A course discussion board is the online equivalent of a classroom, so behave as if you were face to face in the same room.

- **Be prepared to participate in discussions.** Do the assignments and readings so you will be able to contribute to the "conversation."

- **Read before writing.** Read what is already posted so you do not repeat what others have already written. Ask questions if you'd like something clarified.

- **Give your post a specific title.** A descriptive title for your message will help people identify the topic of your post.

- **Be brief.** Stick to the point, and keep your messages concise.

- **Watch your language.** Since there are no visual or auditory cues to help people interpret messages, the words of your message become very important. When you write a post, avoid strong or offensive language. You can disagree with another person's ideas, but don't make personal attacks.

- **Use good grammar and spelling.** Write and spell correctly so your readers won't have trouble interpreting your message. Do not use slang, abbreviations, and "NetSpeak" ("u r rite" for "you are right") unless your instructor specifically permits them. AND DON'T USE ALL CAPITAL LETTERS; this is considered rude.

- **Read your post aloud before sending it.** You'll be able to tell whether your message is clear and has an appropriate tone for a classroom, and you can correct grammar and typographical errors.

- **Do not post ads.** Marketing is not appropriate for a class discussion board.

- **Report problems directly to your instructor.** If someone has posted something offensive, let your instructor know. He or she will deal with the problem.

- **The Internet is forever.** Remember that once you press the send button, your message will exist on other people's computers for the foreseeable future. Don't post anything you may regret later.

Your Turn 11–5

EVALUATING A COURSE DISCUSSION BOARD

If you are taking a course with a discussion board, log on and read some posts. Look for posts that follow the guidelines above, and look for posts that violate them. Then answer these questions.

1. Describe one of the "good" posts you found. What made this post effective?

_____

_____

2. Describe one of the posts that violated one or more of the guidelines. What was wrong with it? How would you improve it?

_____

_____

3. What other suggestions do you have for making online discussion boards better?

_____

_____

Leading Groups

In every group there is usually someone who takes charge. The leader may be the person who has formal authority, like the instructor or the highest-ranking manager at a business meeting, or the leader may be a group member who simply directs everyone, like a student who takes charge of a project group. Leadership, then, is more than a title. Leadership is a set of behaviors, beliefs, and values that enables the leader to persuade others to act.

People become the leaders of their groups in several ways. A leader may be elected, such as the president of a parent-teacher association or labor union. A leader may be appointed, as are the members of the president's cabinet, who head various departments of the federal government. Or a leader can simply emerge from the group, as happens in groups of workers, students, or friends.

Qualities of a Good Leader

Some people seem born to leadership. They have a quality known as charisma, a special "magic" to their personalities that inspires great popular loyalty. People with charisma have great self-confidence, personal magnetism, and communication skills. Martin Luther King Jr., Magic Johnson, Princess Diana, and Nelson Mandela are examples of people with this leadership quality.

"*Either lead, follow, or get out of the way.*"

SIGN ON BROADCAST EXECUTIVE
Ted Turner's desk

A good leader need not be charismatic, however. He or she must simply possess a variety of qualities that many ordinary people have. First and foremost, leaders have good human relations skill. The ability to get along well with others is the foundation of true leadership. Second, leaders are very goal oriented and very motivated. They know what they want to accomplish, and they are able to focus on doing what's necessary to achieve their goals. Third, leaders have good self-belief. Their outlook on themselves and on life is positive. They can communicate the confidence they have in themselves and in life to help motivate others.

Basic Leadership Styles

Just as people have different personalities, they approach the task of leading a group in different ways. People differ in the emphasis they put on:[2]

- the task itself—getting a job done
- relationships with others—being interested primarily in people

Democrats Leaders who stress both task and relationships can be called Democrats. They tend to derive their authority from the cooperative ideals and goals of the group. They are good at getting individuals to participate, because they are not overly concerned with maintaining their own authority or power. They are interested in motivating group members to share the responsibility for achieving the group's goals.

Taskmasters Leaders who stress the task over the group's relationships are Taskmasters. They are more concerned about getting the job done than fostering fellowship. They tend to be confident, independent, and ambitious. To get group members to do what's necessary, they try to control behavior with rewards and punishments. This type of leader assigns tasks and responsibilities to group members.

Nurturers Leaders who put relationships over the task at hand are Nurturers. They believe that people come first. They emphasize the personal development of group members. Because of this, they tend to be sympathetic, approving, and friendly. They create a secure atmosphere in which the group can operate.

Bureaucrats Leaders who are oriented neither to the task nor to relationships are Bureaucrats. They behave in a cautious, orderly, and conservative way. They prefer facts and established procedures to risk-taking behavior. Such leaders pay attention to detail and accuracy.

Situational Leadership Which of these four basic leadership styles is best? The answer to this question is: the style that is most effective in a particular set of circumstances. Although each of us may possess traits and values that make us tend naturally to one of the four basic styles, good leaders can adapt their styles to the situation. The ability to adapt your leadership style to different circumstances is called situational leadership.

> "The great leaders are like the best conductors; they reach beyond the notes to reach the magic in the players."
>
> BLAINE LEE,
> author

(© Johnny Crawford/The Image Works)

After the September 11, 2001, attack on the World Trade Center in New York City, Rudolph Giuliani, who was then the mayor, showed exceptional situational leadership skills. Normally a taskmaster in style, Giuliani became strong yet flexible, demonstrating elements of all the leadership styles as the situation demanded. Years later, when he ran for the Republican presidential nomination, his taskmaster style was again evident. Giuliani was unable to convince voters that he had the type of leadership qualities necessary to be president, and he was not nominated.

A team of researchers working together on a long-term project would probably do best with a leader who thinks both task and relationships are important—a Democrat. In this situation the contributions of motivated, creative individuals are important in achieving the best results. In contrast, a factory gearing up for a seasonal crunch would benefit from a leader who stresses task over relationships, assigning jobs and responsibilities as necessary—the Taskmaster.

A self-help group such as dieters needs a leader who stresses relationships over tasks—the Nurturer. Since the achievement of goals is closely related to the psychological well-being of the individuals, the leader must emphasize the interpersonal relations of the group members. In a situation in which neither the task nor the relationships are particularly important, the leader can focus on process and procedure. The Bureaucrat does well in situations in which the means are as important as the ends—government agencies, for example.

Your Turn 11–6

WHICH LEADERSHIP STYLE WORKS BEST?

1. Indicate which of the following leadership styles is best suited to the groups listed below.

   Democrat style: emphasizes cooperation and shared responsibility

   Taskmaster style: focuses on the tasks that need to be done, not on people

   Nurturer style: focuses on group members, not on tasks

   Bureaucrat style: focuses on procedures rather than people or tasks

   a. a platoon of soldiers in battle   _____

   b. employees of a state motor vehicles bureau   _____

   c. the head of a family   _____

   d. a professional association   _____

   e. a church choir   _____

   f. a youth group   _____

   g. a group of volunteers for a neighborhood block party   _____

   h. employees in a research "think tank"   _____

   i. a department in a college   _____

   j. the staff of a college yearbook   _____

2. Which style would you favor for leading a group? Why?

   _____

   _____

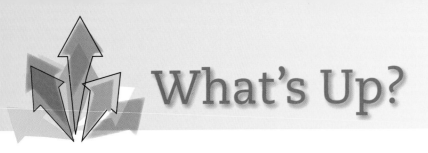
What's Up?

Name _____ Date _____

1. What is the difference between a formal group and an informal group?

_____
_____
_____
_____

2. Briefly state what the cooperative and competitive goals of a basketball team might be.

_____
_____
_____
_____

3. What are norms?

_____
_____
_____
_____

4. Describe these group communication patterns:

   Chain _____
_____
_____

   Wheel _____
_____
_____

   All-channel _____
_____
_____

5. What is conformity?

_____
_____
_____
_____

Name _____ Date _____

6. What is groupthink?

_____

_____

_____

_____

_____

7. Why do people generally observe quietly when they first join a new group?

_____

_____

_____

_____

_____

8. What is the purpose of an agenda?

_____

_____

_____

_____

_____

9. What is leadership?

_____

_____

_____

_____

_____

10. Why is situational leadership effective?

_____

_____

_____

_____

_____

Case Studies

The Case of the Garbled Messages

Alex, Gayle, Jennifer, and Keith were assigned to a class team to write and present two papers. The group met once to plan the first paper. A few days later, Alex told Gayle what he needed from her. Gayle, in turn, explained to Jennifer what she had to do. Jennifer then coached Keith about his share of the work. There were several drafts because each of them made mistakes or forgot to tell the next person something critical. The process was frustrating, and they dreaded doing the second paper.

1. Describe the communication pattern this group used when they prepared the first paper.

_____

_____

2. How would you change the way the group operates in order to make the preparation of the second paper less frustrating and more efficient?

_____

_____

_____

The Case of the Inexperienced Teacher's Aide

Jamika got a part-time job as a teacher's aide in a daycare center. She loved helping the teacher lead the four-year-olds in the various activities of their morning. One morning, the teacher called in sick, and Jamika was on her own. Many of the children seemed cranky that day, and Jamika tried to soothe each one affectionately. She spent a lot of time with a little girl who wouldn't take her coat off. By the middle of the morning, some children were fighting over a toy, the little girl still had her coat on, and another group refused her suggestion that they clean up the toys they had played with. Jamika was getting upset. It was clear to her that she had lost control of the class.

1. What leadership style is Jamika using?

_____

_____

2. To get the group back on track, what leadership style might Jamika try? Why?

_____

_____

_____

_____

Journal

Answer the following journal questions.

1. Describe the role you play in your family and the norms for your behavior. To what extent is having a role and norms useful? To what extent does it limit you?

_____
_____
_____
_____
_____
_____

2. Have you ever felt prejudice toward someone else and been mistaken about what they were really like? Describe what happened and what changed your attitude.

_____
_____
_____
_____
_____
_____

3. What was the least successful group you've been in? What made the group function poorly? How might its group dynamics been improved?

_____
_____
_____
_____
_____

4. Describe a person who has played a great leadership role in your life. What qualities made this person an outstanding leader?

_____
_____
_____
_____
_____
_____

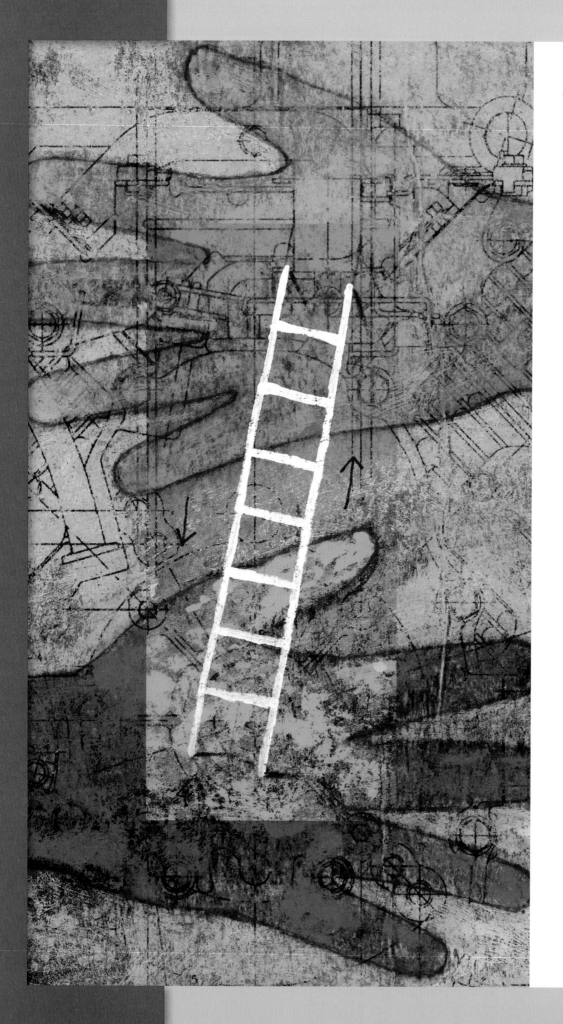

Developing Your
Action Plan

In previous units, you learned how to make the most of your emotional, intellectual, physical, and social potential. Now you are going to put these aspects of yourself to use. In the following chapters, you will learn some practical tips for managing change, stress, and money, and you will use all you have learned to start planning your career.

CHAPTER 12 HANDLING CHANGE AND STRESS

In this chapter, you will be...

...developing your self belief:
- I will remember that good self-belief helps protect me from feelings of stress.
- I will cope with stress and emerge as a stronger person.

...reframing your thoughts:
- I will think positively to help me cope with stress.
- I will view change as an opportunity rather than a threat.
- I will learn to say no to extra tasks for which I have no time.

...setting goals:
- I will develop a social network to help me in times of stress.
- I will make at least one lifestyle change to help me cope with stress.

...envisioning a compelling future:
- I will imagine a world in which I have dealt with the source of my stress.

...achieving personal mastery:
- I will cope with the symptoms of stress by eating and sleeping well, exercising, relaxing, and seeking support from friends and family.

CHAPTER 13: MANAGING MONEY

In this chapter, you will be...

...developing your self belief:
- I will view money as a tool, not as a measure of my self-belief.

...reframing your thoughts:
- I will make money decisions based on more on fact than emotion.

...setting goals:
- I will prepare a budget for my everyday expenses.
- I will set a long-term financial goal based on my values and beliefs.

...envisioning a compelling future:
- I will imagine having enough money to live securely and do the things I would like to do.

...achieving personal mastery:
- I will acquire the personal finance skills that will help me throughout life.

CHAPTER 14: PREPARING FOR YOUR CAREER

In this chapter, you will be...

...developing your self belief:
- I will view work as an activity that will challenge and satisfy me as well as earn money.

...reframing your thoughts:
- I will take inventory of the personal qualities, experience, skills, and interests I can offer.
- I will match my aptitudes and background to suitable occupations.

...setting goals:
- I will investigate career information resources on campus.
- I will participate in job-shadowing or internships programs.
- I will prepare a resume and career portfolio.
- I will set at least one long-term career goal.

...envisioning a compelling future:
- I will find a good job with career potential.

...achieving personal mastery:
- I will acquire the education, skills, and experience that will help me be flexible and successful in the global economy.

Handling Change and Stress

One person's stress is another person's sport.

Two factory workers learned that in six months their plant would shut down. Both felt extremely stressed about losing their jobs. The first, after a brief period of feeling angry and anxious, decided he would go back to school and acquire skills that would enable him to get off the factory floor and into a more promising career. The second worker tried to get factory work elsewhere, but no one was hiring. After months of job hunting, he lost the motivation to look for a job. Two years after the plant shut down, one man is on his way to a new career and another is counted among the "permanently unemployed."

Why did one person become energized by the prospect of a layoff and another become demoralized? Many psychologists think that, like beauty, stress is in the mind of the beholder. Most events in and of themselves are not traumatic enough to cause stress. Rather, **stress** is the psychological and physical reaction that results when a person has trouble *coping* with a situation, event, or change. People feel stress when they interpret the situation as likely to overtax their ability to deal with it. Thus, one person's stressful situation may be another person's enjoyable challenge. To give an extreme example, most of us would feel tremendous stress if we were pushed out of an airplane with a parachute on our back. Skydivers, on the other hand, would find this experience exhilirating.

Despite the potentially serious effects of long-term stress, it's a mistake to think that stress is a completely negative experience. Stress has positive aspects as well. Many people experience growth when they seek new experiences they are not sure they can handle. When you start a new job, choose a difficult course of study, or decide to get married, you are seeking stress, whether you are aware of it or not. On the other hand, if you constantly played it safe and never tried something new or challenging, you would never reach your potential. You would stop growing. To live a successful life, you must handle the stress you seek and the stress that comes unpredictably.

Experiencing stress is an inevitable part of life, and you can learn to manage it. By studying this chapter, you will:

- learn about the causes of stress;
- discover our responses to stressful situations;
- understand the relationship of personality and environment to stress; and
- discover some strategies for coping with stress.

Finally, you will learn how to deal with a modern source of stress—"technostress."

Natural disasters can be extremely stressful events.

The minor hassles of daily life can cause anxiety. For example, a traffic jam can be stressful, especially when you don't expect it or it makes you late.

What Causes Stress

As we've already seen, what causes stress for one person may be routine or even stimulating for someone else. Nevertheless, we can make some generalizations about the types of events that cause stress for most people:

- **Major negative events,** like losing a loved one or a job, being the victim of a serious crime, or having a life-threatening illness
- **Minor daily events,** like traffic jams, school deadlines, rushed schedules, noisy neighbors, and missing keys
- **Catastrophic events,** like major natural disasters, acts of war, terrorism, or torture.

All these types of events can vary in their intensity. There are some characteristics that make a particular event or situation more stressful for most people.[1]

- **Unpredictable events are more stressful than predictable events.** Getting sick unexpectedly causes more stress than an annual case of hay fever.
- **Uncontrollable events cause more stress than controllable events,** Being expelled from school is more stressful than quitting.
- **Uncertain events are more stressful than definite events.** Not knowing whether you've gotten a job causes more stress than knowing whether you've gotten it or not.
- **Long-term events cause more stress than brief one-time events.** Having a chronic disease causes more stress than having a serious but short illness.

Your Turn 12-1

The following questions ask about your feelings and thoughts in the last month. For each item, check how often you felt or thought that way.[2]

1. In the last month, how often have you felt that you were unable to control the important things in life?

☐ never (0)   ☐ almost never (1)   ☐ sometimes (2)   ☐ fairly often (3)   ☐ very often (4)

2. In the last month, how often have you felt confident about your ability to handle your personal problems?

☐ never (0)   ☐ almost never (1)   ☐ sometimes (2)   ☐ fairly often (3)   ☐ very often (4)

3. In the last month, how often have you felt that things were going your way?

☐ never (4)   ☐ almost never (3)   ☐ sometimes (2)   ☐ fairly often (1)   ☐ very often (0)

4. In the last month, how often have you felt difficulties were piling up so high that you could not overcome them?

☐ never (0)   ☐ almost never (1)   ☐ sometimes (2)   ☐ fairly often (3)   ☐ very often (4)

Add the point values of the answers you checked off. The scores range from a maximum of 16, which indicates you feel very stressed, to a minimum of 0, which indicates you feel no stress.

What common thread runs through all these stressful events? *It's the feeling that we have lost control and cannot cope.*

Responses to Stress

All of us respond to stressful situations both psychologically and physically. We begin by assessing the situation—a psychological response—and almost immediately react physically as well.

Psychological Responses

We first react to stressful events by assessing them. We ask ourselves:

1. Is the situation good, neutral, or bad?
2. Do I have the resources to cope with it?
3. What will the consequences be if I fail to cope?
4. What would failing to cope with the event mean for my self-belief?

Exams are a common source of stress for students, especially when a lot is at stake and they feel they are not well prepared.

Let's take an example. Suppose Kaylee is barely passing a course in which the final exam is coming up. If she doesn't pass the exam, she will flunk the course. Clearly, this situation is not good or neutral; the fact that she might fail a course is bad (question 1). But can Kaylee pass the final exam? Can she catch up with the reading, study the material, and go into the exam prepared enough to pass (question 2)? What would happen if she does fail the exam and thus the course (question 3)? What would failing do for her self-belief (question 4)? The way Kaylee answers these questions will affect the amount of stress she feels. In this case, Kaylee does feel threatened by the possibility of failing, she's so far behind she thinks she can't catch up, the course is in her major so failing has important consequences, and she feels that any failure means she is a total loser. Clearly, Kaylee is going to be very stressed out about this exam.

People vary in their appraisals of similar situations. Another student, Megan, is in the same course and has the same problem. But Megan thinks that if she reads and studies nonstop until the exam, she can pass. Anyway, she reasons, failing wouldn't be so bad—she needs the course for her major, but she can always ask her advisor for help. Perhaps he'll suggest that she repeat the course next term if she does fail. And finally, Megan doesn't think that failing a course means she is failing at life. She figures that in the worst case scenario, her parents would be angry for a while, and she might have to reconsider her major.

These differences in thought patterns between Kaylee and Megan help explain how people can have such different reactions to the same types of events. As we saw in Chapter 1, whether our thought patterns are usually negative or positive can affect our self-belief and well-being. This is especially so when we are experiencing stress.

Physical Responses

The physical responses to stress begin while we are assessing the situation. The immediate physical reactions include increased levels of stress hormones, which help the body produce more energy, higher blood pressure, and faster heart rate. These responses can help us deal with stress in the short run by improving our "fight or flight" ability. For a while, the body can keep up the "high alert" of the stress response, but eventually we become exhausted.

The "fight or flight" response provides the surge of energy that helps people and animals deal with immediate danger. It is less useful, however, to cope with long-term stress.

Long-Term Responses to Stress

Psychologists think that the fight or flight response works well for short-term physically threatening situations, like being attacked in a dark alley. Unfortunately, the response works less well for the psychologically threatening situations of modern life, like a tough final exam or rush hour traffic. In these situations, our bodies overreact to the actual threat we face. As a result, the stresses of modern life can take a long-term toll on our physical and mental health. When stress continues over a long period, it can weaken the body's ability to fight infection and contribute to heart disease and cancer.

When people have serious symptoms of stress that impair their ability to carry out the normal tasks of daily life, they may be suffering from a psychological disorder. They may have posttraumatic stress syndrome (common among war veterans and victims of disasters or violent crimes) or clinical levels of anxiety or depression. Stress that interferes with daily life calls for seeking professional help.

Signs of Stress

The responses to stress are varied, and different people experience different combinations of symptoms. Learning to recognize the many signs of stress, which include physical symptoms, mental changes, emotional changes, and behavioral changes, will help you identify and cope with stress.

- **Physical signs.** The most common physical manifestations of stress are shortness of breath, increased or irregular heart rate, chest pains, fatigue, headache, insomnia, muscle tension (especially in the neck and shoulders), abdominal cramps, and nausea. People who experience stress over a long period often get colds.

- **Mental signs.** Stress changes the way people think and perceive. Common changes in mental functioning include negative thought patterns, decreased concentration, increased forgetfulness, indecisiveness, confusion, and the mind racing or going blank.

- **Emotional signs.** People under stress can experience anxiety, nervousness, depression, anger, frustration, and fear. They may become irritable and impatient, and their tempers may grow short.

- **Behavioral signs.** All these physical and psychological changes often show themselves in behavioral changes. Typical behaviors of those under stress include pacing, fidgeting, and nail biting; increased eating, smoking, and drinking; crying, yelling, swearing, and blaming; and throwing things or hitting.

Your Turn 12-2

STRESS SIGNALS CHECKLIST

Are you suffering from stress? More than two or three of the following signs may be an indication that you should examine your life for sources of stress. Place a check mark next to any symptoms that apply to you.

Physical Signs
- ☐ Shortness of breath
- ☐ Fast or irregular heartbeat
- ☐ Muscle tension
- ☐ Nausea
- ☐ Insomnia

Mental Signs
- ☐ Difficulty in concentrating
- ☐ Increased forgetfulness
- ☐ Confusion
- ☐ Mind racing or going blank
- ☐ Indecisiveness

Emotional Signs
- ☐ Anxiety
- ☐ Depression
- ☐ Anger
- ☐ Frustration
- ☐ Fear

Behavioral Signs
- ☐ Pacing, fidgeting
- ☐ Nail biting
- ☐ Changes in eating, drinking, or smoking
- ☐ Crying, yelling, or swearing
- ☐ Throwing things or hitting

Stress, Personality, and the Environment

As we have seen, individuals have different reactions to the same stressful events. In the case of the two factory workers who were laid off, one saw the loss of his job as an opportunity to grow; the other became paralyzed and unable to act. The same event held a very different meaning for each of their lives. One man was able to take risks, think positively, and adapt well to his new situation. The other man avoided risk, became demoralized, and adapted poorly.

What factors contribute to such dramatic differences in responses to potentially stressful situations? There are factors that increase our vulnerability to stress, and factors that help protect us:

- **Factors that increase the likelihood that we will feel stress** include a dislike of change or risk, negative self-belief, poor coping and time management skills, and a lack of social support.

- **Factors that help protect us from stress** include a positive attitude toward change, good self-belief, resilience and good coping and time management skills, and a good social network.

"*Change of fortune is the lot of life.*"

Proverb

WHATEVER IT TAKES
Sylvia Harris

(© Peter Wynn Thompson/Redux Pictures)

Growing up in California, Sylvia Harris always loved animals, especially horses, and wanted to be a veterinarian. However, while she was attending Santa Rosa Junior College, her parents divorced. Harris believes the stress of the divorce triggered her first bout of bipolar disorder. With periods of manic activity followed by depression, Harris suffered for years. Her health deteriorated, and in 1995, she was sent to a psychiatric hospital for three months.

With medication, Harris was able to control her disorder, and she moved to Florida to go back to school. There, in 1999, Harris hit bottom when her car was stolen, she lost her job and apartment, and she wound up homeless on the streets of Orlando. When a minister at a homeless shelter asked her about her interests, Harris told him she liked horses. He arranged for her to move to Ocala, Florida, an area known for its racing horses. There Harris landed a job grooming the horses at Quail Roost Farm. "I still had never been on a horse, and I was 35 years old," Harris says. She told the owner she wanted to be a jockey.

In the months she spent at Quail Roost, Harris learned how to ride. But then the owner died, and the farm was shut down. Harris moved on to other centers of horse racing, working as a groom and exercise rider but always wanting to qualify for a jockey's license.

In 2005, she wound up in Chicago, with an empty tank of gas and $55 in her pocket. She went to Arlington Park, where she found steady work with the horses. In 2007, she was occasionally offered a horse to race, more as a favor than because anyone thought she would win. But in November, a horse she was riding—a horse no one else wanted to ride because they thought he was infirm—placed third at Hawthorne Race Course. In his next race with Harris on December 1, the horse actually won. This victory made Harris the second African American woman to win a thoroughbred horse race; the first was Cheryl White, who rode in the 1970s.

At 40, Harris understands she is at an age when most jockeys are retiring rather than starting out. Still, she is happy with what she has accomplished. "I've proved that I can do this and it has given me confidence," she says. "The horses have changed my life."

Sources: "Black Female Jockey Reborn After Being Homeless," Associated Press, Jan. 23, 2008, <http://NBCSports.com>, accessed May 19, 2008; Bill Finley, "Becoming a Jockey Changes a Life," *New York Times,* January 9, 2008, p. C13; "Jockey Harris Earns First Career Win," ThoroughbredTimes.com, 2008, accessed January 11, 2008; Jason Shandler, "Harris' Long Climb to the Top," BloodhorseNOW.com, January 7, 2008, accessed May 18, 2008.

Attitudes to Change

Some people find change to be threatening. They are much more comfortable when life settles into a predictable routine. The thought of doing something new and different makes them very anxious. Risk avoiders feel that new situations threaten their fragile self-belief. So they use up more energy trying to maintain the status quo. Ironically, the effort to avoid risk also creates stress.

On the other hand, some people believe that change is the fundamental condition of life. They feel that new things are challenges rather than threats. Such people tend to be open and flexible, and they take risks when necessary. Risk takers accept that they will feel a certain amount of stress. They have positive self-belief, and they are confident in their ability to cope.

Negative and Positive Thought Patterns

As you recall from Chapter 1, your beliefs influence your behavior. People who are in the habit of thinking in negative ways believe they are unable to cope. Because of their negative thought patterns, they find many events stressful. Some typical thoughts of a stress-prone person are:

"I can tell she doesn't like me."

"I must get this right the first time."

"I can't do anything right."

"I'll never get another job."

"It's the worst thing that could happen."

"I'm a loser."

With thoughts like these, it's no wonder that these people feel stressed about their lives. All these thoughts are sending the message: I am helpless. Believing you are helpless means you lose the will to exert control over your life and your surroundings. The feeling of helplessness leads to stress.

People with self-confidence believe they can influence events and take control of their lives. They tend to think things like "This may be challenging, but I can do it." With a more positive outlook, their ability to deal with stress improves.

Resilience: The Ability to Cope

People who feel they are helpless are vulnerable to stress, because they believe they cannot take control and influence their environment. At the other extreme are people who feel they must be in control at all times. Since this is impossible, of course, they react with stress even to the slightest changes they haven't initiated.

People who fall between these two extremes—the helpless and the controlling—are best able to cope with change and stress. They have the ability to change what they can change, adapt to what they can't change, and understand the difference between the two. Such people are hardy and resilient. When they experience stress, they respond with a positive attitude. Their ability to cope with stress enables them to bounce back to a more relaxed state fairly quickly.

> "A pessimist is one who makes difficulties of his opportunities and an optimist is one who makes opportunities of his difficulties."
>
> HARRY S. TRUMAN (1884–1972), thirty-third U.S. president

> "God, give us the serenity to accept what cannot be changed; give us the courage to change what should be changed; give us the wisdom to distinguish one from the other."
>
> REINHOLD NIEBUHR (1892–1971), religious and social thinker

Your Turn 12-3

ARE YOU PRONE TO STRESS?

How well are you described in the items below? In the space provided, write one of the numbers 1 through 4 as follows: **1 Never   2 Sometimes   3 Frequently   4 Always**

1. I try to do as much as possible in the least amount of time. _____

2. When I play a game, I have to win in order to feel good. _____

3. I find it hard to ask for help with a problem. _____

4. I'm very critical of others. _____

5. I'm very ambitious. _____

6. I try to do more than one thing at a time. _____

7. I spend little time on myself. _____

8. I am very competitive. _____

9. I get involved in many projects at the same time. _____

10. I have a lot of deadlines at work or school. _____

11. I have too many responsibilities. _____

12. I become impatient with delays or lateness. _____

13. I speed up to get through yellow lights. _____

14. I need the respect and admiration of other people. _____

15. I keep track of what time it is. _____

16. I have too much to do and too little time to do it. _____

17. My friends think I'm very competitive. _____

18. I feel guilty if I relax and do nothing. _____

19. I talk very quickly. _____

20. I get angry easily. _____

Total _____

(continues)

Now total your answers and rate yourself:

Over 70 — You are very prone to stress.

60–69 — You are moderately prone to stress.

40–59 — You are somewhat prone to stress.

30–39 — You occasionally feel stress.

20–29 — You rarely feel stress.

Social Support

Being able to rely on others helps people decrease the impact of stress on their lives. People who are socially isolated are more vulnerable to stress. They tend to be in poorer physical and mental health to begin with, so stressful events add to their troubles. Those who have a strong social network have overall psychological and health advantages that buffer the effects of stress. In addition, they can draw on family and friends to help them cope with specific stressful events.

Coping with Stress

It's important to deal with stress before you suffer from stress overload. There are several basic ways you can cope with stress:

- You can deal with the sources of stress;
- You can acknowledge that friends and family have a claim on your time;
- You can change the way you think about what's causing your stress;
- You can relieve the physical and emotional symptoms of stress; or
- You can turn to friends and family for help and emotional support.

It is usually most effective to use a combination of approaches to manage stress.

Dealing with the Cause

The most direct way of coping with stress is to eliminate its cause. For example, suppose you have a job that's causing you stress. You may have a job that is fast-paced, like working as a short-order cook in a diner. Or you may have a boss who watches every move you make. The most effective way to eliminate stress in these situations is to get another job if you can.

Lack of time and lack of money are common problems that contribute to stress. By improving your time and money management skills, you will be able to decrease the stress that shortages of time and money can cause.

"If a problem has no solution, it may not be a problem, but a fact—not to be solved, but to be coped with over time."

SHIMON PERES,
president of Israel

(For more details on how to manage your time effectively, see Chapter 2. For money management, see Chapter 13.).

Acknowledging the Demands of Others

When people have busy schedules, sometimes they forget that they are certain to be interrupted by friends, family, and colleagues. In reality, the people you live with, work with, and socialize with have a right to some of your time and attention. Ignoring this fact will cause you a lot of stress, because your plans will constantly be falling apart and your relationships with others will suffer.

Therefore, you should plan to be interrupted. Leave what's called "response time" in your schedule: a cushion of time you can use to respond to the people around you. If you plan more time than you think you'll actually need to finish a task, you will still be able to finish it by your deadline even if you are interrupted. And you will remove a source of stress—the conflict between your plans and someone else's needs.

Learning to Say No

There are just so many hours in a day; therefore, we need to develop the ability to say no to additional projects, responsibilities, or demands when accepting them would mean being overcommitted. You need to know how much stress you can cope with, and set priorities on the demands for your time. Developing assertiveness and the willingness to say no will help you accomplish your tasks and goals.

Reframing Your Thoughts

You can also cope with stress by changing how you think about a stressful situation (see Figure 12–1). The meaning that an event has for us depends on the frame through which we see it. By reframing your perceptions, you can change the meaning of an event.

Often people reframe an event or situation by using one of the defense mechanisms we discussed in Chapter 10. Withdrawing, rationalizing, displacing, fantasizing, and projecting are ways in which we try to deal with anxiety-provoking situations. These may be effective in the very

> "Adopting the right attitude can convert a negative stress into a positive one."
>
> HANS SELYE (1907–1982), Canadian scientist and stress researcher

FIGURE 12–1

Stress involves an event and the way you perceive the event. By changing the way you think about a stressful event, you can reduce the stress you feel.

Negative Thought Pattern

Positive Thought Pattern

short term, but they do not relieve stress in the long run. They just drive it deeper.

Instead of trying to escape or focusing on the fear, worry, or anxiety you are feeling about something, try to focus on something you can positively influence or control. For example, if you are feeling stressful about an exam, instead of worrying about it, reframe your thoughts and focus your energy on studying and preparing. In this way, you can acknowledge your nervousness without letting it take control.

Positive self-talk can be helpful in changing your approach to stressful situations. As you recall from Chapter 1, telling yourself about a situation in positive terms encourages constructive behavior. You can increase your resilience—your ability to cope with change and stress—by focusing on positive rather than negative thoughts.

You can also help change your thinking by taking a time-out from a stressful situation. Even something as simple as a short walk can provide a break and allow time for stress levels to diminish. After the break, you will feel refreshed and have a new perspective on the problem.

News & Views

DRUGS TO RELIEVE STRESS: A TREATMENT, NOT A CURE

People who are suffering from anxiety and stress are sometimes prescribed anti-anxiety drugs by their physicians. Although these drugs can be effective in reducing anxiety, they do not reduce the *causes* of anxiety. They are relieving the symptoms of stress but not curing it, much as a cold tablet can relieve congestion but not cure a cold. And unlike exercise, relaxation, and rest, which can also relieve the symptoms of stress, anti-anxiety drugs have side effects and other risks.

The most frequently prescribed anti-anxiety drugs are Valium and Xanax. Both are benzodiazepines, a type of drug that relieves anxiety symptoms without causing extreme drowsiness. Benzodiazepines act by slowing down the activity of the central nervous system. This has the effect of calming people. If used properly, benzodiazepines are effective for treating a general, chronic state of anxiety. They are less effective for treating the stress associated with a specific event, like a death in the family or giving a speech.

Benzodiazepines have undesirable side effects. First, they can cause drowsiness and lack of coordination. People taking benzodiazepines should not drive or operate machinery. Second, they can interfere with thinking and cause memory loss, so taking benzodiazepines when you are studying is not a good idea. Third, benzodiazepines can multiply the effects of other drugs such as alcohol. When taken in combination with those drugs, they can cause coma or even death. Benzodiazepines can also be addictive. Patients who stop taking it can experience tremors, nausea, and hallucinations, and their anxiety returns.

So benzodiazepines, although helpful for some people, must be used with caution under the supervision of a physician. It's important not to abuse these or any other drugs, because the results of abuse can be deadly.

For some people, the physical and emotional symptoms of stress can be relieved through activities like yoga, which can be relaxing.

"*Friendship ... lessens adversity by dividing and sharing it.*"

CICERO (106 BCE–43 BCE),
Roman statesman and orator

Relieving the Symptoms of Stress through Lifestyle Changes

The third basic way to cope with stress is to make lifestyle changes that can relieve the symptoms of stress. There are changes you can make to your diet, exercise regimen, and sleep patterns that will improve your ability to cope with stress.[3]

- **Decrease or cut out caffeine.** As you recall, caffeine is a stimulant; it has some of the same effects on the body that stress does. Avoiding coffee, tea, colas, energy drinks, and chocolate will reduce the physical symptoms of stress.

- **Eat a well-balanced diet.** A healthy diet will improve the body's ability to cope with stress. Avoid junk food, which is high in sugar and fat. In addition, you can eat certain foods such as grains, fruits, and vegetables; these are thought to have a calming effect.

- **Eat slowly.** Try to relax and enjoy your meals rather than racing through them.

- **Get enough sleep.** You know how many hours of sleep you need to feel good the next day. Try to get that amount every night. Lack of sleep makes people more susceptible to stress.

- **Get regular physical exercise.** Aerobic exercise such as walking, jogging, or swimming has been shown to decrease stress levels (see Chapter 6). Regular physical activity or sports can decrease tension and improve your strength and ability to cope.

- **Do relaxation exercises.** Activities such as resting, meditation, yoga, stretching, and deep breathing help relax the body and calm the mind.

- **Take a break each day.** Put a few minutes aside for yourself each day as a respite from the pressures of life. Pursue interests and hobbies that are a source of pleasure and distraction. Even a short rest can leave you relaxed and better able to cope.

Seeking Social Support

If you have family or friends, you will be able to cope with stress better than people who are on their own. Your family or friends may help you with the cause of your stress. For example, if you are overwhelmed by the conflicting demands of studying and housework, someone may take over a few of your chores. They may give you information that you need to solve a problem. In some cases, they can offer emotional support, reassuring you that someone cares about you.

It's interesting to note that women feel more comfortable about asking for help than men do. In times of stress, they are more likely to turn for help to their family or friends. Men tend to try to deal with stress on their own.

Your Turn 12-4

YOUR SUPPORT GROUP

To whom would you turn if you were feeling stress? Use the circles below to represent members of your support group.[4] Write the names of the people to whom you feel closest in the circles that touch the central "me" circle. In the outer circles, write the names of those to whom you feel connected. The people you choose may live near or far or be from the past or present; they may even no longer be alive except within your memory.

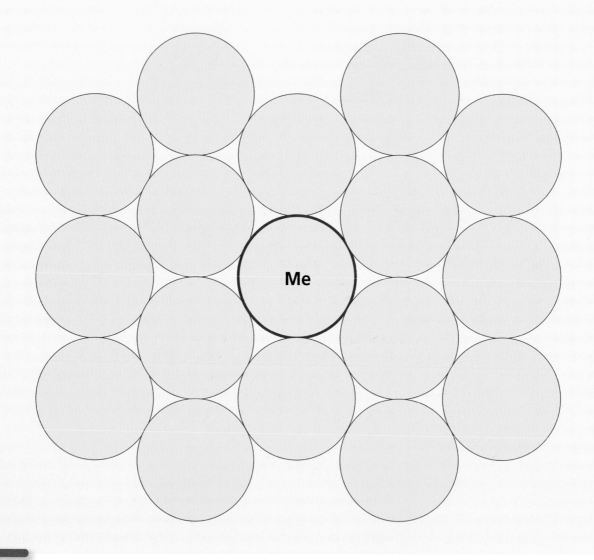

Tech Tips

TECHNOLOGY AND STRESS

We depend on technology in so many areas of our lives that when it fails us—or when we fail to use it properly—we can experience "technostress." But technology can also help us relieve stress. Following are 10 suggestions for minimizing technostress and as well as using technology to cope with stress:

1. **Use anti-virus software.** Keep your computer free of destructive viruses and spyware by installing protection software and keeping it up to date. Running these programs regularly will help keep your computer performing smoothly.

2. **Use file folders.** Organize the files on your computer's hard drive so you can find them easily. Use a separate folder for each course, and give your files descriptive names so you can identify their contents. This way you won't "lose" files or waste time searching for them.

3. **Back up your work.** When you are working on a computer, save your work periodically. That way, in the event of a power failure, you won't lose too much. Furthermore, you should back up important files onto a flash drive, external hard drive, or a storage site on the Web. If your computer fails, you'll have backups of your work.

4. **Try again.** When a computer or other device does fail to perform properly, don't always assume that you have done something wrong. The network or Web site may be down, the software may have a problem, or you may have made a typo. Try again.

5. **Follow computer prompts carefully.** If you get an error message, don't panic. Instead, take your time, read it carefully, and follow the directions. Often, you can solve the problem this way.

6. **Reboot.** If the problem persists, try shutting down and restarting an electronic device. This often resets the machine to the state it was in before the problem occurred.

7. **Get help.** If you cannot correct a problem on your own, ask a tech-savvy friend for help. Pay attention to what he or she does so you can handle the next problem on your own.

8. **Check the Internet for solutions.** Try finding the solution to technical problems on the Internet. Not only do manufacturers post instructions for using their products, they also have help functions on their Web sites. If this fails, you can get in touch with technical support.

9. **Take a break.** If you are spending most of your waking hours in front of a computer, on your cell phone, checking a PDA, or playing video games, you may be experiencing technology overload. Consider breaking the connection for a while—turn everything off and do something else.

10. **Use technology for social support.** Use technology as a tool to help you cope. Remember that social support helps us deal with stress. Get in touch with friends and family via cell phone, e-mail, chat, and social networking sites to main tain your connections with others.

Technology can be a source of stress when it fails, as well as a means to relieve stress when we keep in touch with friends and family.

(©Jose Luis Pelaez, Inc/Getty Images)

Your Turn 12-5

LOOKING FOR TECH SUPPORT

Select one of your electronic devices or software programs, and explore its technical support resources.

1. If you still have the instruction booklet or CD that came with the device or software program, skim it. What types of problems are covered in the troubleshooting section?

2. Go online and search for the technical support section of the manufacturer's Web site. How is the technical support information organized? How can you communicate with the company's technical support staff?

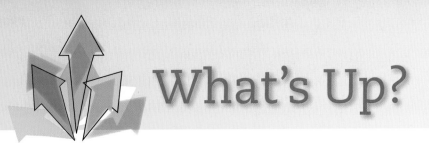

What's Up?

Name _____   Date _____

1. What is stress?
_____
_____

2. Describe the three categories of events that cause stress for most people, and give an example of each.
_____
_____

3. What characteristics do stress-producing events have in common?
_____
_____

4. What are the psychological and physical responses to stress?
_____
_____

5. List physical, mental, emotional, and behavioral signs of stress.
_____
_____

6. How does a person's attitude to change influence his or her experience of stress?
_____
_____

7. Why do people with negative thought patterns experience a lot of stress?
_____
_____

8. How does reframing your thoughts help you cope with stress?
_____
_____

9. What are three lifestyle habits that help you cope with stress?
_____
_____

10. How can people in your support group help you cope with stress?
_____
_____

Case Studies

The Case of the Woman Who Was Too Lucky

Right after she got her associate's degree, Heather got a job in a firm downtown. Two months later, she got married and moved from her parents' house into a new apartment with Diego. She also started taking courses toward her bachelor's degree at night.

Heather thought she should be happy about how well her life was going, but in reality she felt overwhelmed and tense much of the time.

1. Why was Heather feeling jumpy and anxious about her life?

_____

_____

2. What might Heather do to cope with the stress she is feeling?

_____

_____

The Case of the Stressful Job

Arjun had been working at a high-pressure job filled with daily deadlines for about three years. At the beginning of the fourth year, his workload increased when a colleague took a leave of absence. Arjun began experiencing shortness of breath and irregular heartbeat. When these symptoms persisted, he became convinced he was going to have a heart attack. He went to the doctor for a checkup and was told he was healthy. But the symptoms didn't go away.

That summer Arjun's boss talked him into taking three weeks off. By the end of the three weeks, Arjun's symptoms had disappeared.

1. What was the cause of Arjun's shortness of breath and irregular heartbeat?

_____

_____

2. Why did Arjun's symptoms disappear when he took time off from work?

_____

_____

3. What might Arjun do to cope with his stress?

_____

_____

 # Journal

Answer the following journal questions.

1. What everyday hassles cause you stress? How can you use the coping skills described in this chapter to deal with them?

_____

_____

_____

_____

_____

2. Describe someone you know who has a resilient personality that enables him or her to recover quickly from stress. What does this person do to cope?

_____

_____

_____

_____

_____

3. What situation at home, at school, or on the job is causing you stress? How might you cope with the situation? What problem-solving, thinking, lifestyle, and social skills can you use to reduce the stress you are experiencing?

_____

_____

_____

_____

4. To what extent is technology a source of stress for you? How can you use technology to help you cope with stress?

_____

_____

_____

_____

_____

San Francisco Giants pitcher Barry Zito founded StrikeoutsForTroops to raise money for wounded soldiers and their families. He donates $400 each time he strikes out a batter, and he persuaded other baseball players to join him.

(© Mark J. Terrill/AP Photo)

W hat are your dreams and goals? Do you want to start your own business, take a vacation in the Caribbean, or go to school full-time? The chances are that no matter what your goals and dreams are, you will need money to achieve them. And that's money over and above the amount you need for the basics of life—food, shelter, clothing, and so on.

For almost all of us, money, like time, is a limited resource. We earn or receive a limited amount, and with that we try to get by—often from paycheck to paycheck. But just as you must manage your time to get the most out of it, you must learn to manage money for the same reason.

This chapter covers the basics of money management. As you study this chapter, you will:

- assess your attitudes toward money;
- see how the financial pyramid, with your values and goals at its base, provides a model of lifelong personal money management;
- track your income and expenses and prepare a budget;
- review the basics of banking, savings, debit and credit cards, debt, and insurance;
- weigh the pros and cons of home ownership; and
- learn about the importance of investing now for large future expenses.

Finally, you will explore the personal finance resources of the Internet.

© 2011 Wadsworth, Cengage Learning

Attitudes toward Money

Money is a resource that carries a high emotional charge for many people. Time, or lack of it, can cause anxiety and stress, but attitudes toward money are often tangled up with a person's self-belief. American culture places great importance on achieving material success. In this view, the possession of money is often equated with a person's inner worth. The more money you have, the better you are as a person. When money defines self-belief, people depend on possessions to boost their feelings of worth. And possessions, although nice, are not a solid foundation for a positive self-belief.

How do you feel about money? Do you see money as making you a better person? Or do you view money as a tool, something you can use to achieve your goals, whether educational, professional, or personal? Your Turn 13-1 will help you define your attitudes about money.

> "*Make money your god and it will plague you like the devil.*"
>
> HENRY FIELDING (1707–1754), English novelist

Your Turn 13-1

HOW DO YOU FEEL ABOUT MONEY?

This exercise will give you an idea about your attitudes toward money. Circle the answer that corresponds most closely with your feelings.

- When you think of having money, you imagine it
    1 coming from your parents.
    2 belonging to your spouse or significant other.
    3 belonging to you.

- As a child, you spent your allowance or pocket money on
    1 anything you wanted.
    2 necessities.
    3 birthday and holiday presents for your relatives.

- When you were younger, you hated math and did poorly in it. Now that you need to make money decisions, you
    1 figure you can't balance a checking account, much less use your money wisely.
    2 put off making money decisions because you dislike math.
    3 tell yourself that math has nothing to do with your ability to handle money.

- You have just $40 to spend on food and other necessities until payday, four days from now. Passing a pizza place, you

    1 splurge on a pizza with all the toppings.

    2 keep going, because you can't even afford to look in the window.

    3 promise yourself to stop in after payday to buy a pizza.

- You get an unexpected gift of $500. You

    1 buy an expensive watch and new clothes.

    2 invest in bank certificates that will tie up the money for 30 months.

    3 put the money in a savings account to which you have access any time.

- You want to go back to school. You have enough money for only a quarter of the total tuition for the degree or program. You

    1 enroll anyway. Something will come up to pay for the other three quarters.

    2 enroll for a couple of courses, even though they're likely to be your last.

    3 make a plan for financing the whole program through work, grants, and loans.

- You won $30,000. You desperately need a new refrigerator and TV. You

    1 hold off until the refrigerator breaks down and TVs go on sale.

    2 put all the money in the bank and do without a new refrigerator and TV.

    3 buy both.

- Word of your luck has spread at school. The first time your fellow students don't ask you to join them at lunch, you

    1 feel sorry you won the money.

    2 spend lunch time buying them presents.

    3 ignore them and visit a financial planner during your lunch.

    To get your score, add up the numbers you circled. Check the results below.

Your score	What it means
8–10 points	You tend to be very emotional about money. You should beware of making sudden money decisions.
11–17 points	You are shaky about making money decisions. Although you probably won't make major mistakes, you also won't get the most out of your money.
18–24 points	You have an objective attitude toward money and its uses. Be sure you consider all the consequences before making a money decision.

The Financial Pyramid

Now that you have thought about your attitudes toward money, try putting these aside for a while. You'll be a better money manager if you can separate your decisions about money from your feelings. In the remainder of this chapter, we will focus on various aspects of money management. First we will look at the big picture of money management, and then we will consider some of the details that will help you make financial decisions.

The big picture of personal money management is shown by the financial pyramid (see Figure 13–1). The financial pyramid provides a visual model of the main aspects of personal finance. At the base of the financial pyramid are your values and goals. These should be the foundation of all your money decisions. The next step up is your basic living expense—shelter, food, clothing, and so on. Before you can go on to spend money on other things, you must take care of your basic living costs. Once you've budgeted for the basics, you can move up a step to consider savings, credit, and insurance. When these are incorporated in your financial plan, most people are ready to move up a step to home ownership, the main investment of many families. Finally, people devote resources to long-term investing. Common goals for long-term investment are saving for their children's education and saving for retirement.

The financial pyramid helps people set priorities on using their money resources and provides a reminder of important long-term financial goals that people need to act on even when they are young. However, the financial pyramid model may not apply equally to everyone.

> "Money is not the only answer, but it makes a difference."
>
> BARACK OBAMA, forty-fourth president of the United States

FIGURE 13–1

The financial pyramid provides a model for financial planning. The foundation of the pyramid is your values and goals. All decisions about money should arise from that foundation.

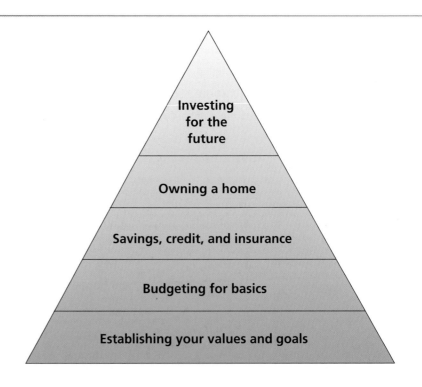

Investing for the future

Owning a home

Savings, credit, and insurance

Budgeting for basics

Establishing your values and goals

For example, some families never own a home; others do not use credit. In addition, the model is not always sequential. Although most people consider these aspects of financial planning in the order shown, from bottom to top, this sequence does not always apply. For instance, if you are living with your parents, you may not need to contribute to basic household expenses, but you may already have dealt with credit when you applied for a credit card or student loans. Once families are well established; however, they are probably making personal finance decisions on each level of the pyramid—at the same time.

Budgeting for the Basics

Planning how you will use your money is called budgeting. A budget is a plan based on your short-, intermediate-, and long-term financial goals. The purpose of a budget is to keep your spending within the limits of your income and to distribute your spending appropriately.

Budgeting has important benefits. The first, of course, is that you will have a better idea of exactly where your money comes from and where it goes. But just as important, budgeting helps you focus on your goals and set priorities for achieving them. Right now you probably don't have enough

Your Turn 13-2

REVIEW YOUR VALUES AND GOALS

Now is a good time to turn back to Chapters 1 and 2 and review your values and goals. Summarize your most important values and goals following. Underline the goals that involve money.

1. Most important values

_____

2. Short-term goals

_____

3. Intermediate-term goals

_____

4. Long-term goals

_____

If not managed properly, money can be a source of conflict in families. Here a couple goes over their bills and budget.

money for all the things you want to do. Does it surprise you to learn that you will probably never have enough money for all the things you want to do? Even though your income may increase in the future, so will your financial responsibilities and your wants. This means you must think about your goals and decide what's most important to you. Budgeting forces you to make choices, plan ahead, and control your spending.[1] But before you can budget, you must have a thorough knowledge of your income and expenses.

Income and Expenses

If you are like most people, you have a pretty good idea of where your money comes from. Your income is the total amount of money coming in. You may have just one or several sources of income:

- a salary you earn by working
- an allowance from your family
- alimony or child support payments
- welfare payments or food stamps
- social security payments
- disability payments
- student financial aid
- tax refunds
- gifts
- interest earned on savings
- investment income and gains

The total amount of your income, from all sources, is called your gross income. If you are working, your employer withholds amounts from your paycheck to pay income taxes, social security (FICA) tax, Medicare tax, group insurance premiums, union dues, 401K retirement account contributions, and other deductions. Thus the amount of money you actually receive, called your net income, is less than your gross income.

Far harder to account for—at least for most people—is where the money goes. The amounts you spend are called expenses. Most people have fixed expenses that are the same from month to month or are due quarterly or yearly. Examples of fixed expenses are rent or mortgage payments, car payments, phone and utility bills, cable TV bills, installment loan payments, savings plans, and insurance payments. Variable expenses differ from one period to another. Food, clothing, entertainment, gas, repairs, gifts, furniture, and education are just a few examples of variable expenses.

Needless to say, if your expenses are greater than your income, or if you are unable to put away money to achieve long-term objectives, you have a problem; however, you can improve your money situation by budgeting.

The Four A's of Budgeting

Budgeting has four basic steps, called the four A's of budgeting.[2]

1. Accounting for income and expenses
2. Analyzing your situation
3. Allocating your income
4. Adjusting your budget

Accounting for Income and Expenses The first step of budgeting is accounting for your income and expenses. What this means, in practice, is that you have to keep track of income and expenses for a couple of months. You keep track not only of big expenses like car payments but small expenses like renting a DVD or buying a snack. If you have a checking account or make most purchases with a credit or debit card, you will have good records of many of your expenses.

To track income and expenses, you can keep a record using a computer spreadsheet or a paper notebook set up as shown on pages 302–303. Divide the record into two sections—a small section for income and a large section for expenses. When you get paid or receive money, enter the date, source, and amount in the income section. When you spend money—even 50 cents for a pack of gum—note the date, what you bought, and how much you paid in the expenses section. Remember to enter items you purchase with a credit card. For example, if you charge a pair of shoes, enter the amount you charge in the clothing column. To make record keeping easier, you can divide your expenses into categories such as rent, phone, utilities, food, clothing, transportation, medical/dental, entertainment, personal items, gifts, and so on. At the end of each month, total your income and expenses by categories. These figures will be the basis for your budget.

Your Turn 13-3

TRACK YOUR INCOME AND EXPENSES

Use the income and expense record on pages 302–303 to keep track of all your income and expenses for two months. You can remove the chart from your book and carry it with you for convenience.

Income and Expense Record, Month of _____

Income

Date	Source	Net Amount
	Total	

Expenses

Date	Rent/Mortgage	Telecom.	Utilities	Insurance	Loans & Credit Payments	Transportation	Food
Totals							

Date	Clothing	Household	Medical	Education	Savings/Emerg.	Personal	Other
Totals							

Total expenses for month _____

Income and Expense Record, Month of _____

Income

Date	Source	Net Amount
	Total	

Expenses

Date	Rent/Mortgage	Telecom.	Utilities	Insurance	Loans & Credit Payments	Transportation	Food
Totals							

Date	Clothing	Household	Medical	Education	Savings/Emerg.	Personal	Other
Totals							

Total expenses for month _____

Analyzing Your Situation After you've kept track of income and expenses for a couple of months, you should analyze your situation. Ask yourself some questions:

- Did your expenses exceed your income?
- Were you able to pay all your fixed expenses?
- Did a large periodic expense such as an annual insurance premium or tuition bill throw you off?
- Are you spending too much money on some types of things?
- Did you pay off all your credit card balances, or did you get by with the minimum payment?
- Were you able to save money for one of your goals (vacation, tuition, a new computer, a car, down payment on a house, retirement, etc.)?

Your answers to these questions will point up any weaknesses in your current money situation.

Allocating Your Income Now comes decision-making time. You've kept track of income and expenses for a couple of months and you've reviewed your spending patterns. You probably think that at this rate you'll never have money to reach your goals! But there are things you can do.

First, figure out how much you must allocate to each of your monthly fixed expenses. You must allocate money for bills you pay monthly (such as rent, electricity, and credit card payments), as well as bills you pay quarterly, semiannually, or annually (insurance premiums, tuition, excise taxes, real estate taxes, and so on). Perhaps you noticed that you were unprepared to pay that semiannual auto insurance premium or some other periodic large bill. If you set aside a certain amount of money each month, you would be ready to pay those large, occasional, but regular expenses. For example, if the cost of your auto insurance premium is $600 a year, you should be allocating $50 each month toward that expense ($600 divided by 12 months equals $50).

After you've budgeted your fixed expenses, review your variable expenses to see where you are overspending. You must make judgments between what you really need and what you want. For example, are you spending a lot more than you thought on personal items and restaurant meals? If you could cut down on these expenditures, you could use the money you save to pay down your credit card balance or start saving. Try to allocate money for things that are really important to you in the long run.

Next, consider what you would do if your car broke down and needed a $400 repair. These things happen all the time, but if you haven't set aside money in an **emergency fund**, you'll be caught short when something unexpected happens. Two to six months' income is recommended for your emergency fund. That will help cover unplanned expenses such as repairs and loss of income through disability or unemployment. Remember to replenish the fund as soon as you can if you take money out of it.

> "Some people are masters of money, and some its slaves."
>
> Russian proverb

Your Turn 13-4

MAKE UP A MONTHLY BUDGET

Use the information you gathered and analyzed to allocate your income on a monthly basis. In the space below, enter the dollar amounts you plan to spend on each of the following expenses for a period of one month.

Item	Budgeted Amount
Rent or mortgage	_____
Telecommunications (telephone, cell phone, Internet, TV)	_____
Utilities (gas, oil, electricity, water, sewer)	_____
Insurance (auto, health, life, homeowners', etc.)	_____
Car payments, other loans, credit cards	_____
Transportation (gas, maintenance, repairs, parking, carfare)	_____
Food (groceries and restaurant meals)	_____
Clothing	_____
Household items and repairs	_____
Gifts	_____
Medical/dental	_____
Education (tuition, books, fees)	_____
Personal (include entertainment)	_____
Emergency fund	_____
Taxes not withheld (self-employment, excise, real estate)	_____
Savings toward goals	_____
Other	_____
_____	_____
_____	_____
_____	_____
Total _____	_____

Finally, consider your goals. If you want to take a vacation in Europe or buy a house, start saving now—even if you can only afford a few dollars a month. (If your goal is more important to you than anything else, you might want to start the allocation process with money toward the goal. Then you'll have to reduce your other expenditures until your goal is met. Some people live frugally for years in order to meet an important financial goal, such as paying for an education, buying a house, or starting a business.)

Adjusting Your Budget   A budget is not carved in stone. As you try out your budget you may find that you haven't planned realistically or you've forgotten some items altogether. Your income will change, your expenses will change, and your goals will change. For these reasons, you should plan to review your budget periodically and revise it as necessary.

Savings and Debit Cards

Savings and Banking

Most people find it's not safe or convenient to have all their money in cash. They put the money they don't need for day-to-day expenses in a bank or financial institution. The institution may be a commercial bank, savings and loan, or credit union. When selecting a financial institution to deposit your money, you should consider

- up to what amount your deposits are insured and by whom. Federal insurance, such as the FDIC, is a better risk than state insurance funds, some of which have gone broke in the past.
- interest rates.
- the accessibility of your money.
- convenience of location, service, and online banking.
- the types of accounts that are offered.
- fees charged for various services.

You may need more than one account to manage your money. Most people need a checking account to pay routine bills. They have their pay deposited in the account, and write checks or authorize online payments to pay bills, keeping a record of each transaction (see Figure 13–2). Checking accounts vary a great deal. Some pay interest if you keep a minimum balance. Some charge you for each check, payment, and ATM transaction; others charge a monthly fee with unlimited service. Many allow you to pay bills online. You should shop around to find the best services for your needs.

Large sums of money shouldn't be kept in a checking account, especially an account that pays no interest. Instead, you can put extra money into a savings account that pays compound interest. With compound interest, you get interest both on the money you deposited and

FIGURE 13–2

People keep money in checking accounts for cash and for paying bills. Most banks provide online access to account records so you can double-check transactions and see your balance.

(© Tony French/Alamy)

the interest it has already earned. Over time, that can add up. A quick way to figure out how long it will take for your savings to double is called the "rule of 72." Just divide 72 by the interest rate you expect to earn. So, for example, if you are earning 4 percent interest, it will take 18 years for your money to double (72 divided by 4 equals 18).

There are a variety of savings options to choose from:

- **Passbook accounts** can be opened with very little money; they pay the least interest.

- **Money market accounts** have interest rates that vary with market rates, but some may require a minimum balance or limit your access to the money.

- **Certificates of deposit** (CDs) offer the highest interest rates, but they tie up your money for a stated period. If you need to withdraw your funds before the certificate comes due, you will pay a penalty.

- **Individual retirement accounts** (IRAs) are used to put aside money for retirement. If you withdraw the funds at an earlier age, there may be a stiff penalty.

As your financial responsibilities increase, you may need more than one savings account. If you are unsure which type of account is right for you, ask your financial institution's customer service representative for advice.

Debit Cards

Most American households now use a **debit card** as a convenient form of payment beyond cash and checks. A debit card allows you to pay for something with money from your checking or savings account without using cash or a check. When you use a debit card, the amount of the payment is automatically subtracted from the balance in your checking or savings account.

Your Turn 13-5

You just received a tax refund of $1,625 from the IRS. What are you going to do with that money? Choose a general plan:

- Keep a certain amount of cash—your choice—to spend immediately.
- Open an IRA (minimum amount, $500).
- Save the rest in one or more types of accounts.

Use the space below to list specifically what you are going to do with the money.

_____

_____

_____

"Money is like a sixth sense, and you can't enjoy the other five without it."

SOMERSET MAUGHAM (1874–1965),
English writer

In addition to their convenience, debit cards help you keep to a budget. With a debit card, unlike a credit card, you cannot spend more money than you have.

Credit

Buy now, pay later. Sounds wonderful, doesn't it? Credit is a financial arrangement that gives you the right to defer payment on merchandise or services. In essence, you are using someone else's money to pay for something. But—you must pay back what you borrowed, plus a charge for using the money, called interest. So anything you buy on credit will cost you more than if you pay cash.

There are times when using credit is worth the price you pay. A genuine emergency like a large medical bill, a genuine necessity like a car repair, or paying tuition for a degree program are all examples of situations in which it is appropriate to borrow money. On the other hand, buying a luxury item because the credit terms look easy and borrowing when you have no prospect of being able to pay the money back are two situations in which you should not use credit.

So be careful when you are considering using credit. It's tempting—and easy—to borrow money and use credit cards. But unless you keep tight control on the amounts you borrow and charge, the debt mounts up until you can't manage the monthly payments. In that situation, your creditors can repossess the merchandise, garnish your salary (get a portion of what you make until the loan is paid), and give negative information about your creditworthiness to a credit bureau. Credit may be attractive, but misusing it can lead to stress and financial crisis.

The Cost of Credit

Because buying something on credit costs more than paying cash, you should shop around when you're taking out a loan or applying for a credit card. Different retailers and financial institutions lend money on different terms. The total cost of credit may vary widely.

When you use credit, make sure you know the **annual percentage rate** (APR), which is the interest rate you will be charged per year on the amount you finance. Also make sure you know the **finance charge**, the total of all costs associated with the loan or credit card—interest, fees, service charges, insurance, and so on—before you sign anything. APRs and fees vary widely, so you should shop around for the best deal. Never sign a credit card application or loan contract unless you fully understand its terms.

Credit Cards

Credit cards allow you to buy merchandise and services and borrow cash up to a certain dollar amount, called your **credit limit**. All you do is sign your name. In return for this convenience, you agree to pay for your purchases in full once a month or in part over an extended period. If you pay your credit card account balance on time and in full each month, you are not charged interest on your purchases. If you pay for only part of your purchases, the unpaid balance is treated as a loan. You pay interest on it, often at a very high APR. In addition, credit cards charge annual fees, fees for late payments, and cash advance fees. In short, a credit card is *not* free money although it may feel that way.

Banks and other financial institutions aggressively market credit cards to students, offering "free gifts" for signup and "teaser" rates like 0 percent for six months. Once the introductory period is over, the interest rate jumps to 10 to 25 percent. With rates like this, even if you make the minimum payment each month, your debt can grow quickly. For example, in 2004, the average outstanding balance on a college student's credit card was $2,169.[3] Thus, unless you pay your balance in full each month, a credit card is actually a high-interest loan.

Still, if you use them carefully, credit cards have many advantages. Like debit cards, they relieve you of the need to carry large amounts of cash when shopping. They allow you to charge travel, entertainment, and merchandise all over the world. They make ordering merchandise by phone or on the Internet easy. Unlike debit cards, they allow you to buy items even when you don't have the cash. Thus credit cards can lull you into a false sense that you have lots of money—until you get the bill. So while they have many advantages, credit cards should be used cautiously. In fact, if you think you might get into financial trouble with a credit card, use a debit card instead.

Most retailers and restaurants accept payment by credit card or debit card. The ease with which purchases can be made without cash has contributed to both the rise in consumer debt and the popularity of debit cards for those who prefer to "pay now."

Loans

In addition to having a credit card for day to day use, people borrow money for large, long-term purchases or uses. Among them are financing an education, buying a house, and buying a high-ticket item such as a car.

Student Loans

If you need money for your education, your first choice should be a federal student loan—a loan whose interest rate is subsidized by the federal government. Financial institutions make loans to students on the condition that the students will repay the loans after they graduate. The lender assumes that the education will make the student employable, so he or she will be able to pay the loan back. The government insures these loans, so banks are paid back even when a student defaults. If you are not eligible for federal student loans, you can borrow from a private lender, but you will pay a higher interest rate since the loan is not insured.

Although you may be reluctant to borrow money to pay for most things, borrowing to finance a college education usually pays off in the long run. A college education is an investment in your future. As you can see in Figure 13–3, the lifetime earnings of people with college degrees and beyond is far greater than those of high school graduates.

If you are interested in applying for federal student grants and loans, check with your school's financial aid office or visit the U.S. Department of Education's financial aid Web site at <http://www.fafsa.ed.gov>.

Installment Loans

Installment loans are paid back in monthly installments for a fixed period of time. The most common installment loan is the auto loan. When you take out an installment loan, you sign a contract agreeing to pay the loan back on the terms outlined in

> "If you would know the value of money, go and try to borrow some."
>
> BENJAMIN FRANKLIN (1706–1790), statesman, scientist, and writer

---

FIGURE 13–3

According to the U.S. Census Bureau, on average, college graduates make almost twice as much as high school graduates over the course of a lifetime. People with professional degrees (such as doctors and lawyers) make almost four times as much.

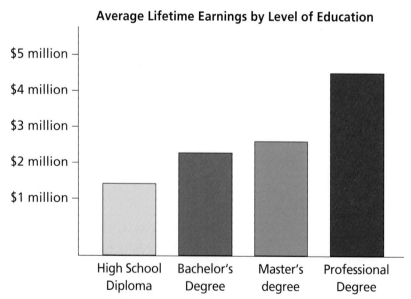

Average Lifetime Earnings by Level of Education

Source: U.S. Bureau of the Census

the agreement. If possible, you should not have more than one installment loan at a time, so your monthly payments for credit are not too high.

Sources of Loans   When you need to borrow money, you must look around for someone who thinks you are a good credit risk and for the lowest APR you can find. Some sources of loans are:

- Your relatives, although this can be an uncomfortable situation; If you do borrow from relatives, you should write a contract and plan a payment schedule.
- Credit unions, if you are a member
- Banks and savings institutions
- Licensed small loan companies such as payday loan companies, which often charge extremely high interest because they take on riskier customers

Whatever you do, avoid taking cash advances on your credit card and borrowing from pawnbrokers and loan sharks. Credit card cash advances have very high interest rates and fees. Pawnbrokers lend small amounts, keep your assets, and charge extremely high interest rates. Loan sharks often operate outside the law.

Credit Records and Your Rights

The first time you apply for a credit card or loan, you may be refused because you have no credit record. You have no credit record, of course, because you have never been given credit. How can you get out of this loop? You can try one of several approaches to establish a credit record:

- Apply for a credit card with a low credit limit and other features designed especially for students (but see the cautions about using credit cards, above).
- Take out a small installment loan and ask someone with a credit record to cosign with you. The cosigner will be responsible for paying if you do not.
- If you have a savings account with a bank, use it as collateral to borrow money from the same institution. Collateral is property—in this case, money—that you give the lender access to as a guarantee that you will pay back the loan.
- Sign up for utilities in your own name, even if you have to pay a large deposit.
- Pay your bills on time.

Credit records are maintained by companies called **credit bureaus**. In recent years, these companies have been criticized for making errors in credit records and being slow to correct them. You have the right to see your credit record and to know who else has seen it in the previous six months. A small fee is charged for this service unless you were recently denied credit or were the victim of identity theft (see News & Views, page 313). If the information is inaccurate, you can have it investigated and corrected, and copies of the corrected report will be sent to anyone who received an incorrect report. You may also add a notation to your file about any information you consider unfair. You can help prevent some errors if you always use the same form of your name on all contracts, accounts, credit cards, and other documents.

Your Credit Obligations

When you use credit, you are obliged, legally and morally, to pay back what you have borrowed. There may be times when for some reason you miss a payment or series of payments. If this happens, you should notify your creditor immediately and explain your situation. Many creditors will help you work out another payment schedule to give you time to recover.

Dealing with Debt

Owing more money than you can pay back is sometimes the result of poor money management: People simply borrow more money and charge more purchases than they can repay. Sometimes people are conned into taking on high-interest debt without understanding the terms they are agreeing to. And sometimes debt becomes unmanageable when income drops because of events such as divorce, unemployment, or illness. No matter what the cause, however, debt can easily grow until it is too large to pay off. In fact, almost 600,000 Americans filed for personal bankruptcy in 2006, because they couldn't resolve their debt problems in any other way.[4]

How can you regain control of your finances? The first step is to know how much you earn, how much you spend, and how much you owe. If you can't get a handle on these three things on your own, you need help. In addition to consulting with your creditors, you can consult organizations whose purpose is to help people having financial difficulties. For example, American Consumer Credit Counseling <http://consumercredit.com> and the National Foundation for Consumer Credit <http://nfcc.org> are two organizations that provide credit counseling services (either free or for a small fee; the organizations are financed by lenders). Credit counselors help people work out long-term debt payment plans while learning how to budget and change their spending habits.

Insurance

Why do you need insurance? You need insurance to protect yourself and your dependents against financial ruin in the event of illness, accident, theft, fire, or death. Insurance works on the principle that not everyone who buys it will actually need it. People pay premiums to an insurance company in case an unforeseen event occurs—an illness, hospitalization, accident, fire, and so on. If a misfortune does occur, the insurance

News & Views

IDENTITY THEFT ON THE RISE

Identity thieves don't steal from you directly. Instead, they steal personal financial information and use it for a spending spree that leaves you, the victim, with a financial mess and a ruined credit rating.

Everyone is vulnerable to identity theft, including students. Commonplace transactions like purchasing items online or applying for financial aid involve sharing information like social security numbers, driver's license numbers, dates of birth, and account numbers that may get into the wrong hands. But beyond these normal risks, some students make particularly good targets for identity thieves. That's because they often throw away preapproved credit offers without destroying them first, pay credit card bills without double-checking them, and neglect to balance their checking accounts.

Even if you aren't careless with your financial information, you still need to take precautions to prevent identity theft. Following are some suggestions:

Shredding documents that contain important financial information helps prevent identity theft.

- Don't give out personal financial information to people who call or e-mail you and ask for it. They may be "phishing," or attempting to get personal data in order to commit fraud or theft.
- Never enter personal information like social security or credit cards numbers on a public computer. Use your own personal computer for online transactions, or call a company directly to place an order.
- Protect your personal computer, especially your laptop (which might get lost or stolen), by using "strong" passwords that have a combination of lowercase letters, uppercase letters, numbers, and symbols. Don't store your passwords on the laptop, either.
- Use a shredder to destroy documents that contain personal and financial information. This includes mail offers of preapproved credit, which contain personal data and can be used to open accounts in your name.
- Take your date of birth off your online profiles.
- Protect your personal data at home as well. Almost half of all identity thefts are committed by people who know the victim.

If you think you have been a victim of identity theft, you need to take some steps to protect your finances and your credit rating:

- Place a fraud alert on your credit file by calling one of the three credit bureaus: Equifax (1-800-525-6285), Experian (1-888-EXPERIAN), or TransUnion (1-800-680-7289). Then check your credit report for inaccurate information or suspicious activity.
- Close any accounts you think may have been threatened, and inform each company of the risk of fraud. If fraudulent charges have already been made, ask for forms to dispute them, or write letters to the company disputing them. When you open new accounts, use new personal identification numbers, user names, and passwords.
- File a complaint with the Federal Trade Commission, which helps coordinate antitheft activities across the nation, at <www.consumer.gov/idtheft>.

Sources: Federal Trade Commission. "ID Theft: What It's All About," June 2005. <http://www.ftc.gov>, accessed June 5, 2008; Lents, Danny. "Identity Theft and College Students," <http://idtheftawareness.com/docs/CollegeStudents.php>, accessed June 5, 2008; Office of Inspector General. "Identity Theft," Feb. 22, 2005. <http://www.ed.gov/about/offices/list/oig/misused/idtheft.html>, accessed June 5, 2008.

Your Turn 13-6

Well before people get to the bankruptcy stage, they should be aware of the warning signs that financial trouble may be getting serious. Take this test to see if any of the warning signs apply to you.

Do you:	Yes	No
• pay only monthly minimums on your credit cards?	☐	☐
• skip some bills to pay others?	☐	☐
• panic when faced with an unexpected major expense, such as a car repair?	☐	☐
• depend on overtime or moonlighting to pay your monthly bills?	☐	☐
• borrow from friends and relatives to cover your basic expenses?	☐	☐
• owe more money on your mortgage than your house is worth?	☐	☐
• have a variable rate mortgage whose payments will rise beyond your ability to afford them?	☐	☐

If you answered *yes* to any of these questions, you may be headed for financial trouble. But instead of waiting for the situation to get worse, you need to take action.

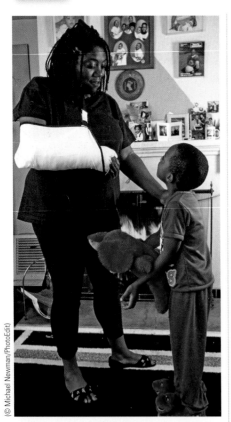

(© Michael Newman/PhotoEdit)

Health insurance helps protect you from high medical bills from accidents and illness.

company pays the insured person under the terms of the insurance contract.

There are many types of insurance available, including health insurance, medical coverage, auto insurance, life insurance, disability insurance, renter's insurance, and homeowner's insurance.

Medical Coverage

An accident or serious illness can mean paying medical bills for years if you are not insured. Yet because of the high cost of medical coverage, millions of Americans are uninsured. Most people who have medical coverage have it through their employers. In some cases the company pays the full premium, but in most cases the employee pays part or all of the cost. There are several types of medical coverage:

- **Traditional health insurance.** When the insured person sees a doctor or is hospitalized, the insurance company covers a portion of the cost, usually 80 percent. With this type of insurance, you pay your health care bills up front and are then reimbursed by the insurance company. Traditional health insurance is usually the most expensive type of medical coverage because insured people can go to the doctor and hospital of their choice.

- **Managed care plans.** Managed care plans are similar to traditional health insurance, except that the insured person is limited in his or her choice of physicians and hospitals to those in the managed care network. Health care providers in the network handle the claims paperwork for you and are reimbursed at fixed rates by the insurer. Managed care coverage usually costs less than traditional health insurance.

- **Medicaid and Medicare.** Low-income people are often eligible for Medicaid, and elderly and disabled people are usually eligible for Medicare, which are federally financed health insurance plans. In addition, some states provide free or low-cost health insurance for children.

Auto Insurance

Each year, thousands of people die, millions of people are injured and disabled, and billions of dollars are spent as the direct result of automobile accidents. Most states require that car owners buy liability coverage, which protects you against the claims of others in case you cause property or other damage while operating a motor vehicle. In addition to liability coverage, auto insurance policies can include:

- Collision coverage to repair damage to your car if a collision occurs; You agree to pay a deductible—$500, on average—and the insurance company pays the balance. If your car is very old, it's not worth buying collision coverage. The insurance company will not pay any claim higher than the total book value of the car.

- Comprehensive coverage in case your car is stolen, catches fire, or is the victim of other perils such as flood; Again, if your car is very old, it's not worth buying comprehensive coverage.

- Medical coverage for your health care bills if you are injured while riding in your car; and

- Uninsured motorist coverage in case you are killed or injured, or your car is damaged in an accident caused by a driver who has no insurance.

Some states have "no fault" auto insurance. Under this type of insurance, your own insurance company pays you benefits, regardless of whose fault the accident was.

The cost of auto insurance varies widely, with young male drivers in urban areas paying the highest premiums. When you buy auto insurance, it pays to shop around and compare coverage. You can economize on the cost of a policy in several ways:

- Buy a less-expensive or used car.
- Buy a car with airbags, an alarm system, or another antitheft device.

Auto insurance helps protect car owners from large expenses resulting from accidents, theft, and natural disasters. Even a fender bender can result in expensive repairs.

- Choose the highest deductibles on collision and comprehensive coverage that you can afford. (The **deductible** is the amount you pay before the insurance company starts paying. The higher the deductible, the cheaper the coverage.) A week's salary is a good rule of thumb.

- Don't buy collision or comprehensive coverage if your car is very old.

- Participate in approved driver education courses to get a "good driver" discount.

- Keep your grades high to get a "good student" discount.

What happens if you are turned down for insurance or your policy is canceled because of a poor driving record? In that case, you go into your state's assigned risk pool and get insurance from a company servicing high-risk drivers. The cost of this insurance is greater than regular auto insurance. If your driving record is good for a few years, you should be able to buy standard insurance again.

Other Types of Insurance

Other types of insurance that you may need now or as your financial responsibilities increase are:

- Renter's insurance, which protects against damage or loss of personal property and liability claims

- Homeowner's insurance, which protects against property damage and liability claims

- Life insurance, which provides financial protection to your dependents in case of your death

- Disability insurance, which pays you a certain amount per month in the event you are injured or too sick to work

- Long-term care insurance, which provides coverage for lengthy nursing home stays.

Owning a Home

Buying a home—whether it is a house, condominium, or cooperative apartment—is the biggest investment most people make during their lifetimes. Despite the high cost of finding, buying, and maintaining a home, most Americans still regard home ownership as part of the American dream. Thus, the decision to buy a home is complicated and involves both financial and emotional factors. Before you take the plunge, it's important to consider the advantages and disadvantages of buying a home.

Your Turn 13-7

YOUR PERSONAL INSURANCE PLAN

Think about your current circumstances. What kind of insurance do you need? For each of the following, indicate why you do need this form of insurance or why you don't need it.

1. Medical coverage

_____

2. Auto insurance

_____

3. Renter's insurance

_____

4. Homeowner's insurance

_____

5. Life insurance

_____

6. Disability insurance

_____

Advantages of Home Ownership

Home ownership has many advantages, not the least of which are the emotional advantages. For many people, owning a home is the realization of a dream. It provides them with a sense of security and control over their lives. In general, homeowners have a greater commitment to their communities than do renters. They tend to be more involved in civic issues such as education and community improvement.

Home ownership can have financial advantages. The biggest advantage is that paying off a mortgage (the loan you take out when you buy a home) is a way to build a nest egg for retirement. Mortgage payments are a form of forced savings because you build equity (ownership) in your home. In addition, the interest on your mortgage and the property taxes on your home are tax deductible, meaning that your

Home ownership is a major financial commitment. Most people need to plan and save for several years before they are ready for this step.

income tax bill will be less. If you have enough equity in your home, you can borrow against its value with a home equity loan. Finally, if you own the home over a long period of time and then sell it, you may make some money on the sale.

Disadvantages of Home Ownership

Home ownership does have a down side. First, you may be in a stage of life that is full of uncertainty, such as during college, at the beginning of a marriage or after a divorce, or when your work requires frequent moves. In these situations, your housing needs may change rapidly, and home ownership would restrict your mobility.

Second, home ownership is expensive. In many cases, you need to make a down payment—5 to 20 percent of the price—to qualify for a mortgage. If you get a variable rate mortgage, when the "teaser" rate expires, your payments may increase sharply. In addition, the mortgage payment is just part of the monthly cost. Owning a home means paying for property taxes, insurance, routine maintenance, and repairs.

Last, owning a home is not a sure way to make money. Home prices rise and fall in the short term. There are periodic real estate "bubbles," when speculators drive prices up sharply. When the "bubble" bursts, home values drop. If you are unlucky enough to buy during a bubble, you may wind up "under water," having a mortgage that is greater than the value of the house. If you sell during the bust, you can lose a lot of money.

If you have the discipline to invest the money you'd save by renting, you may do better financially in the long run than someone who depends on rising home values. Most financial advisers suggest that people view their houses primarily as a homes, not as investments.

Making the Decision to Buy or Rent

If you need help in making the decision to buy or rent, you can consult one of the many books or Web sites devoted to home ownership or personal finance. Many of these have worksheets or calculators that help you estimate costs and benefits. In addition, there are software packages on the market that help you with financial analysis and lead you through the decision-making process.

Investing for the Future

In the long term, you will encounter situations in which you need a lot of money. For example, you may want to start a business or pay for your children's college educations. These are large expenses that most people cannot cover with current income. Later, during your retirement years, you will need money to supplement social security benefits and pension plans, if any.

Your Turn 13-8

SHOULD YOU OWN YOUR HOME?

1. What are your feelings and attitudes toward owning your own home?

_____

2. At this stage of your life, does it make sense to own your own home? Explain.

_____

3. Do you have the financial resources to own a home? Explain.

_____

> "*It's better to do nothing with your money than something you don't understand.*"
>
> SUZE ORMAN,
> financial adviser

People save money for many reasons. These two women used their savings to open a boutique.

Long-term financial planning is critical, but it is something that people find very difficult to do. A woman in her twenties usually does not have retirement on her mind. A father holding his newborn baby may worry more about the cost of diapers than college. Still, the sooner you start to plan and invest for the future, the better off you will be. If you start young, the amounts you need to invest will be smaller because they have more time to grow. If you start late, you will have to invest large amounts each year, which may seriously interfere with your lifestyle. It is crucial to get in the habit of investing regularly, even if the amounts are small.

Home ownership can be one form of long-term savings, as we have seen. However, there are other ways to invest money for long-term goals such as financing your children's education or building a retirement fund. Some of the most common long-term investments are:

■ **Stocks.** When you buy stock, you become a part-owner of a corporation. Your profit may come from dividends paid when the company does well, or from selling the stock at a price higher than you paid. Needless to say, you may not profit but may lose instead. Still, over the long run, stocks have been the best choice for long-term increases in value. For most people, it is best to buy stock through stock index funds, which own shares of all companies on a stock exchange. Buying individual company stocks is riskier.

WHATEVER IT TAKES

Manuel A. Henriquez

(© Courtesy of Manuel A. Henriquez)

When he was two years old, Manuel Henriquez moved from the Dominican Republic, where he was born, to Florida, with his mother and two sisters. For the first few years, the family moved back and forth between Florida and the Dominican Republic. But when Henriquez was in junior high school, he and his sisters rebelled at all the moves. They asked their mother to pick one country. She chose the United States.

Henriquez's mother encouraged him to join Junior Achievement, a national after-school program in which high school students role-play business executives. That experience exposed Henriquez to business, and he was hooked. While at Northeastern University, he started two businesses that sold computer services at a time when personal computers were not commonplace. The first sold off-site connections to his school's mainframe computer so students could use the computer to do homework. The second offered word processing services to students, typing papers and resumes. When his mother's dog got cancer, Henriquez also started HealthyPets, an online company offering links to pet-related information.

Because of his entrepreneurial experience, Henriquez was encouraged to go into the venture capital side of banking after college. Venture capitalists invest money in new research and businesses, a high-risk endeavor that can lead to great losses as well as great gains. In 2003, Henriquez co-founded a company, Hercules Technology Growth Capital, which invests in technology and life science companies. Two years later, the company began selling its shares to the general public. The company's success happened so fast that Henriquez says, "Now I have to find a bigger dream."

Sources: Patricia R. Olsen, "Ever the Entrepreneur: Manual A. Henriquez." *New York Times,* Sept. 23, 2007, p. BU17. "Manual A. Henriquez: Co-Founder, Chairman and CEO." Hercules Technology Growth Capital, <http://www.herculestech.com/team> accessed June 10, 2008. "Profiles in Leadership: Manuel Henriquez." Northeastern University, <http://www.northeastern.edu/leadershipprofiles/1980s/henriquez.html> accessed June 10, 2008.

- **Bonds.** When you buy a bond, you are lending money and will be repaid on a specific date, usually with interest payments in the meantime. Bonds usually involve less risk than stocks, but they do not have as much profit potential.

- **Mutual funds.** Mutual funds pool the money of a group of people and make investments on their behalf. There are stock funds and bond funds as well as funds that combine various types of investments.

- **IRAs, SEPs, and 401(k) plans.** These are all plans for retirement savings. The money in these plans is usually invested through mutual funds or banks.

- **Education Savings Accounts.** Coverdell and other education savings accounts are designed to encourage people to save for tuition and other school expenses. The money in these accounts grows tax-free and is not taxed when withdrawn for educational expenses.

Keep in mind that all these forms of investment pose some risk. Unlike money in a savings account in a bank, the money you invest in stocks, bonds, and mutual funds is not insured by the federal government. Therefore, when you invest you must be prepared to lose money as well as to make money.

Choosing the right types of investments means balancing risk and reward. One way to decrease risk is to diversify. That means you spread your investments in different types of stocks, bonds, and mutual funds. If one of your investments does poorly, it is likely to be balanced by another doing well.

Your Turn 13-9

WHAT ARE YOUR LONG-TERM FINANCIAL GOALS?

Think about large expenses you are likely to have in the future. Then answer the following questions.

1. List some future events or situations for which you will need large amounts of money.

_____

2. What have you done, if anything, to prepare for these events?

_____

3. How can you improve your long-term financial planning?

_____

Tech Tips

USING ONLINE PERSONAL FINANCE RESOURCES

The Internet is a gold mine of sites devoted to personal finance management. Many of them are interactive, allowing you to input your personal data and come up with financial projections. Following are some sites to explore:

■ **Yahoo! Finance <http://finance.yahoo.com/personal-finance>** and **Kiplinger.com <www.kiplinger.com>.** These are two general personal finance sites that offer a range of information, advice, news, and other resources.

■ **Student Aid on the Web <http://studentaid.ed.gov/>.** This U.S. Department of Education site provides information that can help you find funds for your college education. It also provides a link to FAFSA, the federal financial aid application site.

■ **FastWeb <http://www.fastweb.com>.** This is an online database of scholarships maintained by fastWEB (*financial aid search through the Web*). You input your personal profile, and the site generates a list of scholarships and grants for which you may be eligible.

■ **Cardratings.com <http://www.cardratings.com/>.** This site provides ratings for various credit cards. Run by a consumer advocacy organization since 1998, the site allows you to find top-rated credit cards, search its database to see how your own credit card ranks, as well as read consumer reviews of specific cards.

■ **Financial Calculators <http://www.dinkytown.net/>.** Maintained by KJE Computer Solutions, this site offers 300 financial calculators to help you plan. There are calculators for savings, budgets, mortgages, auto loans, credit card debt, taxes, investments, retirement, and business.

■ **Quicken.com Glossary <http://www.quicken.com/glossary>.** If you encounter a financial term you don't understand, look it up on Quicken's glossary site.

Your Turn 13-10

EXPLORING ONLINE PERSONAL FINANCE RESOURCES

Select one of the sites listed previously, or another personal finance site of your own choosing, and explore what it has to offer. How could you use this site to help you manage money?

_____

_____

_____

_____

_____

_____

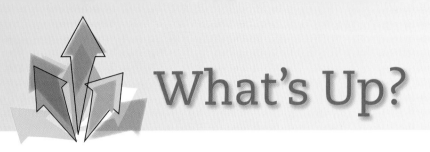

What's Up?

Name _____ Date _____

1. Sketch the financial pyramid in the space below.

2. List five possible sources of income.

_____

_____

_____

3. What is the difference between fixed and variable expenses?

_____

_____

_____

4. What is budgeting? Why is budgeting important?

_____

_____

_____

5. What are the four basic steps of budgeting?

_____

_____

_____

6. What is a checking account used for?

_____

_____

_____

Name _____ Date _____

7. Why is it important to read the details about a credit card offer before applying for the card?

_____

_____

_____

8. How can you establish a good credit history?

_____

_____

_____

9. What is the purpose of insurance?

_____

_____

_____

10. Describe two ways to cut the cost of auto insurance.

_____

_____

_____

11. Describe two advantages and two disadvantages of home ownership.

_____

_____

_____

12. Why is it important to invest now for large future expenses such as a child's college education?

_____

_____

_____

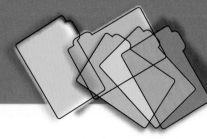

Case Studies

The Case of the Big Spender

When Felipe got his first full-time job, he was thrilled with having his own money. His mother asked him to pay room and board, and he willingly agreed. In the first month he was working, he bought a laptop and clothes for work on his new credit card. He borrowed money to buy a new car. He was stunned at how much he would have to pay for auto insurance. His extra cash was spent on restaurants and entertainment.

Within a few months, Felipe discovered he was constantly broke. The great feeling he had had about earning his own money was replaced by a sinking feeling of being broke—and worse, in debt. Room, board, credit card payments, auto loan payments, insurance, dates—there simply was not enough money for it all.

1. Felipe has two basic problems with his handling of money. What are they?

2. When Felipe first started working, what should he have done about money for the first few months?

3. What can Felipe do to improve his present situation?

The Case of the Laid-Off Assistant

Noreen moved into a new, much larger apartment and bought a kitchen table, chairs, and two sofas on the installment plan. Although her rent was higher and she also had car payments to make, she had enough room in her budget to take on the additional monthly payments on the furniture.

Several months later, Noreen lost her job as an administrative assistant. For the first time in her life, she missed a loan payment—on the furniture. Noreen was frantic. She didn't know what to do until she found a new job. Her unemployment checks were not large enough to cover her expenses.

1. What is Noreen's problem?

2. What should Noreen do about her auto loan and furniture loan?

3. How will Noreen solve her problem in the long run?

 Journal

Answer the following journal questions.

1. Describe your family's attitudes toward money. Is money discussed openly, or is it considered a private topic? Who controls the family finances? How are decisions made? What role do you play?

_____

_____

_____

2. What are your three most important financial goals? What are you doing to reach these goals?

_____

_____

_____

3. Do you have a budget? Do you follow it? What improvements can you make in your budgeting?

_____

_____

_____

4. Describe your use of banks, if any. What types of accounts do you have? What do you use them for? What savings goals do you have?

_____

_____

_____

5. What is your attitude toward credit? How can you use credit more wisely?

_____

_____

_____

6. If you won a huge sum in the lottery, what would you do with it? How would it change your life?

_____

_____

_____

CHAPTER

14 Preparing for Your Career

Your college can be a lifelong source of career information and contacts. For example, many schools hold job fairs, like this one at Miami Dade College, at which companies recruit students and alumni for internships, entry-level jobs, and mid-level positions.

F or many people, work is drudgery, a place to which they drag themselves each day. Others enjoy themselves so much on the job that they hardly consider what they do work. Indeed, highly successful people often think that is that "work is play." As you prepare yourself for a career, keep in mind that you'll be spending a large part of your waking hours working. Wouldn't it be better to be paid to do something you are good at and enjoy?

A large part of reaching your potential can take place in the context of work. If your work is satisfying, the satisfaction you feel at work will spill over into your personal life. If your career makes good use of your abilities and interests, you will feel you are contributing to the world. If your work is challenging, you will grow and develop as a person. In short, a satisfying career can help you reach your potential as a human being.

You may be thinking that this is a very idealistic view of work. Real jobs aren't like that, you say. Perhaps you are remembering a boring job you had—or still have. A job that required a tenth of your brainpower and had no future, perhaps. True, there are many jobs like that out there. But why should you settle for a job like that?

Now turn your mind away from that boring job. Think instead about something you once did that you really enjoyed. When you were working on this activity, you were absorbed. Time flew by. You got a great feeling of satisfaction when you were done. Work should be like that. It can be, too, if you take the time to make some discoveries about yourself and about the world out there before you start job hunting.

You can use the time you have now to prepare yourself for a career. By studying this chapter, you will get ready for your job search. You will:

- figure out what you have to offer as well as what you want out of a career;
- learn where to find economic, technology, and career information;
- match yourself to a suitable career;
- pull together a resume and career portfolio;
- learn about job-search resources;
- prepare for job interviews; and
- start planning your short- and long-term career goals.

Finally, you will explore a variety of career resources on the Web.

What Can You Offer?

A lot of people, including students, homemakers returning to work, and people changing careers, think they have little or nothing to offer employers. "But I can't do anything. I have no skills or experience" is the common refrain. If you think of yourself this way, now is the time to stop. The fact is, everyone has skills, interests, education, and experience that would be of value to some employer. Many employers will train new employees if they feel they have basic skills, the ability to learn, and the commitment to do well.

Personal Qualities, Skills, and Interests

When you are thinking about jobs and careers, the place to start is with yourself. Look at the personal qualities and foundation skills listed in Table 14–1. In 1990, the U.S. Department of Labor appointed a commission to determine the skills people need to succeed in their careers. Although the Secretary's Commission on Achieving Necessary Skills (SCANS) published its work 20 years ago, its findings regarding the worker qualities and skills needed for a high-skill, high-wage economy are still relevant for solid job performance in the modern workplace.

Which of these qualities are you confident you possess? Which of the foundation skills have you developed during the course of your life? A well-prepared person should have most of these qualities and skills. They are necessary for any type of employment, from sales clerk to nurse to computer systems analyst, although particular occupations will require more of some qualities and skills than others. Many of them are qualities and skills you have developed through your upbringing and your education. In addition, you have been improving these qualities and skills in the course of working through this book.

The skills you use in a favorite activity or hobby can sometimes be the basis for a career. For example, a dancer may find work as a dance teacher.

TABLE 14–1 Personal Qualities and Foundation Skills Needed for Solid Job Performance

Personal Qualities	Individual responsibility	
	Self-belief	
	Self-management	
	Sociability	
	Integrity	
Foundation Skills (Transferrable Skills)	*Basic Skills:*	*Thinking Skills:*
	Reading	Ability to learn
	Writing	Reasoning
	Arithmetic	Creative thinking
	Mathematics	Decision making
	Speaking	Problem solving
	Listening	

Source: U.S. Department of Labor, Secretary's Commission on Achieving Necessary Skills (SCANS), *Learning a Living: A Blueprint for High Performance*, Washington, D.C., 1992, p. 3.

"Work saves us from three great evils: boredom, vice and need."

VOLTAIRE (1694–1778),
French writer

The next set of general skills considered necessary for success on the job by the Department of Labor are the workplace skills (see Table 14–2). These are skills involving the use of resources, interpersonal relationships, information, systems, and technology. Like the foundation skills, the workplace skills are very general and are needed in varying degrees for different occupations. For example, a computer technician should have lots of technology skill, but some of the interpersonal skills, such as negotiating, are less important in that occupation.

In every job, workers must deal to a degree with all five skill categories—resources, interpersonal, information, systems, and technology. Yet most jobs are weighted toward one or two skill categories. That is, the skills that are critical for success in the job fall into one or two of the five categories. For example, it is critical that a teacher have a high level of interpersonal skills, because teaching involves working with people. But he or she should also possess information skills, because a teacher must interpret and communicate information (the content of a course or subject). In addition, a teacher must have systems skills in order to deal with a social system (the class and the school) and to monitor and correct performance (of students).

When you read over the workplace skills in Table 14–2, you may be alarmed by how grand and abstract they sound. Don't be. What you have to consider when thinking about careers is how your own specific skills fit into these general categories. For example, you may be skilled at running a forklift and other heavy machinery. How does that very specific skill fit into the workplace skills in Table 14–2? In fact, what you are using when operating a forklift is a technology skill. You are applying technology to a specific task. Let's consider another example, that of a

TABLE 14-2 Workplace Skills Needed for Solid Job Performance	
Resource Skills	Allocate time, money, materials, space, and staff
Interpersonal Skills	Work on teams
	Teach others
	Serve customers
	Lead
	Negotiate
	Work with people of diverse backgrounds
Information Skills	Acquire and evaluate data
	Organize and maintain files
	Interpret and communicate
	Use computers to process information
Systems Skills	Understand social, organizational, and technological systems
	Monitor and correct performance
	Design or improve systems
Technology Skills	Select equipment and tools
	Apply technology to specific tasks
	Maintain and troubleshoot equipment

Source: U.S. Department of Labor, Secretary's Commission on Achieving Necessary Skills (SCANS), *Learning a Living: A Blueprint for High Performance,* Washington, D.C., 1992, p. 3.

woman with little paid work experience who has served as president of a parent-teacher association. In that role, she has developed resource skills by fund-raising, interpersonal skills by leading and working with people of diverse backgrounds, and systems skills by managing the PTA, a social system.

Having a skill is not quite enough, however. You must also enjoy using it. Let's consider a computer technician as an example. He has a high level of technology skill, acquired through education and on the job. He is very good in repairing computer systems, but he is bored by his work. What he really enjoys are the occasions when he helps a customer and explains things. Perhaps this technician would be happier in a job that requires more interpersonal skill, such as computer sales or training.

So when you think about skills, don't think just about what you are good at. Think about what you enjoy as well.

Education and Experience

In addition to your skills and interests, you can offer employers the benefit of your education and experience. Your education is an indication not only of what you know but also of what foundation skills you have—reading,

Your Turn 14-1

What skills do you use when you are enjoying yourself the most? First think of three activities you really enjoy: they can be work, school, sports, recreation, home, or community activities. List them following:

1. _____

2. _____

3. _____

For each activity you listed, write down the skills you enjoyed using as you performed that activity. Use the skills described in Tables 14–1 and 14–2.

Skills You Enjoyed Using in Activity 1:

_____

_____

_____

Skills You Enjoyed Using in Activity 2:

_____

_____

_____

Skills You Enjoyed Using in Activity 3:

_____

_____

_____

Which skill or skills do you use the most during activities you enjoy? How might these skills be used in a work environment?

_____

_____

_____

writing, computation, and thinking skills. In addition, your education shows that you have the ability to learn and to manage yourself, important qualities that employers look for.

Your work experience is also something you have that's of value. If you have never worked for money, worked only part-time, or worked a long time ago, you may think you have nothing to offer in this area. Yet

When taking inventory of your abilities, don't overlook volunteer work or internships. For example, these students have developed skills from their work building houses for a community service agency.

you should think of work experience as something broader than full-time paying jobs. Work experience can also include:

- part-time or summer jobs
- baby-sitting, newspaper delivery, yard work
- community or church work
- other volunteer work
- internships and apprenticeships

Many people develop significant skills through occasional or unpaid work experiences. You shouldn't overlook these activities when you are taking stock of your background.

What Do You Want?

The skills, interests, education, and experience you bring to your job hunt are critical from the employer's point of view. But there are other factors you must also consider—factors that are critically important to you.

There are millions of jobs in this country in thousands of occupations. By taking a careful inventory of your skills, interests, education, and experience, you can narrow your focus. And by carefully thinking about what you want in a career, you can eliminate many more occupations from consideration. In essence, you must evaluate what factors are important to you in a career.

- your preference for working with resources, people, information, systems, or technology
- the type of resources, people, information, systems, or technology that you prefer; For example, money or natural resources, children or immigrants, numbers or words or images, social or technological systems, hand tools or electrical engineering?
- the region of the country where you would prefer to live
- your preference for urban, suburban, or rural lifestyle
- your preference for a large corporation, small company, startup venture, or self-employment (note that many people become self-employed after gaining experience by working for companies)
- your preference for casual or formal environment for work
- your match to the values associated with the work or company (for example, competitiveness, excellence, helping others, creativity, and so on)
- your focus on job security (an increasingly scarce factor in a global economy)
- your salary requirements

"*Focusing your life solely on making a buck shows a certain poverty of ambition. It asks too little of yourself. Because it's only when you hitch your wagon to something larger than yourself that you realize your true potential.*"

BARACK OBAMA,
forty-fourth president
of the United States

Your Turn 14-2

TAKE A SELF-INVENTORY

Take some time to consider what you really want from a job or career. Answer the following questions.

1. Do you prefer to work primarily with resources, people, information, systems, or technology?

   _____

2. With what type of resources (environment, money, employees, etc.) would you enjoy working?

   _____

3. With what groups of people (children, peers, travelers, elderly people, lower-income, etc.) would you enjoy working?

   _____

4. With what type of information (books, Internet, pictures, video, video games, numbers, words, etc.) would you enjoy working?

   _____

5. With what type of systems (social groups, work processes, information systems, etc.) would you enjoy working?

   _____

6. With what type of technology (computers, hand tools, cooking equipment, manufacturing, etc.) would you enjoy working?

   _____

7. In what area of the country would you like to live?

   _____

8. Would you like to work in an urban, suburban, or rural environment? Would you like to work indoors or outdoors?

   _____

9. Are you interested in a casual or formal work environment?

   _____

(continues)

10. What values are important for you in your work (truth, beauty, competence, risk, stability, ambition, helping others, etc.)?

_____

11. How much job security is necessary for you?

_____

12. How much money do you need or want to make?

_____

By making choices in each of these areas, you will be able to focus more clearly on occupations that could be right for you.

What Trends May Affect You?

Knowing what you are good at and what you want is important. But when thinking about occupations, you should also keep up with the news.

For example, when you think about your career, you should consider economic trends. In the last several decades, companies have moved jobs overseas, and people have also been migrating, everyone seeking economic advantages in an increasingly global labor marketplace. For the last 40 years manufacturing jobs have steadily moved overseas, first to Mexico and then to China and East Asia. Ask yourself, what occupations are likely to remain in the United States over the next few decades? It won't do you much good to select an occupation that's being outsourced, or moved to countries with cheaper labor. (For a projection of U.S. job growth over the next decade, see the News & Views on page 337.)

In addition to being mindful of economic trends, you should keep up with technology news. Technology poses both a threat and an opportunity for all of us. While technological advances can put some people out of work, they can also create new jobs, better ways to do existing jobs, and new business opportunities.

Finally, in addition to being aware of developments in the economy and technology, you should keep up with local news as well. Local newspapers, television stations, and Web sites cover economic and business news that affects employment in your area.

News & Views

WHERE THE JOBS WILL BE IN THE YEAR 2016

The Bureau of Labor Statistics regularly publishes employment trend information on their Web site, <http://www.bls.gov>. The graph below is based on data from this site; it shows the number of new jobs expected over a 10-year period in the 20 occupations with the largest job growth. Jobs in the service industries dominate, with the largest growth in some of the lowest paying sectors, such as food preparation and retail sales. These figures underscore the need for higher education to compete effectively for better paying jobs that may be less numerous.

Among the occupations with the largest projected *declines* during this 10-year period are clerks, cashiers, packers, farmers and ranchers, sewing machine operators, and machinists. Most of these occupations are declining because of advances in technology.

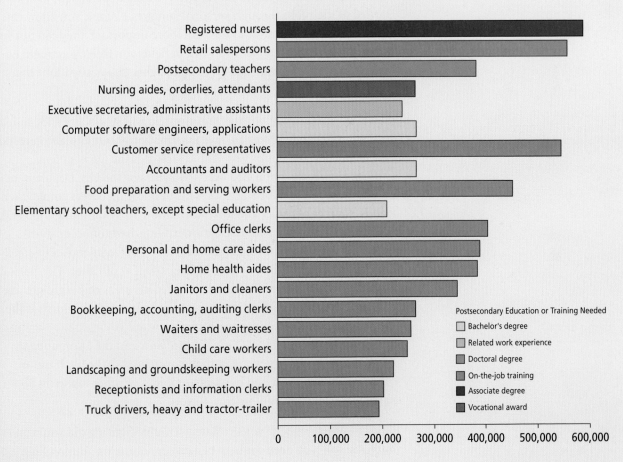

Occupations with the Largest Job Growth, 2006-2016

Matching Yourself to an Occupation

Now that you have spent some time thinking about your skills, your wants, and the economic and technological factors that may affect you, you are ready to match yourself to suitable occupations. Many career information resources are available to help you do this. In addition to using these resources, you should keep up with economic and job news. If you do your "homework," you will be able to come up with a career that's right for you.

Using Career Information Resources

Personal contacts, libraries and career centers, counselors, professional organizations, government agencies, and the Internet are all sources of information about careers.

People You Know   Your friends, relatives, coworkers, instructors, and fellow students are good resources for job and career information. (In fact a U.S. Department of Labor survey showed that 48 percent of job hunters learned of their jobs through personal contacts.) People you know can answer questions about what they do. More important, they can put you in touch with other people who work in fields you think you might be interested in. Networking can give you insights into occupations that may be hard to get from written descriptions.

Libraries and Career Centers   Your public and school libraries and your school's career center all have information about jobs and careers. One of the first references you should look at is the *Occupational Outlook Handbook,* published every two years by the U.S. Department of Labor's Bureau of Labor Statistics. This publication covers employment trends, sources of career and job information, tips on finding a job and evaluating a job offer, and descriptions of hundreds of occupations. Some libraries and schools may subscribe to the *Occupational Outlook Quarterly,* also published by the U.S. Department of Labor. This periodical describes trends in the job market and predicts areas of job growth and decline. Both these publications are available in searchable form at the Department of Labor Web site <http://www.dol.gov>.

Both the *Occupational Outlook Handbook* and the *Occupational Outlook Quarterly* are general in their coverage. Ask the librarian or office staff to help you find books, pamphlets, or other resources about particular occupations of interest to you.

Career Counselors   If you are having trouble figuring out your career interests, you may need the help of a career counselor. You can find counselors in several places:

- high school guidance offices
- career planning and placement offices in colleges and vocational/technical schools

- community organizations
- private counseling firms
- government employment service offices

Counselors are trained to help you discover your strengths and weaknesses. They can administer aptitude and interest tests and interpret the results, helping you match your aptitudes and interests with suitable occupations. Although counselors won't tell you what to do, they can guide your assessment of yourself and your work experience. They may also be able to offer advice about the local job market and educational and training opportunities.

If a career counselor is not available, you can find free interactive job aptitude tests on the Internet to help you narrow your career focus. You input personal data, and the site provides job suggestions that match your profile. These tests may or may not be reliable; however, so using a professional career counselor is preferable.

Professional and Other Organizations   Professional organizations, trade associations, labor unions, and large businesses all provide career information, much of it online. In addition, there are organizations that provide career information for specific groups, such as veterans, women, the handicapped, minority groups, and older workers. To find these organizations, you can check the *Encyclopedia of Associations* in the reference section of your library or do an Internet search. If you need further help, ask the reference librarian.

Government Employment Agencies   Federal and local government employment agencies are another source of career and job information. State employment services coordinate their efforts with the U.S. Employment Service. There are more than 2,000 local offices whose primary function is to help job hunters find jobs. They also provide counseling and testing for those who are exploring their futures.

Internet Career Sites   Almost all of the career resources mentioned so far are available on the Internet. In addition to these specific resources, there are several Internet sites devoted to general career and job information and searches. Job board sites such as CareerBuilder, Careers. com, and Monster.com provide a variety of career resources and advice in addition to job search capabilities (see page 362).

Job Shadowing

Once you have narrowed your career interests, you may want to spend a few hours or a day "shadowing" someone in your chosen occupation. By observing firsthand what a job involves, you will get a better idea of whether the occupation would be a good match for you. To find someone to shadow, ask people you know or your school placement office to help you.

Internships

For a more in-depth view of a field than job-shadowing offers, an internship is ideal. Internships are short-term positions that are designed to acquaint students with particular careers. Internships may be paid or unpaid, for academic credit or extracurricular. They offer inside looks at a companies and industries. A few months of work can help you decide whether you are interested in pursuing employment in that field. Internships sometimes lead to offers of full-time employment after graduation. They also help to build the work experience section of your resume while you are a student.

Internships can be found through your school career center, by networking, and by searching on the Internet. Treat applying for an internship as seriously as you would treat applying for a "real" job, and start early—in the winter for summer internships.

Setting an Occupational Objective

The result of all this thinking, research, and on-the-job experience is that you should be able to narrow your career objective to one or two occupations. Knowing what you are looking for will help you when you begin your job search. For a person with a job objective, job hunting is a self-directed activity. You will be much more likely to find a job that you will like if you look for a specific type of work.

Taking Action on Your Job Search

Once you've got an objective, you are ready to start job hunting. Occasionally, a lucky person finds a good job within a few days. But most people job hunt for weeks or months before finding something suitable.

Your Turn 14-3

IDENTIFY YOUR OCCUPATIONAL OBJECTIVE

If you've done your thinking and research, you should be ready to name some occupations that would suit you. Use the space below to list a few occupations that interest you.

_____

_____

_____

_____

Be prepared: job hunting is itself a job. It can also be a severe test of your self-belief. Most job hunters experience rejection and disappointment before they get a job offer. It's important not to feel too discouraged when this happens to you.

When you've been job hunting for a while and feel that you're getting nowhere, you have to motivate yourself to keep going. First, remember the power of positive self-talk: Praise yourself for the job-hunting tasks you handle well. For example, if you get an appointment for an interview, congratulate yourself. That's an accomplishment in and of itself! And second, use the technique of visualization to keep your motivation high. Imagine yourself at work, doing the job you want. Picture what you're wearing, your coworkers, the office or other place you can call yours. Keep these images in mind when your job hunt plateaus and you feel you're not making progress. If you keep at it, you *will* get a job.

There are several tasks associated with job hunting: preparing a resume, preparing a career portfolio, looking for job leads, filling out employment applications, going on interviews, and handling a job offer.

Preparing a Resume

A **resume** is a short summary of your experience and qualifications. Employers often use resumes to screen job applicants or as an agenda for the employment interview. From the job hunter's point of view, preparing a resume is a good way of presenting past experiences and skills.

How Resume Databases Affect Resume Formats   Many medium-sized and large companies maintain their own searchable databases of resumes. When you send them a paper or e-mail resume, it will be entered into the database and searched by a computer—it won't necessarily be read by a human being. The scanning and searching technologies of these systems affect how job hunters prepare resumes. There are three important things to keep in mind:

1. Resume databases search by key words such as particular skills, job titles, job functions, and educational degrees; therefore, your resume must include such key words in order to be a "hit" in a search. Read job postings from the industry you are interested in, and incorporate the key words that are used in these listings into your resume.

2. Scanners and other input technology can't deal with fancy formatting or colored paper; therefore, you must have a **plain text resume**, a paper and electronic version saved in "text only" or ASCII format (see Figure 14–1). This is your default resume, to be used in most circumstances.

3. You also should also have a **formatted resume** that is visually appealing, with different fonts, indents, bold and italicized type, and so on (see Figure 14–2). This can be used as part of your career portfolio or sent to a recruiter who asks you for it.

FIGURE 14–1

A plain text, or ASCII, resume is used when the resume will be scanned or otherwise entered into a resume database system. It can be sent to an employer in paper form, as a text file, or pasted into an e-mail message.

```
Marianne Guilmette
134 Dobson Street
Pittsburgh, Pennsylvania 15219
(412) 555-5489
mguilmette@cybermail.com

Summary of Qualifications

Associate's degree in marketing. Marketing experience
including advertising and
special promotions.Retail sales experience including
product display and selling
to customers. Telemarketer of the Month,December 2007 and
March 2008.

Work Experience

June 2008 to Present
Campus Store, Pittsburgh Community College, Pittsburgh,
Pennsylvania

Senior Sales Associate (part-time)
Responsibilities include product display, customer sales,
special marketing
promotions, and using computer to produce marketing
communications and campus
newspaper advertisements.

July 2007 to May 2008
MDS Marketing Group, Pittsburgh, Pennsylvania

Telemarketer (part-time)
Sold magazine subscriptions, books, and DVDs by telephone.

Education

Associate's Degree, Marketing, Pittsburgh Community
College, Pittsburgh,
Pennsylvania, 2009

Associations

Future Marketers Club

References and Career Portfolio

Available upon request.
```

How to Organize the Information in a Resume   Resumes usually contain the following information:

- your name, address, phone number, fax number, and e-mail address
- a brief summary of your career highlights and qualifications that includes key words
- education, including school names and locations, dates you attended, types of program, highest grade completed or degree earned (including GED)
- work experience, paid or volunteer, and for each job, usually the job title, name and location of employer, and dates of employment
- any professional licenses
- military experience, including branch and length of service, major responsibilities, and special training
- membership in organizations
- special skills, foreign languages, honors, awards, or achievements
- an indication that references and career portfolio are available on request

The information on a resume can be organized in two basic ways. The first, and most common, format is the **chronological resume** (see

FIGURE 14–2

A formatted resume uses bold, italic, and display type and other design elements to make a visually appealing document. The information in this resume is organized chronologically.

Marianne Guilmette
134 Dobson Street
Pittsburgh, Pennsylvania 15219
(412) 555-5489
mguilmette@cybermail.com

Summary of Qualifications	Associate's degree in marketing. Marketing experience including advertising and special promotions. Retail sales experience including product display and selling to customers. Telemarketer of the Month, December 2007 and March 2008.
Work Experience	**June 2008 to Present** Campus Store, Pittsburgh Community College, Pittsburgh, Pennsylvania *Senior Sales Associate (part-time)* Responsibilities include product display, customer sales, special marketing promotions, and using computer to produce marketing communications and campus newspaper advertisements. **July 2007 to May 2008** MDS Marketing Group, Pittsburgh, Pennsylvania *Telemarketer (part-time)* Sold magazine subscriptions, books, and DVDs by telephone.
Education	*Associate's Degree, Marketing* Pittsburgh Community College, Pittsburgh, Pennsylvania, 2009
Associations	Future Marketers Club
References/Career Portfolio	Available upon request.

Figures 14–1 and 14–2). It lists your most recent job first, followed by other jobs in reverse chronological order. If you've had a lot of work experience, it is presented before education on a chronological resume. Students with little or no work history generally list education before work experience on a chronological resume.

The second basic organization is the functional resume (Figure 14–3). It presents work experience in terms of the functions and skills used on the job. Functional resumes are often used by people changing careers, because they highlight general skills and functions that can be used in another occupation. They can also be used by people with little formal work experience, because they can highlight skills acquired in nontraditional settings. For example, a homemaker wanting to return to work can list skills acquired in running a home and doing volunteer work for the community, church, or school. Or students with skimpy work histories can show what skills they have acquired from school activities and part-time jobs.

Whichever format you use, the resume should be no longer than one page if possible. It should be perfect: neat, well organized, and without grammatical and spelling errors. Don't depend on your word processor's grammar and spelling check to catch all your errors. Ask someone with experience to help you edit and proofread the resume.

FIGURE 14–3

A functional resume highlights the functions and skills you have acquired on the job and in school. It is a good way to organize a resume if you have little work experience or want to change industries or occupations.

WILLIS L. LeMOYNE
67 West Green Street
Pittsburgh, PA 15220
Telephone: (412) 555-3497
Fax: (412) 555-2803
E-mail: WillisLLeMoyne@aol.com

SUMMARY
An excellent job candidate with a degree in marketing, experience in marketing and promotion, and special training in oral presentation skills and graphic design for marketing communications. Strong background in outdoor activities such as camping.

SKILLS AND ACHIEVEMENTS
➤ As marketing coordinator of the Student Activities Association, implemented a marketing plan that increased student membership by 27 percent
➤ Promoted Student Activities Association through pop-up ads on school web site, direct e-mail, newspaper ads, and posters
➤ Used graphic design skills to create promotional materials
➤ Improved communication skills by earning a certificate for special oral presentation course
➤ As Assistant Scout Master, organized and led Boy Scout troop on camping trips including winter survival camping, ice climbing, and mountain climbing expeditions
➤ As Eagle Scout, mentored younger scouts working up the ranks

EDUCATION
Associate's Degree, Marketing, Pittsburgh Community College, 2009

Marketing courses included:
➤ Consumer Behavior
➤ Marketing Management
➤ Computer Design for Marketing Professionals

ASSOCIATIONS
➤ Future Marketers Club

REFERENCES AND CAREER PORTFOLIO
Available upon request.

In addition, resist the temptation to be funny as a way of getting attention. Attempts at humor rarely impress employers. And finally, *do not lie on your resume.* It's wrong, and if you are found out, you could lose a job offer or your job itself.

Your Turn 14-4

GATHER INFORMATION FOR YOUR RESUME

Use the data sheet on pages 345–346 to gather information in preparation for writing your resume. Make sure you double-check the spellings of all names and the accuracy of dates and addresses. You may not use all this information on your resume, but you will have it handy in case you need it.

DATA SHEET FOR YOUR RESUME

Name _____

Address _____

Phone No. _____ Fax No. _____ E-mail _____

Qualifications, Skills, and Career Highlights (list key words)

_____

_____

_____

Education

College or Other Postsecondary School _____

Address _____

Date Started_____ Date Ended_____

Years Completed or Degree Received _____ Course of Study _____

Courses Relevant to Employment Objective _____

_____

Honors _____

Extracurricular Activities _____

High School _____

Address _____

Date Started_____ Date Ended_____

Years Completed or Degree Received _____ Course of Study _____

Courses Relevant to Employment Objective _____

_____

Honors _____

Extracurricular Activities _____

Work Experience

Job Title _____

Employer's Name and Address _____

Supervisor's Name _____

Date Started_____ Date Ended_____

Description of Responsibilities and Skills Used (use key words) _____

_____

Job Title _____

Employer's Name and Address _____

Supervisor's Name _____

Date Started_____ Date Ended_____

Description of Responsibilities and Skills Used (use key words) _____

_____

(continues)

DATA SHEET FOR YOUR RESUME (*continued*)

Job Title _____

Employer's Name and Address _____

Supervisor's Name _____

Date Started_____Date Ended_____

Description of Responsibilities and Skills Used (use key words) _____

_____

Professional Licenses

Name/Number of License _____

Licensing Agency_____ Date Issued_____

Military Experience

Rank _____ Branch of Service _____

Date Started_____ Date Ended_____

Description of Responsibilities and Skills Used (use key words) _____

_____

Special Training _____

Personal Data

Awards, Honors, and Special Achievements _____

_____

Hobbies and Special Interests _____

Foreign Languages _____

Organizations and Offices Held _____

_____

Volunteer Work _____

References List educational, employment, and character references. No relatives, please.

Educational Reference:

Name and title _____

E-mail address_____ Phone _____

Employment Reference:

Name and title _____

E-mail address_____ Phone _____

Character Reference:

Name and title _____

E-mail address_____ Phone _____

Preparing a Career Portfolio

A good resume lists your skills and achievements. A career portfolio, on the other hand, showcases them. A career portfolio is a collection of documents that illustrate what you have done on the job, in school, or in community service. A resume, letters of recommendation or commendation, certificates, awards, news articles, and examples of your work are items that typically appear in a career portfolio.

The items in the portfolio should target your job objective. For example, the marketing graduate whose resume is shown in Figure 14–3 might include copies of these items:

- a nicely formatted paper resume
- a letter of commendation from the faculty adviser of the Student Activities Association, praising his work to increase membership
- one or two promotional items for the Student Activities Association that he designed
- the certificate he earned from the special oral presentation course
- a list of marketing courses with a brief description of each and his grade

Typically, you take a career portfolio with you to a job interview. When something comes up for which you have a relevant document, you can pull it out of the portfolio binder or case and explain it to the interviewer. He or she may ask you to leave the whole portfolio at the end of the interview, so be sure all the documents are photocopies and not originals. Or, if you have posted your career portfolio on a Web site, the interviewer may prefer to look at it online.

Finding Job Openings

Many jobs are not advertised. If you limit your search to classified ads and Internet job sites, you will be short-changing yourself. So when you job hunt, you need to use as many approaches as you can. The more active you are in searching for a job, the more likely you are to find something. Among the sources of information are networking, employers, school placement offices, Internet job boards, classified ads, employment agencies, and registers and clearinghouses.

Networking When you are job hunting, you should ask your parents, other relatives, friends, fellow students, instructors, and coworkers for leads to jobs that might interest you. If you can list 50 people you know who might be helpful, each of them may be able to give you two or three names. To extend your network even further, join business or trade organizations, local community service groups, and organizations like Toastmasters. Before you know it, your word-of-mouth network may have a thousand potentially helpful people in it.

When you look for a job, you need to check many sources for job listings. This job hunter is checking the classified ads, but she also has checked employment agencies and Internet job boards.

Your Turn 14-5

PLAN A CAREER PORTFOLIO

List at least six items you could include in your career portfolio.

_____

_____

_____

_____

_____

_____

You can also use the Internet for networking. Social networking Web sites like MySpace and Facebook increase the ways you can connect with people who may help your job search. Be cautious about combining personal and professional information on these sites; they do not always mix well. A better bet for job hunting is an online social networking site for professionals, like LinkedIn <http://linkedin.com>. These sites are designed for business-only networking.

Remember, about half of all successful job hunters find their jobs through networking. Being referred to a company by a person who is known there often will open the door to an opportunity.

Employers   You can apply directly to an employer even if you're not sure there is a job available. To find employers that may have positions that meet your job objective, you can:

- check the employers' Web sites on the Internet; many post job openings and online application forms (see Figure 14–4);

Your Turn 14-6

START BUILDING A NETWORK

Most people can easily build a network of a thousand or more people. On a separate piece of paper, list 25 (or more) people you know and the jobs they hold. Then build the network by asking each of the people on your core list for two referrals. Working outward, add to your network. Keep a list of every person and their contact information for use when you begin job hunting.

FIGURE 14–4

Many companies post job openings on their Web sites.

(© Cengage Learning Website, a part of Cengage Learning, Inc. Reproduced by Permission Cengage Learning www.Cengage.com/Permissions)

- check relevant trade associations' Web sites for job listings;
- check the directories of your local Chamber of Commerce;
- Visit flipdog <http://www.flipdog.com>, a Web site that scans the Internet for job openings posted on employer Web sites.

School Placement Offices   Many school placement offices provide job referral services to students and alumni. This is an excellent source of job leads for students, because employers list positions whose qualifications are likely to be matched by students or alumni. In addition, placement offices can put you in touch with alumni who work in the field that interests you. These alumni are happy to share information and job leads with students.

FIGURE 14–5

Even though most jobs are not advertised, it still pays to check the classified ads in your local newspaper.

Leading COSTUME JEWELRY
DISTRIBUTOR

is seeking a

MARKETING ASSISTANT

to help regional marketing manager with sales and promotion.

College preferred. Marketing experience a plus.
Competitive salary and benefits.

E-mail resume to Mia Wall,
MWall@fortaine.com.

Newspaper and Online Classified Ads   Classified ads list job openings, but many do not identify responsibilities, the employer's name, or the salary. Still, some people do find their jobs by responding to classified ads (see Figure 14–5).

You can find classified employment ads in local newspapers and professional and trade publications, both in print and on-line. You can also find them on the Internet classified site Craigslist <http://craigslist.com>. Check the classifieds every day, and if you decide to answer an ad, respond promptly. Some jobs are filled before the ad stops running. Keep a record of all ads you respond to.

Internet Job Boards   In addition to classified ads, which typically list local jobs, there are many Internet job boards that list openings around the world. Some of the most comprehensive job boards are the career sites CareerBuilder, Monster.com, CollegeRecruiter, JobCentral, Yahoo! HotJobs, JobOptions, Job.com, and Career.com (see Figure 14–6). Job sites usually update their listings every day, and you can search for openings by location and/or type of job.

FIGURE 14–6

This is the home page of one of the many commercial job boards on the Internet.

(© courtesy of careerbuilder.com)

Another way to use the Internet for job hunting is to post your resume in a resume database on the job boards or on a personal home page. Employers can find qualified job candidates by doing key word searches. For the job hunter, posting a resume is usually less effective than searching a job site because you are relying on an employer to find you instead of the other way around. Regularly repost your resume because some sites pull up newer resumes before older ones.

A certain amount of caution is needed when you are job hunting online. For example, identity thieves have been known to post false job openings on the larger job boards in an effort to get people's social security numbers and credit card data. So never give out such personal information over the Internet (see Chapter 14, News & Views, page 337). Furthermore, if you are currently employed and want to keep your job search private, be careful where you post your resume online. Make sure you understand the degree of privacy the site will afford you. This can range from no privacy (anyone can access your resume) to sites that allow you to see which companies are interested in your resume before the resume is released. To be safe in general, you can create a resume that does not give your name and lists only an anonymous e-mail address, such as those available on Yahoo! or Hotmail. You can then screen any responses you get before offering further information.

Finally, keep in mind that not all employers use Internet job boards, so do not stop using other job-hunting techniques when you start searching online.

Private Employment Agencies   Private employment agencies can sometimes be helpful. There are temporary agencies, general agencies, agencies that specialize in a particular field, and executive search agencies. The most important thing to remember about agencies is that they are in business to make money. Either you or the employer will have to pay a fee, usually a percentage of a year's salary, if you get a job through the agency. Before you decide to use a private employment agency, make sure you understand the financial arrangements.

WHATEVER IT TAKES
Alfredo Quinones-Hinojosa

(© ABC. / May 1, 2007/Baltimore sun)

When he was a child in Mexacali, Mexico, Alfredo Quinones-Hinojosa's father lost his small business, and the family suffered. Seeing his father in tears because he could not support them, Quinones-Hinojosa vowed that he would do whatever it took to be able to take care of his parents and his future family.

As a result, at the age of 19, Quinones-Hinojosa climbed a border fence and arrived in the San Joaquin Valley of California as an illegal immigrant. He found a job weeding fields and picking tomatoes and cotton. After a year, he decided there was no future in migrant farm work and got a job loading freight cars. That job paid him just enough so that he could afford to take night classes at San Joaquin Delta Community College. There he found his first mentor, the speech and debate coach, who encouraged him to apply for a scholarship to the University of California at Berkeley. At Berkeley, Quinones-Hinojosa took many science and math courses, which did not require a perfect command of English, to raise his G.P.A. Because his grades were so high, his advisor urged him to apply to Harvard University Medical School.

In medical school, Quinones-Hinojosa debated what kind of doctor he should become. Because he was good with his hands, he thought surgery would be a good specialty. Today Quinones-Hinojosa is a brain surgeon and researcher at Johns Hopkins University in Baltimore, Maryland; he is also an American citizen. Known as Dr. Q at work, he runs one of the most racially and ethnically diverse research labs on campus. "As you go up in life," says Dr. Q, "you should always look back and help the people behind you.... The potential is in everybody. The question is, 'How do we harvest that potential?'"

Sources: Claudia Dreifus, "A Conversation with Alfredo Quinones-Hinojosa." *The New York Times,* May 13, 2008, p. D2; "Farmerworker to Surgeon: Immigrant Lives Dream." NPR, May 6, 2007 <http://npr.org/templates/story/story.php?storyId=10013111> accessed June 25, 2008; "Illegal Immigrant Becomes World-Renowned Brain Surgeon." WBALTV, Mar. 5, 2007, <http://www.wbaltv.com/family/11177318/detail.html> accessed June 25, 2008; Deborah Rudacille, "The Remarkable Journey of Dr. Q." *DOME,* Sept. 2006 <http://hopkinsmedicine.org/dome/0609/top_story.cfm> accessed June 25, 2008.

State Employment Agencies   Your state's employment service, sometimes called Job Service, provides free statewide and local job referrals. To find a state employment office, look in the phone book under your state's Department of Labor or Employment, or visit <http://www .job-hunt.org/state_unemployment_offices.shtml> for links to the Web sites of all 50 state employment agencies.

Registers and Clearinghouses   Registers and clearinghouses collect and distribute employment information, both off- and online. There are federal and private clearinghouses, and some specialize in certain fields. Some list employers' vacancies, some list applicants' qualifications, and some list both. The cost to the job hunter varies.

Writing Cover Letters

Most employers don't want to be bothered with handling the phone calls of dozens of job applicants. When you respond to a classified ad or other job listing, or contact an employer cold, you usually e-mail, fax, or mail your resume and cover letter.

The cover letter demonstrates your interest in a particular job or company. Its purpose is to get the employer to look at your resume and call you in for an interview. So one all-purpose cover letter will not do. You must write a cover letter that is targeted to each job you're responding to. Here are some tips for composing cover letters:

- Whenever possible, address the letter to a specific person. Do some research, if necessary, to find the exact name of the person you are writing to.

- If you are e-mailing your cover letter and resume, they should go into one e-mail message. (Many employers will not open e-mail attachments for fear of viruses.) Keep the "cover letter" portion of the message short: just the salutation ("Dear Mia Wall"), an opening paragraph in which you indicate which job interests you, where you saw it advertised, and that you think you would be a good fit for the job. In the second paragraph, indicate your availability for an interview. Finish with a closing like "Sincerely," and add your name, phone number, and e-mail address. Then paste your plain text resume right into the e-mail. Figure 14–7 shows Marianne Guilmette's e-mail response to the ad for a marketing assistant.

- If you are sending your cover letter and resume by fax or regular mail, then use a business letter format. A paper cover letter can have an additional paragraph in which you explain why your skills, education, and experience would be valuable to the employer. Still, keep it short—three paragraphs maximum and no more than one page.

Remember, the cover letter, like the resume, is an advertisement for you. Make it positive and upbeat in tone. And make it perfect: neat, well organized, and without errors. Have someone proofread it for you.

FIGURE 14–7

Marianne's e-mail response to ad

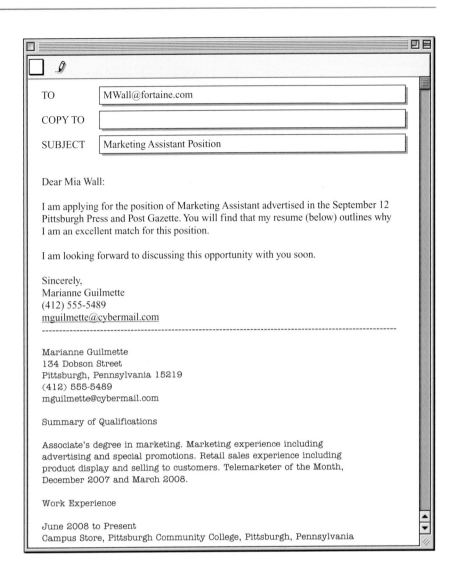

TO   MWall@fortaine.com

COPY TO

SUBJECT   Marketing Assistant Position

Dear Mia Wall:

I am applying for the position of Marketing Assistant advertised in the September 12 Pittsburgh Press and Post Gazette. You will find that my resume (below) outlines why I am an excellent match for this position.

I am looking forward to discussing this opportunity with you soon.

Sincerely,
Marianne Guilmette
(412) 555-5489
mguilmette@cybermail.com

Marianne Guilmette
134 Dobson Street
Pittsburgh, Pennsylvania 15219
(412) 555-5489
mguilmette@cybermail.com

Summary of Qualifications

Associate's degree in marketing. Marketing experience including advertising and special promotions. Retail sales experience including product display and selling to customers. Telemarketer of the Month, December 2007 and March 2008.

Work Experience

June 2008 to Present
Campus Store, Pittsburgh Community College, Pittsburgh, Pennsylvania

Filling Out Employment Applications

When you call on an employer directly, or before you are interviewed, you may be asked to fill out an employment application form. This form includes much of the information that is on your resume but arranged for the employer's convenience. Bring a copy of your resume when you call on employers. You can also use the resume data sheet from "Your Turn" 14-4, page 344, as a handy source of information when filling out an application form.

When you fill out an employment application, follow directions. If it is a paper form, write neatly. Proofread your entries. Remember that spelling and grammar are as important on the application as they are on your resume and cover letter. If there is a section that doesn't apply to you, write a dash (—) or N/A (not applicable) in the space. You need not provide information that may be discriminatory—your age, race, religion, marital status, and arrest record, for example. The employment application form shown in Figure 14–8, page 354, is nondiscriminatory. To prevent identity theft, do not give your social security number on an

FIGURE 14-8

The information
on an employment
application form is
similar to
the information
on a resume.

Fortaine, Inc.

APPLICATION FOR EMPLOYMENT
An Equal Opportunity Employer

PERSONAL INFORMATION

Name _Marianne Guilmette_   Date _Sept. 20, 20—_

Address _134 Dobson St._   Soc. sec. no. _555-2D-0020_

Pittsburgh, PA 15219   Telephone _(412) 555-5489_

E-mail address _mguilmette@cybermail.com_   Fax _—_

Are you 18 years of age or older? Yes ☑ No ☐

Are you either a U.S. citizen or an alien authorized to work in the United States?   Yes ☑ No ☐

EMPLOYMENT DESIRED

Position applied for _Marketing Assistant_ Full-time only ☑ Part-time only ☐ Full-time or part-time ☐

EDUCATION

Type of School	Name of School	Address	No. Years Completed	Major and Degree
High School	West Central H.S.	Fromer Rd., Pitts.	4	College prep
College	Pitts. Com. Coll.	East Main, Pitts.	2	Marketing, A.S.
Bus. or Trade School				
Prof. or Grad. School				

WORK EXPERIENCE

Dates (Month and Year)	Name and Address of Employer	Position(s) Held	Highest Salary	Reason for Leaving
June 2003 – present	Campus Store, Pittsburgh CC, East Main St., Pittsburgh	Senior sales associate	$7/hr	—
July 2002 – May 2003	MDS Marketing Group, Pittsburgh, Pa.	telemarketer	$6/hr +	Company relocated.

List work-related skills you have or special accomplishments. _retail sales, special promotions, product display, telemarketing. Was Sales Associate of the Month twice._

REFERENCES Give the names of three people, not relatives, who have known you for at least one year.

Name	Address	Phone	Relationship
Beth Martingale	Campus Store, PCC	(412)555-2051	Employer
John Hoisington	Dept. of Mktng, PCC	(412)555-3124	Professor
Rev. Wm. Starzyk	Trinity Church, Pitts.	(412)555-9024	Minister

I hereby certify that all information is true and complete and authorize Fortaine Inc. to contact former employers and references regarding this application.

Applicant Signature _Marianne Guilmette_   Date _Sept. 20, 20—_

application form; if you do get the job, you can give your employer the number at that point.

Interviewing

If your resume and application have made a good impression, you will be invited for an employment interview.

There are three basic types of employment interviews:

1. A gatekeeping interview screens a large group of applicants. Typically this is done by an employment agency, recruitment firm, or human resources department. You must do well in this interview to go on to the next stage.

2. A job interview, with one or more people in the company, explores your qualifications, personal characteristics, and suitability. This interview is usually conducted by the person supervising the position. If you do well in this level of interview, you are passed to the next stage.

3. In a final interview, a higher-level executive assesses how well you would fit with the company and discusses any problems that may have come up during previous interviews.

If you are applying for a job at a large company, you are likely to go through all three types of interviews. In a small company, you may be interviewed by just one or two people.

Most interviews are done in person, but some are done over the phone to save the employer time and money. During an interview, the interviewer will evaluate your skills, experience, and character in order to decide whether you are a match for the job. Although an interview may last only 15 minutes, those minutes are very important. You should take time to prepare carefully for each interview. During the interview, you should try to make a good impression as well as learn as much as you can about the job. And after an interview, it's important to follow up to show your professionalism and interest.

> "Work is life, you know, and without it, there's nothing but fear and insecurity."
>
> JOHN LENNON (1940–1980), British rock musician

These two young men are applying for the same job. Which one is likely to make the better impression?

Before the Interview The interview is your big chance to impress someone who has the authority to approve you or give you a job. Because people know that interviews are so important, they get nervous. To minimize your nervousness and increase your self-confidence, prepare yourself for the interview beforehand. Here are some suggestions that will help you arrive at an interview well prepared.

■ **Do some research about the company.** Get information from the company's Web site, public relations department, or from the library. Find out what it produces or sells, how big it is, what its reputation is, and what its problems are. Be ready to ask questions about the company.

- **Do some research about the job.** Make sure you understand the duties and responsibilities of the position. You can check the *Occupational Outlook Handbook* for a general description of the position. Be aware, however, that different employers use different job titles and job descriptions. Check the careers section of the employer's Web site for details about the job.

- **Be ready to explain why your experience and skills qualify you for the job.** Which of your skills and experiences can be useful to the employer?

- **Be prepared to answer the questions that almost always come up.** These are variations on "Tell me about yourself: What are your strengths? What are your weaknesses? Why should we hire you? What have you accomplished? What do you want to do in five years? How much salary do you want?" Be specific, and be ready with examples.

- **Be prepared to handle discriminatory questions.** Although employers cannot legally ask questions designed to reveal your race, nationality, age, religion, marital status, or sexual orientation, sometimes they do. You can either answer the question directly or try to return the interview to its proper focus, the requirements of the job. For example, you can respond with something like, "I know your company is committed to diversity by the statement posted in the lobby. I want to show you how hiring me will help you meet your company's business goals."

- **Make sure you are neat and well groomed and that your clothing is appropriate.** For most job interviews, stick to the basics. That usually means a clean, well-pressed suit for both men and women. Avoid extremes—trendy or skimpy clothes, gaudy colors, large jewelry or lots of jewelry, body piercings (except small earrings for women), lots of makeup, sunglasses, and sneakers. Do not wear perfumes or aftershave. In general, it's better to dress conservatively, because it projects a professional image.

- **Bring several copies of your resume, your career portfolio, a pen, and a small notebook.** You may want to take some notes.

- **Be prepared to take one or more tests.** You may be asked to take an intelligence test, a personality test, a role-playing test, and/or a drug test.

- **Know exactly where the interview is and how to get there.** Plan to arrive 10 minutes early.

- **Turn off your cell phone once you are there.** You don't want a call or message to interrupt the interview.

Getting ready for an interview is a lot like getting ready for an exam. The more you prepare, the less nervous you will feel, and the better you will do.

During the Interview The moment has come. You look great, you have done your homework, and you even got there with a few minutes to spare.

"The sense of being perfectly well dressed gives a feeling of inward tranquillity."

RALPH WALDO EMERSON
(1803–1882), writer

The employment interview is your chance to convince an employer that you are the right person for the job. It also gives you the opportunity to ask questions about the job and the company.

Remember the importance of first impressions and act accordingly. You should be professional with everyone you encounter, including security guards and receptionists.

When you're called in for the interview, it's time to follow the interviewer's lead. After you have introduced yourself and shaken hands, if offered, wait to be seated until the interviewer shows you a chair. Put your things on a nearby chair—never on the interviewer's desk. While you are getting settled, the interviewer is usually reviewing your resume or application. Let the interviewer begin the conversation when he or she is ready.

Interviewers are individuals, too, so the interview process may be quite different each time you undergo it. Some interviewers ask very specific, directed questions and expect short, to the-point answers. Others talk so much you hardly have any time to speak yourself, although you may learn a lot about the company. Still others just say, "Tell me about yourself," and expect you to start talking. So you have to be flexible enough to adapt to the interviewer's style.

Basic Types of Interview Questions   In an interview, you may be asked three types of questions:

1. **Informational questions.** These questions are about your credentials—your experience, education, and skills. They are the easiest to answer. An example of an informational question is "What are your qualifications for this job?" Many job interviews consist only of informational questions.

2. **Problem-solving questions.** These questions are more difficult because they are hypothetical. Interviewers may give you a problem scenario and ask what you would do. For example, he or she may tell you that Employee X arrives late three times a week and ask how you, as his supervisor, would handle the situation. He or she may ask you to role play. For example, if you are applying for a sales job, interviewers might indicate an item on the desk and ask you to sell it to them.

3. **Behavioral questions.** These questions are designed to assess your character, traits, habits, and attitudes by discovering how you handled challenging situations in the past. A typical behavioral question is, "Tell me about a time when you made a big mistake," or "Tell me about a time when you made a great sale." You answer such a question by telling a story about a past experience. Even if the experience was negative—such as making a big mistake— you should frame it positively. "Although the client was upset that the installation was late, I learned the importance of good communication and follow-up."

Handling Personal and Discriminatory Questions   What happens if an interviewer asks you a sensitive or personal question? Saying that it's none of his or her business (even though it may be true) won't work. Instead, you must try to respond in a way that will put the interview back on track without embarrassing the interviewer. For example, if the interviewer asks how old you are, you can simply answer, if it doesn't bother you. Or you can say something like, "Your ad didn't indicate that you were concerned about age but rather focused on familiarity with Microsoft Excel. I'd like to explain to you how I have used Excel in my past jobs."

Remember, questions having to do with your race, sex, age, religion, and marital status are discriminatory; however, some interviewers do ask such questions. If you find yourself in an interview that seems to dwell on these subjects, it might be an indication that you wouldn't want to work for that company.

Asking Questions about the Company   During the interview, keep in mind that you are there for two purposes. The primary purpose, of course, is to sell yourself to the employer. You want to convince the interviewer that you are the right person for the job. The second purpose is for you to assess the company and the job. The interview affords you a brief opportunity to get a feel for the company and to learn more about the job. Be sure you ask questions that show you've done your homework about the company. You may find, after an interview, that you really are enthusiastic about the possibility of working at that company. On the other hand, what you learn about the job and the company may convince you that you would be better off elsewhere.

Interview Tips   Here are some suggestions to make the most of the opportunity provided by the interview:

- Don't eat, chew gum or candy, or smoke.
- Don't criticize former employers or complain about them.
- Don't discuss any of your financial or personal problems.
- Avoid potentially controversial topics like politics and religion.
- Don't make up answers that you think the interviewer wants to hear. This may backfire on you.
- Listen carefully, and be sure you understand each question. Remember that open-ended questions require more than a *yes* or *no* answer. It's okay to ask for clarification or to take time to think about your response. (Review your listening skills in Chapter 8.)
- Be courteous. Make sure you have the interviewer's name right. Listen carefully, and don't interrupt.
- Ask open-ended questions about the company and the job. In addition to gaining information, you will demonstrate your interest and enthusiasm.
- Let the interviewer bring up the subject of money. If you are asked what salary you expect, you can turn the question around by

Your Turn 14-7

ROLE PLAY AN INTERVIEW

Choose a partner from your class and role-play an interview. One of you will be Marianne Guilmette, whose resume appears on page 354. Marianne is looking for a marketing job. The other will play the part of the interviewer, who is looking for someone to fill the vacancy shown in the classified ad on page 349. Take a few minutes to prepare, and then role-play the interview.

indicating you know what the average starting salary is in the industry and by asking what the company's salary range is. Try not to mention a specific salary first, because you may be too high or too low.

At the End of the Interview   Interviewers can bring the interview to a close in several ways. You may be thanked for your time and told you will hear from them. When this happens, it sometimes means that the interviewers do not think you are suitable for the job. They may let you know at a later date that someone else was hired. Try not to take it personally. Remember that the employer is looking for someone who fits into the organization.

Another way the interview can end is with your being invited back for a placement or other test or to talk to someone else in the company. If you're asked to take a drug test, find out which types of tests they are using and which foods or medications could trigger a false positive. (Three-quarters of large and medium-sized companies test for drugs.) When you are invited back, make sure to write down the details of your next appointment. Don't rely on your memory, because you may be too excited to remember things correctly.

And last, the interview may actually end with a job offer. If this happens, *and you are absolutely sure you want the job at the salary offered,* then say yes. But in most circumstances, you should ask for a day to think it over. That extra time will give you a chance to decide whether the company, job, salary, and potential for the future are what you want.

After the Interview   Even if the interview does not result in a job offer, you should send interviewers a letter or e-mail message to thank them for their time (see Figure 14–9). A brief thank-you note serves to demonstrate courtesy and interest on your part. Although you may not get the particular job you interviewed for, at some time in the future you may wish to apply to that company again.

After each interview, you should review your performance. What seemed to impress the interviewer? What could you have done better? Use each interview as a rehearsal for the next. That way you will improve your

FIGURE 14-9

Writing a thank-you note or letter to each interviewer demonstrates your interest in the company and the job.

TO   MWall@fortaine.com

COPY TO

SUBJECT   Interview for Marketing Assistant Position

Dear Mrs. Wall:

Thank you for taking the time to speak with me yesterday about the Marketing Assistant position in the Middle Atlantic region. I was very impressed with your company, and the job sounds wonderful. I'm more than ever convinced that my marketing experience can benefit your company.

Sincerely,
Marianne Guilmette
(412) 555-5489
mguilmette@cybermail.com

interview skills. Remember, you may have a dozen or more interviews before you get a job offer. Ideally, you will have more than one offer and can choose the job you prefer.

Your Career: A Lifelong Enterprise

Your working life will be long—40 or 50 years for many people. Your working life will also be varied: Gone are the days when a person worked at the same job for the same company for life. When you consider a job offer, you must think of long-range as well as short-range consequences. Sometimes an offer of immediate employment is tempting simply because you've been job hunting for a while or need the money. While these are certainly factors influencing whether you take a job, you should try to evaluate how a job fits into your long-term professional goals. Essentially, if the job you are considering will help you achieve your career goals, then you should take it.

Do you remember the long-term professional goals you set in Chapter 2? Now that you have spent some time thinking about yourself and setting an employment objective, you should reevaluate your long-term goals. Perhaps you need an entirely new professional goal, or a slightly modified goal. Perhaps your action plan for achieving your long-term professional goal needs an overhaul.

Goal-setting in the context of a career is an ongoing process. As you gain experience, you may find that the goals you set at the start of your career no longer interest you, were unrealistic, or have become outdated. You may find that your jobs are taking you in unexpected but interesting new directions. You will also find the world around you changing so fast that you must adapt to keep up. Changes in technology and the world

Your Turn 14-8

YOUR LONG-TERM PROFESSIONAL GOALS

Take this opportunity to review and change your long-term professional goals, if necessary. Whether your goals have changed or not, answer the following questions. Renew your commitment to achieving your goals.

1. What is your long-term professional goal?

_____

_____

_____

2. By when do you expect to reach this goal?

_____

3. What actions must you take to reach your goal?

_____

_____

_____

_____

_____

economy have automated and globalized many companies. If you don't keep up with these forces, your skills and experience may become obsolete. Continuing education and retraining are becoming a lifelong process.

The process of self-evaluation and learning that you have undertaken in this course is an ongoing process. It doesn't end when the course is over or when you get your first job. Rather, to reach your potential, you will use your inner resources and abilities to meet the challenges of your personal and professional life.

Tech Tips

EXPLORING INTERNET CAREER RESOURCES

As you have discovered while reading this chapter, there are many career- and job-related Web sites. In addition to the sites we've already mentioned, the following sites offer valuable job-related information.

- **Education and Careers** <http://www.collegeboard.org>. The College Board site devotes a section (Majors and Careers) to information about college majors, degrees, and the careers they can lead to.

- **Occupational Information at O*NET OnLine** <http://online.onetcenter.org>. An interactive site from the U.S. Department of Labor that allows you to match your skills and other criteria with occupations, find detailed information about occupations (including average pay), find technology-related jobs, and link to other government databases with job-related information.

- **Career Information by Industry** <http://www.careermag.com>. One section of the Career Magazine Web site provides information and job searches organized by industry.

- **Resume and Portfolio Advice** <http://career-advice.monster.com>. This Monster site is devoted to general career advice, including how to prepare good resumes and portfolios.

- **Federal Government Student Jobs** <http://www.studentjobs.gov>. For high school, college, and graduate students interested in working for the government while in school, this searchable database contains 60,000 nationwide job listings.

- **Internships and Entry-Level Jobs for Students and Recent Graduates** <http://collegerecruiter.com>, <http://www.monstertrak.com>. All of the Internet job boards can be used by students (see page 347), but CollegeRecruiter.com and MonsterTrak have sections of particular interest. You can search special listings of internships and entry-level jobs on these sites.

Your Turn 14-9

Visit two of the sites listed earlier, and explore their offerings. Then answer the following questions.

1. List the type of resources available on the site.

   _____

   _____

   _____

   _____

   _____

2. How could you use this site for your own career research and job search?

   _____

   _____

   _____

   _____

   _____

What's Up?

Name _____   Date _____

1. List and describe the five categories of workplace skills.

_____
_____
_____

2. What career resources can be found in a school career or placement office?

_____
_____
_____

3. How can you use the Internet to find career information?

_____
_____
_____

4. Why should you keep up with job trends and economic and technology news?

_____
_____
_____

5. What is a resume? What is its purpose?

_____
_____
_____

6. What is a career portfolio? How does it differ from a resume?

_____
_____
_____

continues

Name _____ Date _____

7. Describe three ways of finding a job.

_____

_____

_____

8. What is the purpose of a cover letter? a thank you letter?

_____

_____

_____

9. List three things you can do to prepare for a job interview.

_____

_____

_____

10. What are the two main purposes of a job interview?

_____

_____

_____

11. List and give an example of the three basic types of interview questions.

_____

_____

_____

12. Why should you keep reviewing and changing your professional goals?

_____

_____

_____

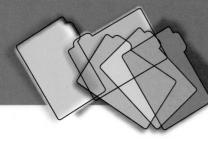

Case Studies

The Case of the Self-Important Applicant

Jeff's uncle knew someone at the telecommunications company where Jeff wanted to start his career. As a favor to Jeff, who was about to graduate, Jeff's uncle set up an interview for him.

Jeff prepared his resume, took his only suit to the cleaners, and went to the interview full of confidence. He was surprised to hear the interviewer describe the entry-level position. Although he had never had a telecommunications job, he was sure he was too qualified to start at such a low-level job. When he heard what the starting salary was, he informed the interviewer that he was not interested. Later that evening, Jeff told his uncle about the interview. He couldn't understand why his uncle became annoyed when he heard what had happened.

1. Was Jeff's uncle justified in being annoyed at Jeff?

2. Why are Jeff's expectations about his first job so unrealistic?

3. How would doing some research into the company and the industry have helped Jeff on his first interview?

The Case of the Discouraged Job Seeker

When Abby finished school, she started looking for her first full-time job. Every day, she checked Craigslist for want ads. Every Sunday, she looked through the newspaper classified ads and circled any that looked interesting. She applied for several jobs but with no results. After three weeks, she was discouraged and decided it was no use to check the ads.

1. What should Abby have had before she even started her job hunt?

2. What's wrong with Abby's job search technique?

3. What should Abby do to get her job search on track?

Journal

Answer the following journal questions.

1. Describe the worst job you ever had. What did you learn from it? How did this job affect your career goals?

_____

_____

_____

_____

_____

_____

_____

2. What is your ideal job? What aspects of this job appeal to you? What "real world" work might this ideal job be similar to?

_____

_____

_____

_____

_____

_____

_____

3. Describe someone you know who loves his or her job. Why does this person enjoy work? How does this enjoyment affect the rest of her or his life?

_____

_____

_____

_____

_____

_____

4. What is your career goal? What are you doing now to prepare yourself to reach this goal?

_____

_____

_____

_____

_____

_____

After You're Done: Self-Assessment

Now that you have worked through *Reaching Your Potential,* it is time to assess your progress. Read each of the following statements. Then circle *yes, maybe,* or *no* to indicate whether the statement is true of you at this time.

Read each of the following statements. Then circle *yes, maybe,* or *no* to indicate whether the statement is true of you at this time.

As a Lifelong Learner...

1. I can name and describe the four areas of potential that each of us has.	Yes	Maybe	No
2. I have good self-belief, the foundation of success.	Yes	Maybe	No
3. I can learn new things and change my beliefs to change my behavior.	Yes	Maybe	No
4. I can set, pursue, and achieve realistic goals.	Yes	Maybe	No
5. I can envision a compelling future for myself.	Yes	Maybe	No
6. I have achieved personal mastery over at least some aspects of my life.	Yes	Maybe	No

UNIT 1   Developing Your Emotional Potential

Chapter 1   The Power of Self-Belief

7. I can explain my most important values and beliefs to another person.	Yes	Maybe	No
8. I usually think about things in a positive way.	Yes	Maybe	No
9. I recognize my good qualities and always make the most of them.	Yes	Maybe	No

Chapter 2 Setting Goals and Managing Time

10. I have a dream for my future.	Yes	Maybe	No
11. I have written personal, educational, professional, and community service goals.	Yes	Maybe	No
12. I have action plans for achieving my goals.	Yes	Maybe	No
13. I set priorities on the things I need to do.	Yes	Maybe	No
14. I use a planner to organize my time.	Yes	Maybe	No
15. I have the motivation needed to achieve my goals.	Yes	Maybe	No

UNIT 2 Developing Your Intellectual Potential

Chapter 3 Improving Your Thinking Skills

16. I use techniques to improve my memory.	Yes	Maybe	No
17. I am able to think critically.	Yes	Maybe	No
18. I try to solve problems in a systematic way.	Yes	Maybe	No
19. I use techniques to improve my creative thinking.	Yes	Maybe	No

Chapter 4 Improving Your Study Skills

20. I know my learning style and try to use it whenever possible.	Yes	Maybe	No
21. I have good study skills.	Yes	Maybe	No
22. I use special reading techniques when I read to learn.	Yes	Maybe	No
23. I take good notes on my readings and in class.	Yes	Maybe	No
24. I have good test-taking skills.	Yes	Maybe	No
25. I know how to use the resources of a library and the Internet.	Yes	Maybe	No

UNIT 3 Developing Your Physical Potential

Chapter 5 Eating Well

26. I can list the basic food groups and their nutrients.	Yes	Maybe	No
27. I eat a balanced diet.	Yes	Maybe	No
28. I maintain a healthy weight.	Yes	Maybe	No

Chapter 6   Staying Healthy

29. I am physically fit because I exercise regularly.	Yes	Maybe	No
30. I do not abuse drugs, including alcohol and tobacco.	Yes	Maybe	No
31. I understand how to prevent the spread of sexually transmitted diseases.	Yes	Maybe	No

UNIT 4   Developing Your Social Potential

Chapter 7   Communicating Effectively

32. I can explain the basic elements of communication.	Yes	Maybe	No
33. I know what my own communication style is.	Yes	Maybe	No
34. I use techniques to improve my communication with others.	Yes	Maybe	No

Chapter 8   Improving Your Listening Skills

35. I am an active listener, with respect for the speaker and comprehension of the message.	Yes	Maybe	No

Chapter 9   Improving Your Speaking Skills

36. I am a good speaker, with good voice qualities and a good command of Standard English.	Yes	Maybe	No
37. I am good at conversing with another person.	Yes	Maybe	No
38. I can prepare and deliver an oral presentation.	Yes	Maybe	No

Chapter 10   Getting Along with Others

39. I am assertive without being aggressive.	Yes	Maybe	No
40. I have ethical values that I try to live by.	Yes	Maybe	No
41. I am good at understanding the needs of other people.	Yes	Maybe	No
42. I give feedback tactfully and receive feedback openly.	Yes	Maybe	No
43. I use conflict resolution techniques to defuse angry situations.	Yes	Maybe	No

Chapter 11   Functioning in Groups

44. I can describe the basics of group dynamics.	Yes	Maybe	No
45. I function well as a member of a team or group.	Yes	Maybe	No
46. I can use different leadership styles in different situations.	Yes	Maybe	No

UNIT 5   Developing Your Action Plan

Chapter 12   Handling Change and Stress

47. I understand the causes of stress and the responses to stress.	Yes	Maybe	No
48. I know the signs of stress and watch out for them.	Yes	Maybe	No
49. I can reduce my feelings of stress by using coping techniques.	Yes	Maybe	No

Chapter 13   Managing Money

50. I know my values and goals and base short- and long-term financial decisions upon them.	Yes	Maybe	No
51. I have a written budget.	Yes	Maybe	No
52. I understand and use savings institutions, debit, credit, and insurance wisely.	Yes	Maybe	No
53. I know the factors that influence whether I should rent or buy a home.	Yes	Maybe	No
54. I invest now for large future expenses such as retirement.	Yes	Maybe	No

Chapter 14   Preparing for Your Career

55. I can match my skills and interests to one or more suitable occupations by using career resources.	Yes	Maybe	No
56. I have a good resume and career portfolio and can write a good cover letter.	Yes	Maybe	No
57. I know how to use various job-hunting resources.	Yes	Maybe	No
58. I am good at preparing for and undergoing employment interviews.	Yes	Maybe	No
59. I can evaluate whether a job fits into my long-term professional goals.	Yes	Maybe	No

Now look over your self-assessment. Underline the statements to which you replied *maybe* or *no*. These statements reflect areas in which you may not yet have reached your potential.

Compare this self-assessment with the one you did before you began working through this book (see pages 000–000). Then answer the following questions.

1. List the five areas you identified as needing work on page 000. Evaluate your progress in each area.

   a. _____

   _____

   b. _____

   _____

   c. _____

   _____

   d. _____

   _____

   e. _____

   _____

2. Which of these five areas would you still like to improve?

   _____

   _____

   _____

   You should review the chapters in which these areas are covered to increase your knowledge and skills.

3. What did you accomplish during this course to help you reach your potential?

   _____

   _____

   _____

Glossary

A

accented English English spoken by many Americans for whom English is a second language

aerobic exercise activities that improve cardio-respiratory endurance; for example, walking and swimming

agenda a list of topics to be discussed at a meeting

alcohol an addictive drug that decreases brain activity and lowers blood pressure

all-channel pattern a communication network in which each group member communicates with every other group member

amphetamine a drug that stimulates the brain

anabolic steroid an artificial form of a male hormone that stimulates the growth of muscle

annual percentage rate (APR) the interest rate charged per year on the amount borrowed

anorexia nervosa an eating disorder in which a person starves himself or herself because of a fear of being fat

assertiveness the self-belief and determination to make your needs or opinions known

associative thinking a method of problem solving in which a person allows his or her mind to wander in order to get fresh insight

auditory learning learning new material by listening; for example, by attending lectures

B

backburner thinking putting a problem aside and allowing your unconscious mind to take over solving it

barbiturate a type of depressant drug, also called *barbs*, *reds*, and *yellows*

beliefs specific opinions about yourself, other people, situations, things, or ideas

benzodiazepine a type of depressant drug, such as tranquilizers and sleeping pills

blog an online journal (from Web log)

binge drinking consuming an excessive amount of alcohol in a short period of time; specifically, having five or more alcoholic drinks in a row (four or more for women) at least once in the previous year

bodily-kinesthetic intelligence the ability to solve problems or make things by using your body or parts of body

body composition the proportion of the body made of muscle compared with fat

body mass index a measure of weight in relation to height

brainstorming a process by which a group of people comes up with many ideas about a problem or issue

budget a plan for using your money in order to spend less than income and meet financial goals

bulimia an eating disorder in which a person consumes large amounts of food and then induces vomiting to avoid gaining weight

C

call number a unique identification number that indicates where a book or other item is shelved in the library system

calorie the amount of heat needed to raise the temperature of one kilogram of water one degree centigrade

carbohydrate a chemical substance that provides energy for the body; for example, sugar

cardio-respiratory endurance the ability to do moderately strenuous activity over a period of time without overtaxing the heart and lungs

career portfolio a collection of documents that illustrate what one has done on the job, in school, or in community service; used in employment situations

certificate of deposit (CD) a type of bank account in which your money is tied up for a period of time ranging from 30 days to 5 or 10 years

chain a communication pattern in which messages are passed from one person to another without skipping over anyone

charisma a special quality of personal leadership that inspires great loyalty

checking account a bank account used to write checks and pay bills

chlamydia a sexually transmitted infection of the genital and urinary tracts

cholesterol a fatty acid found in animal products such as meat, cheese, shellfish, and eggs

chronological resume a resume format that lists a person's most recent job experience first, followed by other jobs in reverse chronological order

circadian rhythm an inner daily clock that governs the operating of our bodies

citation a reference to a published work, including author, title, publisher or periodical, date, and page numbers

closed-ended question a question that can be answered with a simple *yes* or *no*

club drug any of a wide variety of drugs used at parties, dance clubs, raves, and bars, especially by young adults

cocaine an addictive drug that increases brain activity and makes the user feel happy and excited

cognition mental processes such as thinking and remembering

cohesiveness in a group, the degree to which members stick together

communication the exchange of messages, either verbal or nonverbal

community service goals objectives that relate to improving conditions in your neighborhood, town, or city

compelling future the driving force from your current reality to a future reality

complex carbohydrates complex sugars such as starch and whole grains, which usually contain fiber

conformity changing opinions or behavior in response to pressure from a group

course management system a Web site that allows instructors and students to organize and post course materials, handle course-related administrative tasks such as grading, and communicate with one another

cover letter in job hunting, the letter that accompanies your resume, demonstrates your interest in a company or job, and asks for an interview

crack a powerful form of cocaine whose name derives from the sound that rock cocaine makes as it melts

creativity the ability to see things in a new way and to come up with unusual and creative solutions to problems

credit a financial arrangement in which you can defer payment on merchandise or services

credit bureau a company that maintains credit records

credit card plastic identification card that allows the holder to buy merchandise and services up to a certain dollar amount and pay for them later

credit limit the highest amount of money you can charge against a particular credit card

D

debit card a card that allows a person to pay for something by deducting money from his or her checking or savings account

deductible the amount an insured person pays to settle a claim before the insurance company starts paying

deductive reasoning a type of logical thinking in which the conclusion that is reached is true if the information it is based on is true

defense mechanism a mental process used to reduce anxiety and protect self-belief

depressant any drug that decreases brain activity and lowers blood pressure

depression a disorder characterized by sadness and difficulties in eating, sleeping, and concentrating

dialect a variation of Standard English that is spoken in a particular geographic area or by a particular social group

dietary fiber indigestible matter in whole grains, fruits, and vegetables that aids digestion

discussion board a special interest discussion group on the Internet, often used in online courses

displacement reacting to a negative situation by substituting another person for the person who aroused your anxiety or anger

drawing a visual image of something

drug a chemical substance that creates a physical, mental, emotional, or behavioral change in the user

drug abuse the non-medicinal use of a drug, which results in physical, emotional, or mental harm to the user

E

eating disorder a condition in which eating habits are out of control; for example, bulimia

educational goals objectives that relate to learning or training

e-mail a method of exchanging messages over the Internet

emergency fund an amount of money, usually at least two months' salary, set aside for unplanned expenses or loss of income

empathy experiencing another person's feelings or ideas as if they were your own

enunciation the clarity with which words are spoken

expenses amounts of money you spend

extrinsic motivation needs and incentives that come from outside ourselves and make us act in particular ways; an outside reward for behavior

F

fact something that can be shown to be true

fantasy a form of withdrawal from a negative situation in which daydreams provide a boost to self-belief

feedback a response to a message; fundamental to two-way communication

finance charge the total of all costs associated with a loan or credit card

fixed expenses amounts of money you spend that are the same all the time and/or occur regularly; for example, rent

flexibility the ability to move a joint through its full range of motion

flowchart a diagram used to show the steps in a process or procedure

formal group a group with clear goals and established rules

formatted resume a visually appealing resume saved as a formatted document with bold, italic, and other type; used when a paper resume is needed

functional resume a resume format in which work experience is presented in terms of the functions and skills used on the job

G

genital herpes a sexually transmitted disease caused by a virus

gonorrhea a sexually transmitted infection of the genital mucous membranes

gross income the total amount of money, from all sources, coming in

group the conscious interaction of two or more people

group dynamics the study of the patterns of response or adaptation that occur when people interact in groups

groupthink an uncritical acceptance of a group's beliefs and behaviors in order to preserve its unanimity

H

hallucinogen a drug that distorts perceptions and creates images of things that are not really there

heroin an addictive drug that affects the brain and lowers blood pressure

HIV-AIDS (human immunodeficiency virus–acquired immune deficiency syndrome) a collection of diseases and conditions resulting from the destruction of the immune system

home page the main page of a Web site

I

idea diagram a diagram that shows the relationship of secondary ideas to a main idea and to one another

income money coming in, such as salary or child support

individual retirement account (IRA) a type of account used to set aside money, usually for retirement or education

inductive reasoning a type of logical thinking in which the conclusion that is reached is probably true

informal group a loose association of people without stated rules

installment loan a loan that is paid back in monthly installments for a fixed period of time

interest a charge set by the lender and paid by the borrower of money

intermediate-term goals objectives that can be accomplished in one to five years

Internet a worldwide computer network that enables people to communicate electronically

interpersonal intelligence the ability to understand other people and to work cooperatively with them

intrapersonal intelligence the ability to assess yourself and use that assessment to live an effective life; self-knowledge

intrinsic motivation needs and incentives that come from within us and make us act in particular ways

J

jargon specialized words used in a particular field

Johari window a model showing the effect of mutual understanding in a relationship between two people

K

key words the words you enter when using a search engine to find information on the Internet

kinesthetic learning learning new material through movement; for example, by building a working model

L

leadership a set of behaviors, beliefs, and values that enables a person to persuade others to act

leading changing aspects of another person's communication style by getting them to imitate you

liability coverage a type of insurance coverage that protects the insured against the claims of others in case the insured causes property or other damage

linguistic intelligence the ability to use language and words well

logical-mathematical intelligence the ability to think logically, mathematically, and scientifically

long-term goals objectives that can be achieved over a long period of time—more than five years

long-term memory the third stage of memory, in which material is stored for years

M

marijuana a mild hallucinogen that alters the mind in many ways

mental set an overreliance on old ways of seeing and doing things

methamphetamine a highly addictive stimulant that can be smoked, snorted, injected, or taken orally

method of loci a system using images of places that can be used to help memorize information

mind-mapping a creativity technique that involves sketching the problem or topic

mineral a chemical that is needed for life and growth

mirroring to imitate another person's behavior or expressions

mnemonics devices, such as poems or acronyms, to help people remember

money market account a type of bank account whose interest rates change with market rates

monounsaturated fat a type of fat that is liquid at room temperature and found in peanut and olive oil

motivation the needs and incentives that make us act in particular ways

muscular endurance the ability to repeat movements or to hold a position for a long time without tiring

muscular strength the ability to exert force using a muscle once

musical intelligence the ability to hear musical sounds and make music

N

net income the amount of money actually received after amounts are withheld for taxes and other deductions

neurons the nerve cells that make up the brain and nervous system

neurotransmitters chemical substances that pass from one neuron to another, such as dopamine and serotonin

nicotine an addictive drug found in tobacco

norm in a group, the rules by which people in particular roles are expected to behave

nutrients substances used by the body for growth, maintenance, repair, and energy

O

one-way communication a form of communication in which a sender transmits a message, a receiver gets the message, and the process is complete

online social network a Web site such as Facebook or MySpace that allows people to post profiles and other material and to communicate with one another

open-ended question a question that requires an explanation as a response

opinion a belief based on values and assumptions that may or may not be true

P

P.Q.R. system a method of reading for information that involves three steps: previewing, questioning, and reviewing

passbook account a type of bank account with low interest

pegword method a system using numbers and words that can be used to help memorize information

perceive to see, hear, smell, taste, or become aware of something through the senses

periodicals publications, such as magazines and newspapers that appear at regular intervals

periodicals index a directory, organized by subject that provides citations for articles about each subject; can be in book, CD-ROM, or online format

personal goals objectives that relate to your personal life

personal mastery the ability to achieve specific results with consistency

physical fitness the ability to carry out daily tasks without tiring and with enough energy left to enjoy leisure activities and to handle an emergency requiring physical exertion

pie chart a diagram that shows the relationship of the parts (wedges) to the whole (pie)

pitch the level of sound on a musical scale

plain text resume an unformatted resume saved as an ASCII or plain text file; used when a resume will be scanned or otherwise input into a database

planning a thinking process in which an orderly and systematic approach to achieving an objective is devised

polyunsaturated fat a type of fat that is liquid at room temperature and found in corn, safflower, and soybean oil

positive psychology a branch of psychology that studies positive aspects of human behavior

potential the capacity for development into reality; a state of possibility

preface a short essay at the beginning of a book that often summarizes the author's point of view

prejudice a negative attitude toward people solely because of their membership in a certain group

premises Vinformation upon which reasoning is based

previewing scanning a reading selection before reading

priority a task that is important and should be done first

procrastination postponing a task that should be done now, or putting off until tomorrow what should be done today

professional goals objectives that relate to your work life

R

projection attributing your own unacceptable behaviors and feelings to another person

pronunciation the correctness with which words are spoken

protein a chemical substance that is part of all body cells

R

rationalize to explain or excuse an unacceptable situation in terms that make it acceptable to yourself

recall words in note taking, important words that provide cues for the main ideas

receiver in communication, the person who gets a message

reframing changing a belief that one holds in order to change the meaning

respect valuing the worth of another person

responsiveness the degree to which people are closed or open in their dealings with others

resume a short summary of your experience and qualifications, used in job hunting

role in a group, the set of expected behaviors for a particular position

S

saturated fat a fat that is solid at room temperature and found in meat and dairy products and palm and coconut oils

search engine a computerized index such as Google or Yahoo! that can be used to find information on a particular topic on the Internet

self-belief confidence in and respect for your own abilities; also called *self-esteem*

self-fulfilling prophecy a belief that comes true because it is believed

sender in communication, the person who sends a message

sensory memory the first stage of memory, in which material lasts a couple of seconds and then disappears

short-term goals objectives that can be achieved in a brief period of time—a year or less

short-term memory the second stage of memory, in which material lasts about 20 seconds

simple carbohydrates simple sugars such as table sugar, corn syrup, and other sweets

situational leadership the ability to adapt leadership styles to different circumstances

spatial intelligence the ability to form and use a mental model of a three-dimensional world

Standard English the English spoken by news broadcasters, actors, and others who have no regional accents

state specific the quality of being associated with a particular state of mind or place

stimulant any drug that increases brain activity and other body functions and makes the user feel more awake

stress the physical and psychological reactions to events or situations that a person has difficulty coping with

student loan a loan made to students to cover educational costs; payment is deferred until students complete their education

substandard English English spoken with poor pronunciation, enunciation, grammar, and vocabulary

syphilis a sexually transmitted disease caused by a bacterium

T

table of contents an outline of the main ideas of a book (chapters), along with page numbers

tactile learning learning new material through touch; for example, by note taking or handling objects

time line a diagram that shows the sequence of historical events

trust reliance on another person

two-way communication a form of communication in which a sender transmits a message, a receiver gets the message, and the receiver responds by giving feedback

U

unsaturated fat a fat that is liquid at room temperature, such as vegetable oil

URL (uniform resource locator) an Internet address, such as www.cengage.com

Usenet discussion forums a system of discussion groups on the Internet

V

values your deepest feelings and thoughts about yourself and life

variable expenses amounts one spends that differ from one period to another; for example, vacation expense

visual learning learning new material by seeing; for example, by reading

visualization a motivational technique in which one imagines the results of achieving a goal

vitamin a chemical that is needed for life and growth

volume the intensity or loudness of a sound

W

Web page a document on the World Wide Web, part of the Internet

Web site a collection of related Web pages on the World Wide Web; it is maintained by an individual or a group

wheel a communication pattern in which a person at the hub communicates with each person on the spokes, but the people on the spokes do not communicate directly with one another

withdrawal escaping from negative feedback

World Wide Web a part of the Internet that consists of millions of interlinked documents called Web pages

References

TO THE LIFELONG LEARNER

[1]Senge, Peter M. *The Fifth Discipline*. New York: Currency, Doubleday, 1990, p. 14.

[2]O'Malley, Brian. "The Quest of Mt. Everest." Presentation, no date.

CHAPTER 1

[1]McNally, David. *Even Eagles Need a Push: Learning to Soar in a Changing World*. New York: Delacorte Press, 1990, p. 153.

[2]CBS News/New York Times Poll, September 2–5, 2002. Cited on The Polling Report, Inc., Web site, <http:// www. pollingreport.com/news.htm>, accessed January 16, 2003.

[3]Rosenthal, Robert, and Lenore Jacobson. *Pygmalion in the Classroom: Teacher Expectation and Pupils' Intellectual Development*. New York: Irvington, 1989, pp. 46–51.

[4]Braiker, Harriet B. "The Power of Self-Talk," *Psychology Today,* December 1989, p. 24.

[5]Coombs, Patrick. *Major in Success*. 3rd ed. Berkeley, Calif.: Ten Speed Press, 2000, pp. 31–32.

CHAPTER 2

[1]Canfield, Jack. "Improving Students' Self-Esteem," *Educational Leadership,* September 1990, p. 48.

[2]Goleman, Daniel. "Hope Emerges as Key to Success in Life," *The New York Times,* December 24, 1991, pp. C1, C7.

CHAPTER 3

[1]Ferguson, Tom. "Empowerment: The Heart of Wellness," *Self-Care Journal,* May/June 1991, unpaged.

[2]Wolfe, Patricia. *Translating Brain Research into Classroom Practice*. Washington, D.C.: Association of Supervision and Curriculum Development, 1996.

[3]Hammond, John S., Ralph L. Keeney, and Howard Raiffa, *Smart Choices: A Practical Guide to Making Better Decisions*. Boston, Mass.: Harvard Business School Press, 1999, pp. 5–8.

[4]Gilbert, Randy. *Success Bound*. Mt. Jackson,Va.: Bargain Publishers, 2001, pp. 86–88.

CHAPTER 4

[1]Coffield, Frank, David Moseley, Elaine Hall, and Kathryn Ecclestone, "Learning Styles and Pedagogy in Post-16 Learning: A Systematic and Critical Review," London: Learning and Skills Research Centre, 2004, pp. 22–23.

[3]Kelley, Tina. "How to Separate Good Data from Bad," *New York Times,* March 4, 1999, p. E9.

CHAPTER 5

[1]*KFC Nutrition Guide*, revised July 30, 2007, www.kfc. com. McDonald's USA Nutrition Facts for Popular Menu Items, undated, www.mcdonalds.com. *Subway Nutrition Facts—U.S.*, revised January 2008, www.subway.com, all accessed on March 8, 2008.

[2]U.S. Department of Health and Human Services and U.S. Department of Agriculture, *Dietary Guidelines for Americans, 2005*. www.healthierus.gov/dietaryguidelines, accessed March 9, 2008.

[3]U.S. Census Bureau, *Statistical Abstract of the United States 2008*. Table 199, Age-Adjusted Percent Distributions of Body Mass Index Among Persons 18 Years Old and Over by Selected Characteristics: 2003–2004.

[4]Ramage, John D., John C. Bean, and June Johnson. *The Allyn & Bacon Guide to Writing*, 3rd ed., New York: Longman, 2003, p. 612.

CHAPTER 6

[1]Centers for Disease Control and Prevention. *Early Release of Selected Estimates Based on Data from the 2002 National Health Interview Survey.* Data Table for Figure 9.1, Percent of Adults Aged 18 Years and Over with Excessive Alcohol Consumption: United States: 1997–2002. <http://www.cdc.gov/nchs/data/nhis/earlyrelease/200306_09.pdf>, accessed March 28, 2008.

[2]Wechsler, Henry, et al. "Trends in College Binge Drinking During a Period of Increased Prevention Efforts," *Journal of American College Health,* Vol. 50, No. 5, 2002.

[3]Hingson, Ralph, et al. "Magnitude of Alcohol-Related Mortality and Morbidity among U.S. College Students Ages 18–24: Changes from 1998 to 2001," *Annual Review of Public Health,* Vol. 26 (2005): 259–279.

[4]Based on "Self-Test 1: Early Signs of Alcohol Abuse" adapted/developed by Leonard Hickman, Ph.D. <http://www.nd.edu/~ucc/ucc_alcohol2.html> accessed March 29, 2008.

[5]Maugh, Thomas H., II. "Teens Quickly Hooked on Smoking," *Denver Post,* August 29, 2002, p. 2A.

[6]Centers for Disease Control and Prevention. "Annual Smoking—Attributable Mortality, Years of Potential Life Lost, and Productivity Losses—United States, 1997–2001," *Morbidity and Mortality Weekly Reports,* Vol. 54, No. 25. July 1, 2005. <http://www.cdc.gov/tobacco/data_statistics/MMWR/2005/mm5425_highlights.htm> accessed March 28, 2008.

[7]Centers for Disease Control and Prevention. *Early Release of Data from the 2007 National Health Interview Survey.* Data Table for Figure 8.1, Prevalence of Current Smoking among Adults Aged 18 Years and Over: United States, 1997–June 2007. <http://www.cdc.gov/nchs/data/nhis/earlyrelease/200712_08.pdf> accessed March 28, 2008.

[8]Weinstock, H., et al. "Sexually Transmitted Diseases among American Youth: Incidence and Prevalence Estimates, 2000," *Perspectives on Sexual and Reproductive Health,* Vol. 36, No. 1 (2004): 6–10.

CHAPTER 7

[1]Adapted from David W. Merrill, and Roger Reid. *Personal Styles and Effective Performance.* Radnor, Pa.: Chilton, 1981.

[2]Adapted from W. J. Reddin, *Managerial Effectiveness,* New York: McGraw-Hill, 1970.

[3]Iacoboni, Marco. *Mirroring People: The New Science of How We Connect with Others,* New York, Farrar, Straus, and Giroux, 2008.

[4]Carducci, Bernardo. *Shyness: A Bold New Approach,* New York: HarperPerennial, 2001.

CHAPTER 8

[1]Conaway, M. S. "Listening: Learning Tool and Retention Agent," In A. S. Algier and K. W. Algier (eds.), *Improving Reading and Study Skills,* San Francisco: Jossey-Bass, 1982, pp. 51–63. Bommelje, R., et al. "Personality Characteristics of Effective Listeners: A Five Factor Perspective," *International Journal of Listening,* Vol. 17 (2003), pp. 32–46. Cited in Janusik, Laura, compiler. "Listening Facts," International Listening Association. <http://www.listen.org/Templates/facts.htm>, accessed April 17, 2008.

[2]Zuker, Elaina. *The Seven Secrets of Influence,* New York: McGraw-Hill, 1991, p. 143.

CHAPTER 9

[1]Krotz, Joanna L. "Cell Phone Etiquette: 10 Do's and Don'ts," Microsoft bCentral, January 3, 2001 <http://www.bcentral.com/articles/krotz/165.asp>, accessed August 27, 2003.

[2]Arredondo, Lani. *How to Present Like a Pro,* New York: McGraw-Hill, 1991, pp. 16–22.

CHAPTER 10

[1]Luft, Joseph. *Group Processes: An Introduction to Group Dynamics,* With permission by Mayfield Publishing, Mountain View, Calif., © 1984, 1970, 1969 by Joseph Luft.

CHAPTER 11

[1]Asch, Solomon E. "Studies of Independence and Conformity: A Minority of One against a Unanimous Majority," *Psychological Monographs,* Vol. 9, 1956, p. 416.

[2]Adapted from W. J. Reddin. "What Kind of Executive?" *Journal of the Institute of Directors,* December 1966, pp. 448–453; and W. J. Reddin, *Managerial Effectiveness,* New York: McGraw-Hill, 1970.

CHAPTER 12

[1]Papalia, Diane E., and Sally Wendkos Olds. *Psychology,* 2nd ed. New York: McGraw-Hill, 1988, p. 567.

[2]Cohen, S., T. Kamarck, and R. Mermelstein. "A Global Measure of Perceived Stress," *Journal of Health and Social Behavior,* Vol. 24, 1983, pp. 385–396.

[3]Posen, David B. "Stress Management for Patient and Physician," *The Canadian Journal of Continuing Medical Education,* April 1995 <http://www.mentalhealth.com/mag1/p51-str.html>, accessed March 28, 2003.

[4]Ferguson, Tom. "Your Support Group," *The Self-Care Catalog,* Emeryville, Calif.: Spring 1992.

CHAPTER 13

[1]Porter, Sylvia. *Your Own Money,* New York: Avon Books, 1983, p. 12.

[2]Wyss, B. O'Neill. "Dollars and Sense," *TWA Ambassador,* April 1991, p. 85.

[3]Weisbaum, Herb. "College Credit Cards Seen as Risky," MSNBC.com, Aug. 11, 2006, <http://www.msnbc.com/id/14031324> accessed June 3, 2008.

[4]"Bankruptcy Statistics," U.S. Courts, <http://www.uscourts.gov/bnkrpctystats/bankruptcystats.htm>, accessed June 4, 2008.

CHAPTER 14

[1]Dixon, Pam. *Job Searching Online for Dummies,* 2nd ed. Foster City, Calif.: IDG Books Worldwide, 2000.

Index

Note: Pages followed by *f* and *t* indicate figures and tables.

385